Hoover Institution Publications

THE MAKING OF A MODEL CITIZEN IN COMMUNIST CHINA

THE MAKING OF A MODEL CITIZEN IN COMMUNIST CHINA

Charles Price Ridley
Paul H. B. Godwin
Dennis J. Doolin

The Hoover Institution Press
Stanford University
Stanford, California
1971

The Hoover Institution on War, Revolution and Peace, founded at Stanford University in 1919 by the late President Herbert Hoover, is a center for advanced study and research on public and international affairs in the twentieth century. The views expressed in its publications are entirely those of the authors and do not necessarily reflect the views of the Hoover Institution.

Hoover Institution Publications
© 1971 by the Board of Trustees of the Leland Stanford Junior University
All rights reserved
Library of Congress Catalog Card Number: 73-170203
Standard Book Number 8179-1031-X
Printed in the United States of America

To our "little friends,"
the Schoolchildren of China

TABLE OF CONTENTS

ACKNOWLEDGMENTS

The original research on which this study has been based was supported by a grant from the Office of Education, U. S. Department of Health, Education, and Welfare (Project Number 7-1137). The Office of Education bears no responsibility for the findings or the opinions of the authors as expressed here.

We acknowledge with special thanks the invaluable advice and suggestions provided at various stages of this study by Professor Michel Oksenberg of the East Asian Institute of Columbia University, Professor Robert D. Hess of the School of Education of Stanford University, and Mr. John Ma, Curator-Librarian for the East Asia Collections at the Hoover Institution.

A NOTE ON THE SCHOOL TEXTBOOKS

The texts analyzed in this study were contained in ten lightweight paper-bound books, each roughly 5¼" x 7¼" in format and averaging 110 pages in length. See pp. 10-11 for detailed data concerning publishing and distribution.

The books contained 385 lessons in all. Of that total, 155 selections (about 40 percent of all the material in the ten textbooks) appear in translation at the end of this volume.

THE MAKING OF A MODEL CITIZEN IN COMMUNIST CHINA

ONE

THE CITIZEN AND THE MODEL

INTRODUCTION

This study of the making of a model citizen in China, and the role of elementary education therein, proceeds under the assumption that the elementary school *Readers* analyzed below reflect the basic or core values in which the Chinese leadership wishes to inculcate its citizens—at least the values held until the period of the Great Proletarian Cultural Revolution. Further, we assume that the *Readers* reflect the basic value orientations of the Chinese leadership. The development of political attitudes in children is a learning process, and a major part of this process of political socialization occurs in a society's formal educational system. Educational systems are designed, in fact, to socialize their students—to teach them the values of the society and to teach them to accept these values.[1] Education, then, is a tool of politics; in China, it is a tool of the political leadership.

Through the exploration of the kinds of values and the structure of values that the Chinese leadership is trying to inculcate in its primary school students, we hope to identify some of the particular problems which the Chinese Communists face in socializing their children and to develop a specific profile of the structure of these values as revealed in the textbooks.

3

POLITICAL SOCIALIZATION OF CHILDREN IN COMMUNIST CHINA

Studies of American children and children in other Western societies have demonstrated that political learning and political socialization begin before the age of five or six; that is, before the beginning of a child's formal education. This learning is acquired from parents and other adults and forms the basis of an early and emotional attachment to the society and, in the simple form in which it is perceived by the child, the political system of the particular society.[2] It should be observed, however, that Western nation-states have stable societies and political systems in which the adult members tend to accept the basic values of the polity. In mainland China, the adult members are themselves still adjusting to the demands of the communist political system and to the values of its leaders and may not, in fact, pass on to their offspring a positive attachment to the communist system and the values and goals of the political elite.

We do not, however, have information which permits us to make any judgment about this particular problem, but studies of political socialization in more accessible societies do permit us to discuss the probable impact and content of early childhood political learning in China and to make certain speculations concerning the impact of such socialization on a child's experience in elementary school.[3]

The Chinese have a strong sense of historical continuity, and it is almost certain that early childhood attachments to a vague notion of "China" have been established prior to the beginning of elementary schooling, especially where formal pre-school training is available (see below, pp. 36-37). This speculation is reinforced by the content of the information which Chinese children receive about China in the first two grades of primary school, as later chapters will illustrate. The texts we analyze show an awareness of such early learning in that they contain clear distinctions between imperial China, China under the Kuomintang, and China under the Communists. There is a definite attempt to build upon an early awareness of China as an abstraction by indicating the historical continuity of China, while at the same time the texts stress the evil of the past as well as its glory. Thus, the path is prepared for informing the children of the significance of the new China built by the Communist Party under the leadership of Mao Tse-tung. Similarly, the authoritarian nature of Chinese family life[4] may well be a strong and effective basis for introducing the child to the authoritarian nature of the communist political system.[5]

Early learning in the family may not, in fact, prove to be a stumbling block to the political learning that composes so much of Chinese education today. Our analysis will demonstrate that in the first two grades of primary school the *Readers* introduce the student to discrete *information* about the political system, while during the subsequent three years stories are presented to inculcate the child in a positive set of *pre-dispositions* toward the political system, the revolutionary history of the Chinese Communist Party, and the leadership of the "new China." Thus, the early learning experiences of the child prior to entering elementary school may not hinder subsequent political learning and may in fact reinforce it.

Our study, however, will be restricted primarily to the content of direct political education in elementary schools. The Chinese leadership is well aware of the task it faces as it attempts to transform the political attitudes of the adult members of the society, but the texts we analyze were written for the first generation of children to be born and educated under the new order. The creation of a universal education system under the control of the Chinese Communist Party and its use as a political tool to create citizens loyal and dedicated to the new China and its leaders is a significant step toward the creation of a "New Chinese Man."

THE PROBLEM OF EXCESSIVE POLITICIZATION

The distinct problem for China, however, is that the degree of political socialization required goes far beyond that which is necessary for basic loyalty to the state and its political processes. It requires a commitment to Mao Tse-tung and the Chinese Communist Party that at times appears to be excessive, such as the current deification of Mao. The Chinese educational system is charged with producing citizens to be used in the modernization of the state with both specific levels of expertise and a deep, extremely personal commitment to Mao Tse-tung.

As indicated by Mao's destruction of the educational system during the Great Proletarian Cultural Revolution and its subsequent "reform," one of Mao Tse-tung's most immutable beliefs is that intellectuals have proclivities that make them suspect as members of his new society. Mao's distrust of the intelligentsia is of long standing and is based upon the realization that the core of China's intellectuals was educated in the West. Thus the intellectual is either the product of a "bourgeois" society or, for graduates since 1949, a product of an educational system dominated by the "bourgeois" intelligentsia and therefore contaminated by non-proletarian values. Students educated in the Soviet Union are, for obvious reasons, equally suspect. Mao's deep-rooted suspicion of the intellectual comes into conflict with another of his major goals: the rapid industrialization of China necessary to achieve the status of a first-class power in the world. To achieve this goal, China needed, and still needs, to develop the technical and managerial skills upon which a modern industrialized state is built. Such skills are the product of the educational system of the society that seeks to create them and are held and manipulated by persons whose values tend to be pragmatic and universalistic. Such values are an anathema to Mao Tse-tung.

Mao's suspicion of the intellectual did not change the reality that China after "Liberation" had to depend upon intellectuals to staff technical, scientific, administrative, and managerial posts in the Party and Government as well as to fill the entire range of societal roles requiring specific expertise. The educated professional man was needed by the new China, and his indispensable role gave him elite status within the society. Such status brought him into conflict with Mao's preferred elite—the revolutionary leader whose status was to a large extent determined by his political role as a member of the Chinese Communist Party. To some extent the conflict was mitigated by the recruitment of intellectuals into the Party, but intellectuals in the Party were never fully trusted. It was evident that two major elite groups were coming into existence: a political elite composed of Party members and an elite of educated professionals. It is within this bifurcated elite structure that the Chinese communist concept of "Red and Expert" emerges, with the Party elite characterized as "red" and the educated professional elite characterized as "expert." Ideally there should be no conflict between "red" and "expert," for the ideal Chinese communist leader should be both "red" and "expert." To the extent that the "expert" was perceived by Mao as developing a set of professional values that distinguished him from the Party elite, he was a member of a competing elite, competing for leadership of the society. Much of the conflict over educational policies, especially higher education, derives from the "red" and "expert" conflict and from Mao's attempt to resolve the conflict by introducing high levels of political training into the educational system.

The "Red and Expert" conflict is compounded by Mao's quest for "revolutionary successors." Following the retreat from the disastrous effects of the Great Leap Forward, Mao Tse-tung began to show more and more concern for the kinds of persons who would inherit his revolution. At the Tenth Plenum of the Central Committee of the Chinese Communist Party in September 1962, Mao stated that "class education for youth must be strengthened to ensure that our nation will remain revolutionary and incorruptible for generations and forever."[6] Mao viewed the retreat from his policies as a move away from communism and toward bourgeois capitalism. In his July 1964 polemic "On Khruschchev's Phony Communism and its Historical Lessons for the World," Mao again raised the question of revolutionary successors. This question, Mao wrote, is "... a matter of life and death for our country."[7] An article in a national newspaper a month earlier had observed:

> Young people in the new China, under the care and education of the Party, have since early childhood grasped revolutionary truth and have been travelling along a correct road.

The article continued, stating that political training must be intensified and:

> In our view, in the socialist new China, the people's teachers not only have the job of spreading knowledge but, more important still, have the task of fostering the moral qualities of their students.

Moral education had been defined earlier as consisting "principally of socialist and communist education, class education and labor education."[8] "Moral qualities" in this case obviously refers to political education. Political learning on the part of the student is quite evidently more important than any other kind, and in Mao's view political education stands higher and is of greater importance than the "spreading of knowledge."

"Moral qualities" is not merely a euphemism, for the concept of public virtue is a distinct and crucial aspect of the Maoist view of the new China. Chinese domestic and foreign propaganda has led to a canonization of the Chinese revolution and the Chinese Communist Party, and the deification of Mao Tse-tung. Mao's call for "revolutionary successors" is intimately tied to this process of canonization and deification. Political socialization in China is not intended merely to unify China and gain positive attitudes toward the political system and its institutions and processes. Political socialization in China is directed at gaining the total commitment of the population to Mao's vision. Mao's vision is that under the leadership of the Chinese Communist Party, China should become a totally selfless society in which all individual, group, and factional interests are absent. There is more than just a hint of Confucian "virtue" in this goal, and in this sense Mao may be seen as culture-centric. Yet such a utopian goal is not unique to China and has been sought by other civilizations,[9] and the use of the concept of morality in Chinese Communist discussions of the function of the education system is not designed to hide the basic goal of political indoctrination.

Mao's search for "revolutionary successors" is central to an understanding of the content of political learning in China.

The ideal revolutionary has been defined by one scholar as an "ascetic, fearless, disciplined fighter-ideologue."[10] This is the kind of model which Mao would set for Chinese students, and it is this model that the Chinese have raised up in various political campaigns for the Chinese people to emulate.[11]

SCOPE AND METHOD

To the leaders of China, the current younger generation represents perhaps their last hope of preserving the spirit of the Revolution. It is small wonder, then, that so much attention is lavished on the young in an attempt to instill in them an awareness of their importance as "successors to the revolution." Although it is doubtful that the regime can in the long run succeed in stemming the tendencies away from the original revolutionary spirit that motivated it in its drive to power, the effort is nevertheless being made to kindle a revolutionary spirit in the young, as our collection of elementary school readers clearly indicates.

As other investigators have noted, the content of children's readers and textbooks often bears a close relationship to the apparent needs of a society under given conditions of development. McClelland[12] has shown that a high percentage of imagery concerned with "achievement" is found in the writings of developing societies and economies and that the percentage of imagery of this kind declines as the vitality of the society diminishes. As he points out, "achievement imagery" in significant proportions appears in children's readers of a given country prior to spurts in economic development. It is obvious that the imagery and themes of children's readers are concerned either consciously or unconsciously with molding patterns of behavior and thought that the writers feel are desirable within the context of their society. In the case of the Chinese Communist *Readers,* the material is developed with the definite intention of influencing children to develop certain attitudes and characteristics.

In accordance with McClelland's thesis, one would expect to find a good deal of "achievement-oriented" material in these Chinese texts, and, indeed, we do find an emphasis on behavioral characteristics that are beneficial to a nation striving to modernize. The picture for Communist China is made more complicated, however, by the need felt by the leadership to nurture attitudes of loyalty to a political cause as well. Therefore, the emphasis in these *Readers* is, essentially, divided between attempts to mold those characteristics required in a modernizing nation and those characteristics required for a realization of a thorough political and social revolution.

THE DATA SOURCES

The *Readers* which are the subject of this study are a set of elementary school grammar readers (*yü-wen*) used in mainland China in conducting instruction in the Chinese Language, that is to say, the so-called "Mandarin" dialect, which is based on the Chinese of the Peking region. This set contains ten volumes and covers the first five Grades of elementary school, there being two volumes per year. The Chinese texts comprise about 1100 pages.

Under the system of elementary school education for which these readers were designed, division is made at the end of the Fourth Grade, the first four Grades being known as *"ch'u-chi hsiao-hsüeh,"* or Junior Elementary School, and the Fifth Grade being a part of *"kao-chi hsiao-hsüeh,"* or Senior Elementary School. Thus, Volumes One through Eight are entitled simply Junior Elementary School Reader, Volume One, and so on. For convenience sake, we have referred to Senior Elementary School Volumes One and Two as Volumes Nine and Ten.

The texts in our possession are reprints published by the People's Publishing House, Shanghai, of editions prepared under the direction of the Elementary School Language Editorial Office of the People's Education Publishing House, Peking. The dates of publication of the texts and the cumulative total press runs at the time of publication are as follows:

Volume	*No. Publ. (cumulative)*
1. Sept. 1964 7th printing of 1963 edition	928,000

Continued

2.	Nov. 1963 1st printing of new edition	300,000
3.	July 1964 2nd printing of 1964 1st edition	390,000
4.	Dec. 1964 1st printing of 1964 1st edition	386,000
5.	July 1964 15th printing of 1964 7th edition	1,960,000
6.	Jan. 1964 9th printing of 1964 6th edition	1,598,500
7.	May 1964 14th printing of 1964 6th edition	1,774,000
8.	Nov. 1964 11th printing of 1964 6th edition	1,771,000
9.	July 1964 17th printing of 1964 7th edition	1,634,500
10.	Nov. 1964 10th printing of 1964 7th edition	1,579,000

As to the problem of how extensively the *Readers* have been used outside of Shanghai and Peking we have little information, and we can only conjecture on the basis of scattered references in various educational writings that reprints of these editions or of materials similar to them may have been in use in other parts of China as well.

When it comes to when these texts were in use, we are on firmer ground. For Volumes 5 through 10, that is, those used from Grade Three through Grade Five, we have first edition dates as follows:

Volume 5 1957
Volume 6 1957
Volume 7 1958
Volume 8 1958
Volume 9 1957
Volume 10.........................1957

This indicates that the materials in the six volumes above were probably in use in schools in Peking and Shanghai, at least, since 1957, or 1958 at the latest. This corresponds well with information we have on changes in the structure of educational institutions in China at that time, there having been a drastic revision of the system in 1957 involving a step away from the Soviet model and the initiation of considerable experimentation, including accelerated programs in the Chinese language. As a result, new textbooks appeared, and it is clear that those studied here are among these.

The remaining texts for the first two Grades all bear first-edition dates of either 1963 or 1964. Whether they represent revisions over previous editions is not clear. However, there is some additional evidence that some stories and poems used in these editions of the *Readers* have their origin in material created at earlier times. For this reason, the problems of authorship and sources of the stories in the *Readers* have been deferred to Appendix 1 for more detailed treatment.

DETAILED DESCRIPTION OF THE READERS

There is a considerable difference in the presentation of materials in Volumes 1 through 4 (Grades One and Two) and those in Volumes 5 through 10 (Grades Three through Five). These differences reflect, in part, the fact that instruction in the first two grades is devoted essentially to the acquisition of basic language skills, whereas instruction in the higher grades is concerned with development of reading skills. They no doubt reflect as well the Chinese educational psychologist's concern with developing varying approaches based on differences in age levels. For these reasons, the texts in these two major groups should be considered separately.

Volumes 1 through 4 (Grades One and Two). A considerable portion of Volume 1 is concerned with introducing the "pinyin" (or phonetic) alphabet which the Chinese have adopted as a tool in teaching the written language. The letters of the alphabet are introduced, accompanied by pictures illustrating the words which contain the appropriate sounds. (See page 13). Once the alphabet is sufficiently mastered, the Chinese word for "dog," for example, is printed in "pinyin" transcription together with a picture of a dog. Finally, Chinese characters themselves are introduced as individual entities, the

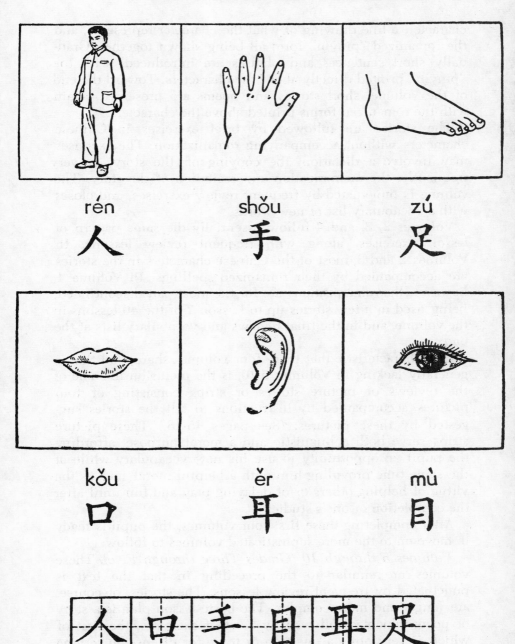

rén   shǒu   zú

人   手   足

kǒu   ěr   mù

口   耳   目

人 口 手 目 耳 足

character, a line drawing of what the character represents, and the romanized "pinyin" form all being shown together. Gradually short sentences and phrases are introduced, with the "pinyin" printed directly above the characters. Toward the end of the volume, short stories and poems are presented, again with the romanized forms printed above the characters.

The stories are followed by brief exercises in Chinese characters without accompanying romanization. The exercises may involve a dictation, the copying of the story, or very frequently, the memorization and recitation of the story. The volume is punctuated by frequent review exercises, and closes with a vocabulary list of new words.

Volumes 2, 3, and 4 follow essentially the same pattern of lesson exercises, along with frequent review lessons. In Volumes 2 and 3, most of the Chinese characters in the stories are accompanied by their romanized spellings. In Volume 4, however, the romanizations are for the most part discontinued, being used in a few stories up to Lesson 7 of the 40 lessons in the volume, and in the final reviews and vocabulary lists at the end.

One characteristic that these four volumes share, and that is generally lacking in Volumes 5-10, is the inclusion in some of the reviews of picture stories or strips consisting of four pictures accompanied by instructions to tell the stories suggested by these pictures. (See pages 15-18.) These picture strips serve both a linguistic and a moral purpose, affording the pupil an opportunity to use his new vocabulary while at the same time providing him with a helpful moral such as the virtue of helping others or of delaying play and fun until after the completion of one's studies.

After completing these first four volumes, the pupil is ready to move on to the more sophisticated volumes to follow.

Volumes 5 through 10 (Grades Three through Five). These volumes are similar to the preceding in that the text is punctuated by frequent review lessons. The stories, of course, are longer and more complex. The basic lesson plan is a story or poem which is followed by a set of exercises, the first of which is very often a question or topic for discussion serving to point up the moral of the story. This may be followed by

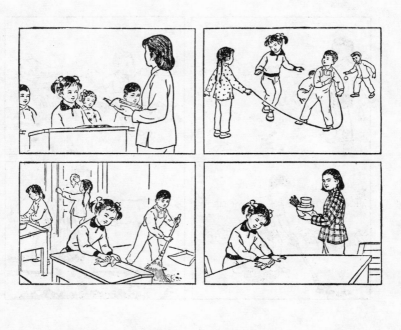

vocabulary dictation, instructions to memorize and recite the text, or various other exercises primarily for the purpose of language practice.

In Volumes 9 and 10, the stories become much longer and the review exercises less extensive. One picture story occurs in Volume 6 and one in Volume 8.

It should also be noted that most of the stories are illustrated with line drawings, although these become less frequent in Volumes 9 and 10.

CATEGORIES OF STORIES*

Although the material presented in the *Readers* varies considerably in form, when one views the selections from the standpoint of their probable intent, it can be seen that they fall generally into three major types:

1. Stories that are primarily *informative*, or informational.
2. Stories that have *the development of specific political attitudes* as their primary intent.
3. Stories that have *behavioral modeling* as their primary intent.

1. Informational stories. Informational stories account for the smallest number of selections among the three categories above. They deal primarily with basic agricultural knowledge, basic knowledge about physiology and hygiene, and basic scientific knowledge. In addition, a number of lessons take up the proper forms for writing letters and other forms of communication. However, the content of the latter may very often have a political or behavioral orientation so that these selections are not always strictly "informational" in a neutral sense.

2. Stories aimed at the development of specific political attitudes. Stories in this category include those concerned with molding the child's attitude toward Chinese society and the organs of the Chinese Communist state, as well as his attitudes toward the former Nationalist regime and toward foreign countries. This category also includes themes of social and international conflict as manifested in war.

*The reader should note that the categories and topics to be discussed later were not subjected to statistical reliability tests during the process of content analysis.

Foremost among stories of this type are those concerned with the "benevolence of the new society." Other stories take up the themes of devotion to Mao Tse-tung, of loyalty and devotion to the Party and to the communes and to building Socialism.

There is a high proportion of stories dealing with the theme of military conflict, and particularly with that of defense against invaders and enemy occupation. In these, there is often an additional element which we refer to as the "deception" theme, in which the child is made aware of techniques of deception such as spying, both in purely military and in non-military contexts.

Also included in this category are stories emphasizing anti-Americanism, anti-imperialism, and proletarian internationalism.

3. *Stories aimed at behavioral modeling.* The Chinese *Readers* differ little from their counterparts in other countries in their emphasis on moral training. The stories in these categories usually exemplify behavior that is considered good and thus worthy of emulation, the Chinese as a rule favoring teaching by "positive" example to teaching by "negative" example, although a few stories of the latter type do occur.

What can be said in general about the content of the three categories of stories described above is that it is clearly relevant to a predominantly agricultural society that is consciously attempting not only to transform itself into a modern, industrial society, but also to one that is attempting, through education of its masses, to eradicate an old social order and to establish a new society based on radically different principles.

STORY FORMS

With the exception of a number of poems, most selections are in narrative form. A few appear in the guise of first person narratives. Stories may be either about events in the lives of actual persons, or, as is very often the case when a moral example is being set, they may be fables. Thus, we find a fairly large assortment of fables from Aesop, such as the story about the boy who cried wolf, as well as traditional Chinese fables. Neither stories from Western sources nor from traditional Chinese sources are appreciably altered in their retelling here.*

From a purely subjective viewpoint, there are very few selections that are dull, most of the longer narratives being well told and often extremely moving. Those that are dull are most often purely informational in content. Furthermore, the stories are apparently factual when dealing with incidents from actual history or from the lives of actual persons. Thus the stories are generally believable and do not appear to distort reality. Having said this much, however, it is necessary to call attention to a number of cases in which the texts are fictionalized. This is seen clearly in three stories, all of which share one point in common in that they describe events purported to have taken place outside of mainland China. The three stories concerned are *Incidents from Taiwan* (Vol. 6, No. 3), in which bad relations between American soldiers and Chinese are portrayed, *Two Louises in America* (Vol. 6, No. 14), a fictional situation involving a New York city slum girl, and *Sambo* (Vol. 10, No. 31), in which an African Negro falls prey to a European movie maker who photographs him as he is being attacked and killed by a lion.

THEMES

As indicated above, we have distinguished between stories that have as their intent simply the imparting of information from those concerned primarily with the inculcation of specific political attitudes, and these two types in turn from those concerned primarily with the development of individual moral and general group-oriented social behavior. For this reason, the stories are assigned to three major thematic categories: informational, political, and behavioral.

Informational themes. Informational themes are those concerned with imparting specific (usually non- or apolitical) information about given subjects. In themselves, informational themes are generally lacking in political or behavioral coloration. Although they are, in this sense, essentially neutral, they

*For a discussion of story forms and of educational philosophy in teaching of literature, see Chapter Three.

nevertheless are revealing in the range of subject matter that is represented.

Political themes. Political themes are those concerned with inculcating specific sets of political attitudes toward the domestic political system, but also in part toward the international system as well.

Behavioral themes. Behavioral themes are those which have as their central purpose defining how an individual should act. That is, they are designed to enable the individual to distinguish between "good" and "bad" behavior. The stories illustrate, by means of negative as well as positive example, what the regime wishes to portray as approved behavior.

Subthemes. Each selection from the *Readers* was assigned a central theme determined by the primary concern of the story. A small number of selections, usually poems in which there were stanzas of differing thematic emphasis, were assigned more than one central theme. Few selections, however, were ever purely informational, political or behavioral in intention. For this reason, each selection was assigned a subtheme or a number of subthemes. Thus, each major theme has a corresponding subtheme which enables us, for example, to classify a given selection as having a specific central theme and one or more subthemes that differ from the central theme.

TOPICS

The concept of topic, or the context within which the themes are transmitted, is an analytical tool designed to determine what kinds of stories are used to transmit the themes and subthemes. Our topical analysis, therefore, is a description of the kinds of stories used to transmit values and behavioral modeling. By determining the degree of emphasis given to different categories of stories, such as stories about rural life and agriculture, war stories, or stories depicting Mao Tse-tung, we shall be able to compare the story topics with the kinds of values and behavior models the stories contain. This comparison permits a fuller discussion of the kind of model child-citizen which the leaders of Communist China wish to create by comparing the value orientation of the themes with the image orientation toward China and the outside world created by the story topics.

As with the thematic analysis, each selection is assigned a central topic according to the primary concern of the story. Few of the stories can be assigned only one topic; therefore the topic central to the story is designated the central topic, and those receiving lesser emphasis are designated as subtopics. Through comparisons of themes and topics an attempt is made to elaborate upon the broader values and goals which the Chinese leadership wishes to develop within its primary school children.

SUMMARY

The object of the study is to determine the significance of the *Readers* as a means of socialization. As we cannot determine with any precision the kinds of responses children have made to the values and value structure in which the Chinese regime has attempted to inculcate them, our observations will be restricted to the kinds and structure of values reflected in the texts and to what kind of model citizen the Chinese leadership hopes to create.

Our concern with political learning is based upon the hypothesis, drawn from many other studies but most notably from Greenstein's *Children and Politics,* that it is during the preadolescent stage of his life that an individual learns his basic orientations to the state and society. It is unfortunate that we can only work with a shadow of the political profile the Chinese Communists wish to create in their young children, but by analyzing what young Chinese are taught—even though this is but one part of their interaction with the society—the outline of the shadow can be brought into sharper resolution.

TWO

THE SPIRIT AND
CONTENT OF
ELEMENTARY
EDUCATION SINCE 1949

INTRODUCTION

From the establishment of the People's Republic of China in 1949 to the present, education has been a key concern of the national leaders. The Communist regime created in 1949 was the first true re-unification of China under one viable government since the fall of the Ch'ing Dynasty in 1911. During the intervening years of internal dissension and war with outside powers, China was a divided nation. Thus, the Communist Chinese leaders were faced with an enormous problem of popular re-education. Not only was it necessary to instill an allegiance to the new regime and to develop an awareness of what the regime stood for, but it was also necessary to inculcate the concept of China as a unified nation. The dominant concern of the Communist leaders was "socialist revolution" and "socialist re-construction," the building of a new Communist state populated by a new Communist man, and this was conceived of not merely in the narrower sense of modernization, but more significantly in the spiritual sense of building a new society and of cultivating individuals actively dedicated to that society.

Education, obviously, was vital to this process, and it is not surprising to find that it was subordinated to these national goals. The intention to use education in this manner is clear from Articles 41 and 42 of the "Common Program of October 1949:"

24

Article 41. The culture and education of the People's Republic of China are new democratic, that is, national, scientific, and popular. The main tasks in raising the cultural level of the people are: training of personnel for national construction work; liquidation of feudal, comprador, and fascist ideology; and developing an ideology of service to the people.

Article 42. Love for the motherland and the people, love of labor, love of science, and protection of public property shall be promoted as the public spirit of all nationals of the People's Republic of China.[1]

These Articles are interesting in that they clearly imply a conscious concern with the "ideological" and moral content of education. On the one hand, old ideas must be uprooted, and on the other, new virtues of civic morality must be nurtured.

This process of education, of course, was not one restricted merely to school children, but involved the entire range of Chinese society. For the older groups, already grown to maturity and educated under the institutions of the deposed society or in Western institutions (either in China or abroad), this meant undergoing re-education or "thought reform," in order to come to an understanding of the ideology and ideals of the new regime. Re-education of the older generation could never hope to bring about the total transformation of personality desired by the leadership. Patterns of behavior and attitudes established during childhood and reinforced by the social practices of pre-Communist society could not be extinguished overnight in response to pressure or exhortations to change even when there was a conscious desire to do so on the part of the individual; behavioral and attitudinal manipulation could never be sufficiently intensive to achieve a permanent and thorough reformation.

The hope of transforming the ideals of the new society into practical realities manifested in the behavior of its citizens lay in the young whose ideology had not yet become fixed. Elementary school education thus became a matter not only of providing persons trained in the basic skills required by a nation struggling to modernize, but a serious business of nurturing "successors to the revolution" who in later years could be trusted to take over power from the aging generation of genuine revolutionaries. The pupil entering elementary school in 1949 or thereafter would be maturing and learning in a period during which he should, ideally, be insulated from pre-1949 values.

It is one thing to enunciate goals of nurturing love of country and concern for public property, or of service to the people, in public documents, and another to translate these into practical action in the classroom. The period 1949 to 1952 was, consequently, one both of consolidation and unification of China's diverse educational institutions and curricula, and, perhaps more important, a time when techniques were developed by which the provisions of the "Common Program" concerning education could be put into practice. Teachers as well as students had to be re-educated if they were to fulfill their mission under the new order.

CONFLICTING EDUCATIONAL GOALS

The goal of transforming a society and of using the formal education process as a tool to achieve political aims resulted in a basic conflict of educational priorities. Essentially the conflict was one of values: a conflict between the necessity of developing a society capable of creating a modernized, industrialized nation-state, and the necessity of creating true "revolutionary successors." On the one hand, the new China needed professional, managerial, and technical skills with which to build the modern, industrialized China; on the other hand, Mao was deeply committed to the creation of a New Chinese Man dedicated to the "revolution." This conflict in values was ideologically solved by establishing the "red and expert" individual as the ideal type to be produced by China's educational system. Nevertheless, vacillation between emphasis on "redness" and emphasis on "expertness" has characterized China's educational policies since 1949.

When the Communists took power in 1949, they inherited the educational system developed by the Kuomintang government. The system of primary and secondary education was characterized by a six-year primary education cycle and a six-year secondary education cycle, both of which were in turn divided into two parts. The six-year primary cycle was divided into four years of junior grades and two years of senior grades, and the secondary cycle was divided into a three year junior middle school (high school) division followed by three years of senior middle school. Beyond middle school were the general and specialized colleges and universities that formed the structure of China's higher education. The Communist regime recognized, however, that if it were to achieve its goals education would have to be expanded. The expansion took two forms: the normal, full-time educational structure was expanded, and an additional process was added to the educational system. The addition was the introduction of part-time vocational and literacy schools. These schools are known as "part-time" schools and "half-work half-study" schools. Thus, education in China was expanded both by increasing the capacity of the full-time system and by adding a second educational process.

The spare-time schools were designed to raise the literacy rate and the general level of technical competence of the vast majority of the Chinese population. They were quite flexible in form, ranging from open-air literacy classes to quite specific technical training for farmers, industrial laborers, and middle level managers. Both the students and the teachers in these schools had regular full-time occupations, with their learning and teaching responsibilities carried on while they were not required to work.

Half-work half-study schools also drew from the fully employed but were more formally organized than the spare-time schools. They were usually based in middle schools under the supervision of governmental agencies which provided students from local technical institutions and industrial units or farms. The half-work half-study schools were more specifically designed to raise the technical competence of the Chinese population. Often there was a functional exchange between the factories and the middle school, for while the factory workers (or farm workers in rural areas) were receiving an education in the school, the student body was receiving technical training on the farms and in the factories. The division of time between study and production does not appear to have been uniform, the exchange occurring on a half-day, half-week, or occasionally on a half-month basis.[2]

There were many varieties of spare-time and half-work half-study schools, but essentially they were designed to complement the full-time educational system and to provide China with the cheapest road to both a universal educational system and higher levels of technical and managerial competence. This approach to education, known as the policy of "walking on two legs," received emphasis at different times during the past twenty years but was most emphasized in 1958-1960 during the Great Leap Forward.

The "walking on two legs" approach to education, however, reflects the basic value conflict in the Chinese educational system of the late 50's and middle 60's. "Walking on two legs" could be viewed, and probably was viewed by many, as a rational approach to China's basic need to develop a literate population capable of achieving the range of technical competence requisite for modernizing industry and agriculture. There is, however, an ideological aspect to the half-work half-study system that reflects Mao Tse-tung's particular concerns and his suspicion of the intellectual. Mao's concern with "revolutionary successors" and with the creation of "red" experts leads him to view half-work half-study as a technique for eliminating the distinction between intellectual pursuits and manual labor, a prime requisite for the creation of his particular utopia. The *Kwangming Daily* in 1965 carried a discussion entitled, "On Experiment with the Part-Work and Part-Study Educational System," in which the *ideological* goals were stated in the following manner:

> To prepare in particular for the elimination of the differences between mental and manual labor as one of the important conditions for the realization of the communist system ...[3]

This ideological role also has a definite place in the full-time educational system. Manual labor is one of the distinctive characteristics of even elementary education and becomes particularly significant in middle and higher education.

EDUCATIONAL POLICY SINCE 1949

Vacillation between emphasis on "red" and emphasis on "expert" since 1949 has been reflected constantly in Chinese educational policies, and the symbolic role of manual labor in the various policies pursued is an indicator of the degree of emphasis at any given time. During the period of the First Five-Year Plan (1953-1957), the Chinese emphasized the general development of the educational system and a relative stability prevailed. 1957 marked a turning point in educational policy, for it was the year in which the Party received severe criticism from the intellectuals during the latter period of the "Hundred Flowers" campaign. By 1956 the regime had become aware that if its goals of modernization were to be achieved, it needed the active support of the intellectuals. The political campaigns of the 1950's had eroded the initial base of support the Party possessed within the ranks of the intelligentsia, and the "Hundred Flowers" campaign was a bid to regain this support. The initial bid in 1956 received only carefully limited responses to the call to criticize the Party's policies. In 1957, when Mao delivered his address "On the Correct Handling of Contradictions among the People," in which the call for criticism was repeated, the response from the intellectuals was still carefully stated. In early May the Party became even more insistent that its defects be criticized, and this demand opened the flood-gates. For five weeks highly critical commentaries and complaints flowed into the Party from across the country. In response the Party leadership clamped down, and the "Hundred Flowers" movement was terminated in June. The greatest shock to the Party was perhaps that the youth in China had offered among the most damning criticisms of Party policies. It was the youth of China that had been subjected to the most continuous indoctrination, and it was upon the youth of China that the Party had been, and was, placing its hopes for a new China.[4] This criticism of the regime led to an increase in political education in the schools and increasing emphasis on political criteria for entrance into middle and higher education.

The increasing emphasis on "redness" received further impetus with the introduction of Mao's Great Leap Forward in 1958. Formal academic education was to be combined with manual labor. Industrial units and other production units were to establish and maintain their own schools, as were local communities. These schools were to follow the basic pattern of part-time and half-work half-study schools, while the formal full-time educational system was ordered to contribute to production by using its manual labor projects to create limited kinds of production facilities of one form or another. The result was a rash of many different kinds of schools or experimental schools, many of which were sub-standard, and an extremely large growth in the number of students attending school. The Great Leap Forward came to its final end in 1960 as the excesses of the policies themselves combined with natural disasters to bring China to the brink of economic and political disaster.

As the Chinese leadership attempted to recover from the impact of the Great Leap Forward in 1961 and 1962, the educational system began to dismantle many of the 1958-1960 experiments. Essentially, the emphasis was once again placed on expertness, the sub-standard schools were closed, and within the full-time educational system primary focus returned to academic preparation.

This respite was to be relatively short, and in 1963, physical labor and political education began to receive more emphasis. Half-work half-study schools once again were the subject of considerable discussion in the press, and "walking on two legs" became a central policy for the educational system. Nevertheless, there was no apparent attempt to reinstitute the more extreme policies of the Great Leap Forward, even though the experimentation with, and probable expansion of, part-time and half-work half-study schools continued until the education system was closed in 1966.

This continual shifting of emphasis from academic training to political training and back again must have created considerable confusion in the minds of the professional educator in China, but in spite of the highly centralized structure of education there appears to have been considerable flexibility within the educational system itself. Directives emanating from Peking were implemented and supervised by the Party organization in each province, city, county, town, village, and school in the country. The implementation, however, does not appear to have been uniform in that considerable leeway was permitted as schools experimented with various techniques for achieving the goals set in the central directives. Thus, there were in China in the 1960's many different kinds of schools following diverse educational practices in face of shifting emphases from Peking on the nature of education, for the trend of policy at a given time could be either for the production of political activists or for the production of individuals suited for a society seeking rapid industrialization.[5]

Within this rather confused pattern of education, primary education played an important if not critical role. The young Red Guards who rampaged across China in 1966, 1967, and most of 1968 were the first generation of Chinese educated entirely by the Communist regime, and their first exposure to a Communist education in a formal sense came when they were in primary school.

ELEMENTARY EDUCATION[6]

Elementary education in China, as we stated above, is divided into two parts, four years of junior primary school and two years of senior primary school. There has been some experimentation with an elementary school process in which the 4-2 sequence is reduced to a single five year sequence. There are no indications that this reform went much beyond the experimental stage,[7] thus at the time our texts were being used, elementary education was generally divided into two parts. In the rural areas especially, it is quite unlikely that the majority of the students went beyond junior primary school.

Although the principle of free universal education is accepted in China, the economic consequences of such a policy are so burdensome that most students paid fees in one form or another. In some cases the parents contributed to the teachers' board by preparing food, and in other cases actual fees were collected from parents able to pay. No doubt the parents did this willingly, for education in China has traditionally been highly valued as the key to social, political, and economic mobility. This same basic value was reinforced by the Communists, who stressed the need for higher levels of education when they came to power in 1949. Such propagandizing and the existence of a widely and strongly held traditional value put definite strains on China's ability to expand education to the extent sought by the people of China after the Communists came to power. Thus in 1949 there were 24,391,033 students in elementary schools, but by 1959 this number had risen to a reported 90,000,000.

Table I: ENROLLMENT IN ELEMENTARY SCHOOLS [8]

Year	Number of Schools	Enrollment
1949	346,789	24,391,033
1950	383,647	28,923,988
1951	502,189	43,154,440
1952	551,942	49,999,944
1953	—	51,664,000
1954	—	51,218,000
1955	—	53,126,000
1956	—	63,000,000
1957	—	65,810,000
1958	—	86,000,000
1959	—	90,000,000

These figures are not exact due to the sources, but they do present an idea of the trend of growth.

The expansion of elementary education under the Communists necessitated the building of new facilities together with the nationalization of private schools that had existed under the Nationalists. In 1952 the Ministry of Education announced that it was going to take over the private schools, but by 1953 it was realized that the government alone was incapable of directly supporting a drastic increase in students and facilities. The regime then began to encourage the creation of schools outside the state supported system. The policy was continued as villages, factories, and other enterprises and communities were encouraged to create and support their own schools.

Nevertheless, even though these "min-pan" (established by the people) schools were responsible for the curriculum, "political education" and "social activites" were to be under the direct control of local Party organizations. Economic necessity required the expansion of education to be financially supported by local governmental and economic units, but the all important areas of political education were to be under Party supervision.

The emphasis on political education was expanded beyond formal political classes to include physical labor. Such labor had at its political root the goal of symbolically combining intellectual and manual labor, even at the primary school level. Apart from political education, the other major goal of primary education was to establish a common spoken language (known in the West as "Mandarin") to replace the various dialects spoken across China. Such a goal has obvious implications for political integration and was a goal sought by the Nationalists for just this purpose.

Beyond these very basic objectives, elementary education would ideally prepare the elementary school student in history, geography, arithmetic, and other primary studies; but for most schools, language, politics, and basic arithmetic probably remained the core of the curriculum. And of these subjects, political education was clearly the most important.

Apart from the Party cadre or organization in a given school directing political education, Party-sponsored youth organizations played an important role in supervising and creating the political life of the student. The officially sponsored youth organization in elementary schools for students too young to join the Communist Youth League (CYL) was the Pioneers. Their mark of recognition was the Red Scarf, a Party symbol the students were taught to regard with respect. The Pioneers, although they were primarily designed to be activists and organizers of the political life of the student body, participated in all areas of school activity. During the winter and summer vacations they organized activities for the students, and during the school year they assisted in preparing and organizing the students to celebrate Communist holidays. In addition they functioned as informers, reporting on the behavior of students and their families.

The Pioneers, along with the Communist Youth League, were an important source of recruitment to the Party, and the Party in turn was committed to raising the prestige of these organizations. The Party, therefore, was not only present in the directly political aspects of the curriculum, but its presence throughout the daily life of the student was made evident by the activities of the Pioneers. Political indoctrination, manual labor, and the omnipresent Red Scarf raised the political consciousness of the students throughout the school year and during vacations. Although it is difficult to ascertain with any precision how many elementary students were members of the Pioneers, figures for 1959 and 1960 are reported as 44 million and 50 million respectively[9]—approximately fifty per cent of the reported student population of elementary schools in that year.

Even though the Party most definitely saw education as essentially a political tool, the students and their parents saw it as an avenue of political, social, and economic mobility. Certainly such mobility could be, and for many probably was, sought for altruistic purposes, but education was also perceived as one of the most important keys to a successful career. By opening the doors of elementary schools to many more students than before, the pressure on middle schools was bound to increase. In 1953 a campaign was launched to discourage elementary school graduates and their parents from expecting entrance into middle school as the next logical step in a student's life. The campaign stressed that elementary schools were designed to produce literate workers, not budding scholars, and that the student should normally expect to enter the ranks of the workers upon graduation. In 1954 the regime emphasized that no more than one-third of all elementary school graduates would enter middle schools, and the government has continued this policy of stressing the limited number of places available in the middle schools and centers of higher education. Elementary education is designed not as a jumping off point to a higher education, but as a preparation for becoming a skilled contributor to production. For many Chinese today, therefore, the only exposure to full-time education has been primary school; while for the Party, primary school is the most effective place in which to control the education of the majority of China's youth.

The basic goal of Chinese elementary education has been to produce students acquainted with the rudiments of reading, writing, and arithmetic while at the same time establishing the highest possible level of political awareness. At times, political training appears to have been excessive, but the regime has demanded a level of discrete political consciousness which will grant its particular goals and styles of rule a high level of legitimacy. It seeks, as we will demonstrate, a commitment of a highly self-sacrificing kind, and elementary education is the first step of the way.

THE ROLE OF THE TEACHER AND PARENT

Before proceeding, it might be well to consider for a moment how the teacher, the elementary school teacher in particular, conceives of his role in the educational process. This role, naturally, is related to the function of education itself within the society. In *Professional Study Lectures for Elementary School Teachers*,[10] Chang T'eng-hsiao quotes Mao Tse-tung's *On the New Democracy* (1940): "Economics is the foundation of a society and politics is the concentrated manifestation of economics." For Mao a "given culture" is the reflection of the politics and economics of a given society. The book then goes on to place education within the context of Mao's formulation:

> Thus, a given economy first determines a given politics, and after this determines a given education. Education is thus derivative of and secondary to politics. Therefore, education is determined not only by economics but by politics as well. On the other hand, education performs a definite service to economics and to politics (regardless of its subjective content or of its intentions). That is to say, the political ideals of a given society are its educational ideals, and its political mission is its educational mission.[11]

What is the role of the teacher in this process? As the author points out in a chapter entitled "Function and Mission of the Teacher," it follows logically that the role of the teacher is one of conscientious implementation of government and Party directives on education and of closely linking his own work with "ideology." More specifically, it is the further duty of the teacher:

> To arm the pupil with systematic scientific knowledge, and, on the basis of this, to cultivate in the pupil a correct world view and philosophy of life. Bringing the child to recognize study as creative labor is the glorious mission with which the nation and the people have entrusted him (i.e., the teacher). The completion of his study mission is the concrete expression of a child's patriotism. The more closely, the more clearly, and the more concretely that the teacher can link a child's study with political struggle and with the cause of reconstruction, the more lofty will be the quality of the child's study and labor and the more conscientious and responsible his study attitudes will be.[12]

Statements of this sort do not provide much practical guidance to the working teacher on how to go about the process of cultivating these desired objectives in the pupil. How was a teacher to implement Article 42 of the "Common Program" calling for the nurturing of love of the motherland, love of labor, love of science, love of the people, and protection of public property, or the "Five Loves," as they came to be known in the popular slogans? In response to the problem presented by these demands, various Chinese educators produced manuals and guidebooks in which they set out concrete programs for teaching patriotism and instilling the "Five Loves" into the minds of elementary school pupils. These guidebooks are an invaluable source for assessing the temper of education at that time.

In writings in the early 1950's, it was recognized that education in the "Five Loves" or in "patriotism" had to begin early in life:

The cultivation of these civic virtues should begin in childhood and their basis should be established especially in elementary school. Consequently, the implementation of "Five Loves" education is the central task of the elementary schools in the cultivation of children to become good citizens.[13]

It was further recognized that if these aims were to be carried out at the elementary school level, the groundwork had to be laid even before the pupil began his formal education. The task of preparing the pupil for formal education in the civic virtues fell on parents and, in a more organized way, on the nursery school. A good example of the pervasiveness of this moral and political training is found in a brief guide for nursery workers and parents compiled by the Shanghai City Democratic Women's Federation in 1951. The book, entitled *A Handbook of Child Training,* outlines the course of physical and psychological development for the child from the age of two through the age of six and lists what he should be able to do and know at each stage.[14]

It is during the third year that the compilers introduce the first hints of political socialization. The main concern, of course, at this age, is with training the child to take care of himself, with developing in him a spirit of independence, enriching his knowledge of the world, satisfying his curiosity, and enlarging his spoken vocabulary. Heading the list of items with which the three-to-four-year-old should be familiar, however, is the "the picture of Chairman Mao and the national flag."

During the child's fourth year, it is recommended that the supervisor give attention to fostering the child's cooperative habits and to strengthening education in love of labor and love of his companions. In terms of political socialization he should

1. Know stories about how Chairman Mao and Stalin love children and (should) love and respect them;

2. Know a few stories about how the Liberation Army fought the reactionaries.

During the fifth year it is advised that the child's concepts of love of country, love for the leaders, love of labor, love of science, and protection of public property be intensified.

During the sixth year, emphasis should be on "fostering an enthusiasm for service, on understanding the significance of thrift and of observing rules, on hating reactionaries and American Imperialism, on loving the Soviet Union and other peace-loving friendly nations, on loving the new China, and on loving the Communist Party and the People's Liberation Army, which serve the people." Among the items of information that the six-year-old should possess are the following:

1. To know that the People's Republic of China is his motherland.

2. To know, love, and respect the leaders of the Chinese people.

3. To know what the Communist Party does and what the People's Liberation Army does.

4. To know the birthday of the Communist Party and the birthday of the Liberation Army.

It is with this sort of background that the child, at about the age of seven, would begin his formal schooling. Training in good citizenship and love for country is, of course, common to most nations. It is interesting to note, however, the scope which Chinese educators, as instruments of Mao, envisioned for education of this kind. As we shall see, from limited beginnings at the pre-school levels, political indoctrination assumes ever increasing importance as the child grows older. Hu Yen-li, in the book cited above on the *"Five Loves"*, discusses this problem of the scope of education for "good citizenship," defining it as an all encompassing task not only of the school itself but of other social institutions as well:

There are those who say that *Five Loves* education should be a part of the political information course and should be taught by the political information teacher.

True, the political information teacher should indeed have this responsibility. However, it cannot be considered sufficient for *Five Loves* education to consist merely of obtaining a few dogmatic items of knowledge about the so-called *Five Loves* as happened in the former ethics and citizenship courses. It must be united with actuality. Not only should the child obtain a knowledge of the *Five Loves*, but he should also be able to put them into practice, extending the virtues of the *Five Loves* into his daily life and conduct, putting their highest ideals into practice. Consequently, the implementation of *Five Loves* education is not the responsibility of the political information teacher only, but is the common task of the entire body of teachers. Moreover, this is not a form of education that should be carried out only in political information classes. Rather, education should be carried out in all subjects, in all classes, and in all extra-curricular activities, with the *Five Loves* as core. Furthermore, it is not only school education that must have the *Five Loves* as its core, but the family and society also must carry out education with the *Five Loves* as its core. It is only in this way that it can truly be united with actuality, and through the cultivation of a new democratic youth, the objectives of *Five Loves* education attained.[15]

The foundation of the "Five Loves" was, of course, "patriotism," or in a more literal translation of the Chinese term, "love for country." It was from love for country that the other four loves would naturally spring. For this reason, we shall concentrate here on the means and techniques by which it was proposed to instill the virtue of love for country.

In terms of the "psychology of patriotism," Chinese educational theorists appear to have taken their cue from their Russian colleagues. According to the latter, a patriotic state of mind and patriotic conduct are inseparable from and have their beginnings in love for parents and relatives. On the basis of these fundamental relationships, the child can be led from a love of the family to a love for his village and the natural environment. From a love of his teacher he can be led to a love for the school and for society, and through a love of his own organization—the Pioneers for the Chinese—he can be led to a love for the Party and for the leader, Mao Tse-tung. In turn, he can then be directed into a love for the new China that the Party and Mao have created.[16] In his book, Hu Yen-ti suggests a similar process of relating family and village, for which one has a natural love, to the concept of the "motherland," which functions to protect these basic entities.[17]

One of the ways that Hu suggests for building a spirit of love for country is to invoke a spirit of national pride. For this purpose he lists a number of examples of Chinese superiority. We shall list here a few of the seventeen items he presents to give a flavor of the program.[18]

1. We have the Himalayan Mountains, which are the highest in the world, and the Kunlun mountain range, which is the longest in the world.

2. Our country contains the longest river in Asia—the Yangtze.

3. Our country's t'ung, oil, tea, pig bristles, and silk are famous the world over.

4. Our country made the compass during the Southern Sung period and used it in maritime navigation.

5. During the Han Dynasty, our country invented paper.

Hu then presents an extremely detailed program for education for patriotism. Before touching on this, however, it may be of greater help in achieving an over-all perspective of this sort of education, to examine a report on actual practice at the elementary school level. The program outlined below, according to the author, was that carried out at the elementary school of the Nanking Normal School around 1950.[19]

The objectives of the program were as follows:

1. Lectures on the superior culture and the abundant local products of the motherland, and on the great-

ness of the strength of the motherland and on the elevation in her international position in order to cultivate in the child a high degree of national self-respect and self-confidence and to cause him to love his motherland.

2. Instruction on the historical facts of aggression against, and oppression and exploitation of, peoples by imperialism, feudalism, and bureaucratism to cause the child to hate the enemy, particularly American imperialism and the Kuomintang reactionaries.

3. Introduction of the main points of the Common Program, to cause the child to know the correct leadership of the Chinese Communist Party and of Chairman Mao, as well as to love the Communist Party and Chairman Mao.

4. Explanation of the great strength of the world peace camp to cause the pupil to know that the Soviet Union is the fortress guarding the peace of the world, that Stalin is the leader of the peaceful peoples of the world, and (to cause him) to love the Soviet Union, Stalin, and the laboring peoples of the world.[20]

In order to carry out this program, the elementary school in question carried out a broad program of activities, involving the following three phases:

1. Classroom education
2. Extracurricular activities
3. Life guidance[21]

From this general outline, it can be seen that patriotic education permeated most of the activities of the pupil and was not confined to the classroom. Let us now discuss in greater detail how this type of education was carried out under each of the above categories.

1. *Classroom education.* As was suggested in the quotation from Hu Yen-li, the work of patriotic or "Five Loves"

education was not a task to be relegated only to courses in political or ideological instruction. Instead, it was to permeate the entire curriculum. This is what we find in the Nanking Normal College's elementary school program. The author here emphasizes history as a key course in patriotic education as "study of history and patriotism are inseparable."[22] He also discusses, however, how patriotic education was infused into political information, language (i.e. Chinese), arithmetic, geography, science, music, physical education, art, and labor classes. An outline of these procedures follows:[23]

a. History. In teaching history, the elementary school emphasized the following six points:

1. Causing the child to become aware of the outstanding traditions of industriousness and courage of the Chinese people.

2. Causing the child to understand the course of the bitter struggle of the working people in transforming their natural environment.

3. Causing the child to understand the history of the solidarity, mutual help, and cooperation of the Chinese laboring people in their struggle for survival and freedom.

4. Causing the child to understand the deep wisdom of the Chinese laboring people and the great contributions that they have made.

5. Causing the child to know the strength of the people and to get rid of fear and worship of imperialism.

6. Causing the child to be thoroughly aware of the reciprocal character of the Chinese revolution and of the world revolution.

The author continues, quoting examples from history texts demonstrating oppression under feudal society and imperialism.

b. Political information. In this field, the program emphasized the development of the child's trust in and feeling for his motherland as well as guidance in putting these into practice. The points emphasized in instruction were:

1. Cultivating the child's spirit of the *Five Loves*.

2. Forming the child's spirit of solidarity and mutual help in the service of the masses.

3. Causing the child to have a correct knowledge of enemies and friends.

4. Lectures on the Treaty of Friendship between China and the Soviet Union (February 1950) in order to strengthen the child's faith in the preservation of world peace and the building of a new China.

c. Language. In the language courses, that is, those classes concerned with learning to read and write Chinese, patriotic themes were introduced in the following ways:

1. Telling stories about labor, combat, production economy support of the front lines, and patriotic stories in order to arouse the child's patriotic emotions.

2. Compilation of supplementary teaching materials about commemoration days and social campaigns in order to strengthen the child's knowledge.

3. Guiding the child in writing letters of comfort to Chinese and Korean soldiers and to the Liberation Army in Tibet in order to arouse the child's respect and love for the soldiers of his motherland.

4. Guiding the child in the practice of speaking in order to develop him into a powerful young propaganda worker.

As this guidebook was written at a time when educational materials had not yet been standardized, the teachers themselves wrote various supplementary reading exercises on national holidays, resistance to American "aggression," secret agents of reactionary parties, and other relevant materials. In addition, they wrote a small collection of anti-American stories in which they used various literary forms "to describe the record of American imperialistic aggression against China and to reveal the internal decadence of American imperialism."

d. Arithmetic. Arithmetic lent itself to the task of cultivating patriotism in yet another way, as the following program of instruction at the school indicates:

1. Calculations of the prizes of war obtained by the Liberation Army at each victory.

2. Calculation of production and construction in this city for the past two years.

3. Calculation of the losses of American imperialism in its invasion of Korea (soldiers and weapons).

4. Calculation of the strength of the camp of world peace (population, area, products, military).

e. Geography. In geography classes, the following points were given emphasis:

1. Lectures on the valuable resources of the nation and on local products in order to elicit the child's love for the motherland and for his own local region.

2. Introduction to the ways of life of minority peoples within the nation in order to strengthen the child's knowledge of minority peoples.

3. Lectures about the geography of the nations of the two great world camps and about the lives of their peoples.

4. Causing the child to become aware that the natural environment can be used to develop the productive power of human society.

f. Science.

1. Establishment of attitudes of research and science in the child, and the destruction of superstitious concepts.

2. Causing the child to know the correct uses of science. Causing him to know furthermore that the purpose of science is to serve politics.

3. Cultivating the child's spirit of creativity and interest in science and research.

4. Forming the child's awareness and habits of respect for individual health and public sanitation.

g. Music. In music classes, the school employed the following philosophy and technique:

In music classes, emphasis was given to the teaching of songs sufficient to arouse patriotic emotions and to foster revolutionary ideology. The following songs were selected for teaching: *A New China Has Been Born, Sing of Chairman Mao, The Rising Sun Shines in All Directions, Our Country's Rivers and Mountains are Made of Iron, Our Country's Frontier River, Walking on the Road toward Peace, Peace Signature Song, People of Taiwan Arise, Red Scarf, Anti-Spy Song, When Our Motherland Is in Need, Bestriding the Yalu River, Kill Those American Wolves, The Fall of American Imperialism,* and *Great is the Strength of the Chinese and Soviet People's Solidarity.* We ourselves composed the following songs: *A Great Happy Day, Speaking of Korea, The Korean People Can Manage Their Home, A Model Child, Relieve Brothers in Distress,* and *The Song of Willing Conscription.*

h. Physical Education.

1. Cultivating the child's interest in and habits of exercise.

2. Forming in the child a spirit of solidarity, mutual help, courage, and activeness.

3. Selection of teaching materials having revolutionary ideology and educational significance. We ourselves compiled the following teaching materials:

> "Exercise for maintaining peace and a healthy body"
> "Striving to Enter the Corps"
> "Liberate Taiwan!"

i. Art.

1. Cultivating the child's creative abilities and ability to use art.

2. Guiding the child in drawing propaganda cartoons.

3. Guiding the child in using the *Red Star* and various work tools in his drawings.

4. Guiding the child in writing artistic characters and propaganda slogans.

j. Labor.

1. Fostering the child's constructiveness, capacity for planning, and creativity as well as fostering his labor viewpoint and habits.

2. Guiding him in common methods of cultivating plants and caring for animals.

3. Using the waste materials to make various kinds of tools (such as blackboard erasers, chicken feather brooms, mops, book satchels, etc.).

4. Guidance in making various teaching tools (such as counters, cards, simple geometric forms, etc.).

From this outline, it can easily be seen that political

education was introduced into and adapted to the characteristics of each branch of the curriculum. In addition to these techniques of formal instruction, the school also carried out a varied program of extracurricular activities aimed at promoting patriotism. Let us now examine these in detail.[24]

2. *Extracurricular activities.* The school conducted six types of extracurricular activity related to patriotic education. These were for the purpose of "aiding the child to broaden his social and political horizons and strengthen his knowledge and understanding." The following discussion indicates the scope of these activities and suggests the uses to which they were or could be put.

a. Visiting exhibitions. Here the author reports comments from pupils after visits to an exhibition on the history of the American "invasion" of China and another on "the great motherland." The first exhibition evidently depicted both American and Japanese aggression against China, for as one pupil said:

> After going to the exhibition, I hate Japan because she invaded China. I hate American imperialism even more because America helped the Japanese army to burn Chinese people to death.

Yet another student spoke of the "debt of blood" that America owes to China for her part in "aggression" against China a hundred years ago. If the purpose of the exhibition on American "imperialism was to fan hatred of America, that of the exhibition on the "motherland" was clearly to inspire devotion, as well as other emotions. As one little girl is reported to have written in her composition about the exhibition:

> How great and lovable our Motherland is! Each one of the 450 million people of China is one particle of force in protecting world peace! Now under the leadership of the Chinese Communist Party and Chairman Mao, we have overcome American Imperialism and her running dog reactionaries and have liberated all China so that the people have attained a happy life.

She went on to describe her determination to study and work hard so that she could contribute her strength to national construction. As a result of such experiences, the authors felt that attendance at exhibitions serves to raise the level of a child's ideology and awareness.

b. Organizing children to watch moving pictures. According to the authors of the program, moving pictures are among the best of educational tools:

> Whenever a motion picture having political and educational significance arrived, we organized the children in collective viewing. Sometimes after watching the movie, we held discussions.

In reporting on the favorable response, both verbal and behavioral, of pupils after watching suitably selected motion pictures, the author concluded that "motion picture education" also results in a rapid elevation of a child's awareness.

c. Organization in reading the *Hsin Shao-nien Pao* (New Youth Newspaper). This activity, which was considered of benefit to the children, was accompanied by encouraging them to contribute their own articles.

d. Holding commemoration meetings. This involved holding gatherings on revolutionary commemoration days and festivals to which the teachers were invited and at which special reports were made. The meetings were followed by publication of the main points of the meeting and by discussions.

e. Holding debates on current events. The authors report that as the result of one debate held the previous year, the children's hatred of American "imperialism" was intensified and that their speaking abilities were raised.

f. Listening to radio broadcasts. The children were organized to listen to radio broadcasts on current events and to broadcasts having "political, ideological, and educational significance." On one occasion, for example, the school organized the pupils to listen to a broadcast in which representatives of various groups in the city accused counter-revolutionaries of their crimes. As one pupil was reported to have said afterward:

Spies kill people, set fires, spread poisons, make ru-
mors, dishonor women, destroy the revolutionary order,
and destroy our schools. They are truly abominable,
and we must stamp them out.

Another pupil said:

Only when we have completely exterminated spies will
we live in security.

3. *Life guidance.* As a supplement to these activities, the
school also carried out a program of what was termed "life
guidance." This had as its primary objectives

The cultivation of the child's capacity for self-aware-
ness and autonomy, his revolutionary ideology, and his
spirit of patriotism and internationalism.

It involved

The fostering of superior character and habits in the
child through the organization of student life and
activities.

In order to carry out these objectives, the school made use of
the provisions for political and ideological training as set forth
in a Ministry of Education program of "life guidance" for
elementary school pupils.[25]
Attention was also given to the following seven points:

1. Inspiring the child to draw up a patriotic pact and
   frequently assisting the child in a genuine self-
   examination.

2. Guiding the children in organizing class clubs, with
   attention to cultivation of cadre from among them.

3. Cultivating activist children in helping and uniting
   the ordinary children.

4. When necessary, and on the basis of actual conditions, holding centralized training.

5. Adopting the methods of competitions and challenges in order to elevate the children's initiative and enterprise.

6. Strengthening corps training and widening the influence of the corps.

7. Making family contacts.

This is but one of many articles dealing with the subject of patriotic education. The particular program presented by the author, except perhaps for the material concerning the program of life guidance, was not necessarily a universal program. It represents the responses of one group of educators to the problem presented by official policy. It is, nevertheless, representative of the spirit of similar articles. Therefore, it is not illogical to conclude that programs of a similar character were carried out in many elementary schools in Communist China during this period.

As it happened, historical circumstances presented Chinese educators with a far more powerful psychological basis for instilling patriotism: the Korean War. With American soldiers fighting on the mainland of Asia and pressing dangerously close to the borders of China, it was only natural to single out the United States as the prime villain of international politics, and a villain that might well invade Chinese territory. This is reflected in the "Oppose America, Aid Korea" campaign that arose under official prompting in China at that time. Clearly, the threat of American invasion could serve as an excellent motive for patriotism. This can be seen to some extent in the materials from Nanking elementary school quoted above, as for instance in the curriculum in arithmetic and in some of the songs used in the music classes.

With the intensification of the Korean War, however, concentration on America as the major enemy and the infusion of this theme into the curriculum appears to have been equally intensified. The words of Hu Yen-li in the introduction to his detailed teacher's guide on carrying out "Five Loves" education on the basis of the "Oppose America, Aid Korea" campaign, are suggestive of this:

> When our children learned of the destruction, killing, and invasion taking place on the land, seas, and in the air of our People's Republic by the airplanes, warships, and pirate troops of American imperialism, they wanted to gnash their teeth in their hatred for the enemy invading us, and struggle to protect their homes and their nation.[26]

With this preface, he introduces a program of patriotic education based on anti-Americanism. This reflects the philosophy noted earlier of the mission of education being equivalent to the political mission of the state. The program he presents is that of the Elementary Department of Nanking University, (November 1950). Because of the detail of the program, which is essentially a teacher's guide, we can discuss here only its major points, with particular reference to applications in language classes.

The objectives of the program were as follows:

1. Through this instruction in current events to cause the child to have an initial understanding of the present situation and of the savageness of American imperialistic aggression and to intensify in the child a psychology of hatred for American imperialism.

2. By means of various educational activities, to solve some of the child's ideological problems and to cultivate his spirit of patriotism and internationalism.[27]

The points to be given emphasis in instruction were the following:

1. The development of the Korean War

2. Internal contradictions existing in America

3. The historical facts of American imperialism's invasion of China

4. The question of the atomic bomb

5. Opposing America and siding with Korea protects our homes and nation

6. Opposing spies and traitors, and raising vigilance

7. Protecting world peace and striving for world victory.[28]

Aside from actual classroom instruction, it was recommended that the children be organized in such activities as making propaganda posters, slogans, picture strips, and maps, as well as in preparing reports and synopses of current events.

The programs for classroom education are similar in spirit to those used in the elementary school of Nanking Normal College, except that here the major emphasis is on the war and the evils of American "imperialism." The suggested study activities for each subject at the upper elementary level is as follows:

1. Language	Stories of the bravery in battle of the Chinese People's Volunteers and of the Korean People's Army.
2. History	The major historical facts of the invasion of China by American imperialists.
3. Science	What we know about the atomic bomb.
4. Political Information	What kind of a country imperialist America is.
5. Geography	Discussion of the weakness of American imperialism's strategy from the relation-

ship between the geography of China, Korea, and America.

6. Arithmetic

Statistics on the populations, troops, production ... of the two camps.

7. Art

Co-ordination with other classes in drawing cartoons and propaganda posters.

8. Music

"Oppose America, Aid Korea" songs.[29]

Further comments about the conduct of the language courses are of particular interest in the context of the analysis of the *Readers* presented in this study:

> In language classes, we selected for reading essays concerning (the theme of) "Oppose America, Aid Korea" and such vivid materials as stirring and moving stories, poems and songs about the heroic fighting of the Volunteer Army in Korea and about the friendship of the Korean people. The children studied these excitedly as they were of much more value and interest than the wooden materials in the textbooks. They learned the poems and songs with loud, clear voices, and studied Oppose America, Aid Korea social studies propaganda. In composition class, everyone wrote letters of comfort to the Oppose America, Aid Korea Volunteer Army and to the Korean People's Army.[30]

The programs of instruction quoted above represent the first phase in the development of the content of Chinese moral and patriotic education under the new regime. They were the first response of educators to the problem of moral education and, as we have seen, appear to have been linked very closely with the Korean War once it had broken out. As time went on and as the crisis of the Korean War gave way to other concerns, as seen both from the standpoint of Party pronouncements and writings on education as well as from the vantage point furnished by the texts translated here, the concerns of educators in terms of patriotic or moral education also shifted. Even so, the reader will find a much in the later books that reflects the concerns of the early 1950's. It thus seems that the basic spirit, at least, of "Five Loves" education was carried over into later materials. There is, however, a significant shift in emphasis that is clearly discernible. It is to this shift in emphasis that we will now turn our attention.

EDUCATION FOR COMMUNIST MORALITY

By the mid 1950's, the concern for moral education had broadened to include "communist morality." Actually, of course, the elements of "communist morality" were present in the educational programs of the early part of the decade, particularly as seen in the Ministry of Education's program for "life guidance." The writings from the mid-1950's would appear to be reformulations of these principles in terms of the broader goals of communism. That is to say, the moral principles enunciated earlier, the "Five Loves," for example, or service to the people, are stated in the wider context of their relation to the class struggle and to the establishment of socialism and communism. The essence of the basic principles of "communist morality" are, in the words of one writer:

> To oppose all oppression of man by man; to struggle for the liberation of all workers, irrespective of race or nationality, from every form of exploitation; to place the well-being of the entire society, the whole body of the people, and the whole body of workers before all else.[31]

"Communist morality" is thus primarily a social ethic (a collective conscience) rather than a personal ethic (an individual conscience.) The standard for judgment of a person's behavior becomes how closely it conforms to the principles of "communist morality," or in other words, how well it conforms to the essential requirements of the collective interest. As another writer on this subject explained:

> To evaluate whether a person's behavior toward society and toward other persons conforms to the principles of communist morality, it must be determined whether this behavior in all respects conforms to the interests of creating, consolidating, and completing the great causes of socialism and communism. All behavior that conforms to the interests of this revolutionary struggle conforms to the principles of communist morality; if it does not, it does not conform to the principle of communist morality. In our nation at present, to weigh whether a person's behavior conforms to the principle of communist morality is to see whether a person's behavior conforms to the interests of socialist construction and socialist transformation and to those of protection of the motherland; whether it conforms to the interests of the revolutionary collective; whether it conforms to the interests of consolidating the socialist camp and protecting world peace; and whether the individual is sacredly carrying out his own obligations in these matters. All behavior conforming to these interests conforms to the principles of communist morality; otherwise, it does not conform to the principles of communist morality.[32]

According to this same writer, "communist morality" therefore makes five concrete demands of the individual.

The most important of the demands of "communist morality" is seen as behavior that is in complete conformity to the interests of revolutionary class struggle. In practice this means complete devotion to the cause of communism and immersion in revolutionary struggle. It involves a hatred for enemies of the people, and on the positive side, characteristics of solidarity, organization, discipline, mutual help, resoluteness, and determination. Equally important is a spirit of self-sacrificing "revolutionary heroism." These characteristics are seen as essential to the completion of the revolutionary cause, that is, to the ultimate goal of establishing a communist society. All of this means that a man should be judged according to his involvement with politics, since the two are inseparable. To deny one's "revolutionary responsibility" is to be immoral.

The second demand that "communist morality" makes on the individual is that he place collective and public interests above his own private and selfish interests. In theory, this does not, as the writer says, involve an "insurmountable contradiction," because the collective and the individual interest are to be united, and the assurance of the collective interest in its turn assures the individual interest. This subordination of individual interests involves as well the individual's conscious observance of his obligations to society and to the state.

"Communist morality" also demands that the individual approach his work with a "new socialist work attitude," striving for a high rate of production. This new attitude toward labor is to replace such erroneous views as that of labor being a difficult burden that is to be feared, so that labor is a "glorious, honorable, and courageous" activity, which should be seen as everyone's right and obligation. The individual should take part in labor because it is the basis of the socialist cause. A point of significance for us is an emphasis on the honorable character of physical labor. To disparage physical labor is to hold an incorrect attitude toward labor.

The fourth demand of "communist morality" is loyalty and love for China, attitudes that should be coupled with those of an internationalist spirit, that is, a spirit of respect and fraternity for other peoples. These attitudes are naturally linked to concepts of "proletarian internationalism" and communist solidarity.

The fifth and final demand of communist morality is for a conscious observance of the constitution and of the laws of the state.

From this brief survey of communist morality it can be seen that it does not concern itself primarily with the ethics of a person's private relations with others. Nevertheless, personal conduct in relation to marriage and family falls within the sphere of communistic moral concern to the extent that behavior on that level influences the performance of social duties. Thus, debauchery, hedonism, or failure to fulfill one's duties as a husband and father or as a wife and mother can be termed immoral conduct in that they lessen the individual's social effectiveness. Running off with another man's wife or abandoning one's children are not immoral because they violate some immutable principle of morality, but because they damage the collective and the revolution.[33]

It is within the context of this sort of morality that Chinese writers on education and its purposes appear to have formulated their programs. Unfortunately, we do not have the same sort of detailed teacher's guides and handbooks for this period as we had for the earlier years of the decade. Nevertheless, we do have some fairly detailed statements on educational content which take up the problem of how communist morality is to be cultivated and of how its principles can be integrated into the curriculum.

In the quotation to follow, it is still possible to perceive the basic framework established for the cultivation of the "Five Loves" and for essential patriotic education. There are a number of points worthy of note in connection with this statement.

First, as before, there is a concern for the development of a deep love for China, a love which is to serve as the basic motive in the complete subordination of the individual to the state.

Second, certain qualities essential to the attainment of national goals are spelled out: firmness, courage, humility, sincerity, frugality, and simplicity.

Third, it is stated that the cultivation of these moral qualities is a task not only of classroom education, but of guidance of pupils in their extracurricular activities and in their daily lives. This is again consistent with the viewpoints and practices found in the writings of the early part of the decade.

Fourth, the writer stresses the importance of cultivating in the pupil a love for labor and obedience to regulations and laws.

Fifth, these virtues are conceived of not as superficial adornments of the personality, but rather as a matter of *behavioral habits* in which motives and behavior should be integrated and function without conflict.

Sixth, we can see, as in previous writings, that moral education is not to be relegated to one phase of the curriculum, but rather is to form a part of the content of each subject taught. The important point is that communist moral education is thus not to be a separate subject stuck awkwardly and haphazardly into the curriculum. Rather it should form the basic framework of the educational process into which the curriculum itself is to be integrated. Bearing these points in mind, let us now turn to a discussion of what one author describes as "comprehensive development education:"[34]

THE CONTENT OF COMPREHENSIVE DEVELOPMENTAL EDUCATION

In the cultivation of Communist morality, it is first necessary to devote attention to the cultivation of a patriotic spirit of love for and devoted loyalty to the motherland. This is to cultivate and educate the younger generation to love the Chinese Communist Party and Chairman Mao, to love the Chinese People's Liberation Army, to love the workers and peasants and all people who have struggled on behalf of socialism, to love the brilliant cultural heritage of their motherland, to love our factories and farms, our cities and villages, our rivers, seas, and mountain forests, and to love each blade of grass and each tree of their motherland, in that these make up the wealth and inexhaustible treasure of our motherland. The cultivation of the younger generation in love for the motherland requires that they be cultivated in steadfast mastery of knowledge and in the steeling of their bodies in order to prepare them to offer their entire knowledge and talent to their motherland, to have a violent hatred for all enemies destructive to the cause of socialism, and in times of danger to the motherland to protect her and oppose all enemies with firm resolve.

In cultivating the younger generation to become true patriots, it is at the same time necessary that they be internationalists. The spirit of internationalism is one of seeking to unite the peoples of all nations into a great revolutionary family and one of happiness at the accomplishments of revolutionary movements of other peoples. The firm solidarity of our nation and the Soviet Union together with other people's democratic republics is the basis of internationalism.

The cultivation of patriotism and a spirit of internationalism in the younger generation is one of the important tasks of communist moral education.

To cultivate communist morality in the younger generation, it is necessary to cultivate such superior qualities in them as firmness, courage, humility, sincerity, frugality, and simplicity. (The remainder of the paragraph discusses the reasons why this is necessary and has been omitted).

A person who can truly use the communistic spirit in thought and conduct is also able to form superior communist qualities. In order to cultivate these qualities in the younger generation, it is necessary to consolidate and to develop good qualities and to eliminate and to overcome bad qualities through classroom teaching in each subject, through various extracurricular activities, and through everyday life. This is a meticulous and painstaking educational process.

Labor education is one of the basic elements of communist moral education. Labor is the first necessary condition of human life. Without labor, there would be nothing. Labor is a glorious and great task, but exploitation is shameful conduct. We must cultivate the younger generation to view labor as their principal responsibility toward society, cultivate their love for labor and their love for the working people and cultivate in them the concept of labor and habits of labor so that they will treat labor with a positive and conscious attitude.

This is to say, they must respect labor regulations. However, these regulations differ from those of the past in that they are consciously observed rather than enforced. Unless regulations are consciously observed, socialist production cannot proceed. We must cultivate the younger generation to become persons capable of consciously observing labor regulations. For this reason, in school the pupils should be cultivated in conscious observance of school regulations, in maintaining order, in protecting school property, and in respecting the collective interest. In addition, he should be cultivated in the ideology of obeying state plans, respecting state laws, respecting social order, and respecting social and public morality in order to prepare him to respect labor regulations and military regulations in the future.

A pupil's obedience to rules is the standard for a pupil's rules of study and conduct in daily life. This not only demands of the student that he consciously study rules, assuring the completion of his study tasks, but also raises the pupil's socialist consciousness, cultivating him to become a person having the qualities of communist morality. At the same time, under collectivist education, it results in the over-all development of his personality and in his becoming a conscious and active builder of socialismand protector of our great motherland.

Consequently, the cultivation in the younger generation of a patriotic spirit of love for and of devoted loyalty to the motherland, of communist morality, and of behavioral habits of observance of regulations is an integrative educational process. Behavioral habits are the basic requirements of communist moral practice. It is only in this way that the younger generation can be cultivated to become persons in whom word and deed are consistent and in whom the outer and inner are one.

The author goes on to describe the basic content of technical education, physical education, and esthetic education, which are in his view, the components of a comprehensive education required to produce a well-rounded person. He then proceeds to explain the mutual relationship between these various categories of education. The following passage is instructive in that it provides another general blueprint for the integration of political education into all phases of the curriculum.

Next, we must discuss the mutual relationships between the elements of comprehensive developmental education. As has been said above, the individual elements of a comprehensive developmental education are not independent of each other, but rather have an organic unity. The individual elements permeate and affect each other and, in the actual educational process, are often carried out simultaneously. For example, in the teaching of literature, helping the pupil to develop his powers of cognition and attentiveness is a task of intellectual education, whereas guiding the pupil's life and influencing his conduct by means of the emotions, viewpoints, and ideas revealed in the literary works is a task of moral education. The analysis and study of the artistic form of a literary work, furthermore, serves to develop a pupil's esthetic education. In teaching mathematics, generalization from facts and examples develops a pupil's capacity for logical thought and is a task of intellectual education. Through the development of mathematical exercises on such applied problems as mutual aid and co-operation and increases in agricultural production not only is the student made more skillful in his knowledge, but the student is also brought to understand the superiority of the socialist system. As a consequence, the student is brought to a greater love for his socialist motherland and his concept of collectivism is cultivated as well, thus fulfilling the task of moral education. In teaching about nature, bringing the pupil to a knowledge of natural phenomena and their laws and developing his thirst for knowledge and his powers of thought fulfill the task of intellectual education, whereas bringing the pupil to an understanding, through observation and cultivation of various plants, of the relationship between this and socialist construction, in addition to cultivating his production skills and labor habits, not only fulfills the task of moral education, but at the same time is a factor in comprehensive technical education.

The relationships between each subject are of this kind. For example, in teaching pupils about physiology and hygiene, the pupils are brought to a conscious understanding of the importance of physical education. Further, the correct implementation of physical education not only improves the health of the pupil but also plays a part in the growth of the pupil's moral qualities. In physical education classes, attention should be given to uniformity and beauty of movement, so that it is related to esthetic education.

The mutual relationships between the content of comprehensive developmental education are not only of this kind in classroom teaching but in extracurricular activities and daily life as well. Classroom teaching and extracurricular activities should be united, as for example, in developing extracurricular groups organizing the planting of various crops, putting acquired knowledge to practical use, and organizing pupils in practicing habits of productive labor. This, under the premise of developing intellectual education, develops factors of a comprehensive technical education. Pupils, through labor, develop organizational capacities, division of labor, co-operation, solidarity, and mutual assistance, and give attention to appropriate distribution of work according to physical strength. This serves to develop a spirit of collectivism. Moreover, attention to the development of a pupil's physical strength is also a factor in physical education.

Consequently, a thorough-going implementation of comprehensive developmental education is a basic principle in cultivating the younger generation in becoming adults of a socialist society. This should be the guiding ideology in the organization and conduct of our teaching and education work. However, each subject has its own teaching objectives and tasks, and each activity has his own objectives and content. We must, on the basis of the objectives and tasks of each branch of teaching, and by thoroughly penetrating the content of teaching materials and the objectives and content of each activity, put into effect comprehensive developmental education...

The foregoing materials make up the general context in which the *Readers* available to us were written. Although there was an intensification of socialist education beginning in 1957-1958, and although there were changes in the administration and character of the schools at the secondary level with the creation of the half-study half-work schools, there is little indication that there was any great change in the over-all philosophy of political and ideological education at the elementary level. The *Readers* may well indicate an attempt at intensification of political indoctrination in the formal curriculum, but they are very likely not substantially different from what went before.

As is shown in Appendix 1, there is much "older" material in the *Readers* dating from the early part of the decade and from the preceding decade (1940's) as well. For example, among the categories of war stories and stories about personal heroes, there are a large number dealing with events during the Korean War and with friendship between the Chinese soldiers and the Korean people. Of war stories, apart from those about the Korean War, and with the exception of those about the Quemoy shellings (1958), the largest proportion concern either the Civil War or the Sino-Japanese War. During the period of the Sino-Japanese War many regions had their own elementary school readers which were reported to have used similar materials.[35]

Regardless of when any individual story was written, it is possible to detect in them most of the elements proposed by the various writers quoted above and in the Ministry of Education's program for "life guidance" in political and ideological education. This may not be immediately obvious from the methods of analysis that we have applied to the texts, as we have chosen to delineate the more obvious political and behavioral themes occurring in the stories. Thus, there is no thematic category of "Five Loves." A more careful examination of these categories will reveal, however, that the original "Five Loves" are well represented.

For example, the first of the "Five Loves," love for the motherland, involves a far wider range of themes, as interpreted by the Chinese themselves, than simple patriotism itself. Although it is amply represented in the *Readers*, stories and poems that are representative of the "First Love" have been divided among a number of categories in our analysis. Thus, under the major category of political themes, distinction is made between themes of devotion and allegiance to the new society, the benevolence of the new society, and glorification of Mao Tse-tung. All of these are essentially patriotic themes. To place stories illustrating them in one all-inclusive category, however, is an over-simplification. As the analysis will show, many of these themes dealing with loyalty and patriotism are two-sided. One set of themes emphasizes the goodness of the new regime, whereas another set expresses the loyalty that one should feel toward it.

Similarly, we have treated as essentially "behavioral" themes certain areas that might also be considered to belong to the category of the "First Love" of patriotism. For example, self-sacrifice and heroism are treated under the theme or "altruistic behavior," whereas stories dealing with formation of favorable attitudes toward nature, which might also be treated as part of the love of nation theme, are placed within a thematic category entitled "esthetic aspects of nature and farm life."

Another example of how the treatment of the "Five Loves" varies is that accorded "protection of public property." We have included stories illustrating this concern in a category of behavioral themes entitled "social and personal responsibility."

"Love of labor" is the only one of the original "Five Loves" to which we have accorded a separate category. Here it is frequently joined with a theme of love of study as well. Specific citations of stories involving this theme occur in the section on thematic analysis under behavioral themes.

The original theme of love of science among the "Five Loves" is essentially covered under our behavioral category of "starting from reality in resolving conflict" or "investigation and research." At no point in the *Readers*, however, does one find any overt expression of the concept of "love" for science as one does of "love" for labor.

From this, it is clear that although the "Five Loves" play an important part in the *Readers*, they are not necessarily stated in those terms.

A survey of the *Readers* also indicates that many stories and poems illustrate various points of the original Ministry of Education directive on "Life Guidance" for elementary school pupils within the sphere of political and ideological education. Some of the articles of that program are not necessarily applicable to Language classes and others obviously were eliminated as a result of the Sino-Soviet conflict. Nevertheless, a good proportion are still reflected in the *Readers*. It may be helpful to cite below a number of the 30 articles of the program together with references to stories or poems in which they are illustrated. The reader will, of course, find further examples in addition to those cited below.

4. To respect and love Chairman Mao and to study his spirit of service to the people and of finding the truth from the facts:

Chairman Mao at the Shihsanling Reservoir Work Site (Vol. 6, No. 1)
At the Yenan Central Hospital (Vol. 5, No. 33)
A Wounded Man's Wish (Vol. 7, No. 3)
Carry a Message to Peking (Vol. 2, N. 25)

5. To respect and to love the Chinese Communist Party and to support its correct leadership:

The Party Is My Mother (Vol. 6, No. 12)
Ever Since the Party Line (Vol. 7, No. 2)
A Letter to Comrade Hsü T'e-li (Vol. 10, No. 33)

7. To respect and to love the People's Liberation Army and its honorable soldiers, and to learn from their courageous fighting and spirit and iron discipline:

Uncle, Please Accept (Vol. 5, No. 36)
Mailing Back a Kitchen Knife (Vol. 7, No. 9)
The Watermelon Brothers (Vol. 7, No. 10)
The Little Messenger (Vol. 7, No. 11)
To Save a Fisherman's Life (Vol. 7, No. 12)

8. To guard state secrets and to devote attention to helping opposing traitors and spies:

Examining a Pass (Vol. 3, No. 18)
Liu Wen-Hsüeh (Vol. 6, No. 24), in a sense

11. To be be continually prepared to sacrifice one's life to protect the sovereignty of the territory of the motherland and the interests of the people and of the masses:

Tung Ts'ung-jui Gives His Life to Blow Up a Bunker (Vol. 6, No. 32)
Breaking Through the Wu River Barrier (Vol. 10, No. 16)
Liu Wen-hsüeh (Vol. 6, No. 24)

12. To mourn for the national heroes and revolutionary martyrs who defended the motherland, and to learn from their spirit of courageous and vigorous self-sacrifice:

At the Foot of Mount Mei (Vol. 10. No. 22)
Recollections of Sixteen Years Ago (Vol. 10, Nos. 13 and 14)
The Martyr Fang Chih-min (Vol. 8, No. 31)
Rather Death than Submission (Vol. 8, No. 30)

20. To foster collective life habits of the individual for the group and the group for the individual:

On Duty for the Day (Vol. 1, No. 38)
The Sunflower Smiled (Vol. 6, No. 25)
Giving Convenience to Others (Vol. 10, No. 8)

29. To love and protect public property of the school, of society, and of the nation, and to exert every effort to make repayment:

The Flowers in the Park (Vol. 1, No. 35)
Our Classroom (Vol. 2, No. 1)
In the Wheat Field (Vol. 2, No. 32)
Don't Walk Through Here (Vol. 3, No. 5)
Dialogue of the Tables and Chairs (Vol. 3, No. 24)

The above selection of articles from Section 4 (Politics and Ideology) of the Ministry of Education's program and the lists of stories in the *Readers* that exemplify or are related to them is only partial. The point emphasized here, however, is that there is a definite continuity between the earlier formulations of educational policy and the content of the *Readers*.

In assessing the place of the *Readers* in the continuity of Chinese educational policies for political and ideological indoctrination, however, it is important also to consider not only the past tradition out of which they were developed, but the varying influences working on education during the period in which they were in use.

The Great Proletarian Cultural Revolution brought the schools of China to a close in June 1966. These texts were, thus, presumably in use during the long period from at least 1958 until June 1966. In the wake of the Cultural Revolution, we can expect a considerable re-evaluation of education at all levels and without doubt the adoption of revised volumes. Stories such as the one concerning the goodness of Liu Shao-ch'i (see *A Woolen Blanket*, Vol. 7, No. 4) will most certainly be deleted. The emphasis on eliminating "old culture," "old habits," "old customs," and "old thought" will also no doubt find its place in the texts.

Between 1958 and 1966, however, there were a number of movements that may have served to alter the way in which the stories presented in these readers were utilized in practice.

The two chief movements were the Great Leap Forward and the Socialist Education Movement, the former of which ended in disaster and the latter of which had its beginnings in the fall of 1961. The Socialist Education Movement, in particular, may have brought with it an intensification of political education at all levels of the school system. This, however, is more in the area of conjecture than of fact.*

---

*The issues and policies involved in the Great Leap Forward and the Socialist Education Movement are too complex to be treated within the scope of this study. For an extensive analysis of the Great Leap Forward, see Franz Schurmann, *Ideology and Organization in Communist China* (Berkeley: University of California Press, 2nd edition, 1968). The Socialist Education Movement has been examined by Richard Baum and Frederick C. Teiwes in *Ssu-ch'ing: The Socialist Education Movement of 1962-1966* (China Research Monographs, No. 2, Berkeley: Center for Chinese Studies, 1968).

THREE

TECHNIQUES OF LANGUAGE TEACHING WITH REFERENCE TO THE TEACHING OF READING

INTRODUCTION

In the preceding chapter we have seen the extent to which the school curriculum has been designed as an instrument of indoctrination. As our concern in this study is with the part that language instruction and the teaching of reading play in the process of socialization, it is of considerable interest to consider the views of Wen I-chan, a Chinese educator in this field, who on the basis of his own experiences, those of teachers in Peking, and those of Soviet educators, has prepared a manual for language teachers at the elementary school level.[1]

In his introduction, he states what he views as the three objectives of elementary school language teaching:

1. The carrying out of preliminary instruction in language and literature in order that the pupil may understand and use his native language.

2. Through the medium of language teaching, the implementation of political and ideological education, the cultivation in the pupil of a socialist political orientation, the establishment of the basis for the world outlook of dialectical materialism in the pupil, and the cultivation in the pupil of the qualities of communist morality.

3. The teaching, through the medium of language instruction, of basic knowledge of science, geography, and history.[2]

69

Wen's work naturally covers the entire range of elementary school language teaching. Here, however, we shall consider only his treatment of the teaching of reading. His experiences and suggestions are confined to the level from Grade One through Grade Four, a range that spans most of that of the *Readers* under study here. Below, we have summarized the general content of his discussion.

In terms of mastery of reading, Wen I-chan feels that the major concern at the First Grade level is simply to cultivate basic reading skills so that the pupil can read simple passages correctly and clearly. In the Second Grade the pupil should be instructed in reading selections aloud with expression of emotions appropriate to the text. In Grades Three and Four, these skills should be further developed.

The objectives of the reading class are, of course, far broader than the development of the pupil's mechanical skills in reading. The central concern of the language teacher is the task of bringing the pupil to understand the text he is reading. As a rule, the methods that Wen I-chan advocates are indirect, word-by-word explanations of the text if at all possible. Thus, he also discourages the teacher from drawing out the moral of a selection too abruptly or hastily. Rather, the moral is to be made clear to the pupil in a natural way as a discussion of the selection proceeds.

Wen suggests four methods for clarifying texts:

1. *Conversations taking pictures as their basis.* In this method, the teacher shows pictures related to the selection and asks questions about the pictures in an attempt to draw out information from the pupil and lead him to an over-all understanding of whatever is under consideration. This method is primarily recommended for Grades One and Two.

2. *Story telling to supplement the text.* This method is another recommended for use in Grades One and Two. Because of the limitations on vocabulary and on length of selections at this level, it is possible that a selection in and of itself may not contain enough detail to make its point clear. Thus, Wen I-chan suggests telling further stories related to the topic of the lesson in which the attitudes or experiences touched upon in the lesson are given fuller expression.

3. *Analysis of the text by the conversational method.* This is

clearly the preferred method to be used at all grade levels. The method involves a question-and-answer dialogue between the teacher and the pupils, in which the teacher asks the class leading questions designed to bring out the point the teacher wishes to reinforce. An excellent example of this can be seen in the teaching guide for *The Story of Li Ch'un-hua*, which is presented in Chapter Four.

4. *Direct explanation of the text.* Although the methods described above are the most preferable, Wen I-chan concedes that there are cases when a direct explanation is unavoidable. Such a procedure is necessary when the selection contains a difficult vocabulary, involves complex symbolism, or deals with information with which the pupil would not normally be familiar.

Of the types of selections in elementary school readers, it is the "literary" work that predominates. A "literary" work in the sense that Wen I-chan uses the term includes almost all types of selection excepting the purely informational or didactic. In fact, Wen I-chan defines a "literary work" in terms well familiar to the student of Western criticism as "works ... which reflect actual life and ... instruct the reader." In other words, he sees literature as imitative and didactic. The objectives in teaching a "literary work" therefore become essentially those of broadening the pupil's knowledge, bringing him to a correct knowledge of society and of life, and of teaching him to deal correctly with life. These ends, however, are not to be accomplished by direct means but through involving the pupil emotionally in the story or poem. The forms of "literary works" that Wen considers suitable for these purposes are stories, fables, allegories, poems, songs, riddles, plays, jokes, and everyday sayings. Most of these types are represented in the *Readers.* It is of interest that he feels called upon to defend the fable as a form for use in the elementary school classroom, there having been some objections to the fable on the grounds that it distorts "reality."

As Wen I-chan recommends, and as the analysis of the *Readers* corroborates, an additional function of the elementary school language curriculum is the imparting of a general knowledge of science, geography, and history. This is necessary because there are no formal courses in these subjects in the first four grades and in order to provide a foundation for these courses when they are introduced at the Fifth Grade level.

There are, therefore, some readings that are intended purely as means of imparting knowledge of this kind. The science readings deal mainly with the natural world and with physiology and hygiene. As such they leave little room for ideological content. The readings in history and geography, however, are seen by Wen I-chan as fulfilling the dual function of providing basic information about these fields and of cultivating patriotic feelings. Geography, thus, is primarily the geography of China, and history is primarily Chinese history with the greater emphasis on events leading up to the success of the communist regime.

In addition to classroom work, Wen I-chan also recommends promoting outside reading for the purposes of encouraging the pupil's independence in reading as well as his love of reading. For this purpose he recommends books, magazines, newspapers, and other written material. To be considered "good" these materials must evince qualities of "ideological healthiness," "trueness to life," "appropriateness to the age group in which the reader belongs," and "perfection of form and purity of language."

Another function that Wen I-chan recommends for the outside reading class is that of "literary appreciation." Literary appreciation sessions may be held on particular occasions such as commemorative days and should be devoted preferably to a single topic. The programs should consist of the telling of stories, recitation of poems, the performance of plays, and related activities. Ideally, the works selected for "appreciation" should center about a single topic, which apparently should be political, as for example the topic "Our Great Leader Chairman Mao."

SOME SPECIFIC EXAMPLES OF LANGUAGE INSTRUCTION

A survey of the *Readers* indicates, as noted earlier, that most stories are followed by brief exercises that often include a question or questions related to content. It can be concluded that questions of this sort serve as a starting point for class discussion and various types of class exercises or as the basis for individual compositions by the pupils. It is impossible for us to step into a Chinese classroom and observe what happens there. Teachers' guides, however, like that written by Wen I-chan, suggest uses to which the stories and exercises can be put. Below, we shall quote two examples from his guide. As it happens, the examples selected for illustration by the author occur in the *Readers* under analysis as well.

The first of these is the picture strip *A Little Dog and a Bone*, found in Review 11 of Volume 2. The sequence is as follows:

Picture 1: A dog carrying a bone in his mouth comes to a bridge over a stream.

Picture 2: The dog, standing on the bridge, looks down and sees his reflection in the water.

Picture 3: He jumps into the water, the bone falling from his mouth.

Picture 4: He swims ashore without the bone.

This is how Wen I-chan, writing from his own experiences in using these materials, suggests that the lesson be taught:[3]

Writing a Short Composition Based on the Picture Strip
A Little Dog and A Bone

Teaching materials: The picture strip, *A Little Dog and A Bone.*
Grade: Second term of the Grade One or Grade Two.
Time: One session.
Objectives of Instruction: To cultivate the pupil's capacity to write compositions on the basis of visual aids and to teach him to write short compositions of from three to five sentences.

Course of instruction:

1. Organization of instruction.

2. Initial talk. Today, we are going to write compositions. First, I will show you some pretty pictures, and then I will tell you an interesting story. You will make notes about the story, and then write it out. The title of the story is *A Little Dog and A Bone.*

3. Display the pictures and talk about them. What is drawn in the picture? (A dog). Where is the dog? (On a bridge). What is under the bridge? (Water). Is the little dog holding something in his mouth? What is it? (Yes. It is a bone). That's right. You know that dogs like to gnaw bones very much and think that there's nothing better to eat than a bone. Look again. Where is the little dog looking? (He's looking into the river). Why is he looking into the river? (Pupils cannot answer). Look carefully. Is there anything in the water? (There's a little dog there holding a bone too). What is that? (It's a reflection of the dog on the bridge). That's right. Very good. The water is clear, and the things on the bridge are reflected in the water so that there is a reflection of the little dog and of the bone in the water. Now that we understand these pictures, we can tell an interesting story from them. Do you know what it is? (Do not know). I'll tell you.

4. Teacher tells story. There was a little dog who was holding a bone in his mouth and who was crossing a wooden bridge. He looked into the river, and saw that there was another little dog in the river and that that little dog was also holding a bone in his mouth. He thought, how good it would be if I grabbed that bone down below! He then threw down his own bone and jumped into the river to grab the bone in the river. It fell into the river.

5. Discuss the content of the story simply. Did the little dog grab the bone? (No, he didn't). Why didn't he? (Because it was a reflection in the river. There wasn't actually any bone at all). What was the result for the little dog? (It fell into the river). Was it good or bad for the little dog to do this? (Bad). Why was it bad? (He wanted to grab another person's thing with the result

that he himself came to grief). Would you like to write out this story? (Yes). Fine but there are two words you haven't had before. I'll write them on the blackboard now. (Write the two words 'grab' and 'throw' on the board, read them to the pupils once, and write the stroke order once). Now you can begin writing. (The pupils are already familiar with forms of compositions and know that each sentence must end with a period. No further mention of this is required).

6. The pupils look at the pictures and write their compositions as the teacher walks back and forth between rows giving directions.

Examples of compositions written by pupils. (They all wrote well. Two examples are chosen here.)

1. There was a little dog. He was holding a bone in his mouth. He was about to cross a bridge. He saw that there was also a little dog in the water. It was holding a bone in its mouth. He then let go of his own bone. Then he jumped into the water. He went to grab the bone in the water. He fell into the river. (Lu Ch'iao, Class A, Grade One).

2. There was a little dog holding a bone in his mouth. He was very happy. He found the bone by the bank of the river. His home was on the other side. He wanted to go back home. There was a little stream ahead. There was a single-plank wooden bridge over the stream. Holding the bone in his mouth, he walked to the middle of the single-plank wooden bridge. He looked into the river. There was a little dog in the river. It was holding a bone in its mouth too. He threw down his own bone. Then he went to grab the bone in the river. As soon as he jumped, he jumped into the river. He drowned. (Shih Shu-lung, Class A, Grade One).

This provides a good indication of the use to which the picture strips can be put. It is clear that their primary use in this case was as a tool of language instruction. Even so, concern for the moral content of the picture story was not entirely lacking.

Stories, of course, normally contain more explicit verbal material obviously intended for use in indoctrination. With this in mind, let us consider the lesson plan that the author used for the story *The Story of Li Ch'un-hua.*[4]

The Story of Li Ch'un-hua

Objectives of instruction:
1. To cause the students to know that peasants and their children in the old society suffered oppression and exploitation by landlords, so that they led lives like those of oxen and horses, and to evoke the sympathy of the pupils for the oppressed peasants and their hatred for the oppressive landlords; to cause the students to know that after the Liberation the lives of the people became better from day to day, that the Communist Party and Chairman Mao led the people in destroying the injustices of the old society, and that the lives of the children of the peasants of new China are very happy;
2. To allow the pupils to learn the new characters and compounds in the lesson;
3. To practice reading aloud with emotion.

Preparation for Teaching: Preparation of four picture strips.
1. Li Ch'un-hua Living a Hard Life at Home;
2. Li Ch'un-hua Being Punished at the Landlord's House;
3. The House of Li Ch'un-hua After the Liberation;
4. Li Ch'un-hua's Mother Sending Li Ch'un-hua Off to School.

Period of instruction: Three class sessions. (Note: In the translation that follows, some materials of minimal interest such as discussions of definitions of words have been omitted. Those portions omitted are indicated in all instances.)

Session One

1. Initial talk: Classmates, can you think of a lesson in which you studied about a landlord's oppression of a peasant and of what the peasant's life was like after the Communist Party came? (*Old Uncle Chu.* Before the

Liberation, old Uncle Chu planted rape for the landlord for 18 years and suffered oppression under the landlord. After the Liberation, the tables were turned and the rape garden was given to old Uncle Chu). Do you know about the oppression that the peasants suffered at the hands of landlords? (In the movie *The White-Haired Girl*, we saw how Hsi-erh's father Yang Pai-lao suffered oppression under a landlord. Yang Pai-lao couldn't pay his rent, so the landlord forced him to sell Hsi-erh to him and forced Yang Pai-lao to kill himself). What happened to Hsi-erh? (She was taken away by the landlord). What was Hsi-erh's life like in the landlord's house? (It was hard for Hsi-erh. She served the landlord Shih-jen's mother all day and into the evening and she was often beaten and cursed). Before the Liberation, the hardships suffered by peasants and the children of peasants under the oppression of landlords were more than can be told. Today we are talking about a new lesson. This lesson is the story of a peasant child before and after the Liberation.

The title of the lesson is The Story of Li Ch'un-hua.

Li Ch'un-hua was a girl. Before the Liberation, her life was extremely hard. But after the Liberation, she was happy. This lesson is a story told by Li Ch'un-hua herself about her circumstances before and after the Liberation. If we are to master this lesson, there are a few words that we will have to understand first.

2. Explanation of words: (There is a brief paragraph on the words selected for explanation. Of the five words explained, two are included here because of the "ideological" terms in which they are discussed).

a. "Watch." (*Keng*). The landlord used to be afraid that the peasants would steal his things, so he sent a watchman out during the night. The watchman would hold a rattle in his hands which he struck with a rattling sound. He struck it five times each night. The first time he struck it on the first watch, and the second time he struck it on the second watch. The third time he struck it on the third watch. The third watch was midnight. At the fifth watch, it was still dark and the sky was filled with stars. What is the meaning of "got up at the fifth watch?" (Getting up in the dark before sunrise. Getting up very early). And "sleeping only half the night?" (Going to bed at midnight. Going to bed very late).

e. "To abolish." (*Lo-ch'u*). When it is said in the lesson that unjust conditions were abolished after the Liberation, this means that unjust conditions were done away with.

3. The teacher reads the text with emotion. Do not open your books. Sit quietly and listen to me read. After I have finished you will have to answer my questions.

4. Preliminary questions: Whose circumstances is this lesson about? (The circumstances of Li Ch'un-hua). After listening to the story, what points do you find difficult to bear? (Li Ch'un-hua's being so hungry she cried; her working for the landlord and being beaten and cursed, and Li Ch'un-hua crying and saying to her mother: "I'm not going back again."). At what points did you feel happy? (The Communist Party came. Li Ch'un-hua went to school). After listening to this story, whom do you hate? (The landlord who took advantage of Li Ch'un-hua. I hate the landlord.). For whom are you distressed and for whom are you happy? (I'm distressed for Li Ch'un-hua, and I'm happy for Li Ch'un-hua too). To whom are you grateful? (The Communist Party came, and then Li Ch'un-hua lived well. I'm grateful to the Communist Party).

5. Pupils read the text silently to themselves. Now you understand the general meaning of the story. Are there any words or compounds that you still do not understand? Open your books and take a careful look and mention them.

6. Teaching new words. (Note: At this point, the outline instructs the teacher to write the new words on the blackboard and discuss them. The new words in the outline are presented below and their definitions noted. The discussions on how they are written are omitted).

a. What is the meaning of "very poor?" (Having nothing to eat and nothing to wear; being disastrously poor).

b. What is the meaning of "cooking wild vegetables?" (That's going out into the wilds and digging up wild vegetables which are brought back, cooked, and eaten. Poor people didn't have any rice to eat, so all they could do was eat wild vegetables).

c. What is the meaning of "making tea and pouring water?" (Making tea and pouring water is pouring tea. This indicates serving the landlord).

d. Do you remember the meaning of "getting up at the fifth watch and sleeping half the night?"

e. What is the meaning of "dry weather."

f. What is the meaning of "being punished?" (Being beaten and cursed. Suffering oppression and being treated badly).

After the completion of instructions on new words, the teacher again reads them aloud two times, after which the pupils read them aloud and write them out individually until they are familiar with them.

Session Two

1. Organization of instruction.

2. Review and reinforcement of new words learned in the previous session.

3. Reading and discussion of each paragraph of the lesson.

a. Read the first paragraph aloud and bring up questions for analysis: Before the Liberation, Li Ch'un-hua's family was very poor. How can this be seen? (Her family didn't have any rice to eat; Li Ch'un-hua was so hungry she cried, and all they could do was dig up wild vegetables to eat). How long do you think a person would be hungry before he would cry? (It would certainly be after not having gotten enough to eat for several days and when his stomach would be growling). When Ch'un-hua was so hungry she cried, what did her mother say? (Her mother was very distressed to see her own daughter so hungry that she cried, and her mother also cried. Her mother said: "Ch'un-hua, don't cry. Mother will go and dig up a few wild vegetables and cook them for you to eat."). Why weren't they eating rice but eating wild vegetables instead? Are wild vegetables good to eat? (Ch'un-hua's family was farming the landlord's land. The grain for which they had worked a whole year was taken away by the landlord. They didn't have any rice to eat, and all they could do was eat wild vegetables. Wild vegetables are not good to eat and are not filling. You can get sick even if you eat a lot). Did the landlord eat wild vegetables? (The landlord did not eat wild vegetables. He always ate well).

The teacher opens up a screen at the blackboard, revealing the first picture strip. The teacher talks about the picture strip. What place do you think this is? (The home of Li Ch'un-hua). That's the home of Li Ch'un-hua. The mother is sewing tattered clothes. Ch'un-hua has not eaten for several days and is terribly hungry. She has climbed up onto her mother's lap and is crying. Her mother looks at the kettle. She takes off the cover. The kettle is empty. She looks at the bowls and pitchers. The bowls and pitchers are broken and empty. There is not even a single grain of rice. Then she looks at the bare, run-down room ... "Ai! I've worked bitterly for a whole year, and my child is still barefoot without shoes to wear and hungry without food to eat." At this time, the mother is both grieving for her child and hating the landlord. She is in great distress. She too begins to cry.

Classmates, can you think of a title for this paragraph of the lesson and for this picture strip? (Li Ch'un-hua, Crying, Asks Her Mother for Rice).

b. Read the second paragraph of the lesson aloud. Analyze.

At what age did Li Ch'un-hua go to work at the landlord's house? (She went when she was ten.). What punishments did Li Ch'un-hua suffer in the landlord's house? (She looked after children, washed clothes, and made and served tea for the landlord. She was as tired as a rice sprout during a drought, and she was frequently beaten and cursed). Can a ten year old child manage so many activities? (She wasn't able to, but there was nothing she could do about it. When she couldn't manage them, she was beaten and cursed. She had to manage them even though she wasn't able to). Was Ch'un-hua tired? (Yes). What does it say in the story? ("I got up every day at the fifth watch, sleeping only half the night. I was as tired as a rice sprout during a drought and couldn't raise my head.").

The teacher opens the screen, revealing the second picture strip. Who do you think this is? (The landlord). Who is this? (The landlord's wife). Whom are they beating? (They are beating Ch'un-hua). Ch'un-hua went to the landlord's house to work when she was only ten years old. There were children in the landlord's family, too. They dressed in gay-colored clothes, ate rich foods, and went skipping off to school. They frequently took advantage of Ch'un-hua. The landlord spoiled his own children and never made them cry. But as soon as Ch'un-hua cried, she was beaten and cursed. It was very bitter for Li Ch'un-hua.

Was Li Ch'un-hua able to bear so much bitterness? (She wasn't able to bear it, and ran back to her own home. She said to her mother: "I won't go back again."). What did her mother think at this time? (The mother saw that her own daughter had been beaten black-and-blue by the landlord and she no longer looked like a human being. She was very distressed). What did her mother say to Ch'un-hua? ("Ch'un-hua, you'll have to go back! I only wish that there was something I could do so that you wouldn't have to go back and be punished!"). Her mother knew very well that her child would be mistreated by the landlord's family. Why did she send her back even so? (At home, there was no food to eat and no way to live! Besides, Ch'un-hua had snuck back home and the landlord would have found her, wouldn't he? What could her mother do? All she could do was send Ch'un-hua back). In what manner did Ch'un-hua return to her home? In what manner did she return to the landlord's house? (Ch'un-hua ran home from the landlord's house. She couldn't stand the hardship. Ch'un-hua walked back crying to the landlord's house. She did not want to go back to the landlord's house and be punished).

Give a title to the second paragraph. (Li Ch'un-hua Suffers Punishment in the Landlord's House).

    c. Read the third paragraph aloud. Analyze.

How were things in Li Ch'un-hua's family once the Communist Party had come? (The Communist Party came and led the peasants in overthrowing the landlords. The landlord's house and land were distributed to Li Ch'un-hua). Why was the landlord's land distributed? (The landlord did not work and ate freely. He took away the houses and land of the peasants). How was life in Li Ch'un-hua's family after the houses and land had been distributed? (It got better from day to day). What is the meaning of getting better from day to day? (Things get better each day. She didn't suffer oppression under the landlord anymore).

The teacher opens the screen, revealing the third picture strip. Classmates, whose house do you think this is? What are they doing? (This is the house of Li Ch'un-hua after the Liberation. Li Ch'un-hua's mother is putting new clothes on her. The house they are living in is very nice. Outside, there are cattle and ploughs). That's right. This is the house of Li Ch'un-hua after the tables were turned. It was in this house that Li Ch'un-hua was beaten and cursed by the landlord. The Communist Party came and gave this house to Li Ch'un-hua. There is a house and land, and there are cattle and farm tools. They labor on their own land. How happy they are!

Give a title to the third paragraph. (Li Ch'un-hua's Life Changed for the Good After the Tables Were Turned).

d. Read the fourth paragraph aloud and analyze.

How did Li Ch'un-hua feel when she heard that her mother was going to send her to school? (Happy). In what way was she happy? Read the sentence from the story. ("When I heard, I was so happy I jumped up and down."). Why didn't Li Ch'un-hua go to school before? (Before, her family was poor. They didn't even have any food to eat, and she couldn't afford to go to school). Why was Li Ch'un-hua happy to go to school? (At school she could learn to read and write, to become cultured, and to have knowledge, so that in the future she could build the motherland). What did she think at that time? (She thought: Before, only the children of the landlords went to school. All I could do was work for the landlord family and my mind was not at peace. Now, things have gotten better and I can go to school too. All injustices have been abolished). Can you think of what injustices there were in the old society that have been abolished now? (Landlords not laboring but eating well was unjust. That's been abolished now. The peasants farming the land and handing the grain over to the landlord was unjust. That's been abolished now. Very little children going to the landlord's house and being punished was unjust. That's been abolished now. The fact that only landlord children were able to go to school and that peasant children were not able to go to school was unjust. That's been abolished now). Classmates, what you have said is quite correct. Why has it been possible to abolish these injustices? (Because the Communist Party and Chairman Mao have come).

Show the fourth picture strip. It is the time of spring warmth, and blooming flowers. The weather is exceptionally clear. Ch'un-hua's mother sends Ch'un-hua off to school. Ch'un-hua has her satchel on her back and is wearing new clothes. She is very happy, and walks to school eagerly.

Give a title to the fourth paragraph. (Li Ch'un-hua Goes to School).

4. Read the lesson aloud.

5. Give an assignment. Write the new characters five times. Read the lesson three times.

Session Three

1. Organization of instruction.

2. Review and testing. Choose two pupils to go to the blackboard and write out the new characters, while the remaining students write them in their notebooks. Write: "very poor," "to cook wild vegetables," "to boil tea," "dry weather," and "to be punished."

Choose pupils to read the lesson aloud. One person reads one paragraph and tells the title of the paragraph.

3. Pupils retell the story on the basis of the picture strips. One person tells about Li Ch'un-hua's life before the Liberation and another tells about Li Ch'un-hua's life after the Liberation.

4. Give a summary talk. Li Ch'un-hua's life can be divided into two distinct and different parts. What are these two parts? (Before the Liberation and after the Liberation). What was her life like before the Libera-

tion? What problems can be seen from this lesson? (In the old society, the poor and their children were oppressed and exploited by the landlords. Their lives were very hard. They didn't get enough to eat and they could not dress warmly). Were these things just or unjust? Why were they unjust? (They were unjust. The peasants worked bitterly hard to plant the crops, but the grain they got was taken away by the landlords. The landlords did not plant and did not work, but they had money and power, and they took advantage of the poor people). What has been the peasant's life since the Liberation? (Since the Liberation, the peasant's life has changed for the better and the lives of peasant children have also changed for the better. The injustices of the old society were all abolished). Who brought all these good things? (Chairman Mao and the Communist Party). After studying this lesson, whom do you hate? Why? (I hate the landlords, because the landlords oppressed the peasants). Whom do you love? Why? (I love the Communist Party and Chairman Mao, because they lead the peasants in turning the tables so that they could live happy lives).

5. Lead the pupils in reading the lesson aloud, expressing emotion. This lesson is principally divided into two parts, that before the Liberation and that after the Liberation. With what kind of emotion should the events of Li Ch'un-hua's suffering and punishment before the Liberation be read? (They should be read with grief and sadness). That's correct. But this story is told by Li Ch'un-hua after the Liberation, and not when she is actually being beaten and cursed. Therefore, it is an emotion of sadness in remembrance of suffering in the past. What sentences do you think should be read with sadness? ("Ch'un-hua, mother will go and dig up a few wild vegetables and cook them for you to eat." "Ch'un-hua, you'll have to go back! I only wish that there was something I could do so that you wouldn't have to go back and be punished! ..."). Look again. Where do you think there should be a pause? (In the middle of the first and second paragraphs. The pause should be very long. The pause should be longer between paragraphs and a little shorter between sentences. How should sigh marks be read? (The sighs in

the lesson should be read with a sad, sighing tone).
Give a demonstration reading. Read aloud indicating
emotion.

You have read the first half of the lesson. Now let us
read the final half. The final half of the lesson tells of
circumstances after the Liberation. With what emotion
should it be read? (It should be read with emotions of
happiness and contentment). What sentences should be
read with somewhat greater expression of happiness?
("The Communist Party came and our livelihood improved from day to day." "All injustices were abolished
one by one."). When reading these sentences, the voice
should be raised a little. The word "all" in the phrase
"all" were "abolished" should be emphasized a little.
In general, an emotion of happiness should be used
when reading the final half of the lesson. However,
what emotion should be used when reading "I thought
of the old days when only the children of landlord
families went to school. I wasn't able to go to school.
All I could do was work for the landlord family and I
was not at peace in my mind."? (One should show
emotion of unhappiness). The word "landlord" of "the
children of landlord families" should be read with
greater emphasis, and the "was not able" and the "all I
could do" of "I am not able to go to school. All I could
do was work for the landlord family" should be read
with greater emphasis. Read the last half of the lesson
aloud indicating expression of emotion.

6. Character writing practice. Practice writing new
characters in your notebook. First write looking at the
book. Later, write from memory.

7. Assignment. Use the words "formerly," "now,"
"everyday," and "frequently" to make sentences.

SUMMARY

The preceding lesson outline provides further evidence that
the stories in the *Readers* are used in the classroom for
conscious political ends. The author cites stories in other
lesson plans in which the objectives of instruction include not
only the aims of specifically political socialization but also the
more general socialization goals implicit in the aims of

behavioral modeling as well. For example, the aims of the story entitled *The Mountain of the Sun*,[5] in addition to introducing new characters and providing the student with practice in retelling stories, includes the instruction: "allows the students to learn that avarice is bad and to teach the pupils diligence and simplicity." This serves to exemplify the method of analyzing the texts in terms of behavioral and political themes as the intended input and intended means of interpretation of the *Readers*. There are, in addition, stories that the author treats under the category that we have designated as "informational." That is, they are intended to familiarize the pupil with some facet of life with which he may or may not be acquainted.

As a survey of the stories reveals, the questions and exercises concluding each story follow a very similar pattern. There is frequently one question (i.e., theme) for discussion dealing with the "moral" or "political" content of the article, together with exercises concerned primarily with linguistic skills. Even some of these exercises, however, select politically meaningful words, phrases, or excerpts from the story. In addition, there are often instructions to read the story aloud with expression of emotion or with various students taking parts if dialogue is involved.

It thus appears that the methods presented by Wen I-chan and those of the *Readers* are of a piece. We have no evidence to the extent that such procedures have been carried out in general practice, but we can be sure that the procedures presented here are at least the ideal that it is hoped the teacher will approximate.

FOUR

THEMATIC ANALYSIS

INTRODUCTION

As indicated in Chapter One, for the purposes of analysis we have found it convenient to distinguish between stories that simply impart information, those that are primarily concerned with political socialization, and those that deal with general, non-political behavior. For this reason, the stories fall into three major thematic categories: informational, political, and behavioral.

Informational themes. Informational themes are those concerned with imparting specific information about given topics. In themselves, informational themes are generally lacking in political or behavioral coloration. Although they are, in this sense, essentially neutral, they nevertheless are revealing in the range of subject matter that is presented. (See Table II-A under "Informational Themes" for a list of these themes).

Political themes. As indicated in Chapter One, these themes have as their aim political socialization and are concerned primarily with political and social attitudes on the national level, but also to a certain extent on the international level as well. (See Table III-A under "Political Themes" for a list of these themes).

Behavioral themes. Behavioral themes are those aimed at behavioral modeling and have as their concern some aspect of personal behavior. (See Table IV-A under "Behavioral Themes" for a list of these themes).

In general, each selection was assigned a central theme from one of these three categories, depending on whether its central concern was felt to be simply that of providing information, that of political socialization, or that of behavioral modeling. A small number of selections, usually poems, in which there were individual stanzas of equal strength, were assigned more than one central theme. Few selections, however, were ever purely informational, political, or behavioral in intention. For this reason, each selection was in addition assigned a subtheme or a number of subthemes, depending on its content.

The following table indicates the relative percentages with which each of these thematic categories occurred.

Table I-A: PERCENTAGES OF THEMES
                       BY MAJOR CATEGORIES

Theme	Major Themes		Subthemes		Totals	
	No.	%	No.	%	No.	%
Informational	77	18.33	111	11.62	188	13.67
Political	144	34.29	357	37.38	501	36.44
Behavioral	199	47.38	487	50.99	686	49.89
Totals	420	100.00	955	99.99	1375	100.00

It is clear from the above table that informational themes play a relatively minor role in the fabric of the *Readers*. It is also evident that there is a significantly greater emphasis on behavioral over political themes. This is to be expected, particularly at the lower grade levels.

An examination of the distribution of the major thematic categories by grade level, as shown in Table I-B, indicates that the emphasis on them varies from grade to grade in a consistent manner for each category.

From this it can be seen that informational themes increase to a peak in Grade Three, after which they assume less importance. Political themes, on the other hand, increase continually in frequency through each grade level. This is also generally true of the behavioral themes through Grade Four;

Table I-B: PERCENTAGE OF MAJOR THEME CATEGORIES BY GRADE LEVEL*

Theme	Grade Level 1		2		3		4		5		% Totals
	No.	%	No.	%	No.	%	No.	%	No.	%	
Informational											
Central Theme:	8	10.39	17	22.08	29	37.66	14	18.18	9	11.69	100.00
Subtheme:	17	15.32	18	16.22	21	18.92	23	20.72	23	28.83	100.01
Total:	25	13.30	35	18.62	50	26.60	37	19.68	32	21.81	100.01
Political											
Central Theme:	21	14.58	30	20.83	27	18.75	29	20.14	37	25.69	99.99
Subtheme:	22	6.16	65	18.21	77	21.75	88	24.65	105	29.41	100.18
Total:	43	8.38	95	19.16	104	20.56	117	23.35	142	28.54	99.99
Behavioral											
Central Theme:	38	19.10	39	19.60	44	22.11	44	22.11	34	17.09	100.01
Subtheme:	55	11.30	114	23.41	103	21.15	121	24.85	94	19.30	100.01
Total:	93	13.56	153	22.01	147	21.28	165	24.05	128	19.10	100.00

*All percentages reported are raw percentages.

however, the emphasis on behavioral themes declines in Grade Five as material of a political nature become more predominant.

Before turning now to a detailed account of the analysis of each of these thematic categories, a word of explanation is in order as to the method of analysis employed. As can be seen from the subsequent treatment of the selections in the *Readers*, we have not made use of the concepts of *n*-Affiliation and *n*-Power. We have, however, used the term "achievement," although not the term "*n*-Achievement," as a thematic category under the section on behavioral themes. There are a number of reasons for this procedure. One of the most basic is that we are interpreting the *Readers* primarily as instruments of political indoctrination and behavioral modeling and our central concern is in discerning the probable intent of the writers or compilers. That is to say, we are primarily concerned with the manifest themes which were consciously used in writing the texts and which are in all likelihood brought out in classroom discussion. It is clear from the preceding materials on education that achievement is a manifest theme of Chinese education. On the other hand, it is not as certain that affiliation and power in and of themselves are intended as manifest themes. Themes of affiliation and power are present in the stories. They occur, however, as latent themes underlying many different kinds of stories, and as such they are sufficiently diffuse as to be unimportant in terms of specific themes of political and behavioral indoctrination.

A few examples of this difference in treatment may be of help by way of clarification. McClelland, who has had access to some of these same materials, cites the story *Chairman Mao Sees a Play* (Vol. 3, No. 11), as exemplifying motives of *n*-Affiliation.[1] That affiliative concerns are important in this story cannot be denied. However, from the standpoint of political indoctrination, it is not so much motives of affiliation in themselves that are stressed as motives of affiliation in respect to Mao. The central concern of the story is thus the kindness and benevolence of Mao, which is a part of the thematic complex of the glorification of Mao as the benevolent leader and father figure. Thus, if this story were to be scored in terms of *n*-Affiliation only, we would be missing its central point, namely, political indoctrination.

As another example, McClelland treats stories dealing with repression and cruelty of landlords in terms of *n*-Power.[2] Again, from the standpoint of political indoctrination it is not the true central concern of the story which is the delineation of the "evils" of pre-Communist society. Similarly, McClelland considers the story *I've Come to Escort You to Work* (Vol. 6, No. 26), as an example of a power relationship involving the investment of the "power to help, to guide, and to control others" in the individual.[3]

From our standpoint, the motive of *n*-Power is irrelevant to the central concern of the story as far as behavioral indoctrination is concerned. From the preceding discussion of educational thought in Communist China, it is clear that the story in question was included for the purpose of illustrating one aspect of "communist morality."

There is a further consideration which has prompted the form of analysis that we have adopted; viz., the necessity of considering the *Readers* as an essential aspect of an over-all program of political socialization within China. An analysis of materials such as these cannot be divorced from the milieu that produced them. Thus, to analyze the story *I've Come to Escort You to Work* solely in terms of *n*-Power is to ignore the historical background and philosophical tradition against which it was written. This is, of course, but a reflection of a more general problem in the study of many aspects of Chinese culture, that of achieving an appropriate balance between Western techniques of investigation and analysis and consideration of those distinctive aspects of Chinese culture, both ancient and modern, that, if ignored can lead to misinterpretation. It is our intention in this study to take a middle course between the extremes of treating an aspect of China in Western terms without reference to the Chinese cultural framework and, on the other hand, of dealing with Chinese culture entirely in its own terms without reference to Western standards.

With this in mind, let us now turn to a detailed discussion of the themes found in the *Readers*.

INFORMATIONAL THEMES

Preliminary observations. As we have indicated previously, the language curriculum in the first four grades of elementary school also bears the burden of imparting incidental instruction in history, geography, and science. The fact that such information is incidental, however, should not detract from its focus. In his first years of formal schooling, the child begins to acquire systematic information about the world in which he lives. In political systems where education is viewed as a specific political tool, the child receives information designed to focus his attention on specific attributes of his environment. Thus the information passed on to a child in such an educational system is designed to fit the goals and expectations of the political leadership. Even incidental information, therefore, may be assumed to have at least some political purpose.

The principal concern of the Chinese leadership with political integration and agricultural development is demonstrated by the frequency with which these two themes occur in the informational aspects of the *Readers.* These two themes tend to dominate the informational content of the material to which the students are exposed in the grammar texts. Out of a total number of 188 central themes and subthemes, agricultural themes total 45, themes discussing aspects of Communist China total 41, and information relating to traditional China account for 28 themes. Thus knowledge about China as a cultural and historical entity occurred in a total of 69 themes. Nevertheless, counting the same categories by central theme only, agriculture occurred 26 times, knowledge about Communist China occurred three times, and themes relating to traditional China occurred five times. The dominance of agricultural themes as a central concern of the regime is clearly evident.

Themes that impart knowledge relating to Communist and to traditional China assume dominance only through the large number of subthemes which contain such information. In addition, it is this subtheme dominance which contributes to the steadily rising occurrence of these themes through each grade, thereby placing this particular set of information in the same basic pattern of occurrence as the political themes to be discussed in the following section. The agricultural themes, on the other hand, follow the same basic pattern as the total informational themes, cresting in the Third Grade and tapering off through the Fourth and Fifth Grades. It would appear that even though the information relating to Communist and traditional China is relatively apolitical, the designers of these texts sought to place the material in the *Readers* where it would complement more specifically value-orienting themes.

Description. The following table shows the informational themes in the *Readers* in order of frequency of occurrence both as central and subthemes. Table II-B, which follows the discussion, shows the frequency and distribution of informational themes by Grade level and the total number of times that each theme occurs as a central theme and as a subtheme. Table II-C shows central themes by frequency of occurrence.

Table II-A: INFORMATIONAL THEMES

1. Basic agricultural and/or farm knowledge
2. Knowledge about Chinese Communist institutions, history, and/or personalities
3. Knowledge about traditional Chinese history, culture, and/or personalities
4. Basic scientific and technical knowledge
5. Basic knowledge of physiology and/or hygiene
6. Basic social knowledge and customs
7. Basic knowledge about natural history
8. Miscellaneous general knowledge
9. Knowledge about non-Chinese leaders of the Communist movement
10. Basic academic knowledge
11. Basic knowledge about China

1. *Basic agricultural and/or farm knowledge.* As the designation implies, this category refers to information about basic agricultural processes. A story having this theme may deal, for example, with methods of planting and caring for various types of crops or with matters related to agriculture and farm life. Examples of stories of this sort are *Planting Castor Plants* (Vol. 4, No. 10) and *Our Good Friends* (Vol. 4, No. 14). In

some cases, these selections also contained material which was scored as behavioral in content.

As Table II-B indicates, 26 stories have basic agricultural knowledge as a central theme, and 19 additional selections deal with it as a subtheme. Most attention is given to this theme in the first three grades with highest concentration in Grade Three. In Grades Four and Five, frequency of occurrence falls to a low level.

2. *Knowledge about Chinese Communist institutions, history, and/or personalities.* This category is meant to cover all selections in which there is factual information about any aspect of the Chinese Communist movement and the individuals involved in it, both before and after the establishment of the People's Republic of China in 1949. Although there were only three selections that could be scored for this category as a central theme, the subtheme figured prominently in 38 stories. The story *Rather Death than Submission* (Vol. 8, No. 30) is an example of this. Because the story described the courageous action of its central character, Lin Hsiang-ch'ien, it was scored with "heroic self-sacrifice" as its central theme. In addition, it provided information both about Lin Hsiang-ch'ien and a situation in which he was involved. For this reason, the story was scored with this category as a subtheme.

There is a steady increase in the number of selections having this category as a subtheme as grade level rises. This reflects the growing concern with political themes in the higher grades.

3. *Knowledge about traditional Chinese history, culture, and/or personalities.* This refers to information about matters that would normally be considered to be a part of the lore of traditional China, and covers selections dealing with famous personalities, works of literature, or other material and cultural attainments of ancient China. Examples are the stories about the Ming Dynasty pharmacologist Li Shih-chen (Vol. 8, No. 23), the Great Wall (Vol. 7, No. 30), and the Grand Canal (Vol. 7, No. 31).

It is interesting to note that the incidence of this theme, as a subtheme, also increases in frequency as grade level rises. A closer look at many of the selections scored for this theme reveals that they tend to serve two purposes. The stories about the Great Wall and the Grand Canal, for example, not only depict two of the most magnificent public works of ancient China, but they also describe the oppression of the people that occurred as these structures were being built. Thus, in addition to contributing to a feeling of national pride, they also reinforce feelings of gratitude to the new regime for having brought an end to the "oppression" that existed under the regimes of "feudal" China and of the Kuomintang.

4. *Basic scientific and technical knowledge.* This category involves selections concerning general scientific or technical knowledge. An example of the category is the selection *Plastics* (Vol. 6, No. 35) which is a simple and straightforward discussion of how plastics are made and of their uses.

This theme occurs with far less frequency than does that of basic agricultural and farm knowledge, reflecting the greater emphasis on China as an agricultural nation and on the pupils as future agricultural workers. In addition, most selections scored for this theme occur in the first three grades, with lesser emphasis in Grades Four and Five. This is again related to the increased emphasis on political themes in these latter volumes.

5. *Basic knowledge of physiology and/or hygiene.* Selections in this category deal for the most part with techniques of sanitation or hygiene. A small number discuss basic human physiology. Examples of the former are *How to Prevent Infectious Diseases* (Vol. 6, No. 15) and *Flies, Mosquitoes, and Bedbugs* (Vol. 6, No. 16). An example of the latter is *A Bean's Journey* (Vol. 5, No. 23), which describes the course of a bean through the digestive system. Informational themes in this category are very often linked with behavioral themes emphasizing individual responsibility in matters of hygiene.

This theme occurs in the first three Grades, and is represented at high levels in only one instance as a subtheme in Grade Five.

6. *Basic social knowledge and customs.* Selections in this category usually stress correct social procedure as related to the form of notes for various occasions, or as the designation

implies, information about various social customs. An example of this is the selection *Informal Notes* (Vol. 5, No. 25). This category occurs primarily in the first three Grades.

7. *Basic knowledge about natural history.* This category receives minor emphasis. An example is *The Camel* (Vol. 8, No. 13).

8. *Miscellaneous general knowledge.* This category was designed to cover informational themes that did not fit other categories and that were not in themselves of any particular significance. It includes most selections made up of riddles, as, for example, Vol. 6, No. 36, or selections such as *Why We Must Predict the Weather* (Vol. 7, No. 13), which contain varied information not easily classified. The theme is fairly evenly distributed throughout the grades with the exception of Grade Three in which it was slightly more predominant.

9. *Knowledge about non-Chinese leaders of the Communist movement.* This was scored as a subtheme in all cases, and was slightly more emphasized in the higher grades. An example is the story *Giving Lenin Something to Eat* (Vol. 5, No. 20). The low frequency with which this theme occurs obviously reflects the greater concern devoted to China and her institutions and the general neglect of events outside of China.

10. *Basic academic knowledge.* This theme, which occurs with surprisingly low frequency, covers for the most part selections dealing with writing and reading. An example is *Write Much and Revise Much* (Vol. 8, No. 7). The low score refers to the content of the selections themselves, and it should be noted that each lesson in the *Readers* is accompanied by vocabulary and writing exercises.

11. *Basic knowledge about China.* This category was reserved for selections dealing essentially with a physical description of China. Examples of this are *Food Crops* (Vol. 7, No. 16) and *Economic Crops* (Vol. 7, No. 17), both of which were scored for this category as a subtheme. It occurs with low frequency and only in the higher grade levels.

Summary. From the above description and discussion of informational themes in the *Readers,* it can be seen that the major emphasis falls on agriculture, Chinese Communist institutions and personalities, and traditional Chinese culture. By contrast, scientific and technical information is of lesser importance.

Thus, the analysis to this point indicates that the content of the *Readers* is on the one hand designed to emphasize the fact that China is primarily an agricultural society and on the other hand to emphasize Chinese culture, be it traditional or Communist, to the exclusion of foreign cultures. These tendencies obviously serve to reinforce Chinese ethnocentrism as well as to present a highly one-sided view of the world. In short, the information available to the Chinese elementary school pupil is essentially limited in scope and imposes upon him a world view having China as its center with very little consideration for what lies beyond the borders of China.

In the analyses of the political and behavioral themes that follow, we shall see how this primary ethnocentrism is combined with the political attitudes and standards of behavior with which the "ideal" young person in China would be equipped were he to adopt these standards as his own.

Table II-B: FREQUENCY AND DISTRIBUTION OF INFORMATIONAL THEMES*

Theme	*Distribution by Grade Level*				
	1	*2*	*3*	*4*	*5*
1. Basic agricultural and/or farm knowledge	45	9	9	17	6	4
Central Theme:	26	2	5	12	5	2
Subtheme:	19	7	4	5	1	2
2. Knowledge about Chinese Communist institutions, history, and/or personalities	41	2	7	9	10	13
Central Theme:	3	0	1	1	0	1
Subtheme:	38	2	6	8	10	12
3. Knowledge and traditional Chinese history, culture, and/or personalities	28	0	3	4	9	12
Central Theme:	5	0	0	2	3	0
Subtheme:	23	0	3	2	6	12

Table II-B continued:

4. Basic scientific and technical knowledge	17	5	5	4	0	3
Central Theme:	8	0	4	3	0	1
Subtheme:	9	5	1	1	0	2
5. Basic knowledge of physiology and/or hygiene	15	4	5	5	0	1
Central Theme:	12	2	5	5	0	1
Subtheme:	3	2	0	0	0	1
6. Basic social knowledge and customs	13	1	4	3	2	3
Central Theme:	7	1	1	2	1	2
Subtheme:	6	0	3	1	1	1
7. Basic knowledge about natural history	7	2	0	0	2	3
Central Theme:	6	1	0	0	2	3
Subtheme:	1	1	0	0	0	0
8. Miscellaneous general knowledge	7	1	1	4	1	0
Central Theme:	6	1	1	3	1	0
Subtheme:	1	0	0	1	0	0
9. Knowledge about non-Chinese leaders of the Communist movement (subtheme only)	7	0	1	3	2	1
10. Basic academic knowledge	4	1	0	0	3	0
Central Theme:	3	1	0	0	2	0
Subtheme:	1	0	0	0	1	0
11. Basic knowledge about China	4	0	0	1	2	1
Central Theme:	1	0	0	1	0	0
Subtheme:	3	0	0	0	2	1

*Underscored numbers represent total occurrences as both central themes and sub-themes.

Table II-C: CENTRAL THEMES BY FREQUENCY
OF OCCURRENCE

Order	Theme	Number of Occurrences	
		No.	%
1.	Basic agricultural and/or farm knowledge	26	33.77
2.	Basic knowledge of physiology and/or hygiene	12	15.58
3.	Basic scientific and technical knowledge	8	10.38
4.	Basic social knowledge and customs	7	9.09
5.	Miscellaneous general knowledge	6	7.79
	Basic knowledge about natural history	6	7.79
6.	Knowledge about traditional Chinese history, culture, and/or personalities	5	6.49
7.	Knowledge about Chinese Communist institutions, history, and/or personalities	3	3.89
	Basic academic knowledge	3	3.89
8.	Basic knowledge about China	1	1.29
		77	99.96

POLITICAL THEMES

Preliminary observations. The informational themes demonstrate the concern of the Chinese leadership with two basic problems: the need for agricultural development and the need for political integration. The informational themes, however, consist primarily of description in that they were designed to impart knowledge about farming and agriculture in general. The themes dealing with the Chinese polity, too, were to a large extent "factual." On the other hand, the political themes analyzed below are primarily an attempt to gain the loyalty of the young Chinese. The children are told about the benevolence of the new society and the "evils" of Kuomintang and traditional China; the themes are designed to give the children a rationale for the loyalty that is demanded of them. Thus, the informational themes, when they referred to China, were designed to locate the child's political focus. The political themes demand devotion and allegiance and give a reason for demanding loyalty.

Two patterns appear which confirm what we would anticipate. The primary emphasis is upon China, and only in a secondary way on the international Communist system or the Communist movement in general. At this early age the development of core values would be emphasized, and these core values would be designed to develop the child's political attitudes toward the new China and its leadership. Thus, as Table III-G indicates, the central themes are focused on the benevolence of the new society, the requirement of devotion and allegiance to the new society, and the glorification of Mao Tse-tung—the single Chinese leader deemed most responsible for the development of the new society and polity.

The frequent occurrence of the central themes places the category "Benevolence of the New Society" above "Devotion and Allegiance to the New Society," but when subthemes are included the order of these two categories changes. Evidently, and again as we would anticipate, devotion and allegiance are the goals of the Chinese leadership and therefore receive the greatest amount of attention. Nevertheless, the emphasis is not upon China as such, but upon the "new" China—the China built by Mao Tse-tung and the Chinese Communist Party.

Referring to the over-all curves of the three categories of themes, as the level of introductory *information* about the society and polity decreases, the attempt to *focus* loyalties increases. Thus, in terms of intensity, the child in the first two or three Grades is given basic information and in the final two or three Grades is subjected to increasingly intense political indoctrination.

Studies of childhood political socialization in the United States have demonstrated that the political attitudes developed early are positive and indiscriminate.[4] We cannot demonstrate that such positive orientations necessarily occur among Chinese children, but it seems a reasonable assumption. Certainly the stress placed in the *Readers* on the benevolence of the new society supports such an assumption. Thus, if a child's early experiences produce indiscriminately positive attitudes, the structure of the political themes should reinforce the attitudes developed prior to entering school. Similarly, the political themes designed to produce positive attitudes toward Mao Tse-tung in China make him a highly visible political figure for children; thus, the *Readers* serve as reinforcement for the indoctrination children receive from the radio and other forms of mass communication.

The themes themselves are designed to develop not only positive attitudes to the new regime and its leaders, but also to develop categories of negative attitudes. Looking at the frequency of negative-attitude-producing themes, we find that the "Evils of Republican China," is the most common. We also find that this thematic category follows the same frequency of occurrence pattern through the Grades as the positive attitude-producing themes, in that it becomes more frequent as the student moves from one Grade to another. Thus, as indoctrination of positive themes increases, so does the indoctrination of negative themes. Political themes designed to inculcate negative attitudes toward aspects of traditional or Imperial China are somewhat less prominent. Kuomintang China is a much more recent political experience, and the Kuomintang government in Taiwan is in a sense competing with the Communists for the allegiance of the Chinese people. For this reason the creation of negative attitudes toward Kuomintang China is a real and specific goal. With the obvious exception of continuing traditional values, Imperial China is no threat, but the Chinese Communist leadership undoubtedly believes it necessary to indicate that the "new" China is superior to any of its predecessors.

The inclusion of negative political themes calls for some specificity in the attitudes of children. Themes that involve the development of negative attitudes toward external political systems, such as that of United States, would not be difficult to create. To require children to distinguish between three Chinas is somewhat more difficult. Nevertheless, the Kuomintang experience is relatively common among the parents of the children studying the *Readers*, and Kuomintang China represents the challenge to the efforts of the Chinese communists that would most likely occur in the home. Political learning occurring prior to a child's entrance into primary school is of great significance, and the Communist leadership is undoubtedly trying to change positive attitudes toward Kuomintang China that may have been created by the family.

Dawson and Prewitt have referred to the problem of differing political values taught by different socializing agents as "discontinuity."[5] In this particular case, the children may be taught inconsistent values in the home and in school. For a Chinese parent to teach his child that Kuomintang China was "good" and that China under Mao is "bad," however, is quite unlikely, and if it does occur the behavior is probably not very widespread. Such a parent would soon be discovered, and he would become at best a "counter-revolutionary" and at worst a "class enemy." His doom would be sealed. In addition, most parents would certainly recognize the effect such teaching would have upon their child's future and would refrain for this reason alone. Thus, we may safely assume that the negative attitudes taught in relation to Kuomintang China receive no challenge from the family learning experience and are part of the basic or core orientations which the Chinese leadership is attempting to create in order to influence future political attitudes.

Description. Table III-A shows the political themes identified in the *Readers* in order of decreasing frequency of occurrence as both central and subthemes. In the discussion that follows we shall treat each major category individually. Table III-F, which follows the discussion, shows the frequency and distribution of political themes by Grade level and the total number of times that each theme occurs as a central theme and as a subtheme. Table III-G shows central themes by frequency of occurrence.

Table III-A: POLITICAL THEMES

1. Devotion and allegiance to the new society
   Devotion to the Revolution
   Dedication to building the new society and to national reconstruction
   Devotion to the Party
   Devotion to the communes
   Devotion to the People's Liberation Army
   Devotion to the Pioneers
   Devotion of minority peoples to the new society

Devotion to communism
Devotion to the new society
Devotion to socialism
Devotion to the militia

2. Benevolence of the new society

Improved conditions under the new society
Modernization under the new society
Benevolence of the Party
Benevolence of the People's Liberation Army
Benevolence of the communes
Devotion of leaders to the welfare of the people
Benevolence of socialism
Benevolence of the militia

3. Glorification of Mao

Devotion to Mao
Mao as leader
Love of Mao for the people

4. Evils of Republican (Kuomintang) China

Kuomintang oppression
Poverty and suffering of the people
Landlord oppression
Capitalist oppression
Warlord oppression

5. Military conflict

Defense against invaders
Liberation of the Chinese people
Liberation of Taiwan
Peasant uprisings

6. Social conflict

Oppression of the weak by the strong
Conflict with remnants of the old society
Liberation of the masses

7. Deception

Cleverness in deception
Vigilance against destructive elements in society
Spying and spies
Vigilance against spies

8. Love for the people

Love for the laboring people

Learning from the masses
Inherent virtues of the laboring people

9. Nationalism
National pride
Love for China

10. Evils of traditional Chinese society

11. Anti-Japanese sentiment

12. Internationalism
Friendship between the Chinese and Korean peoples
Common interests of the oppressed peoples of the world
Support of liberation movements of other peoples
Friendship between the Chinese and Russian peoples

13. Anti-Americanism

14. Anti-imperialism

15. Unity of theory and practice

16. Anti-capitalism

17. Dedication to the revolutions of other peoples

18. Anti-Chiang Kai-shek sentiment

19. Liberation of women (latent)

---

1. *Devotion and allegiance to the new society.* By this designation is meant any expression of devotion or allegiance to the society as a whole or to any individual organization that is a part of that larger society. In order to identify those aspects of the society to which proportionally greater emphasis was given, the over-all category was divided into eleven subcategories (see Table III-A). With the exception of subcategory "devotion to new society," these are highly specific. Subcategory "devotion to new society" was included to cover cases in which no specific organ of the society was mentioned.

"Devotion and allegiance to the new society" occurred as a central theme in 32, or about 22 per cent, of the total number of stories having political themes as central themes. This theme occurs with increasing frequency as the grade level rises. It is of considerable interest to note that heavy emphasis is placed on commitment to the active role of *building* the new society and the major organs involved in the "socialist revolution and construction" (subcategories a-f), while relatively little emphasis is placed upon the more abstract notions of communism, socialism, etc. (subcategories g-k). The emphasis, as the themes in general demonstrate, is on active participation in nation-building, rather than passive devotion to political abstractions.

The subcategory "devotion to the Revolution" requires some definition. By this is meant not only allegiance to the "continuing revolution" as envisioned by Mao, but refers as well to the theme of allegiance to the Revolution as expressed by Chinese citizens during the War of Liberation and of allegiance to the Party prior to that. The theme of "devotion to the Revolution" occurs with increasing frequency as the grade level rises.

A clear example of this theme appears in the story *At the Foot of Mount Mei* (Vol. 10, No. 22), in which the heroine sacrifices her life to Kuomintang agents rather than divulge the whereabouts of her husband.

Another subcategory of considerable importance is that of "dedication to building the new society and to national construction." This theme is more evenly distributed throughout the various grade levels. The poem, *A Road is Built With a Pair of Hands* (Vol. 1, No. 37) is illustrative of how this theme is handled at a lower grade level. Here, the emphasis is on the collective nature of the undertaking, stressing the value of the cumulative effect of the small efforts of many individuals. Naturally, the necessity for hard work in building the new society is brought out. As a workman states in *Visiting a Steel Mill* (Vol. 3, No. 32):

> We must smelt even more good steel to support agriculture and to hasten the establishment of Socialism!

"Devotion to the Party" is another important theme. If Mao, as we shall see, is the supreme father figure, the Party emerges as a mother figure, and is, indeed, referred to explicitly in these terms. In *The Party is My Mother* (Vol. 6, No. 12), in which the author discusses his hardships and the mistreatment he received under the old society before "Liberation," he concludes:

> I have often felt that the Party is my mother. If it weren't for the Party, where would today's happiness be? I must work actively and study hard, forever going with the Party.

Other themes under this category that receive major treatment are those of devotion to the People's Communes, the People's Liberation Army, and to the Pioneers. Loyalty to the Party, however, is stressed over loyalty to these other organizations.

2. *Benevolence of the new society.* This is the second of the major political themes that dominate the *Readers.* The term refers to the generally benevolent character with which the Communist regime and its organs are portrayed. As in the case of the theme of "devotion and allegiance to the new society," differentiation is made in terms of specific organs of the society.

The two most important subcategories of this theme, "improved conditions under the new society," and "modernization under the new society" occur more frequently during the first three grades than in the higher grades. A clear example of the former is *We Move into a New Laborers' Village* (Vol. 3, No. 40). In this story, there is merely the description of the pleasant quarters, with a brief final comment of comparison with former days. As can be seen, this theme often involves a direct or implicit comparison with past evils. This is equally true in the poem *The Basket* (Vol. 3, No. 37) which describes the misfortunes of an elderly couple, who, carrying the basket, were badgered by landlords and foreigners, and which closes with a verse telling how the basket is now used for gathering grain.

The theme "modernization under the new society" is exemplified by the story *The Swallows Return* (Vol. 4, No. 18), in which a young swallow flying back north with his mother in the spring thinks that they are lost because he cannot recognize the terrain over which they are flying. There are highways, bridges, and towns that were not there during their flight south in the fall. As his mother says in reply to her offspring's concern:

> Child, there's no mistake. The people have built an iron bridge over the river. The river has changed in appearance.

This theme tends to stress the continual progress that is being made under the new society as well as the need for hard work in order for the goals of modernization to be attained, and is frequently linked with the theme of "dedication to building the new society and to national construction."

A third theme of considerable significance is that of the "benevolence of the People's Liberation Army." Armies throughout Chinese history have traditionally been destructive, living off the land whenever necessary. Furthermore, the military profession was traditionally looked down upon in China, the soldier being placed at the bottom of the social scale, even below the peasant. The leaders of Communist China apparently feel a need to change the traditional image of the soldier. This is very evident in the stories illustrating this theme. In these stories, the People's Liberation Army is pictured as whole-heartedly devoted to the welfare of the common people. A typical story is *Mailing Back a Kitchen Knife* (Vol. 7, No. 9), in which a unit is on the march. One of the cooks, on opening his pack, discovers a knife that had been borrowed from an old man in a town some 30 miles back. On finding it, he goes immediately to the post office in the town nearby to mail it back to its owner. The clerk refuses to charge him postage, and after the soldier leaves adds a note of his own to the address slip:

> The Liberation Army takes not so much as a needle or a thread from the masses.

The very next story, *The Watermelon Brothers*, serves to drive this point home once again. Here, there is an explicit contrast between the benevolent behavior of the People's

Liberation Army and the destructive behavior of the "reaction-ary" Kuomintang troops. Watermelon fields belonging to two brothers lay at opposite ends of a village. When the Kuomin-tang troops pass through on the east, they run into the fields where they pick and eat all the watermelons. Soon after that, the People's Liberation Army arrives. When the brother on the western side of the village hears this, he rushes to his melon field prepared to defend it. To his surprise, although the soldiers praise the appearance of the melons, they do not stop to pick any, nor do they accept those that he himself has picked and holds out to them. At the end of the story, a question for discussion serves to bring out the theme.

The theme next in importance is the "benevolence of the Party," a theme that, in general, tends to increase in import-ance as the grade level rises. With this theme, the reference to the Party is often made in a single line of a poem or in a phrase in which an association is made, either explicitly or implicitly, between a present good and the Party. In *I Love Our Great Motherland* (Vol. 5, No. 18), the Party, Mao, and China are all linked:

> I love our great motherland.
> The Party and Chairman Mao nurture us
>   as we grow.
> We must study hard and labor hard
>   To build our motherland into a paradise
>   of Communism.

In *Ever Since the Party Line* (Vol. 7, No. 2b), the association of the Party with better conditions is clearly seen:

> Gold fills the earth and silver fills
>   the hills;
> Everywhere there are rivers of food.
> Ever since we've had the Party Line,
> The song of the Leap Forward has not ceased.

A similar instance occurs in the poem *Because There is the Communist Party* (Vol. 9, No. 3), which runs:

A happy life has come,
Because there is the Communist Party.

Thus the Party appears as an ever-benevolent institution.

Next in importance as a theme is "benevolence of the communes." This theme tends not to be stressed as the sole theme of a story or poem, and very often occurs in the form of a brief reference in a longer piece. For example, *Autumn Is Here* (Vol. 3, No. 3), is a poem of 24 lines that appears to have as its central theme the description of an abundant autumn harvest. Into this idyllic framework, the author slips concluding lines that attribute this abundance to the commune:

And everywhere voices are loud in song,
Singing about the rich harvest year,
Singing that the commune is good.

The juxtaposition of an often luxuriant description of a rich harvest and of a short phrase attributing this to the commune, as above, is a common means of presenting this theme.

Chu Teh's Carrying Pole (Vol. 5, No. 10) is a story typical of the next category, "devotion of leaders to the welfare of the people." In this story, Chu Teh, during the period on Chingkang Mountain in 1928, went with the soldiers to carry back food, which was in short supply. The story thus illustrates how an important leader behaves as one of the people, not seeking special privileges for himself by virtue of his position. The soldiers, in turn, hold him in high regard and attempt to prevent him from participating in the actual physical labor of carrying food. The same theme of concern on the part of the leaders is equally well exemplified in *A Woolen Blanket* (Vol. 7, No. 4) in which the author of the story gives his blanket to Liu Shao-ch'i during a bivouac in 1942, only to wake in the morning to find the same blanket covering him. The story emphasizes how Liu Shao-ch'i saw to it that the comforts of the soldiers were taken care of before he turned his attention to his own personal problems. As is so often the case in the *Readers*, the point of the story is crystallized for the pupils by a discussion question at the end:

From what passages in the lesson can one see Comrade
Liu Shao-ch'i's concern for the soldiers?

The remaining themes of the "benevolence of socialism"
and of the "benevolence of the militia" occur in isolated
instances and assume very little importance as compared to
other themes under this category.

3. *Glorification of Mao.* The theme of "glorification of
Mao" is fairly evenly distributed throughout the various grade
levels. As indicated by Table III-A, there are three component
subcategories to this theme, those of "devotion to Mao," of
"Mao as leader," and "Love of Mao for the people." In Table
III-B, can be found descriptions of Mao, his behavior, and of
the attitudes of other characters in the stories to him.

The spirit of the theme "devotion to Mao" is nicely summed
up in this sentence from *Study Hard* (Vol. 1, No. 30):

We must be obedient to the words of Chairman Mao
and be good children of Chairman Mao.

In *Carry a Message to Peking* (Vol. 2, No. 25), and elsewhere,
he is referred to as "beloved" Chairman Mao. Again, in
Everyone Loves Mao Tse-tung (Vol. 7, No. 2), there are the
lines:

The people of China, six-hundred-million strong,
All love Mao Tse-tung.

This same feeling is portrayed in *A Wounded Man's Wish*
(Vol. 7, No. 3), in which a dying soldier wants only to see
Mao. In *Mountain Song of a Rich Harvest* (Vol. 7, No. 14), the
emotion expressed is one of gratitude:

The songs are different but the thought is the same: All
thanking Mao Tse-tung.

In some cases, the emotions of gratitude to and love for Mao
resulting from the betterment of conditions that he has

brought about are linked with desires for advancement; advancement, of course, in a collective sense rather than in an individual sense. As the heroine says in *The Story of Sister Li Ch'un-hua* (Vol. 4, No. 40):

> When the communes were set up, I studied how to run a tractor, and became a tractor driver. I am very grateful to the Party and to Chairman Mao. I will certainly labor actively and strive for production.

Under the subcategory "Mao as leader," we find many references to his status, often in the form of glorifying words and phrases. As one reads over the list of phrases in Table III-B by which he is described, one cannot help but think of some sort of Sun God, so glowing is the adulation. Indeed, one gets the impression that he is virtually deified. No other leader is spoken of in these terms. Liu Shao-ch'i, Chu Teh, and Chou En-lai seem pale and insignificant when compared to the sunlike, lustrous Chairman Mao. Not even Lenin, who was highly praised, received such adulation.

This veneration of Mao is, however, but one face of the coin. For although Mao appears often as an exalted godlike being, he is also portrayed as a man of deep feeling and love for people. As shown by stories exemplifying the theme of "love of Mao for the people," Mao, in spite of his status, does not consider himself above the people. Instead, he is shown as being interested in them, treating them with respect and courtesy.

In *A Wounded Man's Wish* (Vol. 7, No. 3), Mao speeds on horseback to the bedside of a dying soldier whose only wish is to "see Chairman Mao." Similarly, in the story *At the Yenan Central Hospital* (Vol. 5, No. 33), Mao visits a comrade who has been wounded. When the nurse, who does not recognize Mao, orders him to leave the man's room, he does so willingly and with good humor. The question at the end of the story asks:

> How did Chairman Mao respect the system in the hospital and in what way was his attitude friendly?

From this, we can see that the *Readers* attempt to foster a complex of attitudes about Mao. On one hand, he is shown as having devoted his life to the betterment of the Chinese people, having in the process become their exalted yet humble and down-to-earth leader. On the other hand, it is shown that the people should respond to him in a spirit of gratitude and love.

Table III-B: ATTITUDES TOWARD AND BEHAVIOR OF MAO

Descriptive terms applied to Mao

Our beloved Chairman Mao
Our beloved leader chairman Mao
Our great leader Mao Tse-tung
The sun of the new China
The helmsman
The lustrous glitter of Chairman Mao
Deepest is the grace of Chairman Mao
Chairman Mao, like the sun
Busy
Like a common laborer
Courteous, friendly, and respectful
A full smile on his face
A tall man, wearing a short jacket, leggings, and a pair of sandals

Behavior of Mao

Leads us in reform
Helps us pull up the roots of poverty
Walks ahead of us
Smiles a smile at me
Loves us
Tells us to study hard and advance upwards
Loves the people
Leads our way
Directed people of village in digging well so they wouldn't have to carry water
Took empty seat at back of hall at a play
Sat down with a little boy on his lap and talked to him

Personally issued regulations on burning of lamps during an enemy blockade

Deferred humbly to a young nurse who asked him to leave the room of an injured man whom he was visiting

Went to worksite to take part in voluntary labor

Picked up an iron shovel and began to shovel up the earth

Refused to accept a basket of eggs offered him by a peasant woman, and instead, took the eggs to the hospital for the wounded

Went from bed to bed in the hospital talking to each of the wounded soldiers

Wrote elegy for girl who was killed resisting the enemy

Mounted his horse and raced to the hospital when he heard that a dying soldier wanted to see him

Bent down, grasped the dying soldier's hand and said: "You are a good comrade of our Party. We will never forget you."

Revitalized morale of the troops after failure of the Autumn Harvest Uprising

Attitudes toward Mao

We must be obedient to the words of Chairman Mao and be good children of Chairman Mao

Always think of Chairman Mao

We send our respects to him

We respect and love you, our leader Chairman Mao

Your grace will never be forgotten

People were overcome with happiness and pleasure at seeing him

Peasant woman presents Mao with eggs saying: "You toil for us common people all day and into the night ..."

The people of China, 600 million strong, all love Mao Tse-tung

Dying soldier's only wish was to see Mao

Everyone thanks Chairman Mao for a bountiful harvest

Tibetan peasant wanted to see Mao with her own eyes

Peasant felt a warm strength in his body on seeing photograph of Mao

We keep in step behind Chairman Mao

The words of Chairman Mao should be remembered

We are forever following Mao Tse-tung

The grace of Chairman Mao is the most precious thing in the world

Always learned from Chairman Mao

The Party has gone on to victory after victory because of the
correct leadership of Chairman Mao
Comrade Mao is not afraid

---

4. *Evils of Kuomintang China.* As the designation indicates,
this refers to injustices portrayed as occurring during the
period from 1911 through 1949. This theme increases in
frequency as the grade level rises. Although only nine stories
are classified with this theme as a central theme, there are 28
additional stories in which it figures predominantly. As can be
seen in Table III-A, differentiation is made between various
types of social inequity. Of these, themes of "oppression" at
the hands of the Kuomintang are the most predominant. It is
interesting that there are comparatively few stories emphasizing oppressive behavior of the capitalists or the warlords.
Thus, the major blame, in the *Readers* is thrown onto the
Kuomintang.

An example of the theme of "capitalist oppression" occurs in
Life in Our Family before the Liberation (Vol. 3, No. 39). The
story describes the poverty and degradation of the writer's
family, and closes with the death of the father, who as a result
of his labor in a coal mine, often spat blood, but kept on
working. Very often, an explicit contrast between the past and
present is drawn in the same story. In this case, the contrast is
provided by the following story, *We Move into a New
Laborers' Village,* which has been discussed as being representative of the theme of "benevolence of the new society." In the
latter story, the coal mine runs a dependent's school for the
families of the workers and the workers live in bright, clean
houses.

Unlike traditional China, in which the *Readers* find both
good and evil, only evil is found in Kuomintang China.

5. *Military conflict.* Like the theme of "evils of Kuomintang
China," that of military conflict (i.e., any form of warfare)
occurs infrequently as a central theme (only six instances), but
very frequently as a subtheme (29 instances). Similarly, there
is a tendency for the theme to increase in frequency as the
grade level rises. As Table III-A indicates, we have differentiated between four cases of military conflict. Of these, the
theme of "liberation of Taiwan" and that of "peasant upris-

ings" assume fairly little importance, whereas more attention is given to "defense against invaders" and "liberation of the Chinese people."

Stories about the "liberation of the Chinese people" are, of course laid during the War of Liberation and involve tales of battles between the Communist forces and Nationalist forces. Stories of this sort very often emphasize the allegiance of the common people to the cause of Revolution and to the People's Liberation Army.

Of far greater significance, is the subcategory "defense against invaders." With the exception of a few stories involving the offshore islands or Taiwan, this theme occurs primarily in stories about the War of Resistance against Japan. A typical story of this type is the two-part story *An Urgent Message* (Vol. 9, No. 28 and No. 29), in which a fourteen year old boy by the name of Hai-wa succeeds in delivering an important message even though he is for a time captured by the enemy.

One case in which the invader is more relevant to the present situation occurs in *Taking a Prisoner* (Vol. 3, No. 21). A Nationalist airplane from Taiwan is spotted over Fukien Province and is shot down by the Communist Chinese air force. The pilot, who bails out, is terrified and meekly surrenders to the militia. The story closes with the sentence:

We have a strong Liberation Army and we have a strong Militia too. Wherever the enemy appears, we will annihilate him.

Many stories in this category also illustrate themes of courage and bravery in battle. *An Extraordinary Forty Minutes* (Vol. 10, No. 19), provides a typical example of this. The story involves an incident in tha summer of 1958 during the Quemoy shellings. A dedicated young soldier, An Yeh-min, was firing a gun when the ammunition behind it was set afire by an enemy shell. He kept to his post and was badly burned by the flames. After the fire was extinguished, he would not leave his post in spite of the severity of his burns until ordered to do so. As this instance suggests, these stories are extremely graphic, and little is left to the pupil's imagination in terms of the violence described.

From this, one can see that obvious importance is attached to keeping the possibility of invasion by an outside enemy continually before the eyes of the young people. By using examples, particularly of heroic actions from the past, it is possible to set up standards of behavior that would be desirable under conditions of invasion. In other words, the *Readers* are saying: This is how a brave and loyal Chinese behaves when his country is attacked.

6. *Social conflict.* Themes of social conflict occur rarely as central themes, with only four cases, but frequently as subthemes, with 28 cases. Again, frequency increases as the grade level rises.

Of the three subcategories shown in Table III-A, that of "oppression of the weak by the strong" appears as the most predominant. This is closely related to themes of the "evils" of Kuomintang and traditional China in which oppression of the people plays an important role.

The theme "conflict with remnants of the old society," although it does not occur frequently, is of some interest in that it calls attention to the fact that not everyone in the society has accepted the new regime and that there is social conflict within present Chinese society as well as in past Chinese society. This is exemplified in the story *Liu Wen-hsueh* (Vol. 6, No. 24), the story of a Fourth Grade pupil who sacrifices his life in trying to apprehend an unreformed landlord whom he catches stealing peppers from the commune. Because of his "love for socialism" and his "love for the people's communes," he resisted the bribes of the landlord and struggled with him to the death. In this way, the pupil is made aware that latent class conflict still exists within Chinese society.

7. *Deception.* "Deception" is a theme that frequently occurs together with "defense against invaders," although not necessarily so. The most predominant of the themes under this category is that of "cleverness in deception." By this is meant any story in which the ends desired by the characters are attained by means of a clever stratagem making use of

deception. This theme is illustrated by the story *Little Hammer* (Vol. 4, No. 21), in which a fifteen year old boy who is scouting for enemy troops is come upon by a Japanese officer. He makes his escape by outwitting the officer, whom he deceives into believing that he is going to water his horse.

This theme is also frequently illustrated by animal stories as well as by war stories. For instance, in *The Fox and the Crow* (Vol. 3, No. 16), which is based on Aesop's fable, the fox flatters the crow into singing, thus causing her to drop the piece of meat she is holding in her beak.

Another theme involving deception is that of "vigilance against destructive elements within the society," in that enemies of the new society are normally portrayed as being secretive about their political sympathies. The story of Liu Wen-hsüeh (Vol. 6, No. 24), which was referred to above in the discussion of social conflict, is also representative of this thematic category. The theme, however, may also be examplified in animal stories. *A Wolf in Sheep's Clothing* (Vol. 3, No. 17) involves a wolf who masquerades as a sheep so that he can get his fill of young sheep. The shepherd boy who discovers him beats him to death with a stick.

It is clear that stories of this kind are interpreted in political terms in the classroom so that the pupil will be aware that there are always "wolves in sheep's clothing" within the society. The hint that this is so comes from the questions that often follow immediately after a story. A typical example of a discussion question of this sort follows two short fables, *The Farmer and the Snake* and *The Cat and the Little Birds* (Vol. 9, Nos. 33a and 33b):

> Discuss the implications of these two fables. What instruction do we receive from them?

In other words, there can be little doubt that through this sort of story the Chinese youngster is taught to be on the watch for deception from any quarter.

The other themes classified under this category are concerned with spies and spying. An example of this occurs in *Examining a Pass* (Vol. 3, No. 18), in which two Pioneers are standing sentry duty. A man comes along with a pass. The Pioneers become suspicious of him and question him. Finally, they take him to the Militia, where it is found that he is actually an enemy spy. Thus, the pupil is trained to be aware of the dangers of both internal and external enemies.

8. *Love for the people.* The theme "love for the people" is differentiated into the subcategories of "love for the laboring people," "learning from the masses," and "inherent virtues of the laboring people." It occurs in fairly even distribution throughout the *Readers*, but receives far less emphasis than the themes discussed above.

An example of the theme of "love for the laboring people" occurs in the poem *A Telephone Call* (Vol. 2, No. 38) in which the children thank their "worker uncles" for the good deeds that they have done. Another good example of the theme occurs in *Thousand-man-cake* (Vol. 5, No. 15).

The theme of "learning from the masses" has also been included under "love for the people" in that it represents a feeling of trust in the wisdom of the peasant. This is shown in *Crossing a Bridge* (Vol. 8, No. 15), in which the wheel of a gun carriage slips over the edge of a bridge. The soldiers turn to a local peasant, who suggests a means for solving the problem.

The subcategory "inherent virtues of the laboring people" was included to cover a limited number of stories. As in the case above, it is classified under "love for the people" because of the attitude of faith in the peasant that it represents. In *The Axe and the Fur Coat* (Vol. 5, No. 29), the virtues of the peasant as contrasted to the weakness of the rich merchant are shown by the results of a contest between two sons of Old Father Winter in which the object is to freeze the peasant and the merchant. The peasant cannot be frozen.

In general, stories classed under this theme show the peasant to be a noble, hard-working, and essentially ingenious individual worthy of respect and love. The non-Chinese reader cannot help but receive the impression, however, that the compilers have in a sense given themselves away in stories of this kind. It is clear that they do not regard themselves as "laboring people," and that they do not see the urban children for whom the *Readers* were prepared as the sons and daughters of peasants. In other words, respect for the peasant is an attitude that ought to be fostered in the pupil, who more often than not, is of a more sophisticated urban background.

9. *Nationalism.* The comparatively low score which this theme has received is misleading in that many if not most of the themes described above are essentially nationalistic in character. For the purposes of analysis, however, we have restricted this theme to overt expressions of love for or pride in China.

The theme of "love for China" is expressed infrequently. One example of it is *I Love Our Great Motherland* (Vol. 5, No. 18). It is, rather, the theme of "national pride" that assumes a greater emphasis. This can be seen in the expression of pride about China in *Autumn in Peking* (Vol. 5, No. 7) or in *National Day* (Vol. 5, No. 8).

Again, it must be recognized that the *Readers* in their pervading culture-centrism are essentially nationalistic documents.

10. *Evils of traditional Chinese society.* Selections in this category emphasize the oppression and suffering of the people of ancient China at the hands of either harsh rulers or cruel feudal lords. The highest frequency of this theme is in Grade Five. Examples of this category are the poems *A Red Sun Blazing like a Fire* (Vol. 9, No. 19a) and *The Silkworm Woman* and *The Brick Burner* (Vol. 9, Nos. 20a and 20b). Both of these poems describe the hard life of the peasant in ancient China.

11. *Anti-Japanese sentiment.* This occurs as a subtheme with fairly even distribution through most grades with the exception of Grade One, in which it does not occur. It usually occurs in conjunction with stories about the War of Resistance against Japan. It also occurs, however, in *Kuang Biscuits* (Vol. 7, No. 32), which is a story concerning the Japanese pirates who attacked the China coast during the Ming Dynasty.

In general, highly antagonistic attitudes are expressed toward the Japanese characters, who are, of course, all soldiers in these stories. Table III-C shows the behavior of the Japanese as depicted in the *Readers* and the attitudes that the Chinese characters displayed toward them.

In assessing the significance of this anti-Japanese feeling, it should be borne in mind that the stories involved are from the period of resistance against Japan. Even so, it is striking, as we shall see presently, that in terms of frequency at least, anti-Japanese themes are more predominant than anti-American themes.

Table III-C: ATTITUDES TOWARD AND
BEHAVIOR OF JAPANESE SOLDIERS

Descriptive terms applied to Japanese soldiers

Japanese bandits
The enemy
Pirates
Dwarf pirates

Behavior of Japanese soldiers

Kicked open door and charged into garden
Murdered members of several families who had contact with the Chinese army
Could not withstand Chinese attack, falling into disorder and knocking into each other like headless flies
Flashed his bayonet
Approached old man menacingly
Shook bayonet at old man
Killed old man with a bayonet thrust to chest
Pressed bayonet to chest of young boy
Tore down elementary school to build an arsenal
Spoke with a sneer to Chinese children
Forced way into village and pounded on every door
Set up machine guns in field, separating men, women, and children
Gave candy to children as a bribe
Threatened children and their families with beheading if children made mistakes in picking out family members
Pirate chief was so frightened on seeing Chinese leader that both of his hands trembled
Could not rise to the defense in time

Chinese attitudes and behavior toward Japanese soldiers

Children carry on studies in secret in spite of enemy presence

Chinese soldiers wanted to charge and attack in their hatred

Chinese soldiers easily defeated Japanese soldiers

Chinese civilians outwitted Japanese soldiers

Chinese were courageous and resolute in the face of threats against their lives by the Japanese

Children clenched fists tightly and did not speak in the face of Japanese threats

Boy remained calm in face of Japanese threats and outwitted Japanese soldiers

Chinese defeated Japanese pirates with clever strategy and captured all of them

---

12. *Internationalism.* By this is meant "proletarian" internationalism, or the feeling of solidarity between the "oppressed" peoples of the world. What is of interest here is the far greater attention given to the friendship between the Korean and Chinese people and the scant attention given to friendship between the Russian and Chinese people. This category also involves themes of the common interests of the "oppressed" peoples of the world and of support of liberation movements of other peoples.

The story *Two Louises in American* (Vol. 6, No. 14), is an excellent example of how the theme of proletarian internationalism is expressed in the *Readers.* Louise, the poor New York slum girl wears "thin, tattered clothes," and, in the story, her hands are "cold and numb." She doesn't get enough to eat and wanders around scavenging cinders and trash, and is aware that only the "rich can have nice things." When she becomes involved in a dispute over a crumb of biscuit with a Pekingese dog, the pet of a rich woman, she is taken away by the police and kept in jail for three days. When she returns home and asks her mother, "Isn't a laborer as good as a dog?" her mother does not answer, only gritting her teeth and clenching her fists.

On the other hand, the story as suggested above, may involve friendship between peoples, as in the case of the interest of the Russian peasant woman in having something Chinese to take home with her as told in *The Chinese and Russian Peoples are Eternal Brothers* (Vol. 8, No. 27).

Table III-D shows the ways in which friendship was

expressed between the Chinese and Koreans during the Korean War in various stories in the *Readers*.

Table III-D: ATTITUDES TOWARD AND
BEHAVIOR OF KOREANS

Descriptive terms applied to Koreans

Old woman:
 Elder sister
 Our Korean mother
Young girl:
 A child as strong as steel
Woman:
 Eldest brother's wife

Behavior of Koreans

Old woman:
 Accompanied Chinese soldiers as they were leaving Korea
 Spent sleepless nights washing and mending clothes for Chinese soldiers
 Brought cakes to Chinese soldiers during battle
 Took care of wounded Chinese soldiers in her home
 Laid aside her grandchild, who was killed as a result, in order to carry wounded Chinese soldiers to shelter
Young girl:
 Cried as Chinese soldiers were leaving
 With her mother, helped Chinese soldiers to escape from an enemy cell
 On hearing that her mother had been killed while rescuing soldiers, drew the corners of her mouth tight and said: "Mother, I'll avenge you for this."
Mother of young girl:
 Killed herself and enemy soldiers with hand grenade
Woman:
 Accompanied Chinese soldiers up steep mountain as they were leaving
 Was wounded by an enemy shell as she was digging wild vegetables for the Chinese soldiers
Korean boys: Stood hand to hand at edge of cliff at night during a heavy rain in order to guide Chinese soldiers on march

13. *Anti-Americanism.* Contrary to what might be expected on the basis of the review of the anti-American curriculum during the Korean War period, themes of anti-Americanism assume minor significance in terms of numbers, there being only two selections with anti-Americanism as a central theme, and six additional selections having it as a subtheme.

The two selections in which anti-Americanism has been scored as a central theme are *Incidents from Taiwan* (Vol. 6, No. 13) and *Open Fire on the God of Plagues* (Vol. 9, No. 34). In the former, the Americans under criticism are soldiers, and thus symbolic of American military presence on Taiwan. In the story, the "Kuomintang reactionaries" are building a road for the American barracks, and to do so, force the residents of the area to leave their homes, which they then burn down. As a result, a boy by the name of Ch'eng-kuei and his friends "deeply hate" both the Americans and the Kuomintang, and throw rocks at the windshields of passing jeeps whenever possible. In one incident, a drunken and discourteous American soldier is beaten up by the boys while a pedicab driver holds the soldier down for them. In these incidents, the callous behavior of the American soldiers is given strong emphasis.

In *Open Fire on the God of Plagues*, a poem expressing Chinese determination to liberate their oppressed brothers and sisters on Taiwan, the command is given:

Open fire!
For our brothers and sisters on Taiwan;
For the fresh blood on the streets of Tokyo;
For the raging fires of Seoul and Pusan;
For the righteous struggles of the peoples of
Asia, Africa, and Latin America.

The discussion question at the end brings the matter to a focus:

Why is it said that the American invaders are gods of plague, evil and barbarous plunderers, the common enemy of the world's peoples, and the number-one war criminals?

Americans are also described as "savage American wolves" elsewhere in this poem. For an over-all view of anti-American

attitudes expressed in the *Readers*, one may consult Table III-
E.

As can be seen from these examples, the anti-American
feeling that is expressed, although minimal in terms of
frequency, is, nevertheless, of a highly virulent quality when it
does occur.

Table III-E: ATTITUDES TOWARD AND
_____   BEHAVIOR OF AMERICANS

Descriptive terms applied to Americans

Rich woman:
  Rich
  Wears fur coat and gloves
Proprietress of restaurant for dogs:
  Plump
  Thick-jowled
Poor slum girl:
  Wears thin, tattered clothes
  Cold, numb hands
  Fatherless
American soldiers:
  Bad eggs
  Thoroughly drunken
American and Americans in general:
  American invaders
  American imperialism
  The god of plague
  Evil and barbarous plunderers
(America and Americans in general):
  Common enemy of the world's peoples
  The number-one war criminal
  Savage American wolves

Behavior of Americans

Policeman:
  Took orders from rich woman
  Ignored poor girl's story
  Arrested poor girl
Rich woman:
  Scolded poor girl angrily
  Struck poor girl

Proprietress of restaurant for dogs:
  Welcomed rich woman's dog attentively
Poor slum girl:
  Lived in New York slum
  Picked up cinders and trash
  Knew that only the rich can have nice things
  Couldn't get full meal
Poor girl's mother:
  Works day and night
  Clenched fists and gritted teeth when daughter asked: "Aren't
  the poor as good as the rich?"
American soldiers (setting is Taiwan):
  Grab Chinese boy and beat him up
  Refused to pay pedicab driver
  Struck pedicab driver in the face
America and Americans in general:
  Invaded Taiwan
  Remain shamelessly on Taiwan

  Chinese attitudes and behavior toward Americans

Chinese boys on Taiwan deeply hated the American soldiers
Chinese boys threw stones at and smashed the windows of
  American cars
Chinese children ran away from American soldiers
Chinese boys knocked American soldier down
Pedicab driver held American soldier down while Chinese boys
  beat and kicked him
Chinese on Taiwan will not stand for oppression
Chinese on Taiwan will resist America as the Koreans did in the
  Korean War

---

14. *Anti-Imperialism.* Anti-Imperialism does not occur with great frequency, there being only two selections in which it appears as a central theme and an additional six selections in which it appears as a subtheme. It tends to occur more frequently at the higher grade levels. The stories involving themes of anti-Imperialism are, interestingly enough, not anti-American in tone, and, in fact, do not specify any particular nation as being guilty of Imperialism. For example, in *Huang-p'u Park* (Vol. 3, No. 38), a boy and some of his classmates are playing in the park, when grandfather comes along. When they ask him, "Grandfather, when you were small did you come here to play often?", he told them how Shanghai had been an

"imperialist empire" when he was a boy and that there was a sign over the gate of the park: "Chinamen and Dogs Keep Out." The nationality of the imperialists in question is not brought out in the story.

Typically imperialist behavior is also evident in *Sambo* (Vol. 10, No. 31), in which Sambo, an African, is tricked into being attacked and eaten by a lion for the edification and profit of a group of European film producers.

15. *The unity of theory and practice.* The unity of theory and practice is, of course, a basic doctrine of Chinese Communism. As might be expected, it is alluded to more frequently in Grade Five than at the other levels.

A direct statement of this theme occurs, however, only in *Man Has Two Treasures* (Vol. 3, No. 26), a poem discussing the relationship between the hands and the brain.

16. *Anti-capitalism.* This occurs as a subtheme in six selections in which the "oppressive" character of capitalist enterprises is depicted. The theme is fairly evenly distributed throughout the grade levels with the exception of Grade One, in which it does not occur. A typical example of the manner in which this theme is presented is seen in *Little Shun-tzu* (Vol. 10, No. 30), in which a teenage boy is mistreated by the owner of a workshop. In the end, little Shun-tzu dies as a result of his mistreatment. The theme is also alluded to in *Two Louises in America* (Vol. 6, No. 14), which was discussed in connection with the theme of internationalism.

Again, what is striking here is that the theme receives the scant attention that it does. However, as suggested, this may well reflect the ethnocentric character of the *Readers* and the greater attention given to positive aspects of the pupil's relationship to the nation.

17. *Dedication to revolution of other peoples.* This category depicts dedication of peoples of other nations to revolution. An example of this is *Lenin's Overcoat* (Vol. 5, No. 19) in which Lenin sacrifices personal comfort for the good of the revolution. This example is typical in that the emphasis in other stories in this category is primarily on the Russian revolution and not on potential revolutions in underdeveloped countries. Again, this is a comparatively minor theme in the *Readers*.

18. *Anti-Chiang sentiment.* Feeling against Chiang Kai-shek appears as a subtheme in four selections. Three of these are at the Grade Five level. As a theme it normally occurs in a story laid during the War of Liberation. It is of minor importance in the over-all structure of the *Readers.*

19. *Liberation of Women.* This occurs only as a latent theme, and is somewhat more pervasive than the low score would indicate.

One aspect of policy of the new regime was the "liberation of woman," that is, to free them from the unequal position that they suffered in traditional Chinese society. This liberation involves legal equality in such matters as marriage, divorce, ownership of private property, as well as the necessary affirmation of their rights to work outside of the home.

Although no overt mention of the liberation of women or of the position of women in Chinese society is made, the implications of this liberation are clear throughout the stories in the texts.

For one thing, there is often no clear distinction made between the types of role that men and women or boys and girls play in the stories. Both boys and girls are depicted performing the same kinds of agricultural tasks, while both men and women are shown sacrificing themselves either under battle conditions or in various phases of the War of Liberation. Again, both men and women are shown sacrificing their lives heroically in non-military situations.

Thus, in terms of such stated goals as becoming "peasant or worker," there are no apparent distinctions of sex. Everyone appears equally capable of becoming a peasant and a worker, and although only men become soldiers, the third of the three acceptable goals under the new society, women also are depicted as functioning in at least para-military capacities. In addition, both boys and girls are shown doing housework or caring for small children in those few stories that deal with these topics. Thus, although it cannot be said that there is no distinction made between the appropriate roles of male and female in the new society, the distinction is at least minimal.

Summary. The major political themes that dominate the *Readers* attempt to influence the young so that they will be dedicated to the new society and the new political system. The goodness and benevolence of the new society is contrasted with the oppressive, cruel society and political system of Kuomintang China. Thus the child's awareness of the "new" is heightened, and his dedication to build the new society is sought. The child is also made aware of "Chairman Mao," the great father figure who is humble and yet a virtually divine eminence from which all the child's present good fortune derives.

The major values are complemented by the themes that occur with less frequency but are also highly salient values for the child-citizen to internalize. He is taught to be ready for military action when requested and, even in the absence of open military or social conflict, he learns to be on guard against those who would deceive and destroy him. His views of the external world should be dominated by the ever-present threat of American "imperialism," and he has been taught to hate America. He will also be aware of the existence of "oppressed peoples" in the world who have yet to throw off the yoke of oppression and who are awaiting the "revolution."

A more detailed profile of the ideal young model citizen will be developed in Chapter Six, for the citizen in the new China is also taught a more general set of values—values designed to teach him how to behave in the new society.

Table III-F: FREQUENCY AND DISTRIBUTION
OF POLITICAL THEMES*

Themes		*Distribution by Grade Level*				
		1	*2*	*3*	*4*	*5*
1. Devotion and allegiance to the new society	138	16	24	26	31	42
Central theme:	32	6	4	5	5	12
Subtheme:	106	10	19	21	26	30
Devotion to the Revolution	31	0	2	4	7	18
Central theme:	10	0	1	0	3	6
Subtheme:	21	0	1	4	4	12

*Underscored numbers represent total occurrence as both central themes and subthemes.

Table III-F continued:

Themes	Distribution by Grade Level				
	1	*2*	*3*	*4*	*5*
Dedication to building new society and to national re-construction	22	3	6	4	3	6
Central theme:	4	0	1	2	0	1
Subtheme:	18	3	5	2	3	5
Devotion to the Party	18	3	2	4	3	6
Central theme:	7	2	1	2	0	1
Subtheme:	11	1	1	2	3	5
Devotion to the communes	19	5	3	3	8	0
Central theme:	2	1	0	0	1	0
Subtheme:	17	4	3	3	7	0
Devotion to the PLA	17	1	4	4	4	4
Central theme:	2	0	0	0	0	2
Subtheme:	15	1	4	4	4	2
Devotion to the Pioneers	9	0	0	1	2	6
Central theme:	1	0	0	0	0	1
Subtheme:	8	0	0	1	2	5
Devotion of minority peoples to the new society	9	0	0	1	2	6
Central theme:	1	0	0	0	0	1
Subtheme:	8	0	0	1	2	5
Devotion to Communism	6	2	1	2	0	1
Central theme:	3	1	1	1	0	0
Subtheme:	3	1	0	1	0	1
Devotion to new society	6	1	2	0	2	1
Central theme:	1	1	0	0	0	0
Subtheme:	5	0	2	0	2	1
Devotion to Socialism	1	1	0	0	0	0
Devotion to Militia (subtheme):	1	0	1	0	0	0

Table III-F continued:

Themes		Distribution by Grade Level				
		1	2	3	4	5
2. Benevolence of the new society	79	5	20	17	20	17
Central theme:	37	4	10	8	9	6
Subtheme:	42	1	10	9	11	11
Improved conditions under the new society	22	2	7	4	4	5
Central theme:	14	2	6	1	1	4
Subtheme:	8	0	1	3	3	1
Modernization under the new society	15	2	7	1	3	2
Central theme:	7	1	3	1	1	1
Subtheme:	8	1	4	0	2	1
Benevolence of the PLA	13	0	2	4	6	1
Central theme:	2	0	0	0	2	0
Subtheme:	11	0	2	4	4	1
Benevolence of the Party	12	1	0	2	3	6
Central theme:	5	1	0	1	2	1
Subtheme:	7	0	0	1	1	5
Benevolence of the communes	8	0	3	3	2	0
Central theme:	6	0	1	3	2	0
Subtheme:	2	0	2	0	0	0
Devotion of leaders to welfare of the people	7	0	1	3	1	2
Central theme:	3	0	0	2	1	0
Subtheme:	4	0	1	1	0	2
Benevolence of Socialism (subtheme only):	1	0	0	0	0	1
Benevolence of Militia (subtheme only):	1	0	0	0	1	0

Table III-F continued:

Themes		1	2	3	4	5
		Distribution by Grade Level				
3. Glorification of Mao	43	11	5	11	10	6
Central theme:	24	7	2	5	6	4
Subtheme:	19	4	3	6	4	2
Devotion to Mao	20	6	1	4	7	2
Central theme:	11	4	0	1	5	1
Subtheme:	9	2	1	3	2	1
Mao as leader	12	2	3	3	2	2
Central theme:	7	1	1	2	1	2
Subtheme:	5	1	2	1	1	0
Love of Mao for people	11	3	1	4	1	2
Central theme:	6	2	1	2	0	1
Subtheme:	5	1	0	2	1	1
4. Evils of Kuomintang China	37	1	7	4	10	15
Central theme:	9	0	2	0	3	4
Subtheme:	28	1	5	4	7	11
Kuomintang oppression	17	0	3	3	3	8
Central theme:	1	0	0	0	0	1
Subtheme:	16	0	3	3	3	7
Poverty and suffering of the people	8	1	2	0	1	4
Central theme:	2	0	1	0	0	1
Subtheme:	6	1	1	0	1	3
Landlord oppression	7	0	1	1	4	1
Central theme:	3	0	0	0	2	1
Subtheme:	4	0	1	1	2	0
Capitalist oppression	3	0	1	0	1	1
Warlord oppression (subtheme only):	2	0	0	0	1	1

Table III-F continued:

Themes		Distribution by Grade Level				
		1	2	3	4	5
5. Military conflict	35	4	7	8	6	10
Central theme:	6	2	3	0	1	0
Subtheme:	29	2	4	8	5	10
Defense against invaders	20	4	5	4	2	5
Central theme:	6	2	3	0	1	0
Subtheme:	14	2	2	4	1	5
Liberation of Chinese people (subtheme only):	11	0	2	3	4	2
Liberation of Taiwan (subtheme only):	3	0	0	1	0	2
Peasant uprisings (subtheme only):	1	0	0	0	0	1
6. Social conflict	32	0	4	6	8	14
Central theme:	4	0	0	1	1	2
Subtheme:	28	0	4	5	7	12
Oppression of weak by strong	29	0	4	4	8	13
Central theme:	4	0	0	1	1	2
Subtheme:	25	0	4	3	7	11
Conflict with remnants of old society (subtheme only):	2	0	0	2	0	0
Liberation of masses (subtheme only):	1	0	0	0	0	1
7. Deception	29	0	9	4	8	8
Central theme:	10	0	4	1	2	3
Subtheme:	19	0	5	3	6	5
Cleverness in deception	17	0	5	1	5	6
Central theme:	6	0	2	1	2	1
Subtheme:	11	0	3	0	3	5

Table III-F continued:

Themes		Distribution by Grade Level				
		1	*2*	*3*	*4*	*5*
Vigilance against destructive elements in society	7	0	2	2	1	2
Central theme:	3	0	1	0	0	2
Subtheme:	4	0	1	2	1	0
Spying and spies (subtheme only):	3	0	1	1	1	0
Vigilance against spies	2	0	1	0	1	0
Central theme:	1	0	1	0	0	0
Subtheme:	1	0	0	0	1	0
8. Love for the people	20	4	4	7	4	1
Central theme:	4	1	1	2	0	0
Subtheme:	16	3	3	5	4	1
Love for the laboring people	12	4	3	4	1	0
Central theme:	3	1	1	1	0	0
Subtheme:	9	3	2	3	1	0
Learning from the masses (subtheme only):	6	0	1	1	3	1
Inherent virtues of the laboring people	2	0	0	2	0	0
Central theme:	1	0	0	1	0	0
Subtheme:	1	0	0	1	0	0
9. Nationalism	19	2	0	9	4	4
Central theme:	4	1	0	3	0	0
Subtheme:	15	1	0	6	4	4
National pride	16	1	0	8	4	3
Central theme:	2	0	0	2	0	0
Subtheme:	14	1	0	6	4	3
Love for China	3	1	0	1	0	1
Central theme:	2	1	0	1	0	0
Subtheme:	1	0	0	0	0	1

Table III-F continued:

Themes		Distribution by Grade Level				
		1	2	3	4	5
10. Evils of traditional Chinese society	11	0	1	0	5	5
Central theme:	6	0	1	0	1	4
Subtheme:	5	0	0	0	4	1
11. Anti-Japanese sentiment (subtheme only):	11	0	3	3	3	2
12. Internationalism	10	0	4	2	3	1
Central theme:	1	0	0	0	1	0
Subtheme:	9	0	4	2	2	1
Friendship between Chinese and Korean people (subtheme):	5	0	3	0	2	0
Common interests of oppressed peoples of world (subtheme):	2	0	0	2	0	0
Support of liberation movements of other peoples (subtheme only):	2	0	1	0	0	1
Friendship between Chinese and Russian people (central theme only):	1	0	0	0	1	0
13. Anti-Americanism	8	0	2	3	1	2
Central theme:	2	0	0	1	0	1
Subtheme:	6	0	2	2	1	1
14. Anti-Imperialism	6	0	2	0	1	3
Central theme:	2	0	1	0	0	1
Subtheme:	4	0	1	0	1	2
15. Unity of theory and practice	6	0	2	0	0	4
Central theme:	1	0	1	0	0	0
Subtheme:	5	0	1	0	0	4
16. Anti-Capitalism (subtheme only):	6	0	1	2	1	2

Table III-F continued:

Themes	Distribution by Grade Level				
	1	2	3	4	5
17. Dedication to revolution of other peoples	4	0	1	1	1	1
• Central theme:	2	0	1	1	0	0
Subtheme:	2	0	0	0	1	1
18. Anti-Chiang sentiment (subtheme only):	4	0	0	1	0	3
19. Liberation of women (latent):	3	0	0	0	1	2

Table III-G: CENTRAL THEMES BY FREQUENCY
OF OCCURRENCE

Order	Theme	Number of Occurrences	
		No.	%
1.	Benevolence of the new society	37	25.69
2.	Devotion and allegiance to the new society	32	22.22
3.	Glorification of Mao	24	16.66
4.	Deception	10	6.94
5.	Evils of Kuomintang China	9	6.25
6.	Military conflict	6	4.16
	Evils of traditional Chinese society	6	4.16
7.	Social conflict	4	2.77
	Love for the peoples	4	2.77
8.	Nationalism	4	2.77
9.	Anti-Americanism	2	1.38
	Anti-Imperialism	2	1.38
	Dedication to revolution of other peoples	2	1.38
10.	Internationalism	1	0.69
	Unity of theory and practice	1	0.69
		144	99.91

BEHAVIORAL THEMES

Preliminary observations. In the preceding sections, we
have seen what a young Chinese pupil is supposed to believe
about his country and the world and what his attitudes toward

these should be. Now our investigation turns to the question of how the individual should behave. What is good behavior or bad behavior from the point of view of the *Readers?* In an attempt to answer this question, we have examined each selection in terms of the behavior exemplified by its characters. As we shall see, the behavioral characteristics presented as desirable in the *Readers* are consistent with those which are the ideals of "communist morality."

The primary emphasis of the behavioral themes, measured by the frequency of occurrence of both central and subtheme, is on social and personal responsibility, achievement, and altruistic behavior. If we measure only the central themes, the order of priorities changes, and altruism becomes the most emphasized behavioral theme, followed by the themes of social and personal responsibility and achievement. This change in ranking is important, in that by measuring central themes only, the less active values are dominant, while the active, goal-seeking value of achievement is relegated to third place. The basic pattern established by the distribution and frequency of the themes indicates that duty and loyalty receive more emphasis in primary school than individual initiative.

The raw scores of the three dominant themes re-emphasize the basic pattern. Altruism has the highest score, totaling 65 central themes; social and personal responsibility account for 39 central themes, and achievement accounts for only 28 themes. Thus, the dominant central themes are designed to inculcate the closely related values of altruism and social and personal responsibility. Achievement, the principal value of a society seeking to promote rapid modernization, is the lowest of the three primary exemplified in the *Readers.* Only a strong subtheme count raises achievement to second place. Thus, as with the political values discussed in the previous section, the concern of the Chinese leadership with creating a dutiful citizen appears to override its concern with the creation of an achievement-oriented citizen.

The distribution of these three primary themes through the five Grades is equally significant. Altruism follows the same distribution curve as the general pattern set by the political themes. The number of themes related to altruistic values increases in occurrence through the Grades, peaking in the Fourth Grade. The values of social and personal responsibility have a more erratic pattern, but these themes also peak in the Fourth Grade and dip in the Fifth Grade. Achievement themes peak in the Fourth and dip in the Fifth Grade, but the number of *central* themes emphasizing achievement is relatively low enough to decrease the actual impact of this particular set of themes. In addition, as indicated below, achievement in the *Readers* is seen in societal terms rather than as an individual or personal attribute; achievement themes, therefore, are also group- or society-oriented.

When the major values of both the political themes and the behavioral themes are compared, it can be seen that the emphasis on political loyalty that occurs in the Fourth and Fifth Grades is complemented by the emphasis on altruism and responsibility that occurs in the behavioral themes in the same grades. An over-all image emerges from the *Readers* in which a definite pattern of increasing intensity in socialization efforts occurs as the student moves from grade to grade.

Description. Table IV-A shows the behavioral themes identified in the *Readers* in order of decreasing frequency or occurrence as both central and subthemes. As in the case of the political themes, we shall discuss each major category individually. Table IV-B, which follows the discussion, shows the frequency and distribution of behavioral themes by grade level and the total number of times that each theme occurs as a central theme and as a subtheme. Table IV-C shows central themes by frequency of occurrence.

Table IV-A: BEHAVIORAL THEMES

1. Social and Personal Responsibility
   Devotion to duty
   Obedience and deference
   Performance of social obligations
   Protection of public property
   Thrift and frugality
   Prudence and foresight
   Hygienic behavior
   Honesty
   Neatness and order

2. Achievement
   Achievement through diligence and persistence
   Desire to achieve
   Achievement cleverness

3. Altruistic Behavior
   Heroic self-sacrifice
   Service to others
   Sacrifice of egoistic motives for higher goals

4. Collective Behavior
   Co-operation in a common endeavor
   Solidarity and anti-individualism

5. Prosocial Aggression

6. Conquest of Natural Environment

7. Role Acceptance
   As worker-farmer-soldier
   General acceptance of social role
   As commune member
   As successor to the revolution

8. Starting From Reality
   Scientific attitude of investigation and research
   Solution of conflict through study of actual situation

9. Esthetic Aspects of Nature and/or Farm Life

10. Willingness to Accept Advice and Criticism

11. Love of Labor

12. Bad Consequences of Improper Behavior

13. Behavioral Techniques for Resisting Enemy
    Invasion and Occupation

14. Internal Reward and Satisfaction
    Satisfaction from accomplishment of a task
    Happiness in doing what is right

15. Love of Study
    Love of study
    Love of school

16. Responsiveness to and Affiliation for Nature
    and Farm Life

17. Anti-Superstition

1. *Social and personal responsibility.* Themes of social or personal responsibility occur with high frequency in the *Readers*, there being 39 selections scored under this category for central themes and another 96 selections scored for subthemes. These themes decrease in frequency in the higher grade levels.

As Table IV-A indicates, themes in this category are generally concerned with the relationship between the behavior of the individual and his group or society as a whole. Some of these, such as "thrift and frugality," "prudence and foresight," and "neatness and order," although essentially matters of personal responsibility, are, in the context of Chinese Communist morality, seen as affecting the welfare of society as a whole and, for that reason, are also considered with the more obviously social virtues.

In general, these themes stress the obligation of the individual to the good of the over-all group or of society. In this, the individual is clearly shown as subordinated to the larger interests of society. In *The Flowers in the Park* (Vol. 1, No. 35), for example, which exemplifies the theme of "protection of public property," the little boy wants to pick the flowers. He is stopped, however, by his older sister, who tells him:

Don't pick them! They are for everyone to look at.

A Story About Borrowing a Picture Book (Vol. 8, No. 25) is concerned with honesty and personal integrity and involves a situation in which a girl must make a decision involving a conflict between loyalty to her family and her duty to a larger social group. The conflict is, of course, resolved in favor of the group, and her correct behavior is amply rewarded.

The conflict presented in the story described above suggests very strongly that there is considerable significance in the prominence given in the *Readers* to themes of social responsibility. The significance of these themes becomes more obvious when it is recalled that traditional Chinese ethics, as exemplified particularly by Confucianism, were primarily family-centered and that the first loyalty of the individual was to his family. There can be little doubt that the inclusion of a high proportion of selections devoted to questions of social responsibility is a deliberate attempt to shift the focus of loyalty from the family to society.

2. *Achievement.* Achievement appears as a theme of almost equal importance as that of social and personal responsibility, with 28 cases as a central theme and 90 cases as a subtheme. A story was scored for achievement when it dealt with examples of actual achievement or with expression of the desire to achieve. It should be pointed out that "achievement" in the sense used here, in keeping with the social character of the Communist ethic, refers not so much to *personal* achievement as an end in itself, but rather to achievement as it is related to wider social goals. Whatever the individual achieves is not for his personal glorification. In other words, personal achievement is portrayed as subordinated to the good of the society.

Of the three subcategories of achievement themes found in the *Readers,* that of achievement through "diligence and persistence" is by far the most emphasized. Stories exemplifying this theme usually involve individuals who attain their goals not so much by virtue of any outstanding ability but rather through keeping at a task until it is at last successfully completed. A typical example of this theme occurs in *Grinding a Piece of Iron into a Needle* (Vol. 4, No. 12), in which the T'ang poet Li Po, as a small boy, comes upon a woman grinding a piece of iron. When he asked her what she was doing, she replied: "Making a needle." Li Po, who was "fond of playing and afraid of hardship," was skeptical that such was possible. But the old woman said:

> All you need is perseverance. If you do not fear hardship, a piece of iron can be ground into a needle.

It was then that Li Po understood the truth of the value of perseverence and hard work. From that time on, he studied hard and made rapid progress.

This is a lesson that is spelled out plainly time and time again as in the following New Year's Motto that appears in Volume 5, No. 38:

Establish a spirit of diligence and frugality;
Develop a spirit of bitter struggle.

Another typical example of the theme occurs in *A Patch* (Vol. 6, No. 6), in which a little boy tears his clothes crawling through a fence and attempts with little success and to the great amusement of his sister to sew on a patch. However, in his shame at his failure, he persists, working slowly until he completes the patching successfully.

The lesson is clear. Success is achieved through patience, perseverence, and diligence. If one works hard enough at something, he will inevitably succeed. Failure springs from lack of effort, and nothing more.

Very often, themes of diligence and achievement are linked with those of collective labor for a common good or for an altruistic end rather than for personal advancement or improvement. Evidence for this is seen in *Cleaning a Wall* (Vol. 7, No. 7). At a meeting of the Pioneers the writer of the selection brings up the problem of a wall near the school on which there was writing and scribbling. The Pioneers agree to go out and clean it up. In the story, a contrast is made between the work styles of Chao Shu-fang, who was "patient and precise," and Lu Chien-wen, who was by temperament "too hasty" and who worked rapidly but inefficiently. The point is reiterated that it is by persistent and patient labor that one attains goals and that working with a group in a spirit of public service is more effective than independent effort.

In other stories, it is not the act of achievement that is emphasized, but rather the desire to achieve. An example of this occurs in *Gathering Rice* (Vol. 5, No. 6).

In contrast to this, there is another type of achievement that figures in many selections. This is not achievement through persistence, but achievement through solving a problem in a clever or ingenious way. To describe this form of achievement, we have adopted the term "achievement cleverness."

Classical Chinese literature abounds in stories of "achievement cleverness," and under this category we find a good number of stories from classical as well as more recent sources. A typical story of this sort is *Szu-ma Kuang* (Vol. 2,

No. 36), in which Szu-ma Kuang saves a playmate who has fallen into a cistern by breaking it with a rock, or *A Crow Gets a Drink of Water* (Vol. 2, No. 17), in which a crow put stones into a bottle of water in order to raise the level of water so that he can drink it. Another example from a classical source is *Weighing an Elephant* (Vol. 7, No. 21), in which Ts'ao Chung, the father of Ts'ao Ts'ao, works out a clever method to weigh an elephant indirectly.

Thus, while it appears that diligence is the key to achieving long-range goals, the clever solution is approved as well. There does appear, however, to be a distinction between the types of situations to which these two forms of achievement are applicable, "achievement cleverness" being portrayed as more appropriate to the solution of immediate problems as opposed to the sustained effort required to attain major goals.

3. *Altruistic behavior.* Themes of altruistic behavior are next in importance to those of achievement in terms of frequency of occurrence, there being 65 selections emphasizing altruistic behavior as a central theme and 32 selections having it as a subtheme. Altruistic themes increase in frequency as grade level rises.

Here, we have differentiated between three categories of altruistic behavior: "heroic self-sacrifice," "service to others," and "sacrifice of egoistic motives for higher goals." It is the first two of these that are of major concern.

Of these themes, it is that of "heroic self-sacrifice" that occurs most frequently. "Heroic self-sacrifice" refers either to sacrifice of one's life to save the life of another or to save public property, or to an act of heroism in which the individual risks his life for these ends. Most often, however, the story involves a hero or heroine who willingly sacrifices his or her life. A typical example occurs in *Lo Sheng-chiao* (Vol. 8, No. 28). In this story, Lo Sheng-chiao, a member of the People's Liberation Army forces in Korea, sacrifices himself in saving the life of a little Korean boy who has fallen through the ice into a river. As soon as Lo Sheng-chiao learns of the accident, he jumps into the cold water without thought for his own life.

This same sort of behavior is characteristic of *Hsiang Hsiu-li*

(Vol. 7, No. 36), a girl who sacrifices her life in preventing the spread of a fire that would have led to a costly explosion. At the hospital, to which she was taken seriously burned, the first thing she asked was: "Did the sodium explode? Was the plant damaged?" She soon died from the severe burns that she had suffered, but as the text remarks:

> Her lofty communist spirit and her heroic self-sacrifice for the people will always live in our hearts.

The question at the end of the story asks:

> In what ways was Hsiang Hsiu-li's lofty Communist spirit exemplified?

The theme of "service to others" is central in 16 stories. A typical example is found in *I've Come to Escort You to Work* (Vol. 6, No. 26), which tells of a small boy who helps a blind woman find her way to work and passes the duty on to his younger sister when he can no longer continue to do it himself. The question at the end of the story serves to bring the point home:

> Why did the brother and sister want to escort Auntie Liu to Work?

Through stories like these, the point is made over and over again that one should think of others before oneself, offer kindness and help to those that need it, particularly the sick and the elderly, and put one's own interest after that of others.

The theme "sacrifice of egoistic motives for higher goals" is well exemplified by the story *Giving Convenience to Others* (Vol. 10, No. 8). Chao Meng-t'ao, who is a model worker, struggles with her conscience and finally swaps spinning machines with an inexperienced girl who cannot meet her quota because of the poor quality of her machine. Chao Meng-t'ao succeeds in overcoming the handicap imposed by the inferior machine, and as a result of her example, a spirit of mutual helpfulness pervades the entire work group, which continues as a model production group year after year.

4. *Collective behavior.* Collective behavior, that is, doing things as part of a group rather than by oneself, is emphasized throughout the text. It occurs more frequently as a subtheme, having been scored only ten times as a central theme but 65 times as a subtheme. We have considered collective behavior under two categories, the first, that of "co-operation in a common endeavor," which is the most frequent manifestation of the theme, and second, that of "solidarity and anti-individualism."

The first of these categories is exemplified by *On Duty for the Day* (Vol. 1, No. 38), in which a group of pupils take care of their classroom together.

An example of the theme of "solidarity and anti-individualism" occurs in *A Bundle of Arrows* (Vol. 3, No. 15), an adaptation of one of the fables of Aesop. Here, an old man's ten sons learn that survival depends upon working together rather than individual activity.

The theme of "collective behavior" together with those of "social and personal responsibility," "achievement," and "altruistic behavior," recur constantly as the dominant themes of the *Readers.*

5. *Prosocial aggression.* Prosocial aggression can be defined as "morally righteous" aggression, thus including such diverse forms of aggressive behavior as the Crusades, the Inquisition, slaughter of an enemy in war for the preservation of freedom, or attacking a dangerous criminal who is threatening the lives of innocent people. It is, thus, any form of aggressive behavior that is conceived of as functioning for the social good. As such, it is opposed to murder or beating up a classmate for no good reason, which are examples of *antisocial* aggression.

The theme of prosocial aggression occurs as a subtheme 43 times in the *Readers,* and increases in frequency as grade level rises. It frequently accompanies war stories.

An interesting instance of this theme occurs in *Incidents from Taiwan* (Vol. 6, No. 13). Here, the aggressive behavior of the American soldiers, who beat up whomever they can lay their hands on, is shown as evil. However, when the little Chinese boys, with the help of a pedicab driver, in turn attack a drunken American soldier, it is clear that the author of the story intends this as justifiable and righteous behavior:

> The pedicab driver, holding the American soldier's head down, clamped him firmly by the neck so that the children could punch and kick him. They gave the rotten thing a savage beating.

The contrast between "antisocial" and "prosocial" aggression is again clearly shown in *Liu Wen-hsüeh* (Vol. 6, No. 24), the story of the Fourth Grade pupil who sacrificed his life fighting with an unreformed landlord who was stealing the commune's peppers. In the end, the landlord was caught and executed by shooting.

A Wolf in Sheep's Clothing (Vol. 3, No. 17) presents another instance of prosocial aggression in which a shepherd boy slays a wolf that has been killing his sheep. As he strikes the wolf, he repeats the sentence: "Death to you, you wolf in sheep's clothing!"

A particularly strong note of violence is sounded in *Open Fire on the God of Plagues* (Vol. 9, No. 34), in which, as the "heroic cannons roar" and "heroic soldiers shout out in rage," the theme of "Open Fire" on the American "invaders" on Taiwan is expressed. As the text states: "Our brothers on Taiwan have lit the flames of hate," and "A debt of blood must be returned in blood."

From these examples, it can be seen that the *Readers* encourage aggressive behavior when this behavior is in the interest of the social good.

6. *Conquest of the natural environment.* This theme has been scored only once as a central theme, but occurs in 27 selections as a subtheme. In general, this theme increases in frequency as grade level rises.

An example of this theme occurs in *The Development of Yen-wo Island* (Vol. 9, No. 9), in which the taming of a previously under-developed area is described. The importance of this theme lies in the fact that it goes against the traditional

Chinese philosophical view of man as "being" in nature by asserting that man can by his efforts control nature.

7. *Role acceptance.* A selection has been assigned this theme when it contains some expression indicating that the central character of the selection accepts his status or role within society. Of the various categories of role differentiated, that of "worker-farmer-soldier" is the most predominant. This indicates that the pupil is encouraged to think of himself as growing up to become primarily a worker, farmer, or soldier if the situation requires it.

A good example of a selction exemplifying this theme is *What Will I Be When I Grow Up* (Vol. 2, No. 3), in which the narrator expresses his wish to become a peasant, a worker, and a soldier.

8. *Starting from reality.* This theme includes two categories, the theme of "scientific attitude of investigation and research" and the theme of "solution of conflict through study of the actual situation." In general, these themes increase in frequency through Grade Four, but assume slightly less significance in Grade Five. "Starting from reality" is the central theme of 19 selections and a subtheme of six selections.

A "scientific attitude of investigation and research" in dealing with problems is an important element of Maoist thought. This is exemplified in *The Secret of the God* (Vol. 6, No. 27), in which the object of investigation is a "god" who lived in a mountain cave and who had the reputation of being able to cure illness on the receipt of an offering. The young people who were interested in investigating the "god" were at first discouraged from doing so by the older people, who feared that it was too dangerous an undertaking. Finally, a group of youths went into the cave, seized the "god," and discovered that he was an unreformed vagabond. Thus a scientific attitude prevailed over superstition.

The theme is stated directly in *General Liu Chih-tan's Notebook* (Vol. 8, No. 32), General Liu always seemed to know more about a village than even the officials of the village, his notebook bulging with information about population and resources. This was because he investigated all aspects of any new place he came to, and, as the story concludes:

Many of his comrades were influenced by him, all coming to respect investigation and research.

The explicit statement of this principle occurs in *Starting from Reality* (Vol. 10, No. 11), which begins with an assertion of the objective existence of external reality:

There is a date tree outside the window even if the window is closed and you can't see it.

As the story states, although the "truth is clear," we often fail to investigate the actual situation, with the result that we depart from reality and that our work is done badly. What is the remedy for this?

In work, one cannot rely only on one's own methods of thought, but must start from reality, emphasizing investigation and research.

At the end of the selection, the pupils are asked:

What is starting from reality? Explain, citing an incident from everyday life as in the text.

The pupil is thus encouraged to apply a philosophy of "investigation and research" to the events of his daily life.

The theme of "solution of conflict through study of the actual situation" is exemplified by *The Gold and Silver Shield* (Vol. 4, No. 24), in which two generals, who are looking only at one side of a shield, get into a dispute over whether it is made of gold or silver. The shield-maker finally turns the shield around, showing them that they were both wrong for looking at only one side of the shield.

9. *Esthetic aspects of nature and/or farm life.* This theme occurs as a central theme in 12 selections and as a subtheme in 13 selections. It occurs most frequently in Grades Two and Three and in Grade Five as well.

The presentation of nature in esthetic terms is bound up with traditional Chinese attitudes toward nature that have played a predominant role in Chinese art and literature and in accordance with which the natural world is pictured in idyllic terms. Thus, this theme, which is exemplified by selections depicting nature in its esthetic aspects, is opposed to the theme of "conquest of the natural environment," in which nature appears in her most violent aspects and in which man is wrestling with nature in an attempt to overcome her. Thus, the *Readers* exemplify both the traditional Chinese and Western attitudes toward nature.

There are selections under this category that are devoted entirely to presenting an idyllic picture of country life, as for example, *Summer Has Gone By* (Vol. 5, No. 1):

Those delightful dawns and dusks
Appear before my eyes like a picture scroll.
Summer has gone by,
But I am still thinking of it.

The theme is also sometimes linked with a political theme such as the "benevolence" of the communes or of the Party. For example, politics and esthetics are blended in *The Abundant Hsi-sha Archipelago* (Vol. 8, No. 20), in which a long description of the archipelago, which is located in the South China Sea, is brought to a close with the message:

In the past, the Hsi-sha Archipelago was very desolate,
but after the Liberation, the Party and the government
sent many scientists and workers to the islands to work.
As a result of their hard labors, the Hsi-sha Archipelago
has become an extremely attractive place.

Nature is thus portrayed in extremely appealing terms, and farm life is shown to consist of esthetic pleasures as well as of hard work.

10. *Willingness to accept advice and criticism.* This occurs primarily as a subtheme, appearing as a subtheme 20 times

and as a central theme twice. It is fairly evenly distributed throughout the grade levels except for Grade One, in which it appears only once, and Grade Three, in which it is most frequent.

This theme stresses the wisdom of accepting advice and criticism from others willingly and depicts either the beneficial results that result from heeding advice or the unfortunate consequences of not doing so.

A typical example of this theme is *The Man Who Lost His Sheep* (Vol. 6, No. 28b), the story of a man who at first does not heed the advice of a neighbor to repair a hole in his sheep pen, but who later realizes his error after having lost several more sheep. The theme is stated explicitly in the final paragraph of the story:

> The man was full of regret, for he should have taken the advice of his neighbor. He patched up the hole at once, and repaired the sheep pen so that it was sturdy. From then on, no more sheep were carried off by the wolf.

The discussion question at the end of the story serves to bring out the point of this story and of the selection preceding it even more explicitly:

> Study these two allegories and discuss what educational value they have for us and how they should instruct us in our daily lives.

Thus the pupil is shown that humility and willingness to defer to the advice of others is a virtue that should be cultivated.

11. *Love of labor.* The theme of "love of labor" occurs more frequently as a subtheme than as a central theme, being scored 18 times for the former and three times for the latter. It is given greatest emphasis in Grades One through Three and assumes less importance in Grades Four and Five.

Love of labor is, naturally, a necessary quality in the young who are to build the "new" China. In Grade One, the theme is stated explicitly in the poem *Studying and Laboring* (Vol. 1, No. 31):

> We love to study,
> We love to labor.

More characteristic than a direct statement of love of labor, however, is the association of the accomplishment of a piece of work with a psychological state of satisfaction and happiness. This, in turn, is often related to themes of achievement. This is exemplified in *Pulling Weeds* (Vol. 5, No. 2):

> The weeds in the turnip patches had all been pulled out! How tasty food is after one has labored.

In this way, the *Readers* stress the joys of labor and satisfaction that results from its accomplishment.

12. *Bad consequences of improper behavior.* This theme stresses the bad results that follow from failure to comply with rules or from failure to heed advice. Eight stories were scored with this category as a central theme and ten with it as a subtheme. The theme appears in highest concentration in Grades Two and Three.

A typical example of this theme is found in *Wait a While* (Vol. 5, No. 27), in which a man who does not bother to fasten the harness of his donkey tightly has two baskets of porcelain that he is carrying fall to the ground and smash.

Another example occurs in *The Wolf and the Cat* (Vol. 5, No. 28), the story of a wolf who can find no one to protect him from a hunter because he has destroyed his reputation by killing and eating the animals of most of the people in the village.

13. *Behavioral techniques for resisting enemy invasion and occupation.* This was scored as a subtheme only in 17 selections. The theme is fairly evenly distributed through the grade levels except for Grade One, in which it was scored only once.

A selection was scored for this theme if it showed forms of

behavior that would be applicable to situations that might occur during a period of enemy occupation. For this reason, many of the stories illustrating this theme are set during the War of Resistance Against Japan.

A good example of a story exemplifying this theme is *I Am the District Chief* (Vol. 3, No. 19), in which the courage of those who resist the interrogation of an enemy soldier is portrayed. The story also illustrates a technique for confusing and outwitting the enemy soldier. *The Hawker* (Vol. 3, No. 20) treats a somewhat similar situation in which a street hawker is actually the village school teacher.

14. *Internal reward and satisfaction.* "Internal reward and satisfaction" was scored as a subtheme only in 16 selections. The theme is fairly evenly distributed throughout the grade levels, with a high concentration in Grade Four.

It is characteristic of the *Readers* that few if any stories show the characters receiving concrete rewards for work accomplished or for meritorious behavior. At best, the characters obtain the admiration and praise of their comrades or superiors. Rather, the reward comes more often in the form of feelings of happiness and satisfaction ("psychic income"). This is illustrated by the designations for the two subcategories under this heading, "satisfaction from accomplishment of a task," and "happiness in doing what is right."

The following are examples of the first subcategory:

> After we finish sweeping, the classroom is very clean, and in our hearts we are very happy. (Vol. 1, No. 38).

> In a little while, all of the snow had been swept up. The children went off to school singing. (Vol. 1, No. 44).

The story *The Day of Joining the Pioneers* (Vol. 4, No. 31) contains an example of the theme of "happiness in doing what is right." In the story, a boy on his way to school finds a schoolbook that belongs to someone in another school. He risks being late to school himself in order to return the book to the boy. He arrives at his own school just as the class bell is ringing:

His heart was pounding hard, his legs ached, and he
was very tired. But he felt a happiness that he could not
express, because on the day that he was to join the
Pioneers he had done the kind of thing that a Pioneer
ought to do.

In this way, then, the pupil is taught not to expect any other
reward for goodness than internal satisfaction.

15. *Love of Study.* "Love of study" as a theme occurs far
less frequently than does love of labor, having been scored as
a central theme only twice and as a subtheme six times.
Greatest emphasis on the theme occurs in Grade One. The
theme has been differentiated into two subcategories, "love of
study" itself, and "love of school." The latter theme occurs
only once in Grade One.

The theme "love of study" is linked closely to those
stressing the goals toward which the pupil should address
himself. As we have seen, these are primarily the down-to-
earth goals of becoming a farmer, worker, or soldier. The pupil
is thus not being conditioned to think of himself as a scholar
or to view the love to learning as something intrinsically
valuable. Learning and study are for the solution of concrete
problems and for the ends of national re-construction. As the
poem quoted earlier, *Studying and Laboring* (Vol. 1, No. 31)
states:

Having learned skills, we go out to plant the fields;
Having learned skills, we go out to work.

The theme is also linked in some cases with that of the
"benevolence of the new society." This is true in *We Must
Prize the Happy Life of Study* (Vol. 9, No. 1), in which an old
laborer describes the hardships of his youth, when labor was
hard and cruel and study was hard to come by for peasant
boys, whom teachers scolded and struck. As the old man says:

I envy you children today. How fortunate you are! The
Party and the government have immense concern for
you and have set up excellent schools for you. The

teachers are warm and pleasant to you so that you can study and learn the skills of labor without fear and anxiety. How you ought to prize such a happy life of study.

The important point, however, is that learning is seen not so much as an end in itself, but as a means of mastering skills that can be turned to the service of society. As in the case of "achievement," realization of one's capacities is subordinated as a goal to the use of one's capacities in the realization of the over-all goals of the society.

16. *Responsiveness to and affiliation for nature and farm life.* This theme was scored only once as a central theme and only seven times as a subtheme. It occurs in fairly even distribution in Grades Two, Three, and Four.

An example of this theme occurs in *Mountain Song of a Rich Harvest* (Vol. 7, No. 14), in which the joys of rich harvest are extolled. This poem also links feelings of responsiveness to farm life with feelings of gratitude toward the communes, Mao, and the Party.

The selections included in this category are usually ones in which individuals are portrayed as responding in a positive manner toward farm life and the natural world.

17. *Anti-superstition.* This theme is the least important in terms of its occurrence, appearing as a central theme only once and as a subtheme only three times. It is evenly distributed through Grades Two through Four. The infrequency of its occurrence may be in part explained by the fact that the *Readers* were intended for use among urban populations rather than in rural areas.

The theme is exemplified in *Kicking a Ghost* (Vol. 7, No. 24), in which the writer, Lu Hsün, investigates what appears to be a ghost in a graveyard at night only to find that the ghost was a very human grave robber. In this story, the theme of a "scientific attitude of investigation and research" is linked with that of anti-superstition. The correct attitude toward superstition is shown by the behavior of Lu Hsün, who, instead of running away, approached the "ghost" and kicked it.

Summary. The attitudes which these themes are intended to develop complement the more definite political attitudes discussed in the previous section. The over-all focus of the behavioral themes is primarily on the ideal behavior required for a collective rather than a nuclear society. The traditional Chinese value structure is family-oriented, whereas, the behavioral and political themes we have analyzed are nation-state and societal in orientation. In addition, achievement themes, as we emphasized above, are not designed to create goals of personal achievement, but to develop values related to wider social goals. Thus, achievement orientation accords with the more highly stressed values of altruism and personal and social responsibility.

This basic orientation to the society is more of a transformation of family oriented values than a direct attack on the more traditional Chinese value structure. This condition becomes clearer when it is understood that the rights and duties of an individual in traditional Chinese society were not so much to the individual home, but to the entire lineage as it was traced through lines of male descent. As Maurice Freedman writes: "From the point of view of the state, a man's obligations to it were, in fact, both qualified and mediated by his kinship relations."[6] The themes we have identified in the *Readers* indicate that the new values are designed to make nation and society the primary focus of individual Chinese citizens, rather than kinship. This is not to say that the individual family has been destroyed as a focus of loyalties, but that loyalty to the family lineage is not a particular value orientation taught in China's schools. The efforts of the Chinese leadership are directed at focusing primary value orientations on the society and its political system. In traditional China, kinship responsibilities was a major value, but this was a far wider orientation than the nuclear family. Thus, the transformation of primary loyalties from lineage to society does not demand a direct attack on the nuclear family.

Only secondarily at the primary school level does another variation in traditional Chinese values occur. The individual is taught to appreciate the concept of reality and to develop systematic approaches to problem solving. The themes of "conquest of the natural environment" and "starting from reality" stress the ability of man to transform his environment and to improve the state of nature through systematic and scientific study. An individual is taught to value change and to be diligent in his efforts to change his environment. In traditional China, man's ideal was to adjust to the natural order in order to be in harmony with it. In Communist China children are taught to work hard and change the natural environment—in all cases for the common good of the society. This value tends to put education into a particular focus, for one should study not to become a scholar, but to contribute to the construction of a new China. At this early age, children are taught to value labor and the role of a worker, peasant, or soldier, rather than intellectual enterprises. But, if one does desire an academic career, then it should not be for scholarship, but for construction of the "New China."

The over-all pattern of the value structure of behavioral themes, as is shown analytically below in Tables IV-B and IV-C, is clear. An individual is taught that he has obligations to society at large, and he should strive to achieve not for himself, but for the common good. Further, at this young age, the individual is taught to value labor not personal achievement, and labor is seen as primarily physical labor as a worker, peasant, or soldier. The model citizen, seen through the behavioral themes, is a person who works well with others, accepts as his goals in life the modest ones of being a worker, soldier or farmer, and approaches the world and its problems in a spirit of objective inquiry.

Table IV-B: FREQUENCY AND DISTRIBUTION
                      OF BEHAVIORAL THEMES*

Theme		*Distribution by Grade Level*				
		1	2	3	4	5
Social and personal responsibility	135	25	31	26	34	19
Central theme:	39	10	12	5	9	3
Subtheme:	96	15	19	21	25	16

*Underscored numbers represent total occurrences as both central themes and subthemes.

Table IV-B continued:

Theme		Distribution by Grade Level				
		1	*2*	*3*	*4*	*5*
Devotion to duty	21	3	1	4	7	6
Central theme:	5	0	0	0	3	2
Subtheme:	16	3	1	4	4	4
Obedience and deference	21	4	3	2	5	7
Central theme:	3	1	1	1	0	0
Subtheme:	18	3	2	1	5	7
Performance of social obligations	20	2	10	5	2	1
Central theme:	7	1	4	1	0	1
Subtheme:	13	1	6	4	2	0
Protection of public property	18	3	5	3	6	1
Central theme:	8	3	2	0	3	0
Subtheme:	10	0	3	3	3	1
Thrift and frugality	14	0	6	4	3	1
Central theme:	5	0	3	2	0	0
Subtheme:	9	0	3	2	3	1
Prudence and foresight	14	1	2	5	4	2
Central theme:	4	1	2	1	0	0
Subtheme:	10	0	0	4	4	2
Hygienic behavior	13	5	4	3	1	0
Central theme:	2	2	0	0	0	0
Subtheme:	11	3	4	3	1	0
Honesty	7	3	0	0	3	1
Central theme:	4	2	0	0	2	0
Subtheme:	3	1	0	0	1	1
Neatness and order	7	4	0	0	3	0
Central theme:	1	0	0	0	1	0
Subtheme:	6	4	0	0	2	0
Achievement	118	17	23	30	32	16
Central theme:	28	6	6	9	5	2
Subtheme:	90	11	17	21	27	14

Table IV-B continued:

Theme		Distribution by Grade Level				
		1	2	3	4	5
Achievement through diligence and persistence	83	12	13	24	23	11
Central theme:	23	3	4	9	5	2
Subtheme:	60	9	9	15	18	9
Desire to achieve	19	2	7	4	3	3
Central theme:	1	0	1	0	0	0
Subtheme:	18	2	6	4	3	3
Achievement cleverness	16	3	3	2	6	2
Central theme:	4	3	1	0	0	0
Subtheme:	12	0	2	2	6	2
Altruistic behavior	97	5	16	21	28	27
Central theme:	65	1	11	17	19	17
Subtheme:	32	4	5	4	9	10
Heroic self-sacrifice	59	0	10	10	20	19
Central theme:	46	0	8	10	14	14
Subtheme:	13	0	2	0	6	5
Service to others	31	4	5	9	6	7
Central theme:	16	1	3	7	3	2
Subtheme:	15	3	2	2	3	5
Sacrifice of egoistic motives for higher goals	7	1	1	2	2	1
Central theme:	3	0	0	0	2	1
Subtheme:	4	1	1	2	0	0
Collective behavior	75	16	18	14	17	10
Central theme:	10	6	1	2	1	0
Subtheme:	65	10	17	12	16	10
Cooperation in a common endeavor	66	16	17	13	14	6
Central theme:	8	6	0	2	0	0
Subtheme:	58	10	17	11	14	6

Table IV-B continued:

Theme	Distribution by Grade Level				
	1	2	3	4	5
Solidarity and anti-individualism	9	0	1	1	3	4
Central theme:	2	0	1	0	1	0
Subtheme:	7	0	0	1	2	4
Prosocial aggression (subtheme only):	43	2	7	10	10	14
Conquest of natural environment	28	3	6	3	8	8
Central theme:	1	1	0	0	0	0
Subtheme:	27	2	6	3	8	8
Role acceptance	26	6	9	2	5	4
Central theme:	8	6	1	0	0	1
Subtheme:	18	0	8	2	5	3
As worker-farmer-soldier	15	3	7	1	1	3
Central theme:	3	3	0	0	0	0
Subtheme:	12	0	7	1	1	3
General acceptance of social role	6	3	2	1	0	0
Central theme:	4	3	1	0	0	0
Subtheme:	2	0	1	1	0	0
As commune member (subtheme only):	4	0	0	0	4	0
As successor to revolution (central theme only):	1	0	0	0	0	1
Starting from reality	25	0	4	6	9	6
Central theme:	19	0	2	5	7	5
Subtheme:	6	0	2	1	2	1
Scientific attitude of investigation and research	20	0	2	4	8	6
Central theme:	16	0	1	3	7	5
Subtheme:	4	0	1	1	1	1

Table IV-B continued:

Theme	Distribution by Grade Level				
	1	2	3	4	5
Solution of conflict through study of actual situation	5	0	2	2	1	0
Central theme:	3	0	1	2	0	0
Subtheme:	2	0	1	0	1	0
Esthetic aspects of nature and/or farm life	25	2	7	6	1	9
Central theme:	12	2	4	1	0	5
Subtheme:	13	0	3	5	1	4
Willingness to accept advice and criticism	22	1	5	8	4	4
Central theme:	2	0	0	2	0	0
Subtheme:	20	1	5	6	4	4
Love of labor	21	6	6	5	2	2
Central theme:	3	2	0	0	1	0
Subtheme:	18	4	6	5	1	2
Bad consequences of improper behavior	18	2	7	5	2	2
Central theme:	8	2	2	2	1	1
Subtheme:	10	0	5	3	1	1
Behavioral techniques for resisting enemy invasion and occupation (subtheme only):	17	1	5	3	3	5
Internal reward and satisfaction (subtheme only):	16	3	3	2	6	2
Satisfaction from accomplishment of a task	10	3	1	2	2	2
Happiness in doing what is right	6	0	2	0	4	0

Table IV-B continued:

Theme		Distribution by Grade Level					
			1	2	3	4	5
Love of study		8	4	1	2	0	1
	Central theme:	2	2	0	0	0	0
	Subtheme:	6	2	1	2	0	1
Love of study		7	3	1	2	0	1
	Central theme:	1	1	0	0	0	0
	Subtheme:	6	2	1	2	0	1
Love of school (central theme only):		1	1	0	0	0	0
Responsiveness to and affiliation for nature and farm life		8	0	2	2	3	1
	Central theme:	1	0	0	0	1	0
	Subtheme:	7	0	2	2	2	1
Anti-superstition		4	0	1	1	1	1
	Central theme:	1	0	0	1	0	0
	Subtheme:	3	0	1	0	1	1

Table IV-C:

CENTRAL THEMES
BY FREQUENCY OF OCCURRENCE

Order	Theme	Number of Occurrences	
		No.	%
1	Altruistic behavior	65	32.66
2	Social and personal responsibility	39	19.59
3	Achievement	28	14.07
4	Starting from reality	19	9.54
5	Esthetic aspects of nature and/or farm life	12	6.03
6	Collective behavior	10	5.02
7	Role acceptance	8	4.02
	Bad consequences of improper behavior	8	4.02
8	Love of labor	3	1.50

Table IV-C continued:

9	Willingness to accept advice and criticism	2	1.00
	Love of study	2	1.00
10	Conquest of natural environment	1	0.50
	Responsiveness to and affiliation for nature and/or farm life	1	0.50
	Anti-superstition	1	0.50
		199	99.95

FIVE

TOPICAL ANALYSIS

INTRODUCTION

Chapter Four discussed the kinds of values in which the Chinese leadership is trying to inculcate its young citizens. Apart from the *themes* of the stories, however, there is the question of the *kinds* of stories used to project the themes: What kinds of topics are used to transmit the themes? or, What are the contexts within which the themes are transmitted? Thus, topics are really descriptions of the stories used to transmit values.

Due to the fact that the Communist leadership is concerned with transmitting behavioral norms as well as value orientations, there is some overlapping between *themes* and *topics*. This is particularly true of the topics "recommended behavior" and "proscribed behavior." We have defined socialization as a learning process in which an individual in a particular society is prepared to meet the attitudinal and behavioral requirements of other members of the society. Thus, it would appear appropriate for given stories to have "recommended behavior" and "proscribed behavior" as topics. To a large extent, socialization, especially the socialization of young children, is a role-learning process in which expectations of behavior in different but specific situations is a crucial aspect. We have included the topical classifications of "recommended behavior" and "proscribed behavior" in our analysis, therefore, even though the distinction between them and the behavioral *themes* is somewhat cloudy.

162

As we explained in Chapter One, each selection was assigned to a given topical category. If, as frequently was the case, it was possible to include a selection among a variety of topics, that topic which was central to the story or poem was designated as the main topic, and those receiving lesser emphasis were designated as subtopics. For instance, a story involving Mao Tse-tung and some particular action during the War of Liberation would be placed under the main topic heading, "Mao," if the central concern of the story turned on the behavior and personality of Mao, with "war situations" as a subtopic. If, on the other hand, Mao figures in an incidental way in the events of the story, the main topic would be "war situations" and the subtopic would be "Mao." The story might also involve other important but non-central subject matter which would also be listed as subtopics.

Table I shows the variety of topics covered in the texts. The topics as listed in Table I are arranged in order of descending frequency of occurrence as both main and subtopics. Below, we shall discuss each of these topics in that order. Table II, which follows the discussion, shows the frequency and distribution of topics by Grade and the total number of times that each topic occurs as a main topic and a subtopic. Table III shows main topics by frequency of occurrence.

The most frequently occuring topics, as Tables I and II indicate, were "recommended behavior," "aspects of Communist China," "rural life and agriculture," and "war situations." Counting only the main topics, "rural life and agriculture" stands ahead of "aspects of Communist China." The initial structuring of values indicated by the thematic analysis is reinforced by the topical analysis in that the child-citizen is directed toward a rural life in which to act out his responsibilities to the new China. Essentially, the contextual units through which the themes are transmitted emphasize a pattern of values in which a child's attention is focused upon rural life in a clearly communist China.

The major distinction between the topical analysis and the thematic analysis is found in the number of war stories used to transmit the themes. War stories, containing descriptions of violence and death, were the fourth most frequent contextual unit. These stories appear to perform two functions. On the one hand, they permit the use of heroes and heroines exemplifying the highest possible sacrifice for one's country, and on the other hand they enable the regime to elaborate on the nature of righteous struggle. As we will discuss later, the war stories do not raise the imminence of the American threat; rather, they describe the struggle through which the new China was born. In essence, they describe the heroism of those who created Communist China, perhaps attempting to show that even if the contemporary demands of constructing the new China are difficult, the sacrifices made in the past were greater.

The topical analysis, generally speaking, indicated a high level of concentration on China and the moral responsibilities of the individual to building a new China. This apparent stress on the individual rather than the group complements the group emphasis of the themes, for the stories are used to transmit highly group-oriented themes. That is, heroes commit the acts of heroism for the good of the group, and individual moral responsibility serves the greater good of the group. The stories, seen as the contextual units for the themes, are designed to guide the individual into group-oriented behavior.

Table I: TOPICS

1. Recommended Behavior
2. Aspects of Communist China
     Communes
     Communist Party
     People's Liberation Army
     Pioneers
     The Long March
     Minority Peoples of China
     China
     Chingkang Mountains
     Peking
     Militia
     Socialism
     Communism

Guerrillas
National Holidays
National Flag
National Anthem

3. Rural Life and Agriculture

4. War Situations
   War of Liberation
   War of Resistance Against Japan
   Korean War
   Nationalist Aggression
   Pre-Modern Peasant Rebellions
   Pre-Modern Defensive Wars
   Wars of Defense of Non-Asian Peoples
   American Aggression

5. Mao

6. Industry and Aspects of a Modern Society

7. Traditional China

8. War Situations Emphasizing Heroes
   War Situations Emphasizing Civilian Heroes
   War Situations Emphasizing Military Heroes

9. Nature and the Natural World

10. Comparison of the Old and New Societies

11. Personal Hygiene and Physiology

12. Personal Heroes in Civilian Life

13. Social Knowledge

14. Proscribed Behavior

15. Non-Chinese Peoples
    Russian People
    Korean People
    American People
    African People
    German People (Military)

16. Pre-Communist Society (1911-1949)

17. School and School Life

18. Inventors, Discoverers, and Scientists
    Chinese Traditional: Lu Pan, Hua T'o, Li Shih-chen
    Non-Chinese: Michurin, Galileo, Watt

19. Social Situations
20. Traditional Founders of Communism
     Lenin
     Marx
21. Basic Chinese Communist Ideology
22. Founders of Chinese Communism and Chinese
     Communist Personalities
     Li Ta-chao
     Jen Pi-shih
     Hsü T'e-li
     Liu Chih-tan
23. Writings of Mao
24. Other Chinese Leadership Personalities
     Liu Shao-ch'i
     Chu Teh
     Chou En-lai
     Ho Lung
25. Life Under the New Society
26. Personal Goals
27. Taiwan

1. *Recommended behavior.* This category includes a wide variety of story types. They all, however, share the common characteristic of illustrating some form of overt behavioral norm that is considered worthy of emulation. Thus, included here are the Chinese retellings of fables of Aesop, traditional Chinese fables, and most stories having as their central purpose the illustrating of desirable conduct.

As seen in Table II, "approved behavior" appears as the main topic in 99 of the 400 selections scored, or nearly 25 per cent of the total of 186 times as both a main and a subtopic. It is thus the most important topical category. As can be seen from its distribution by Grade (Table VI-B), "approved behavior" remains a major topic through Grade Four, but becomes less significant in Grade Five.

2. *Aspects of Communist China.* As Table II indicates, this category contains selections dealing either with China itself or with some aspect of China, as for example, the Party, the Long March, the Pioneers, and so on.

Forty-one, or about ten per cent, of the stories have some aspect of China as their main topic, and an additional 41 have an aspect of China as a subtopic, giving a total of 82 out of 400 selections in this category. The topic is distributed fairly evenly throughout the five grade levels.

3. *Rural life and agriculture.* Selections in this category are very often informational in content, although some do deal with questions of behavior or with political themes. A story was assigned to this category if its central concern was essentially with farm life.

Of the 45 selections having rural life as a main topic and of the eight selections having it as the subtopic, most occur during the first three Grades, there being a considerable decline in frequency of occurrence through Grades Four and Five, a pattern duplicating the distribution of the informational themes in the previous chapter.

4. *War situations.* Selections included under this category have war as a common topic. The category is further subdivided on the basis of particular wars or types of wars. Many war stories also bear a subtopical designation depending on whether civilian or military heroes are the principal characters.

Thirty-nine selections have a war situation as their major topic. It is of significance to note that no war stories occur during Grade One, and that they increase in frequency as Grade level rises. Of equal interest is the fact that the War of Liberation and the War of Resistance against Japan, respectively, receive the major attention, whereas comparatively less concern is devoted to the Korean War. Even the topic of "aggression" by Nationalist China is relegated to minor consideration.

5. *Mao.* Twenty, or five per cent, of the total number of selections have Mao as their central character. He also figures significantly in six additional stories or poems. These stories are distributed quite uniformly throughout the various grade levels. Thus, in terms of frequency of selections in the *Readers* at least, there is strong but not exceptional emphasis on Mao at each Grade level.

6. *Industry and aspects of a modern society.* This is a broad and somewhat loose category that includes selections dealing

with subjects as diverse as steel plants and telephones. The term "modernized society" refers, thus, to anything that represents an improvement over primitive peasant conditions. Sixteen, or four per cent, of the total selections are included in this category are far fewer in number than those under "rural life and agriculture."

7. *Traditional China.* The term "traditional China," for our purposes here, refers to any historical period prior to 1911. Selections under this category include several classical poems from the T'ang and Sung Dynasties depicting the hardships of the laborer and the peasant, as well as a number of traditional stories about such topics as Yü the Great and the building of the Great Wall. The category is thus divided between stories showing the "evil" of traditional China, that is, of feudal China, and stories emphasizing the industriousness and creativity of the Chinese people and the attainments of traditional Chinese culture.

As can be seen from Table II, there are 12 stories, three per cent of the total, that have an aspect of traditional China as their main topic. It should be noted that stories about traditional China increase in frequency as Grade level rises.

8. *War situations emphasizing heroes.* This category occurs only as a subtopic to the category "war situations." The category is further subdivided into stories emphasizing either civilian or military heroes. Of the 23 stories scored for this category, 12 deal with civilian heroes, and 11 deal with military heroes. This reflects, naturally, the high proportion of civilian involvement in wars fought on Chinese terrain. As in the case of "war situations," frequency increases generally as grade level rises.

9. *Nature and the natural world.* This topic appears as the main topic in 18, or 4.5 per cent, of the stories. The category included all selections having a description of nature as their central concern. For the most part, it is usually the esthetic character of the natural world that is emphasized. In some instances, brief references to the communes or other organs of the state are introduced into passages describing the beauty of the natural world in an apparent attempt to link the positive esthetic response to nature to feelings about the state.

As shown by Table II, the topic is stressed in Grade One, assumes less importance in Grade Two, and then increases in frequency through Grade Five.

10. *Comparison of the old and new societies.* Into this category fall selections that make an overt comparison between "bad" living conditions under the Kuomintang regime and the "improved" or "improving" conditions under the Communist regime. Fifteen, or about 4.3 per cent, of the selections have this as their main topic. The topic is fairly evenly distributed between grade levels with the exception of Grades One and Three. The intent of such selections is without exception to draw a contrast between the "oppressive" past society and the "benevolent" present society.

11. *Personal hygiene and physiology.* Selections classified in this category deal primarily with questions of basic sanitation, care of the body, and prevention of disease. A few deal with basic physiology. Some are purely factual, while others involve the moral aspects of proper hygiene.

Thirteen selections, or about 3.2 per cent, fall under this category. As shown by Table II, this topic is emphasized in the first three Grades, but is not dealt with in Grades Four and Five at all, reflecting the greater concern with political topics that occurs at these latter grade levels.

12. *Personal heroes in civilian life.* This includes stories about persons who perform an heroic act in a situation not involving military combat. The hero or heroine often sacrifices his or her life, either in saving the life of another person or in protecting state property.

Six stories, or 1.5 per cent of the total, have this category as a main topic. The emphasis on this topic tends to rise generally through the first four Grades, but receives little attention in Grade Five.

13. *Social knowledge.* Into this category were placed most selections dealing with such matters as writing thank-you notes, receipts, and other forms of communication, or with imparting information that is social in character but that does not involve moral considerations. There are nine selections, or some 2.2 per cent, that have this as a main topic.

14. *Proscribed behavior.* A story classed under "proscribed

behavior" is one that teaches a moral lesson by negative example. In general, such a story involves a demonstration of the bad consequences that follow inevitably from improper behavior. This category is contrasted with that of "recommended behavior" in which the moral lesson is taught by positive example. Eleven stories, or about 2.2 per cent, fall under this category. It receives greater emphasis in the first three Grades, and is of minor importance in Grades Four and Five. The lower frequency of occurrence of this topic, as contrasted with "recommended behavior," reflects the Chinese preference of teaching by positive example.

15. *Pre-Communist society.* For the purposes of this analysis, the term "pre-Communist society" is defined to cover the period from 1911 to 1948. Stories in this category invariably portray the "evils" of the old, that is, Kuomintang, society, whether it be represented by hard working conditions or injustices imposed upon the peasant or laborer by harsh landlords or capitalist shop owners. This category differs from that of "comparison of the old and new societies" in that there is no stated comparison or reference to conditions under the "new" society, although the comparison is, of course, implied and is without doubt brought out in the classroom.

Nine stories have this as their main topic, and the highest proportion occurs in Grades Four and Five.

16. *School and school life.* This is a minor category, there being only five selections having it as a main topic and an additional four having it as a subtopic. As the designation indicates, the category is reserved for selections about school itself or the functions and activities of the school. As Table II shows, greatest emphasis on this topic occurs in Grade One.

17. *Inventors, discoverers, and scientists.* This category is divided between stories about traditional Chinese figures on the one hand and non-Chinese figures on the other. The Chinese traditional figures include Lu Pan, the inventor of the saw, Li Shih-chen, a Ming Dynasty pharmacologist and physician, and Hua T'o, an ancient physician. The non-Chinese figures are Watt, Galileo, and Michurin, the Russian horticulturist. The stories about the Chinese figures tend to emphasize their devotion to the poor, whereas those about the

non-Chinese illustrate the virtues of persistence and/or "investigation and research" as effective means of solving problems.

Stories in this category are distributed uniformly throughout the texts, with the exception of Grade One in which the topic does not occur.

18. *Social situations.* A selection was scored as representing a "social situation" when it depicted behavior involving action between individuals and when it was not possible to score "approved" or "proscribed" behavior as the central concern. Such selections were usually scored with "proscribed behavior" as a subtopic, however.

19. *Non-Chinese peoples.* Stories involving or referring to non-Chinese peoples were extremely rare, there being only four selections scored as having this as a main topic. Seven additional stories made some reference to non-Chinese peoples. These included only the Russian, Korean, American, African, and German peoples, the latter being represented by a group of soldiers only. As a rule, the category is meant to include references to Japanese soldiers; their actions in the Sino-Japanese War were not included in this category. Naturally, the people of Taiwan, being Chinese, were not included, either. The treatment of the "people" of a nation is always sympathetic. It must be borne in mind, however, that the term "people" refers in all cases to the "oppressed masses" of the given nation.

20. *Traditional founders of Communism.* This category includes one story about Marx in Grade Five, and seven stories about Lenin, six of which occur in Grades Three and Four. In all cases, the stories reflect favorably on the attributes of these individuals.

21. *Basic Chinese Communist ideology.* By this is meant any statement of Marxism-Leninism as modified by Mao. There is only one selection which can be classified as having Chinese Communist ideology as a central concern. Five additional selections treat in passing matters that are essentially Maoist dogma.

22. *Founders of Chinese Communism and Chinese Communist personalities.* The selections in this category refer to leaders of the past and include a two-part story about Li Ta-

chao and individual selections describing incidents from the lives of Jen Pi-shih, Hsu T'e-li, and Liu Chih-tan. It should be noted that this category is distinct from that dealing with those current leaders who were also founders of the Chinese Communist Party. The distinction was made in order to focus attention on attitudes to those currently in positions of power (i.e., in power *before* the purges of the Great Proletarian Cultural Revolution.)

23. *Writings of Mao.* These include four selections from writings of Mao which are, generally, excerpts from longer works. As these selections appear only in Grade Five, they have not been rewritten in simplified form.

24. *Other Chinese leadership personalities.* This category includes stories concerning individuals who were in positions of leadership at the time the *Readers* were compiled. There is one story each having Liu Shao-ch'i and Chu Teh as central characters, and there is one story each in which Chou En-lai and Ho Lung appear as minor characters. Aside from these, no mention made of other leaders.

25. *Life under the new society.* This category is reserved for any story dealing specifically with life under the new regime without reference to pre-Communist conditions. There were two stories classified under this heading as a main topic and one as a subtopic.

26. *Personal goals.* This category was reserved for any story in which the central character of the story made overt expression of future life goals. One such instance occurred in Grade One.

27. *Taiwan.* This category includes one story in which Taiwan was the main topic. Scattered references to Taiwan occur in other selections, but not with sufficient emphasis to merit scoring as a subtopic.

SUMMARY

The topics or contextual units through which the values and the structure of values are transmitted to young Chinese reinforce the values determined from the thematic analysis. In addition, the concentration on individual behavior, as such a concentration is exhibited through the frequency of stories related to "recommended behavior," reflects the concern of Chinese educators with the development of basic patterns of individual responsibility. Similar concentration could probably be found in Western or any other primary school texts. China's concern with political integration and economic modernization is also admirably stated in the story topics. Nevertheless, the particular problems faced by China are also reflected in the story topics. The topical analysis, perhaps more clearly than the thematic analysis, states the overriding concerns of the Chinese leadership.

The stories categorized under "recommended behavior" are designed to guide the individual into behavior patterns acceptable to the basic group and societal orientation of the Chinese regime. Following the structure portrayed by frequency patterns, the second concern is that the child should be introduced to the history of the Party together with the symbols and ideology of the new Party-State. Appropriately for China and many if not most developing states, the next level of concentration is on rural life and agriculture. Thus, a child's focus is set on individual responsibility within a Party-State wherein his future life will in all probability be spent in the countryside. This pattern however, receives its particularly Chinese Communist structure with the introduction of war stories as the fourth level of concentration. The emphasis placed upon the War of Liberation and the Sino-Japanese War, rather than the Korean War or United States' aggression, emphasizes the history of the Party rather than an external threat. Thus, war stories are not used to develop the principle of national cohesion against an ever-present external enemy, but to raise the image of self-sacrifice and struggle.

The large number of stories describing rural life, although particularly appropriate for a nation with as large a rural population as China, are quite extraordinary when, to the best of our knowledge, the *Readers* were designed to be used by students in Peking and Shanghai. The extent to which these texts were used outside these two cities is not clear. Scattered references to them are occasionally encountered from other locales. Nevertheless, the emphasis in terms of frequency of topics is significant and suggests a deliberate intent on the part of the compilers of the texts to foster an image of the student as primarily a rural person, or perhaps more accurately as primarily a person having life goals closely associated with agricultural production. When this approach is viewed in contrast to the comparatively lesser emphasis given to stories about industry, the pattern appears to fit the official government policy of the time in which agriculture was viewed as the economic basis and "industry as the leading factor." The stress on rural life is also reinforced by the many line drawings in the *Readers* showing rural scenes. (See page 175.)

The proportion of stories about Mao, although not high relative to the topic "recommended behavior" scores well overall. Thus Mao as a political focus is quite high and indicates the initial phase of the Mao-cult in the formal educational process. It should be remembered that the references to Mao are strongly reinforced through radio broadcasts, images and portraits, and references to Mao, "the great helmsman," by the teacher. Stories about Mao, therefore, probably have a much greater impact on the pupil than the number of such stories initially indicates. In addition, the reforms in education introduced in the latter phase of the Great Proletarian Cultural Revolution will undoubtedly increase the number of references to Mao Tse-tung.

The emphasis placed on the topics discussed above fits well with the requirements of the Chinese nation. China's primary need is the development and modernization of its agricultural base (rural life and agriculture), as well as general industrialization (industry and aspects of a modern society). To accomplish these ends, it needs properly motivated citizens (recommended behavior) with a nationalistic awareness (aspects of Communist China) solidly united behind a charismatic leader (Mao).

The remaining topics require little summarization, but some general observations are prompted by the frequencies of certain topics. The degree to which the *Readers* concentrate on China to the exclusion of the outside world need not reflect on ethnocentric view of the world. The pattern reflects the early concentration on China in which general references to China are refined to give a more deliberate political and national

gēng dì

耕地

fàng yáng

放羊

zhāi mián huā

摘棉花

zhī bù

织布

kāi lù

开路

gài fáng zi

盖房子

focus. The sporadic references to non-Chinese scientists and inventors, and to the "oppressed" peoples in other countries give a sense of China's relationship to the outside world and are indications of a move away from a more traditional ethnocentrism.

The topics summarized above, seen as contextual units for the themes discussed in the previous chapter, reinforce the informational, political, and behavioral themes discussed in the previous chapter. The total impact of the themes and topics cannot be measured because we do not have access to the responses of the students to the stories and the themes they contain. We can, however, discuss the structure of values the Chinese leadership wished to create in its young citizens. Within such an analysis, it is possible to locate contradictions between and among the values, and difficulties created by attempts to transform more traditional values into acceptable modes for a Chinese Communist Party-State. The following two chapters will analyze and discuss the "model child" and the value conflicts created by the structure and content of the themes and topics.

Table II: FREQUENCY AND DISTRIBUTION OF TOPICS*

Topic	Total Scores	Distribution by Grade Level				
		1	*2*	*3*	*4*	*5*
Recommended Behavior	186	36	39	41	41	29
Main Topic:	99	25	22	18	23	11
Subtopic:	87	11	17	23	18	18
Aspects of Communist China	82	15	13	16	23	15
Main Topic:	41	11	3	12	6	9
Subtopic:	41	4	10	4	17	6
Communes	18	4	3	3	8	0
Main Topic:	6	2	1	2	1	0
Subtopic:	12	2	2	1	7	0

*Underscored numbers represent total occurrences as both main topics and subtopics.

Table II continued:

Topic	Total Scores	Distribution by Grade Level				
		1	2	3	4	5
Communist Party	12	4	1	2	2	3
Main Topic:	10	3	0	2	2	3
Subtopic:	2	1	1	0	0	0
Peoples' Liberation Army	12	2	3	1	6	0
Main Topic:	3	1	0	1	1	0
Subtopic:	9	1	3	0	5	0
Pioneers	11	0	3	4	4	0
Main Topic:	3	0	1	2	0	0
Subtopic:	8	0	2	2	4	0
The Long March	7	0	0	0	1	6
Main Topic:	5	0	0	0	1	4
Subtopic:	2	0	0	0	0	2
Minority peoples of China	6	0	0	0	1	5
Main Topic:	1	0	0	0	0	1
Subtopic:	5	0	0	0	1	4
China	3	1	0	2	0	0
Chingkang Mountains	3	0	2	1	0	0
Main Topic:	1	0	1	0	0	0
Subtopic:	2	0	1	1	0	0
Peking	2	0	0	2	0	0
Militia	2	1	1	0	0	0
Main Topic:	1	1	0	0	0	0
Subtopic:	1	0	1	0	0	0
Socialism	1	1	0	0	0	0
Communism	1	1	0	0	0	0

Table II continued:

Topic	Total Scores	Distribution by Grade Level				
		1	*2*	*3*	*4*	*5*
Guerrillas	1	0	0	0	0	1
National Holidays	1	0	0	1	0	0
National flag	1	1	0	0	0	0
National anthem	1	0	0	0	1	0
Rural life and agriculture	53	8	13	18	8	6
Main Topic:	45	6	12	15	7	5
Subtopic:	8	2	1	3	1	1
War situations	46	0	11	8	13	14
Main Topic:	39	0	9	8	10	12
Subtopic:	7	0	2	0	3	2
War of Liberation	22	0	5	4	5	8
Main Topic:	17	0	3	4	4	6
Subtopic:	5	0	2	0	1	2
War of Resistance against Japan	11	0	2	3	4	2
Main Topic:	9	0	2	3	2	2
Subtopic:	2	0	0	0	2	0
Korean War	5	0	3	1	1	0
Nationalist aggression	3	0	1	0	0	2
Pre-modern peasant rebellions	2	0	0	0	2	0
Pre-modern defensive wars	1	0	0	0	1	0

Table II continued:

Topic	Total Scores	Distribution by Grade Level				
		1	2	3	4	5
Wars of defense of non-Asian peoples	1	0	0	0	0	1
American aggression	1	0	0	0	0	1
Mao	26	7	3	5	5	6
Main Topic:	20	5	2	4	5	4
Subtopic:	6	2	1	1	0	2
Industry and aspects of a Modern society	25	5	8	5	3	4
Main Topic:	16	3	6	4	1	2
Subtopic:	9	2	2	1	2	2
Traditional China	24	1	3	3	8	9
Main Topic:	12	0	1	2	3	6
Subtopic:	12	1	2	1	5	3
War situations emphasizing heroes (subtopic only):	23	0	5	6	5	7
War situations emphasizing civilian heroes	12	0	3	3	2	4
War situations emphasizing military heroes	11	0	2	3	3	3
Nature and the natural world	19	5	1	2	4	7
Main Topic:	18	5	1	2	3	7
Subtopic:	1	0	0	0	1	0
Comparison of the old and new societies	16	1	4	2	4	5
Main Topic:	15	1	4	2	4	4
Subtopic:	1	0	0	0	0	1

Table II continued:

Topic	Total Scores	Distribution by Grade Level				
		1	2	3	4	5
Personal hygiene and physiology	14	3	5	5	0	1
Main Topic:	13	3	5	5	0	0
Subtopic:	1	0	0	0	0	1
Personal heroes in civilian life	13	1	1	3	6	2
Main Topic:	6	0	1	3	2	0
Subtopic:	7	1	0	0	4	2
Social knowledge	12	0	3	4	3	2
Main Topic:	9	0	1	3	3	2
Subtopic:	3	0	2	1	0	0
Proscribed behavior	11	2	4	3	1	1
Non-Chinese peoples	11	0	3	1	3	4
Main Topic:	4	0	0	1	1	2
Subtopic:	7	0	3	0	2	2
Russian people	3	0	0	0	1	2
Main Topic:	2	0	0	0	1	1
Subtopic:	1	0	0	0	0	1
Korean people (subtopic only):	5	0	3	0	2	0
American people	1	0	0	1	0	0
African people	1	0	0	0	0	1
German people (subtopic only):	1	0	0	0	0	1
Pre-Communist society	10	0	2	0	3	5
Main Topic:	9	0	2	0	3	4
Subtopic:	1	0	0	0	0	1

Table II continued:

Topic	Total Scores	Distribution by Grade Level				
		1	2	3	4	5
School and school life	9	5	1	2	1	0
Main Topic:	5	3	1	1	0	0
Subtopic:	4	2	0	1	1	0
Inventors, discoverers, and scientists	8	0	2	2	1	3
Chinese traditional	4	0	1	1	1	1
Lu Pan		0	1	1	0	0
Hua T'o		0	0	0	0	1
Li Shih-chen		0	0	0	1	0
Non-Chinese	4	0	1	1	0	2
Michurin		0	0	1	0	1
Galileo		0	0	0	0	1
Watt		0	1	0	0	0
Social situations	8	0	2	3	3	0
Traditional founders of Communism	8	0	1	3	3	1
Lenin	7	0	1	3	3	0
Marx	1	0	0	0	0	1
Basic Chinese Communist philosophy	6	0	2	0	0	4
Main Topic:	1	0	1	0	0	0
Subtopic:	5	0	1	0	0	4
Founders of Chinese Communism and Chinese Communist personalities	5	0	0	0	1	4
Main Topic:	3	0	0	0	0	3
Subtopic:	2	0	0	0	1	1
Li Ta-chao (main topic):		0	0	0	0	2

Table II continued:

Topic	Total Scores	Distribution by Grade Level				
		1	*2*	*3*	*4*	*5*
Jen Pi-shih (main topic):		0	0	0	0	1
Hsü T'e-li (subtopic):		0	0	0	0	1
Liu Chih-tan (subtopic):		0	0	0	1	0
Writings of Mao	4	0	0	0	0	4
Other Chinese leadership personalities	4	0	0	1	1	2
Main Topic:	2	0	0	1	1	0
Subtopic:	2	0	0	0	0	2
Liu Shao-ch'i (main topic):		0	0	0	1	0
Chu Teh (main topic):		0	0	1	0	0
Chou En-lai (subtopic):		0	0	0	0	1
Ho Lung (subtopic):		0	0	0	0	1
Life under the new society	3	0	2	0	1	0
Main Topic:	2	0	2	0	0	0
Subtopic:	1	0	0	0	1	0
Personal goals	1	1	0	0	0	0
Taiwan	1	0	0	1	0	0

Table III: MAIN TOPICS
BY FREQUENCY OF OCCURRENCE

Order	Topic	Number of Occurrences	
		No.	*%*
1	Recommended behavior	99	24.75
2	Rural life and agriculture	45	11.25
3	Aspects of Communist China	41	10.25
4	War situations	39	9.75
5	Mao	20	5.00

Table III continued:

6	Nature and the natural world	18	4.50
7	Industry and aspects of a modern society	16	4.00
8	Comparison of the old and new societies	15	3.75
9	Personal hygiene and physiology	13	3.25
10	Traditional China	12	3.00
11	Proscribed behavior	11	2.75
12	Social knowledge	9	2.25
	Pre-Communist society	9	2.25
13	Inventors, discoverers, and scientists	8	2.00
	Social situations	8	2.00
	Traditional founders of Communism	8	2.00
14	Personal heroes in civilian life	6	1.50
15	School and school life	5	1.25
16	Non-Chinese peoples	4	1.00
	Writings of Mao	4	1.00
17	Founders of Chinese Communism and Chinese Communist personalities	3	0.75
18	Other Chinese leadership personalities	2	0.50
	Life under the new society	2	0.50
19	Basic Chinese Communist ideology	1	0.25
	Personal goals	1	0.25
	Taiwan	1	0.25
		400	100.00

SIX

THE MODEL CHILD

INTRODUCTION

The "model" or ideal child refers to a child who is the perfect exemplar of the knowledge, attitudes, and values set forth by the *Readers.* This child is an artificial creation whose profile is determined by our analysis of the texts. We are unable to take into account neither what the child learned from his experience in the classroom with the teacher nor what effect the rest of his formal training had; and we are equally unable to determine the effect of the input from his home and his peers. In short, we are creating the model child without taking into account the additional or conflicting socialization influences that affect him from the areas of his home, school, and social environment.

The goal of childhood political socialization in most societies is to instill a sense of belonging to a particular political community and to give the child a positive set of orientations toward the symbols, institutions, and personalities valued by the political system. In addition, the socialization process attempts to define the role the child is to fulfill as an adult, politically, socially, and in the terms of his occupation in the future. In the United States a child is typically led to believe that his future is determined by his own achievement level and goals. In China, as we have seen, there was a demonstrable emphasis on rural occupations. Initially, the goals of political socialization and general socialization in China appear to be no different from any other modernizing society providing a formal educational process for its children. Thus, our findings that Communist China should be perceived by children as superior to any other country, and that the child should perceive his government's institutions and personalities as powerful and benign structures and persons worthy of credence, are indicators that China seeks the same goals as other nation-states.

Our orientation to this analysis, however, is somewhat broader than *political* socialization—we have attempted to gain from the *Readers* a more encompassing view of the child. We have sought to glean a value structure from our content analysis which gives indications as to how the child is taught to perceive both Communist China and his role in it. That is, we are concerned not only with how a child in Communist China is taught to view his country and political system, but also what he is taught as his ideal role in the new China.

In contemporary China the search for Mao's revolutionary successors was undeniably aided by education. The closing of China's educational system since 1966 by Mao Tse-tung as part of the catharsis of the Great Proletarian Cultural Revolution demonstrates how closely related Mao perceives the educational and political systems of his new China. As he proceeds to restructure China's political system, Mao is taking steps to create an educational system that will more accurately mold the New Chinese Man. At this time there are too few concrete results from which to predict what new forms the molds will take, but we can view one part of an earlier mold and analyze its form. The outlines are clear enough: the system sought to produce an individual at the primary school level who was aware of the "new" China, who was loyal to it and its leadership, and who was compliant, group oriented, and satisfied with a life in rural China. No doubt the child would be aware of middle school and higher education, but he would also recognize that the probability of his joining this small elite was extremely low. His future, like that of his ancestors, would be almost inevitably tied to agriculture. It is to this child-citizen we now turn.

CHILD-CITIZEN: THE IDEAL

The core values of the ideal child-citizen are those through which he interprets his nation, its leadership and their policies, and his own role within the nation. These values are the bedrock upon which all other values are based. Thus, even though for analytical purposes we have divided our content analysis into three basic types of themes, the result is a clustering of values built into the stories which should not be seen as comprised of three distinct structures—they are complementary structures leading to specific clusters. The basic cluster may be defined as core values, values however that are designed to inculcate a more *cognitive* than *affective* value structure in the child-citizen; and it is within the core values that we can locate a structure of values which order the more salient thrusts of our themes and topics.

Core values. We will use as our basic core value structure the first four categories of themes scored in the informational, political, and behavioral thematic analyses. Initial cluster values are given in Table I.

Table I: <u>CORE VALUE CLUSTERS</u>

Devotion and allegiance to the new society
Benevolence of the new society
Glorification of Mao Tse-tung
Evils of Kuomintang China

Social and personal responsibility
Achievement
Altruistic behavior
Collective behavior

Basic agricultural or farm knowledge
Knowledge about Chinese Communist institutions and history
Knowledge about traditional China
Basic scientific and technical knowledge

The core values provide a definite orientation toward China, emphasizing the "new" society as opposed to traditional China and the "evils" of the Kuomintang interregnum. Within the "new" society, the child-citizen is made aware of his particular social and political responsibility to contribute to the overall good of the community. Any goals of personal achievement must remain secondary to the pre-eminent responsibility of contributing to the common good of the new society. Thus achievement, although possessing a high level of saliency, is clustered with altruistic and collective behavior values. The "new" society being created under the leadership of Mao and the Chinese Communist Party should be perceived of by the child-citizen as a benevolent society and one worthy of the highest dedication. The sharp contrasts raised between the "new" China, and traditional and Kuomintang China, clearly prepare the ideal child-citizen for self-identification as a contributor to the construction of a new society. Similarly, the child-citizen is made aware of the role of the Chinese Communist Party and Mao Tse-tung in the revolution that led to the construction of the "new" China. The factual knowledge the child receives from his primary school experience expands upon these basic orientations.

These core values and their basic structures permit the child to move from an affective orientation to China toward a more completely cognitive orientation. The ideal child-citizen produced at the end of Grade Five is able to identify the source of the "new" China (the revolution), and the leaders of the revolution and the new China (the Party and Mao Tse-tung), the ideal behavior for a Chinese citizen (altruistic and collective), and should be positively oriented toward a life in rural China wherein he would use scientific and technical skills to produce a better life for the society as a whole.

Core values, however important, are at the base of a far wider set of orientations and information. Table II is designed to list the factual knowledge, beliefs, values, and personal characteristics that form the profile of the ideal child-citizen.

Table II:	FACTUAL KNOWLEDGE

1. Familiarity with basic agricultural techniques
     Planting and harvesting crops
     Care of orchards
     Essentials of animal care
2. Basic knowledge of human physiology
   and hygiene

General knowledge of body functions
Knowledge of rules of hygiene
Fundamental knowledge about disease transmission
Understanding of the responsibilities of the individual in
  public sanitation

3. Scientific knowledge
Some knowledge about plant nutrition
Some knowledge about plant grafting
Miscellaneous information about the lives of various
  animals
Some knowledge about marine life
An understanding that it is necessary to investigate reality
  in order to solve problems

4. Knowledge of industry and technology
Steel and iron production
Salt production

5. Basic social knowledge and customs
Communications for given circumstances and occasions
Record-keeping for meetings

6. Knowledge about China
Miscellaneous information about the geography of China
Some knowledge about the lives of the minority peoples

7. Knowledge about traditional China
Knowledge about some ancient Chinese scientists and
  technicians
Knowledge about a few Chinese emperors
Knowledge about peasant military leaders and peasant
  uprisings
Some classical poetry reflecting oppression of the common
  people
Knowledge about cultural and other achievements of
  ancient China

8. Knowledge about the Communist movement
in China
Some knowledge about the Long March
Knowledge about Civil War battles
Knowledge about some key personalities in the Chinese
  Communist movement
Knowledge about some revolutionary martyrs

9. Knowledge about leaders of the world
Communist movement

> Some information about the life and works of Marx
> Incidents from the life of Lenin

10. General knowledge about the outside world

> Some information about the Korean War
> Some information about the Quemoy conflict
> Some information about pre-Communist Russia
> Some information about class conflict in the United States

11. Basic academic knowledge

> Techniques for study
> Techniques for writing compositions
> Knowledge of the most important Chinese characters
> required for reading and writing
> Knowledge of the "pinyin" romanization

BELIEFS

Political Beliefs

1. The "New" Society

> The "new" society is good
> The Party and all organs of the government are devoted to
> the welfare of the people
> The People's Liberation Army was always concerned for the
> people and never pillaged
> Life in the "new" society is better than life in the old
> society and is continually improving
> The minority peoples of China are devoted to Mao,
> Communism, and to the "new" society
> Remnants of the old society who oppose the regime still
> exist and lie in wait either to sabotage the "new" society
> or to stage a come-back
> Continual vigilance is necessary in order to prevent the
> resurgence of the remnants of the old society

2. The "Old" Society

> The old society was bad
> The Kuomintang government oppressed the people
> Police brutality existed under Kuomintang rule
> Kuomintang armies pillaged without concern for the
> common people

Peasants under Kuomintang rule supported the Communist movement

3. Mao Tse-tung

Mao is devoted to the welfare of the people

Mao is concerned for each individual personally

Mao is the guiding spirit of the nation

Mao is responsible for destroying the "old" China and creating the "new" China

4. The nature of society

The working people of all capitalist nations are poor and oppressed

The ruling classes of capitalist nations exploit and oppress the working classes

The masses possess an inherent wisdom from which there is much to be learned

5. Peoples of other nations

The Japanese have, traditionally, been aggressive in their intentions toward China

The Japanese were cruel in their treatment of the Chinese both old and young

The Chinese are superior to the Japanese in military skill and cleverness

Strong friendship exists between the Chinese and the Korean people

Strong friendship exists between the Chinese and the Russian people

The laboring classes of the United States are oppressed by the ruling classes and are to be sympathized with

6. Beliefs about other nations

The United States is an evil, imperialistic nation suppressing the people of Korea and Taiwan

The United States collaborates with the Chinese Nationalists in subjugating Taiwan

Taiwan is a province of China yet to be liberated

There exists a constant threat of invasion from without, particularly from Taiwan, for which defenses must be ready at all times

The Korean War was fought because of U.S. aggression

Imperialists and colonialists exploit the peoples of backward, and particularly non-white nations

Personal Beliefs

1. Beliefs about work

   Any goal can be achieved by hard work
   A scientific approach to problems assures their solution
   Nature can be conquered by study of natural laws and hard
   work

2. Beliefs about personal conduct

   Improper behavior is inevitably attended by bad
   consequences for the individual
   Good behavior is its own reward
   A person should sacrifice himself to the goals of the state
   A person should sacrifice his own personal desires to the
   interests of others, his group, or to the larger society if
   the two are incompatible
   Solidarity and mutual cooperation are superior to and win
   out over individualistic behavior
   Society or the group is more important that the individual
   Superstition has no grounds in reality and must be opposed

VALUES

Positive (responds positively to and perceives as good)

   Mao Tse-tung
   The Communist Party
   The Communes
   Communism
   Socialism
   The Pioneers
   The national leaders
   The People's Liberation Army
   The minority peoples of China
   The revolutionary martyrs
   Leaders of peasant rebellions in Chinese history
   Chinese historical figures who served the common people
   The oppressed masses of other lands (including Americans)
   Work
   Nature and the natural world
   Study
   All aspects of the "new" society
   The past achievements of China
   China herself as the motherland
   The social roles of worker, farmer, and soldier

School
Rural and farm life

Negative (responds negatively to and perceives as bad)
    The injustices of the old society
    Landlords, capitalists, and other remnants of the old society
    The Kuomintang and those connected with it
    Chiang Kai-shek
    Colonialists
    Imperialists and American imperialists in particular
    The Japanese Imperial Army
    Superstitious practices
    The bad rulers and other oppressors of traditional China
    Destructive elements within society

PERSONAL CHARACTERISTICS

Industrious in work and study
Diligent and persistent, especially in the face of hardship
Achievement and goal oriented, desiring to achieve
Dedicated to building the "new" society
Co-operative working with others for common goals
Honest and responsible in his personal affairs, in his
    relations with others, and in his work
Having a sense of responsibility for public property
Behaves with due regard for public sanitation
Willing to accept the advice and criticism of others
Prudent and has foresight
Patient and not hot-tempered
Obedient, deferring to rules and to elders and superiors
Thrifty and frugal
Courageous, being willing to sacrifice his life for others or
    for the state both in everyday life and battle
Altruistic, being kind to others, particularly the aged and
    less fortunate
Expresses anger or behaves aggressively only toward those
    who violate communist social standards or who attempt
    to harm society
Prepared to behave in an aggressive manner to the point of
    taking another's life in defense of the state
Vigilant against enemy attack and deception
Capable of working deception against an occupying enemy
Ingenious in solving problems
Sees happiness and personal satisfaction as sufficient
    recompense for sacrifice or accomplishment

SUMMARY

The four major headings of the above table categorize the whole range of inputs the child-citizen has received by the completion of the Fifth Grade. Inputs are divided into inputs of relatively apolitical factual information; inputs of belief statements or judgments about his environment that the child is taught to believe; value inputs, both negative and positive; and inputs relating to personal characteristics that are deemed desirable. The core values we discussed earlier represent the basic filter through which the child-citizen sorts and judges information; the broader structure we are now considering should be viewed as the principal components of the ideal child-citizen.

Bearing in mind that the limits set upon this analysis of the model child-citizen are highly artificial in that experience beyond that of the *Readers* is not taken into consideration, what emerges is an individual with the foundations of a good general knowledge about the natural world, but also one with both a highly biased and one-sided knowledge of both past and modern Chinese history and a distorted image of the non-Chinese world. He is equipped with the beginnings of the practical knowledge required of him to become primarily a farmer and with an assortment of historical information selected for the purpose of enhancing his commitment to the "new" China, its political and social systems and the men who determine China's future. This selection of historical materials is designed to create a rejection of the "old" China and to convince him that with the exception of a few international friends, the outside world is essentially hostile.

This factual knowledge is in turn coupled with attempts to foster belief in the benevolence of the Party and its leaders, and distrust of forces both within and without the nation that present a threat to the regime. In terms of his personal life, the focus is on fostering a faith in the inevitable success of hard work, and particularly of hard work done in cooperation with others.

He is thus taught to value all phases of the "new" society, work and study, and perhaps most important, the social role of the worker-farmer-peasant. In turn, he is taught to hate and despise much of the "old" society, with the exception of the achievements made by the people, as well as to hate any nation, group, or element that has destruction of his society as its goal.

At the base of this complex of knowledge, beliefs, and values is a personality which ideally would be characterized essentially by behavior of a highly self-sacrificing kind. The individual, in addition to working or studying hard, must not only restrain all emotions and desires not consistent with their beliefs and values, but also be prepared to sacrifice his life if society or circumstance so demands. The only socially approved outlet for expression of frustrated motives is that of aggression against enemies of society. The rewards for his sacrifices are rarely concrete, being rather either those of happiness or satisfaction at having made them or of the praise of his fellows or elders.

That this model child-citizen does not and cannot exist should be obvious. No one child could absorb or remember all of the information presented in the *Readers*, and it is quite improbable that most children could come to accept all of the values and beliefs presented in the *Readers*. This is not to say, however, that the child of average intelligence will not emerge from his school experiences without having been affected by the structure of values thrust at him. In the absence of a significant degree of contradictory signals from his environment, and surrounded by continual intrusions of a similar nature from all other sources of information in his community, it may be assumed that he will become a properly motivated child-citizen of the regime.

For the child of average or below average intelligence there is little reason to doubt the effectiveness of this informational, but value-laden, set of inputs. It is, however, with the above average child that the weakness in the system may occur. To the analytical mind there are inconsistencies to be perceived in the *Readers*. While the presence of these inconsistencies would not entirely undermine the intelligent child's loyalty to his nation or his willingness to devote himself to the tasks of rational construction, they may at least sow seeds of doubt and cynicism in his mind. These internal contradictions in the *Readers* and their possible effects will be discussed in the following Chapter.

SEVEN

CONFLICTING VALUES
IN THE READERS

INTRODUCTION

It should not be surprising to find inconsistencies in a set of school readers compiled at the hands of eight persons, subjected to the review of three additional persons, and drawn from diverse sources both Western and Chinese. When the further requirement of attempted conformity to an ideology that itself is not a model of consistency is added, the possibilities for inconsistency are increased even more.

The analysis shows that the compilers were conscientiously striving to produce texts consistent with official ideology. It is thus perhaps more correct to state that the internal contradictions in the *Readers* have their basis in the contradictions in the political and behavioral models that the texts were written to emulate and in Communist Chinese society itself. To this course of "error" may be added any "incorrect" interpretations of official dogma by the compilers and editors.

With this in mind, let us point out a number of key internal contradictions to be found in the *Readers*.

CONTRADICTIONS INHERENT IN THE READERS

A major conflict in the *Readers* arises from emphasis given to themes of achievement. The basic conflict can be expressed schematically as follows:

Themes of achievement

vs.

Themes of sacrifice of personal motives for the benefit of others or of society

Themes of limited personal goals of becoming a worker-farmer-soldier

Themes of collective behavior

This problem has been pointed out by Lewis.[1] As his sources indicate, the child is trained in such a way as to encourage the development of "achievement motivation" and of individuality and self-reliance. The treatment of "achievement" in the *Readers* corroborates his findings. Ideally, these attempts to instill the individual with the desire to achieve should result in someone who is competitive and personally ambitious. At the same time, however, it is impressed upon him in a spirit of equal approbation that he must sacrifice his desires for personal achievement for the benefit of society. This conflict is explicitly portrayed in *Giving Convenience to Others* (Volume 10, No. 8), in which Chao Meng-t'ao faces a choice between personal achievement and the over-all good of her work group. The conflict is resolved, naturally, in favor of the latter.

This leads one to suspect that the dominance of themes of altruism occurs not only in response to the official doctrine of "communist morality" but perhaps more importantly as an antidote to the equally strong dose of achievement motivation that the child receives. It is perhaps not so much a matter of trying to put out the fires of achievement with altruism, but rather an attempt to redirect the desire to achieve, once established, to achievement for the good of all.

There are other conflicts that arise out of this emphasis on achievement that may pose problems to the more intelligent child as he grows to maturity. One of these is the obvious conflict between the desire for achievement and the limited image of the child as a potential worker-farmer-soldier that the

Readers so clearly extol. This is an extremely important issue both for the individual and for the society as a whole. As long as China must concentrate her efforts on securing her agricultural foundations, there will not be sufficient opportunity within the society for all above-average men and women to attain above-average positions within Chinese society. This is inevitable given the present state of Chinese economic development.

This is obviously the most bitter pill that the ambitious, achievement-oriented child is going to have to swallow. In spite of the glorification of the worker-farmer-soldier, it is difficult to imagine goals such as these captivating the minds of the more able young for very long once they have passed beyond elementary school. This area of conflict is indeed a potential source of very serious frustration, a source of frustration that could well have dangerous consequences in later years. The highly aggressive behavior of the Red Guards in the months immediately following the initiation of the Great Proletarian Cultural Revolution suggests that many young people in China are at present extremely frustrated. Whether these frustrations involve conflicts between desires for achievement and the lack of a medium in which to achieve is, to be sure, a matter about which we cannot draw any definite conclusions. It is nevertheless, a possibility well worth considering.

A closely related source of conflict:

Themes of ingenuity in solving problems

vs.

Themes of obedience to rules and deference to authority

On the one hand, the child is encouraged, as in the example of the story *Szu-ma Kuang* (Volume 2, No. 36), to solve problems by virtue of his own ingenuity and self-reliance. There are many similar stories involving clever and non-orthodox solutions to problems. Standing in opposition to this is the story in which it is emphasized that rules and regulations must be obeyed at all costs. This conflict is, in fact, personified by no less an individual than Lenin himself. In *Bee Guides* (Volume 6, No. 19), Lenin succeeds in finding a beekeeper through his "achievement cleverness," whereas in *Lenin and the Guard* (Volume 7, No. 19), Lenin stands for observance of rules in the most uncompromising of ways. What this amounts to in essence is that the child receives two contradictory sets of signals from the *Readers:* Be self-reliant and ingenious but always obey the rules and defer to authority.

One does not expect even the intelligent fifth grade pupil to become aware that the *Readers* are imparting contradictory values to him. It is, on the contrary, to be assumed that both sets of values are accepted by the child and that both form the basis of his behavior. It is thus highly likely that the conflict will not be perceived consciously but could form the basis of two mutually incompatible types of behavior. This conflict does not present as acute a problem as that between achievement and the limited opportunities of society. On the other hand, it could be of a more pervasive importance in that it could influence the child's attitudes toward authority.

In his behavior toward others, the student is again presented with two conflicting and approved systems of behavior:

> Themes of altruism, kindness, and consideration for others

> vs.

> Themes of "prosocial aggression" allowing unlimited aggression against those deemed to be enemies of society

This does not present, on the surface, as serious a problem as do the conflicts associated with achievement. Here, society provides the child with clear, although not necessarily immutable, signals as to who or what groups of people are dangerous public enemies. He has only to perceive to which group the individual belongs to know whether to approach him with a helping hand or a clenched fist.

Beneath this clear-cut surface, however, this dichotomy does raise serious problems about man's relation to man. Kindness can clearly be extended only to certain persons on the basis, primarily, of their political status and not on the basis of innate human feelings of compassion, as the classical Chinese philosopher Mencius would have urged. On the other hand, the individual might be required by the dictates of the Communist moral ethic either to extend aid to someone he hates or on the other hand to destroy someone he cares for. Although the problem may be remote, as in the case of feelings toward an official figure such as Liu Shao-ch'i who is extolled in the *Readers* but who has since fallen from grace, it becomes intensely personal when the scene shifts to the level of the village or the production team where the conflict between "altruism" and "prosocial aggression" may well involve close friends or even members of one's own family.

Thus the implications of this conflict as it is lived out in the highly political terms of the Chinese environment are perhaps of as equally great importance as those of the conflict between "achievement" and the limited goals open to the child, in that even deeper emotional levels of the personality may be involved. In terms of purely personal relationships, one might expect persons motivated by these conflicting systems to be reluctant to commit themselves to close relationships with others, with the result that a false and cynical camaraderie might be built up between people. One would at the least expect that this would lead to a general emotional shallowness on the part of the individual, who would respond as he knows he should, but who at heart knows he is only playing a game that he must play and that everyone else is playing too.[2]

Another set of conflicting themes in the *Readers* are those concerned with attitudes toward nature:

Theme of conquest of nature

vs.

Theme of nature as something of beauty to be enjoyed

This is in essence a conflict between Western attitudes of

dominance over nature and traditional Chinese attitudes of man's "being in nature." The traditional Chinese aspects of the conflict were pointed out in the discussion of the theme "esthetic aspects of nature and farm life." Here man is clearly presented in these traditional Chinese terms. However, in other stories, nature also appears in its more violent aspects and as a force that must and can be conquered by man. The means whereby nature is to be conquered is two-fold, first by sheer labor and persistence, and second by learning the laws of natural processes and using them to turn nature to man's ends. This latter point is of interest in that, in this connection, an appeal is made to traditional thought concerning man's relation to nature. This is shown in the story *A Man Who Was Good at Butchering Oxen* (Volume 10, No. 29), which is based on an episode from the *Chuang Tzu*, a work from the school of philosophical Taoism.[3] This is the story of a man who is so expert at cutting up oxen that the blade of his knife never needs sharpening. In the original allegory, the man exemplifies the person who is so at one with nature that he achieves whatever he sets out to do spontaneously. The *Readers* interpret his success on the basis of the man's careful analysis of the organization of the ox's body. This theme is, in the *Readers*, thus linked to those of achievement and of "investigation and research," whereas in the context of the Taoist philosophy in which the allegory was written, it represents his state of complete "being in nature," which results in his transcending nature.

Finally, there is the matter of contradictions within the sphere of political attitudes.

One source of difficulty is concerned with attitudes toward China's past:

Themes of the evils of traditional China

vs.

Themes of the accomplishments made in China's past

In the *Readers*, traditional Chinese society is presented as "evil." Feudal rulers oppressed the people, who had to labor hard but live in poverty. The compilers present several poems from classical sources in which themes of oppression and rebellion against oppression are clearly stated. On the other hand, there are stories extolling the achievements of China's past. Typical of these are *The Great Wall* (Volume 7, No. 30) and *The Grand Canal* (Volume 7, No. 31). In both selections, the *Readers* comment on the greatness of these achievements. In contrast, it is made clear that these magnificent projects were completed only through oppression of the masses.

In this way, the child is subjected to conflicting attitudes toward his national heritage, which is seen as both good and evil, good from the standpoint of the superior qualities of the Chinese nation, and evil from the standpoint of the suffering of the people. Thus, conflicting emotions of pride and shame in the Chinese heritage may well be fostered in the child.

A more important contradiction centers about the character of Mao Tse-tung:

Theme of Mao as the supreme father figure

vs.

Theme of Mao as the simple, down-to-earth man of the people

As was pointed out in the thematic analysis, in some selections Mao appears to be virtually deified as the "sun of the new China," while in other places he is described as acting "like a common laborer." Thus, the *Readers* attempt to put Mao on a pedestal and among the masses at the same time, so that the relationship between Mao and the child is both remote and intimate. In actual life, of course, Mao is more likely to be seen as the remote god-like figure, so that the contradiction is not important in practical terms. The contradiction itself is of course related to the larger problem of identifying the child with the leaders of the regime in such a way that they are perceived as kindly, benevolent, and devoted to the welfare of the individual, but, even so, as leaders whose wills are to be obeyed.

CONTRADICTIONS BETWEEN READER VALUES
AND SOCIAL PRACTICE

In addition to the contradictions discussed above, there are other instances in which conflict occurs between values as expressed in the *Readers* and what may be actual social practice. A key conflict of this sort is that of the relationship between the individual, his family, and society or the group:

Themes of devotion to the collective good

vs.

Chinese traditional concepts of primary loyalty and responsibility to the family

"Communist morality," as exemplified by the *Readers*, calls for the individual to subordinate his interests to whose of the collective good. This requirement, however, conflicts with very powerful traditional Chinese patterns of behavior. Of the traditional virtues, loyalty to the family and "filial piety" stood in first place. Of the "Five Relationships" of the Confucian canon, three were concerned with hierarchical relationships within the family (father and son, elder brother and younger brother, and husband and wife), the other two being that between ruler and subject and between friend and friend. The individual's first duty was to his family, and his subordination to his family was complete.

It is this family-centered ethic that acts as a restraint on the society-oriented ethics of Communism. The emphasis in the *Readers* on collective behavior and on self-sacrifice for the higher goals of the state is thus a conscious attempt to shift traditional patterns of loyalty to the family to those of loyalty to the state.

Seen in this light, stories about "heroic self-sacrifice" take on an added dimension, for sacrifice of one's life flies in the face of the traditional virtue of "filial piety," which requires that a person devote himself to his parents. It would, therefore, be "unfilial" to give one's life in battle if this would mean that one's parents would be left without support in their old age. The extent to which themes of self-sacrifice are emphasized in the *Readers* may well be an attempt to alter this traditional concept.

In *A Story about Borrowing a Picture Book* (Volume 8, No. 25), the *Readers* deal explicitly with this conflict. In the story, a little girl who is on duty in the school library struggles with her conscience over whether to break the rules and bring a picture book home to her little brother, who has a broken leg. In the end, civic virtue wins out over family loyalty.

Of equal importance are conflicts between enunciated "Communist moral values" and the actual behavior of those persons in authority:

Ideals of "Communist morality"

vs.

Actual moral practice, particularly of those in positions of authority

The extent to which discrepancies of this sort would be perceived by the elementary school pupil is questionable. He certainly would not be aware of such contradictions at the national level. However, as documents obtained from the commune and production brigade levels of Lien-chiang County in Fukien Province during the Socialist Education Movement of 1962-1963 indicate, communist "moral standards" were not being observed by many individuals and by brigade and team leaders at that time.[4] Team officials were stealing public funds, others were carrying on part-time side businesses, while yet others were building private houses with commune funds. Superstitious practices were also pronounced. This indicates that there is an opportunity for the child to observe "bad" behavior by persons in authority at a local level. To the extent that such practices are general in other areas of China, as the very existence of the Socialist Education Movement suggests, to that extent are the foundations for a later cynicism laid.

Of more serious implications are conflicts that may arise out of discrepancies between what the regime says it is like and what it is really like. As an example, we can select the following case:

Themes of the benevolence of the new society

vs.

Those instances of oppressive practices that may be known

This is, of course, not a problem in which the elementary pupil would be likely to be involved. Rather, it is one that might arise as he grows older. Thus, the perceptive senior high school or college student who inquires into the so-called "Hundred Flowers" episode in which many leading intellectuals were purged or the student who begins to wonder about the reported suicide of the aged writer Lao She during the Great Proletarian Cultural Revolution may suspect that the benevolence of the society is a mask behind which there is a much harder reality.

Another source of conflict may well be the Communist profession of a scientific attitude toward reality:

Themes of the benevolence of the new society

vs.

Doctrinal and/or dogmatic official approaches to problems

The theme of an objective approach to reality in solving both social and scientific problems is a common one in Communist writings. To the older student, it must be obvious that "theory" and "practice" are often far apart. One has only to read Mao asserting in one paragraph that one must be "objective" and then turning around and proceeding subjectively and unscientifically in the next to come to the conclusion that the best young minds in China no doubt realize that official dogma is far from scientific.

SUMMARY

It has been our attempt here, without ourselves wishing to become "dogmatic," to suggest some areas of conflict between the values set by the *Readers* and the realities of Chinese society. Of course, it cannot be assumed that these conflicts are perceived by the elementary school pupil and it cannot be predicted at what point in his growth that the values he has acquired through his training may come into overt conflict with each other or with social practice. We wish only to indicate that the potentialities for such conflict are present, and in as much as the values of the *Readers* reflect dominant official views, that these conflicts by implication may in turn reflect more general sources of value conflict within Chinese society as a whole.

That doubts and uncertainties about Communist values perhaps exist does not mean, however, that the young people of China are not well-motivated by such values.[5] Indeed, reports on the behavior of young Red Guard of high school and college age—the very groups subjected to material such as that of these *Readers*—strongly suggest that some are capable of altruistic acts, that some are capable, as their miniature Long Marches indicate, of sacrificing comforts and of a certain amount of "revolutionary" zeal, that some are devoted to the ideals of Communism and to the new China—in short, that they have taken much of what they have been taught to heart. It is not unsafe to assume that the majority of the young people who may one day be the leaders of China is thoroughly indoctrinated in the ethics of "communist morality" and that they are thoroughly devoted to their nation.

In addition, Solomon's analysis of some thirty young refugees from mainland China indicates that there has indeed been an attitude-change on the part of the younger Chinese when compared to the attitudes of the older refugees interviewed. When responding to a statement that the nation is of lesser importance than the family, the younger refugees, although not uniformly, tended to assert the importance of the nation over the family. Such increasing focus on the nation-state was complemented by the impression that the younger refugees had also internalized the value of active participation in the construction of the new China under the direction of the Chinese Communist Party. Even though the number of refugees interviewed was extremely small and thus any conclusions drawn are quite tentative, it must be remembered that these attitudes were expressed by individuals who had just fled the mainland and were therefore not necessarily predisposed to support the Communist regime. If the nation is displacing family life as the primary focus of loyalty among the younger generations of Chinese, and if the youth of China are positively oriented to active participation in the Party-directed goals of the state, then the efforts of the Chinese leadership in directed socialization are proving to be successful.[6]

One can at the same time, however, also assume that the young of China, no matter how well indoctrinated, are afflicted by a certain amount of doubt and conflict in company with their dedication.

The extent to which the forms of indoctrination used in educating the young of China succeed will depend on the interplay between the personalities and levels of intelligence of the young and events in the larger environment outside the school. Any number of events in the society might reinforce and bring into the open latent doubt and cynicism. A major economic failure or widespread political dissatisfaction with the regime leading to rebellion by a large segment of the population would tend to reinforce dissident feelings in the young, whereas continued economic progress and a generally harmonious state of national affairs would in turn tend to reinforce the values inculcated by the regime.

Another factor that in the future can be expected to play an important role in the attitudes of the young will be the treatment accorded to Mao following his death. If, like Lenin in Russia, he continues to maintain his place as the great founder of the "New China" and continues to be praised in the textbooks and mass media, his person can still serve as a model and an object of veneration for the young. If, however, his successors turn upon him and attempt to destroy his present image, as was the fate of Stalin, the potentiality for mass disillusionment of China's youth becomes an important factor.[7] Thus, any future attempt to displace Mao from his pedestal, and particularly a hasty attempt to do so, might prove fatal to the hopes of the regime in cultivating "revolutionary successors."

A further factor that may lead to alienation of the intellectual youth of China is the displacement of intellectual competence by political reliability as the requirement for advanced study that appears as a possible fruit of the Great Proletarian Cultural Revolution. Should student demands for the revision of university entrance requirements along such lines actually be widely met, those young intellectuals of "bad" background or uncertain political loyalties who would be excluded from realizing their potentialities under such a system will make a significant "pool" of dissident individuals. Their enforced withdrawal from academic life would harm the nation both from the standpoint of their loss to it in the work of modernization and from that of their presence as an articulate but frustrated opposition.

Thus, one cannot arrive at dogmatic conclusions. But, as the examples both of the Soviet Union and Japan through the Second World War suggest, mass programs of indoctrination in ideology and state morality often fall short of their goals in actual practice.[8] Even totalitarian regimes cannot screen out all sources of dissident values within a society. The mere presence of older individuals representing traditional values is one such source of dissidence. Teachers who themselves profess allegiance to the regime and its values but who as a result of their roots in the "old" society may unconsciously exemplify traditional values are yet another source of dissidence, not to mention teachers and elders whose "conversion" may be overt compliance only.

There is, however, an important distinction to be made, and that is the all-important distinction between the deep feelings of patriotism and love for country on the part of the child.

China is, after all, the only country he knows, and it is his feeling for his country that the *Readers* serve to reinforce. Thus, whatever disillusionment he might in later years experience in relation to a specific regime or certain of its leaders, it can only be assumed that he will continue to have a deep and abiding loyalty to and love for his country. Ultimately, then, the mark that China's attempts at indoctrination will leave on the minds of her youth remain in part an unknown to which only the future course of events in that country will provide the key.

APPENDIX ONE

AUTHORSHIP AND SOURCES

Eight persons are listed as having "participated in the work of compiling" Volumes 1, 2, 3, and 4 of the *Readers*. These include Chiang Chung-jen, Lü Ching-shan, Yüan Wei-tzu, Chang T'ien-jo, Ch'ien Ch'in-chu, Lü Mei-ying, Liu Yung-jang, and Liang Chün-ying. In addition, thanks are extended to Wei Chien-kung, Lü Shu-hsiang, and Wang Liao-i for their review of the first draft and for the assistance that they provided. Thanks are also extended to teachers and educational workers from various regions who offered suggestions. No mention is made of what positions the compilers occupy, and, as far as can be ascertained, they are not, as individuals, the authors of books on education. In the lack of evidence to the contrary, it is most probable that they are on the staff of the People's Education Publishing House in Peking. No "compilers" are listed for Volumes 5 through 10.

Wei Chien-kung, Lü Shu-hsiang, and Wang Liao-i the persons who reviewed Volumes 1 through 4, are, however, individuals known in the field of education. Wei Chien-kung was named Vice President of Peking University and Chief Of the Teaching and Research Section for Classical Literature in 1962.[1] Lu Shü-hsiang is a linguist who was formerly editor of the K'ai-ming Book Company and professor at both K'un-ming lien-ho University and Chung-yang University.[2] He has also been on the committee for propagation of a standardized language. Wang Liao-i (also known as Wang Li) is a linguist and specialist in the Mandarin dialect of Chinese.[3]

209

The question of the actual authorship of the stories and poems in the *Readers* is complex. The selections in themselves are of varied origin. A good many are about events in the history of the Chinese Communist movement, some are stories about traditional China, and some are drawn from traditional Chinese literature. The compilers have also drawn on several stories from Aesop. In addition, there is a small number of stories about Western scientists and about such political figures as Marx and Lenin. Others deal with school life and other facets of everyday life.

It is thus clear that the individuals listed above as having "participated in the work of compiling" the *Readers*, were, in fact, essentially compilers or editors, and were not authors. Comparisons of the materials in the *Readers* with the corresponding *Kuo-yü k'o-pen* (1966 editions) in use in the Republic of China (Taiwan) on the one hand and with older materials from mainland China of both Chinese Nationalist and Chinese Communist origin strongly suggest that both the current mainland and Nationalist readers have in many instances drawn on common, previously existing sources.

A good example of this is the story *The Flowers in the Park* (Vol. 1, No. 35). At first glance, one would be justified in assuming that so short and simple a selection was in all probability the creation of the compilers. That the selection in the *Readers* is at best an adaptation by the compilers becomes clear when one turns to Volume 2, Lesson 16 of the Nationalist *Kuo-yü k'o-pen*, a piece entitled *Flowers are Really Pretty*. Here the theme is identical to that of the *Readers*. Furthermore, the Nationalist text contains the sentences: "Don't pick the flowers. Leave them for everyone to look at." The similarity in the wording in the two Chinese versions is too close to be a coincidence. This suggests that both sets of readers have drawn on a similar source for this selection. This view is supported by the presence of a very similar selection in a reader entitled *Ch'u-chi fu-nü-pan tu-pen*, (*Beginning Reader for Women's Classes*), published under the auspices of the Ministry of Education on mainland China in 1946. The selection, *Protecting Public Property* (Lesson 7) deals with the same theme and contains the sentence "The flowers in the park are for everyone to enjoy," which in its Chinese wording differs from the *Readers* only in the use of the more complex characters for "to enjoy" rather than the simpler "to look at."

In addition, the Nationalist *Kuo-yü k'o-pen* of 1966, which are currently in use on Taiwan, contain seventeen other selections that either have their exact parallels in the *Readers* or are sufficiently similar that a common origin can be assumed.

The compilers of the *Readers* have also drawn on textbooks prepared for use in the border regions and liberated areas.

The following table contains a list of previously existing readers in which occur stories similar to those in the *Readers* translated here. Each reader has been assigned a code and is listed alphabetically according to the code designation. The issuing authority and the date of publication, when known, are included for each volume. Table II contains those selections in the *Readers* for which there are previously existing versions in these readers as well as for which there are similar selections in the Nationalist *Kuo-yü k'o-pen* of 1966. The selections from the *Readers* are listed in the order of their occurrence, beginning with Volume 1.

It should be pointed out that we do not have complete collections of each of the series of readers listed below. For this reason, our survey of previous versions of selections in the *Readers* is necessarily incomplete. Were there complete series available, it is to be assumed that there would be an even higher percentage of selections for which previous versions could be demonstrated.

Table I: CODES FOR TITLES
                   OF READERS AND
_____   PUBLICATION DATA

CCKWH   *Chung-chi kuo-wen hsüan (Selections for Inter-mediate National Literature)*, Hsin-hua shu-tien, 1942.

CFT

Ch'u-chi fu-nü-pan tu-pen (Beginning Readers for Women's Classes), Ministry of Education, 1946.

CKCHF

Ch'u-hsiao kuo-yü chiao-hsüeh-fa (Teaching Methods for Junior Elementary National Language), Ministry of Education, Nanking.
Vol. 3: Second edition, 1944
Vol. 5: Second edition, 1944
Vol. 6: First edition, 1943.

CKCKS

Ch'u-hsiao kuo-yü chiao-k'o-shu (Texts for Junior Elementary National Language), Editorial Committee, Office of Education, Peking.
Vol. 2: First edition, 1942
Vol. 3: First edition, 1943
Vol. 6: Revised edition, 1943 (of first edition of 1939).
Vol. 7: Second edition, 1941 (of first edition of 1941).
These texts were in use during the period of Japanese occupation.

KYKH

Kuo-yü: Kao-chi hsiao-hsüeh (National Language: Senior Elementary School), Ministry of Education, East China Military Government Committee.
Vol. 1: Revised edition of January 1951 (of first edition, March 1948).
Vol. 2: Revised edition of January 1951 (of first edition, August 1949)
Vol. 4: Revised edition of January 1951 (of first edition, August 1949).
These are the apparent forerunners of the *Readers* under study here.

KYKP

Kuo-yü k'o-pen (National Language Textbooks), Bureau of Education, Taiwan Provincial Government. Revised editions of 1966.

These readers are currently in use on Taiwan.

NCKW   *Ch'u-chung kuo-wen (Junior Middle School National Language)*, Ministry of Education, Nanking.
Vol. 1: Seventh edition, 1944.

NCKY   *Ch'u-hsiao kuo-yü (Junior Elementary National Language)*, Ministry of Education, Nanking.
Vol. 7: Ninth edition, 1944
Vol. 8: Seventh edition, 1943 (of first edition, 1940).

NKK   *Kao-hsiao kuo-yü (Senior Elementary National Language)*, Ministry of Education, Nanking
Vol. 1: Ninth edition, 1944
Vol. 2: Eighth edition, 1943
Vol. 3: Second edition, 1941 (of first edition, 1940).

PPLY   *Po-p'i lao-yeh (The Oppressive Master)*, T'ao-fen shu-tien, September 1946.

This material was prepared for use in the so-called "winter schools."

SCCHH   *Kuo-yü k'o-pen: Ch'u-chi hsiao-hsüeh (National Language Textbooks: Junior Elementary School)*, Executive Committee, Bureau of Education, Shansi-Chahar-Hopeh Border Region.
Vol. 1: Revised edition of 1948
Vol. 3: 1948

SCK   *Ch'u-hsiao kuo-yü (Junior Elementary National Language)*, Bureau of Education, Shensi-Kansu-Ninghsia Border Region, 1946.

SCKHH   *Kuo-yü k'o-pen: Kao-chi hsiao-hsüeh (National Language Textbooks: Senior Elementary School)*, Executive Committee, Bureau of Education, Shansi-Chabar-Hopeh Border Region, revised editions of 1948.

SCKKY   *Kuo-yü k'o-pen: Kao-hsiao kuo-yü (National Language Textbooks: Senior Elementary School)*, Executive Committee, Bureau of Education, Shansi-Chahar-Hopeh Border Region.
Vol. 2: First edition, October 1946.

SKK   *Kao-hsiao kuo-yü (Senior Elementary National Language)*, Bureau of Education, Shensi-Kan-su-Ningsia Border Region, 1946.

SPKYKP   *Kuo-yü k'o-pen (National Language Textbooks)*, Bureau of Education, Shantung Province un-dated provisional texts for use in the liberated areas of Shantung Province.
Vol. 2: Senior elementary level.
Vol. 6: Junior elementary level.

Table II: SELECTIONS FROM THE READERS HAVING ANTECEDENT VERSIONS OR VERSIONS IN THE NATIONALIST *KUO-YÜ K'O-PEN*

VOLUME 1

No. 35   *The Flowers in the Park*
      CKCKS: Vol. 6, No. 35 (1943) *In the Park.*
      CKCHF: Vol. 6, No. 35 (1943) *In the Park.*
      CFT: *Lesson 7 (1946), Protecting Public Property.*
      KYKP: Vol. 2, No. 16 (1966), *Flowers are Really Pretty.*

No. 41   *K'ung Jung Gives Up a Pear*
      CKCHF: Vol. 5, No. 29 (1944) *A Polite Child.*
      KYKP: Vol. 3, No. 20 (1966) *K'ung Jung Gives Up a Pear.*

No. 42   *I Will Love to Wear My Jacket*
      SCK: Vol. 2, No. 44 (1946) *Loving Clothes.* The theme is similar, but the relationship is tenuous.

VOLUME 2

No. 9   *A Woodpecker*
SCCHH: Vol. 3, No. 12 (1948) *The Tree Doctor.*

No. 17   *A Crow Gets a Drink of Water*
CKCKS: Vol. 3, No. 12 (1943), *A Magpie Gets a Drink of Water.*
CKCHF: Vol. 3, No. 17 (1944) *An Old Crow Gets a Drink of Water.*
SCK: Vol. 3, No. 30 (1946), *A Crow Gets a Drink of Water.*
KYKP: Vol. 3, No. 14 (1966), *An Old Crow Gets a Drink of Water.*

No. 18   *A Ball Floats Up*
SCK: Vol. 3, No. 25 (1946) *Wen Yen-po.*
KYKP: Vol. 3, No. 15 (1966) *An Intelligent Child.*

No. 23   *The East is Red*
SCK: Vol. 2, No. 35 (1946), *He is the Savior of the People.*

No. 35   *The Boy Who Told Lies*
This is the story of the boy who called wolf, and is derived from Western sources.
CKCKS: Vol. 2, p. 36 (1942), no title.
KYKP: Vol. 3, No. 6 (1966), *The Sheperd Boy.*

No. 36   *Szu-ma Kuang*
KYKP: Vol. 3, No. 3 (1966), *Szu-ma Kuang Saves a Companion.*

Review 11   Picture Strip
CKCHF: Vol. 3, No. 13 (1944), *The Dog and the Bone.* This relates the events of the picture strip in story form.

VOLUME 3

No. 15

A Bundle of Arrows (Aesop)
KYKH:　Vol. 1, No. 26 (1951), *Breaking Arrows*. This is the same story as the original Aesop fable, but the characters are members of an ancient Tartar tribe, the Tu-yŭ-hun.

KYKP:　Vol. 4, No. 7 (1966), *An Old Farmer's Sons*. The man has seven sons in this version and ten sons in the *Readers* version.

No. 16

The Fox and the Crow (Aesop)
CKCKS:　Vol. 3, No. 11 (1943), *The Fox and the Crow*.

CKCHF:　Vol. 3, No. 16 (1944), *The Fox and the Crow*.

SCKHH:　Vol. 2, No. 22 (1948), appears as one of two allegories in this lesson.

No. 19

I Am the District Chief
SPKYKP:　Vol. 6, No. 17, *I Am the District Chief*. This is essentially the same story as that of the *Readers* with the exception of a difference in endings.

No. 22

Lenin's Overcoat
KYKH:　Vol. 1, No. 19, (1951), *Lenin's Overcoat*. These are the same stories, but the words for "overcoat" in the titles differ.

No. 26

Man Has Two Treasures
KYKP:　Vol. 7, No. 2 (1966), *The Hands and the Brain*.

No. 28

Why Does the Pot Cover Move?
CKCKS:　Vol. 7, No. 29 (1941), *Watt Invents the Steam Engine*

NCKY: Vol. 7, No. 17 (1944), *Watt Makes Use of Steam*

No. 36   *The Ant and the Cricket* (La Fontaine)
KYKP: Vol. 8, No. 9 (1966), *The Locust Who Wanted to Play*. This story Involves an ant and a locust and is highly similar in its theme to the *Readers* version.

VOLUME 4

No. 4   *Plugging a Hole*
NCKY: Vol. 7, No. 23 (1944), *A Hole in the Dike*. This is the story of the Dutch boy, Peter, on which the *Readers* version appears to be based.
KYKP: Vol. 6, No. 18 (1966), *Saving the Lives of Everyone in the Village*. This is also the story about Peter.

No. 6   *How to Write a Diary*
NKK: Vol. 1, No. 29 (1944), *Methods for Writing Diaries*. This selection is highly parallel to that of the *Readers*.

No. 11   *A Story About Practicing Characters*
KYKP: Vol. 8, No. 4 (1966), *Using Up A Crock of Ink*. This story is about Wang Hsien-chih, and is similar to that in the *Readers* in emphasizing his industriousness.

No. 12   *Grinding a Piece of Iron Into a Needle*
KYKP: Vol. 4, No. 28 (1966), *Grinding a Stick of Iron Into a Needle*.

Review 4   Picture Strip (Spider rebuilding its web after a storm)

CKCKS: Vol. 3, No. 13 (1942), *A Spider Makes a Web.* This selection is in story form.

CKCHF: Vol. 3, No. 28 (1944), *A Spider Makes a Web.* This selection is in story form.

KYKP: Vol. 3, No. 30 (1966), *A Spider Weaves a Web.* This selection is in story form.

VOLUME 5

No. 9   *Chairman Mao Is Like the Sun.*

SCCHH: Vol. 1, No. 41 (1948), *Chairman Mao is Like the Sun.* The first lines are identical, but the remainder of the texts differs.

No. 10   *Chu Teh's Carrying Pole*

SCKHH: Vol. 2, No. 21 (1948), *Stories About Commander Chu Teh.* This selection contains several anecdotes about Chu Teh, one of which is the subject of the *Readers* selection.

KYKH: Vol. 2, No. 24 (1951), *Stories About Commander Chu Teh.* (See above).

No. 15   *Thousand-Man-Cake*

CKCKS: Vol. 7, No. 19 (1941), *Thousand-Man-Cake.*

NKK: Vol. 2, No. 12 (1943), *A Cake Made by More Than a Thousand People.*

No. 34   *Bethune*

SPKYKP: Vol. 2, Contains incidents about Dr. Norman Bethune, one of which is the basis for the *Readers* version.

KYKH: Vol. 4, No. 9 (1951), *Dr. Bethune.* Contains incidents which are the basis for the *Readers* version.

VOLUME 6

No. 19 *Bee Guides*
  SCKHH: Vol. 3, No. 16 (1948), *Bee Guides.*
  KYKH: Vol. 1, No. 20 (1951), *Bee Guides.*

No. 20 *The Horticulturist Michurin*
  CCKWH: Vol. 2, No. 13 (1942), *The Soviet Horticulturist Michurin.* This is a much longer discussion of Michurin than in the *Readers*, with some points of similarity.
  SCKHH: Vol. 3, No. 18 (1948), *The Horticulturist Michurin.* Related to *Readers* and *CCKWH* versions.

VOLUME 7

No. 3 *A Wounded Man's Wish*
  SCKHH: Vol. 3, No. 15 (1948), *Chairman Mao Sees an Injured Soldier.*

No. 10 *The Watermelon Brothers*
  SCKHH: Vol. 2, No. 13 (1948), *The Watermelon Brothers.*
  KYKH: Vol. 2, No. 8 (1951), *The Watermelon Brothers.*

No. 19 *Lenin and the Guard*
  This selection is based on a story by the Russian writer Mikhail Zoshchenko.
  KYKH: Vol. 4, No. 19 (1942), *Lenin and the Guard.*

CCKWH: Vol. 2, No. 1 (1942), *Lenin and a Guard.* This selection is longer and differs in vocabulary from *Readers* version.

No. 21 *Weighing an Elephant*
CKCHF: Vol. 5, No. 30 (1944), *An Intelligent Child.*
KYKP: Vol. 4, No. 9 (1966), *Weighing a Big Elephant.* This selection is simpler than the *Readers* version, which occurs at a higher grade level.

No. 22 *Looking for a Camel*
NCKY: Vol. 8, No. 19 (1943), *Losing a Camel.*

No. 33 *Li Ch'uang-wang Crosses the Yellow River*
PPLY: Page 6 (1946), *Li Ch'uang-wang Crosses the Yellow River.* Authorship is attributed to Li Wen-hsin.

VOLUME 8

No. 3 *The Ta-hsueh Mountains*
SCKHH: Vol. 4, No. 9 and No. 10 (1948), *Record of Crossing the Hsueh Mountains.* These two selections are generally related to the *Readers* version.

No. 8 *Six Ink Bottles*
CCKWH: Vol. 1, No. 25 (1942), *A Story About Lenin Eating His Ink Bottles.* This version is based on a story by the Russian writer Mikhail Zoshchenko.

No. 15 *Crossing a Bridge*
KYKH: Vol. 4, No. 18 (1951), *Crossing a Bridge.*

No. 32

General Liu Chih-tan's Notebook
SCKHH: Vol. 3, No. 17 (1948), *Comrade Liu Chih-tan's Little Notebook*. This selection contains some of the same incidents as the *Readers* version.

No. 34

The Wolf and the Lamb (Phaedrus)
KYKP: Vol. 6, No. 19 (1966), *The Wolf and the Lamb*.

VOLUME 9

No. 4

Sunrise at Sea
Although not so stated in the *Readers*, this selection is from *Hai-hsing tsa-chi (Sea Voyage Notebook)* by Pa Chin (1932).
CCKWH: Vol. 1, No. 3 (1942), *Sunrise at Sea*.
NCKY: Vol. 8, No. 32 (1943), *Seeing the Sunrise at Sea*.
NCKW: Vol. 1, No. 4 (1944), *Sunrise at Sea*.
KYKP: Vol. 7, No. 10 (1966), *Sunrise at the Seashore*. This is not the same selection as those above. However, the high degree of similarity that it shows in its descriptive passages suggests a common origin.

No. 13

Eighteen Brave Soldiers
KYKH: Vol. 4, No. 4 (1951), *Eighteen Brave Soldiers*.

No. 16

The Foolish Old Man Who Removed the Mountains. This is the version of the classical story as elaborated by Mao. The original story is from the *Lieh-tzu*.
NCKY: Vol. 8, No. 27 (1943), *The Foolish Old Man Who Removed the Mountains*.
SCKHH: Vol. 3, No. 19 (1948), *The Foolish Old Man Who Removed the Mountains*.
KYKP: Vol. 4, No. 29 (1966), *The Fool-*

ish Old Man Who Removed the Mountains. This is the traditional version of the story without the embellishment by Mao.

No. 17   *The Reorganization at Sanwan*
    CCKWH: Vol. 2, No. 3 (1942), *The Reorganization at Sanwan.* This selection is somewhat more elaborated than the *Readers* version. The author is listed as Comrade T'an Cheng.

No. 30   *The Song of the Nightingale*
    SCKKY: Vol. 2, No. 23 (1946), *The Nightingale's Song.*

No. 33a   *The Farmer and the Snake*
    KYKH: Vol. 1, No. 13 (1951), *Four Allegories.* The first of these is the same story as that in the *Readers.* The original story is from Aesop.

VOLUME 10

No. 12   *Two Balls Strike the Earth at the Same Time*
    CCKWH: Vol. 1, No. 22 (1942), *Two Iron Balls Struck the Earth at the Same Time.* This is the same story as that of the *Readers.* It is, however, somewhat longer and more elaborate.
    SKK: Vol. 3, No. 31 (1946), *Two Iron Balls Struck the Earth at the Same Time.* Text differs somewhat from that of CCKWH version.

No. 13   *Recollections from Sixteen Years Ago*
and   SKK: Vol. 3, Nos. 5, 6, 7, and 8 (1946),
No. 14   *Recollections from Sixteen Years Ago.*

No. 26b   *Setting Out Early From Pai-ti*
        KYKP: Vol. 3 (Senior Elementary) (1966), *Hsia Chiang Ling*. This is the Li Po poem.

No. 27   *K'ung Ming Borrows Some Arrows*
        NKK: Vol. 3, Nos. 31 and 32 (1941), *Borrowing Arrows With Straw and Boats*. This is written in classical Chinese and is taken from the *San-kuo yen-i (Romance of the Three Kingdoms)*.
        SKK: Vol. 3, Nos. 22 and 23 (1946), *Borrowing Arrows With Straw and Boars*. This selection is also written in classical Chinese.

No. 33   *A Letter to Comrade Hsü T'e-li*
        SCKHH: Vol. 4, Nos. 9 and 10 (1948), *A Congratulatory Birthday Letter*.

APPENDIX TWO
THE PROVISIONS OF THE MINISTRY OF EDUCATION'S "LIFE GUIDANCE FOR ELEMENTARY SCHOOLS"

The following outline is that provided by the Ministry of Education as a guide to individual elementary schools in carrying out "life guidance" and in the preparation of educational materials for this purpose. The outline is divided into four sections:

Section 1. Hygienic habits

Section 2. Organizational discipline

Section 3. Qualities of courtesy

Section 4. Politics and ideology

The individuals provisions under each section are translated below.[1]

Section 1. Hygienic habits.

Bathing and brushing teeth every day. Washing hands before eating, and rinsing mouth after eating.

Drinking much boiled water every day, but not drinking fresh water.

Eating clean, easily digestible foods. Not eating spoiled fruits. Food should be thoroughly boiled and eaten only after boiling.

Not consuming stimulants like cigarettes or alcohol.

Not eating things that sick people have eaten. When sick oneself, not giving what one has eaten to others.

Chewing thoroughly and swallowing slowly, and having set times and amounts to eat. Not eating between meals.

Not sticking anything into the nose and ears and not putting things one cannot eat in the mouth.

Cutting toenails and fingernails frequently.

Protecting the eyes. Not rubbing the eyes with a dirty handkerchief or one used by someone else. Not reading or writing under an improper light.

Brushing, washing, and cutting the hair often.

Frequent bathing, washing of feet, and keeping the skin clean.

When sleeping, keeping the head outside of the covers. The stomach should be covered when sleeping on hot days.

Frequent washing and drying of handkerchiefs, clothes, bedding, and socks in order to keep them clean.

Having enough sleep every day and adequate relaxation.

Having definite times for getting up, going to bed, and defecating every day.

Not being afraid of being vaccinated and of taking preventative innoculations.

Telling parents or teacher when not feeling well. When sick, following the treatment of the doctor or nurse. Not being afraid of taking medicine.

Paying attention to opening and closing doors and windows so that there will be circulation of air in rooms.

Opening the mouth during thunder, bombardment, or when loud noises are made.

Examining the state of body health at fixed times, and giving attention to correcting deficiencies.

When coughing or sneezing, to use a handkerchief or paper as a cover.

Spitting and vomiting into spittoons.

Sweeping out and keeping both the inside and outside of rooms clean at all times.

Dumping rubbish in fixed places, and keeping public places clean.

Not defecating or urinating where one pleases, and keeping toilets and toilet bowls clean.

Exerting effort to kill animals that spread disease germs such as mosquitoes, flies, fleas, lice, and rats.

Not painting on walls or making things for public use dirty.

Frequently playing, relaxing, and breathing fresh air out of doors.

Frequently taking part in such recreational activities as singing, dancing, and acting in plays, and enjoying oneself with others.

Doing calisthenics every morning and exercising the body frequently.

Not moving heavy things. Not doing violent exercise. Not running and jumping before and after meals.

Paying frequent attention to maintaining a straight posture, not stooping or humping the shoulders.

Section 2. Organizational discipline.

Striving to study all lessons well and completing the assignments that the teacher has given on time.

Getting to school on time, going home on time, not skipping classes, not arriving late, and not leaving early.

Requesting leave when having business or being sick, and making up classes that have been missed.

When attending class bringing text books and writing paper and preparing necessary things before going to class.

Immediately entering the classroom and taking one's seat on hearing the signal to go to class.

Listening attentively to lectures in class and paying attention to questions and answers.

Sitting straight, not talking or moving in class and not going in and out of the classroom at one's will.

Raising the hand if desiring to speak in class or at a meeting. Speaking after obtaining the permission of the teacher or chairman.

Respecting the teacher, obeying his instructions, and greeting him on entering and leaving class.

Observing examination rules, not being proud when doing well on an examination, and striving harder when doing poorly on an examination.

Frequently reading books and magazines outside of class, and being diligent in studying current events and various kinds of general knowledge.

Ask others humbly about what one cannot do; enthusiastically help others with what one can do.

Being agreeable to others. Not swearing at others or fighting.

Playing with equipment for public amusement by turns. Not grabbing to be first and not monopolizing it.

When riding on public vehicles, observing rules, paying attention to sanitation, safety, and order, and giving one's seat to the old, the weak, and the sick.

On the road, obeying the directions of the traffic police, watching out for carts and horses, and not loitering about on the streets.

In group activities, the individual complying with the group, the minority complying with the majority, the lower level complying with the upper level, and the local complying with the whole body.

Active participation in student meetings and in the activities of the Pioneers. Obeying the leadership of student cadre and observing group rules.

Taking responsibility for electing those who can serve everyone. After one has been elected oneself, being able to bear responsibility actively.

Protecting the honor of the individual, the group, and the school.

Not losing or lending to others one's badge, identification cards, or passes.

Section 3. Qualities of courtesy.

Greeting teachers and elders on meeting. Calling warmly to classmates on meeting.

Letting elders and guests eat the best food first and not grabbing for food oneself.

Not privately opening and looking at other's letters, packages, or drawers.

First knocking on the door or calling out before entering another person's house. Entering only after receiving permission.

Pay attention to being obedient to others. Not hindering the work of others.

Apologizing to anyone whom one has offended.

Not taking the least thing from others. Asking another's permission before borrowing his things. Returning them on time when finished using them, and bearing responsibility for repayment if one has damaged them.

Exerting great effort to care for sick parents and elders.

Looking after younger brothers and sisters and younger classmates with patience.

Helping others cheerfully, not hoping for a reward in return, and not boasting about one's own meritorious deed.

Not being afraid of difficulties and hardships in work and using all methods to overcome difficulties.

Being enthusiastic, careful, and patient in work, following it through from beginning to end, and not being hasty or losing one's temper.

Bearing responsibility for finishing work that one has already agreed to do.

Not going to dangerous places. Not playing with dangerous things. Striving to help others that one finds in danger.

Being sincere and honest, not spreading lies, not acting hypocritically, not taking advantage of situations, and not being biased.

Cooperating and working together with others, putting determination and suffering of hardship first and enjoyment of pleasure after.

Not being jealous of the talents and endeavors of others, and moreover being willing to learn from them.

When one has been wronged or been deceived, seeking an explanation and not taking private ravenge.

Practicing frugality. Not wasting property, but not being miserly either.

Not gambling for money, not stealing, and vigorously exorting others to stop improper conduct.

Being courageous in criticism and self-criticism, and being conscientious in correcting errors.

Mutual respect and mutual help between boy and girl classmates.

Section 4. Politics and ideology.

Loving their native regions and establishing the determination to expand production and to improve our life environment.

Respecting the national flag, and protecting the dignity and honor of the motherland.

Standing and singing the national anthem with reverence and fostering enthusiasm for love of the motherland.

Respecting and loving Chairman Mao and studying his spirit of service to the people and of finding the truth from the facts.

Respecting and loving the Chinese Communist Party and supporting its correct leadership.

Supporting our people's government and being resolute in carrying out the government's policies and laws.

Respecting and loving the People's Liberation Army and its honorable soldiers, and learning from their courageous fighting spirit and iron discipline.

Guarding state secrets and devoting attention to helping oppose traitors and spies.

Supporting the national united battle line and carrying out the Common Program of the People's Political Consultative Conference.

Studying to accept the rights and privileges of a people's democracy and to understand the citizen's obligations of military service, voluntary labor, and of surrender of grain and payment of taxes.

Continually preparing to use one's own life to protect the sovereignty of the territory of the motherland and the interests of the people and of the masses.

Mourning for the national heroes and revolutionary martyrs who defended the motherland, and learning from their spirit of courageous and vigorous self-sacrifice.

Supporting the Treaty of Friendship and Mutual Assistance and other agreements between China and the Soviet Union.

Supporting the democratic camp of world peace headed by the Soviet Union and strengthening the friendship between the Chinese and Russian peoples; opposing the aggressive camp led by American Imperialism.

Sympathizing with and assisting the revolutionary movements of the world's peoples, particularly the liberation movements of the oppressed peoples of Asia.

Uniting with and having affection for the minority peoples within the nation and respecting the ways of life and religious beliefs of each of these peoples.

Uniting with our international friends and not discriminating against any nationality.

Uniting with and protecting the broad masses of overseas Chinese.

Respecting and loving industrous parents, workers, and peasants' masses, labor heroes, and model workers.

Fostering collective life habits of the individual for the group and the group for the individual.

Not relying on others for what one can do oneself.

Participating actively in productive labor in the home, in school, and in society, and studying production skills.

Supporting the family and participating enthusiastically in mutual assistance labor exchanges and in cooperative movements.

Serving actively as little teachers, assisting in furthering the literacy campaign.

Clarifying right and wrong when something happens, respecting the truth, and opposing superstition and dogmatism.

Observing and investigating carefully at all times and in all places the origin, development, and outcome of events; loving science, learning from people's scientists, and developing a spirit of creativity.

Planning, investigating, and summarizing in living, study, and work.

Respecting time and not wasting one minute.

Curbing all such shameful behavior as destruction, theft, and waste of public property.

FOOTNOTES

CHAPTER ONE

1. Fred I. Greenstein, *Children and Politics* (New Haven: Yale University Press, 1969), pp. 1-17.

2. David Easton and Robert D. Hess, "The Child's Political World," *Midwest Journal of Political Science*, VI (1962).

3. For an analytical survey of the major studies of childhood political socialization see, Richard E. Dawson and Kenneth Prewitt, *Political Socialization* (Boston: Little, Brown and Co., 1969).

4. For a discussion of the authoritarian structure of the Chinese family see: John K. Fairbank, "The Nature of Chinese Society," in Franz Schurmann and Orville Schell (eds.), *Imperial China* (New York: Vintage Books, 1967), especially pp. 32-47.

5. Although we have no data to support this assumption, the argument presented by Hess and Torney in their discussion of "interpersonal transference" is persuasive. See, Robert D. Hess and Judith V. Torney, *The Development of Political Attitudes in Children* (Chicago: Aldine Publishing Co., 1967), especially pp. 20-21.

6. Quoted in Phillip Bridgham, "Mao's Cultural Revolution," *The China Quarterly*, No. 29 (January-March, 1967), p. 9.

7. *Ibid.*, p. 13.

8. "Train Young People to be Staunch Revolutionary Successors," *Kwang-ming jih-pao (Kwang-ming Daily)*, June 1, 1964, in *Survey of the China Mainland Press*, No. 3241, June 18, 1964.

9. See Benjamin Schwartz, "The Reign of Virtue: Some Broad Perspectives on Leader and Party in the Cultural Revolution," *The China Quarterly*, No. 35 (July-September, 1969).

10. Ezra F. Vogel, "From Revolutionary to Semi-Bureaucrat: The Regularization of Cadres," *The China Quarterly*, No. 29 (January-March, 1967), p. 36.

11. For an analysis of the role of hero emulation in China's political

campaigns, see Mary Sheridan, "The Emulation of Heroes," *The China Quarterly*, No. 33 (January-March, 1968).

12. David C. McClelland, *The Achieving Society*, (Princeton: D. Van Nostrand Company, Inc., 1961).

CHAPTER TWO

1. Quoted, with modifications, from Stewart Fraser, *Chinese Communist Education* (New York: John Wiley and Son, Inc., 1965), p. 83.

2. C. T. Hu, "Communist Education: Theory and Practice," *The China Quarterly*, No. 10 (April-June 1962), p. 93.

3. *Kwangming Daily*, January 6, 1965.

4. Dennis J. Doolin, *Communist China: The Politics of Student Opposition* (Stanford, Calif.: The Hoover Institution on War, Revolution and Peace, Stanford University, 1964), especially pp. 11-13.

5. Leo A. Orleans presents an excellent summary of Chinese educational policies in his "Communist Chinese Education: Policies, Problems, and Prospects," in Joint Economic Committee, Congress of the United States, *An Economic Profile of Communist China* (Washington: U. S. Government Printing Office, 1967), pp. 499-518. See also: Leo A. Orleans, *Professional Manpower and Education in Communist China* (Washington: National Science Foundation, 1961).

6. This discussion of elementary education is drawn largely from Theodore H. E. Chen, "Elementary Education in Communist China," *The China Quarterly*, No. 10 (April-June, 1962), pp. 98-122.

7. Robert D. Barendson, "The 1960 Education Reforms," *The China Quarterly*, No. 4 (October-December, 1960), pp. 55-60.

8. Chen, *op. cit.*, p. 102.

9. *Ibid.*, p. 113.

10. Chang T'eng-hsiao, *Hsiao-hsüeh chiao-shih yeh-wu hsüeh-hsi chiang-tso* (*Professional Study Lectures for Elementary School Teachers*) (revised ed., Peking: Ta-chung shu-tien, 1952).

11. *Ibid.*, p. 15.

12. *Ibid.*, p. 108.

13. Hu Yen-li, *Tsen-yang shih-shih wu-ai chiao-yü* (*How to Carry Out Five Loves Education*) (Peking: Shang-wu yin-shu-kuan, 1951), pp. 1-2.

14. Shanghai Democratic Women's Federation, comp., *Erh-t'ung p'ei-yang shou-ts'e* (*A Handbook of Child Training*) (Shanghai: Jen-min ch'u-pan-she, 1951).

15. *Ibid.*, p. 2.

16. P'an Ta-pai, *"Tsen-yang chiao-hao hai-tzu-men ai-kuo* (*How to Teach Children to Love Their Country*)," *Hsin erh-t'ung chiao-yü,* (*New Pedagogy*), Vol. 6, No. 2 (1951) as reprinted in the book of the same title, Jen Yü-wen, ed., *Hsin pei-ching ch'u-pan-she*, (1951).

17. Hu Yen-li, *op. cit.*, pp. 2-3.

18. *Ibid.*, pp. 12-13.

19. Ch'iao I-ch'ien, *"Tsen-yang tui erh-t'ung chin-hsing ai-kuo chu-i chiao-yü, (How to Carry Out Patriotic Education for Children),"* Hsin erh-t'ung chiao-yü (New Pedagogy),* Vol. 6, No. 2 (1951), cited from *Tsen-yang chiao-hao hai-tzu-men ai-kuo.*

20. *Ibid.*, p. 20.

21. *Ibid.*, pp. 21-28.

22. *Ibid.*, p. 21.

23. *Ibid.*, pp. 21-25.

24. *Ibid.*, pp. 26-29.

25. See Appendix 2 for an outline of the program.

26. Hu Yen-li, *op. cit.*, p. 13.

27. *Ibid.*, pp. 14-15.

28. *Ibid.*, p. 15.

29. *Ibid.*, pp. 16-17.

30. *Ibid.*, p. 37.

31. Chou Yüan-ping, *P'ei-yang ch'ing-nien te kung-ch'an chu-i tao-te (The Cultivation of Communist Morality in the Young)* (Peking: Chung-kuo ch'ing-nien ch'u-pan-she, 1956), p. 38.

32. Wu Chiang, *Kung-ch'an chu-i tao-te wen-t'i, (The Question of Communist Morality)* (Peking: Kung-jen ch'u-pan-she, 1955), pp. 25-26.

33. *Ibid.*, p. 42-43.

34. The passage translated here is from Kuo Jen-ch'üan, *Chiao-yü-hsüeh chi-pen wen-t'i chiang-hua (Lectures on Basic Problems in Pedagogy)* (Hangchow: Che-chiang jen-min ch'u-pan-she, 1956), Chapter 4, pp. 50-56.

35. Liu Sung-t'ao, *"Ko-ming chan-cheng chung tui erh-t'ung chin-hsing ai-kuo chiao-yü te tien-ti ching-yen (Experiences in Carrying out Patriotic Education among Children during the Revolutionary War),"* Jen-min chiao-yü (People's Education), Vol.,4 No. 1, reprinted in Jen Yu-wen, *op. cit.*, p. 50.

CHAPTER THREE

1. Wen I-chan, *Hsiao-hsüeh yu-wen chiao-hsüeh ching-yen, i chih ssu nien-chi (Experiences in Elementary School Language Teaching, Grades One Through Four)* (Peking: Pei-ching ch'u-pan-she, 1957).

2. *Ibid.*, p. 1.

3. *Ibid.*, pp. 159-160.

4. *Ibid.*, pp. 143-149. See also *Readers*, Vol. 4, No. 40. The version in the *Readers*, although essentially the same, would appear to differ in a few minor points from that on which this lesson plan is based.

5. Wen I-chan, *op. cit.*, pp. 149-151.

CHAPTER FOUR

1. David C. McClelland, "Motivational Patterns in Southeast Asia with Special Reference to the Chinese Case," *The Journal of Social Issues*, 19, No. 1 (January, 1963), p. 15.

2. *Ibid.*, p. 16.

3. *Ibid.*, pp. 16-17.

4. Dawson and Prewitt, *op. cit.*, p. 45; Greenstein, *op. cit.*, pp. 37-43.

5. Dawson and Prewitt, *op. cit.*, Chapter VI.

6. Maurice Freedman, "The Family in China, Past and Present," in Albert Feuerwerker (ed.), *Modern China* (Englewood Cliffs, N. J.: Prentice Hall, Inc., 1964), p. 28.

CHAPTER SEVEN

1. John Wilson Lewis, "Party Cadres in Communist China," in J. S. Coleman (ed.), *Education and Political Development* (Princeton University Press, 1965).

2. For a more detailed discussion of this problem see: Ezra F. Vogel, "From Friendship to Comradeship: The Change in Personal Relations in Communist China," in R. MacFarquhar (ed.), *China Under Mao: Politics Takes Command* (Cambridge, Mass.: MIT Press, 1966).

3. *Chuang Tzu*, Chapter 3, "Yang Sheng Chu." The original story is about Duke Wen-hui's cook.

4. C. S. Chen and C. P. Ridley, *The Rural People's Communes in Lien-chiang* (Stanford, Calif.: Hoover Institution, 1969).

5. For a study demonstrating the effectiveness of the school in the political socialization of American children, see R. D. Hess and J. V. Torney, *op. cit.*

6. Richard H. Solomon, "Mao's Effort to Reintegrate the Chinese Polity," in A. Doak Barnett (ed.), *Chinese Communist Politics in Action* (Seattle: University of Washington Press, 1969), esp. pp. 338-339.

7. See Jeremy R. Azrael, "Soviet Union," in Coleman, *op. cit.*, pp. 254-257.

8. See Herbert Passin, "Japan," in Coleman, *op. cit.*, pp. 304-312.

APPENDIX ONE

1. *Gendai chūgoku jimmei jiten (Current Chinese Biographical Dictionary)* (Tokyo: Asia Bureau of the Ministry of Foreign Affairs, Kazankai, 1966), p. 180.

2. *Ibid.*, p. 1180.

3. Private communication.

APPENDIX TWO

1. Shen Tzu-shan, *Hsiao-hsüeh sheng-huo chih-tao, (Life Guidance for Elementary Schools)* (Peking: Shang-wu yin-shu-kuan, 1951), pp. 4-13.

STORIES FROM THE READERS

Measures

1 *chin* = 1 catty = 1 1/3 lb. av.

1 *li* = 1 Chinese mile = 1/3 English statute mile (approx.)

1 *mou* = 1/6 English statute acre (approx.)

SELECTIONS FROM
VOLUME 1 OF THE
READERS

(GRADE ONE)

THIRTY. STUDY HARD

Chairman Mao loves us. Chairman Mao tells us to study hard and advance upwards every day. We must be obedient to the words of Chairman Mao and be good children of Chairman Mao.

THIRTY-ONE. STUDYING AND LABORING

We love to study,
We love to labor.
We labor, we study.
We study, we labor.
We study hard at learning skills,
We are diligent from the time we are little.
Having learned skills, we go out to plant the fields.
Having learned skills, we go out to do work.

THIRTY-FIVE. THE FLOWERS IN THE PARK

Elder sister and younger brother went to the park to play.
The chrysanthemums in the park were in bloom. Some were yellow, some were white, and some were red.

Younger brother wanted to pick the flowers. Elder sister said to him: "Don't pick them! Don't pick them! The flowers in the park are for everyone to look at."

1. Why musn't one pick the flowers in a park?

THIRTY-SEVEN. A ROAD IS BUILT WITH A PAIR OF HANDS

> A house is built with a pair of hands,
> Rice is planted with a pair of hands,
> Clothes are sewn with a pair of hands,
> Roads are opened with a pair of hands.
> Each of us has a pair of hands.
> We must build the tall building of Communism.

THIRTY-EIGHT. ON DUTY FOR THE DAY

Today we are on duty. After school is out, we sweep the classroom. Some of us sprinkle water, some of us sweep, some of us clean the blackboard, and some of us wipe the desks and chairs. After we finish sweeping, the classroom is very clean, and in our hearts we are very happy.

FORTY-ONE. K'UNG JUNG GIVES UP A PEAR

Once upon a time there was a little boy named K'ung Jung. One day when he was four years old he was eating pears with his elder brother.

K'ung Jung took one of the smallest pears. His father saw this and asked him: "Why did you take the smallest one?" K'ung Jung said: "I am little, so I should eat the little one."

FORTY-TWO. I WILL LOVE TO WEAR MY JACKET

Hsiao-chu's mother sewed a jacket for her. Hsiao-chu began to sing happily:

"Mother sewed a jacket for me,
A thousand stitches, ten thousand stitches, she sewed fine.
How hard my mother worked to sew my clothes,
I will love to wear my jacket."

Her mother said: "Well sung! Hsiao-chu, I ask you, who planted the cotton? Who wove the cloth?"

Hsiao-chu said: "The cotton was grown by us peasants, and the cloth was woven by the workers."

Her mother said: "That's right! See, how many people must labor to make a piece of clothes! How could we help but love the clothes we wear?"

Why should we love our clothes?

FORTY-FOUR. SWEEPING SNOW

It snowed all night. The ground was white, the trees were white, and the roofs of the houses were white. The sun rose, shining very brightly on the snow.

How cold a day it was! The children, who were not afraid of the cold, got up very early, some of them building snow men and some of them having snowball fights. Quite a few grown-ups were sweeping snow on the road. Some of them put the snow into the fields, and some of them piled the snow beneath the trees. The children went over to help too.

In a little while, all of the snow had been swept up. The children went off to school singing.

SELECTIONS FROM
VOLUME 2 OF THE
READERS

(GRADE ONE)

ONE. OUR CLASSROOM

How really good our classroom is!

A picture of Chairman Mao hangs on the wall facing us. Sitting in the classroom, we raise our heads and look at Chairman Mao's picture.

The blackboard in the classroom is wiped very clean, and the desks and chairs are lined up in order.

Hanging on the classroom walls there are four pictures and a chart of the *pinyin* alphabet. It is very attractive.

I like our classroom. I like our school.

THREE. WHAT WILL I BE WHEN I GROW UP?

When I grow up, I will be a peasant,
And I will build new villages for my motherland.

When I grow up, I will make machines,
And I will send them to the villages.

When I grow up, I will join the Army,
To protect our motherland and fight our enemies.

Workers, peasants, and soldiers are very important and very
    revolutionary.

When we grow up, we will be workers, peasants, and soldiers.

NINE. A WOODPECKER

An old tree became sick, and some of its leaves turned yellow.

A doctor flew up and landed on the tree. He tapped it here and he tapped it there with his beak. When he found a place where there were insects, he pecked a hole. He stuck his long tongue into the hole, and, drawing the insects out one by one, he ate them. After he had eaten all the insects, he spread his wings and flew away.

The old tree, cured by the doctor, slowly began to grow new leaves.

The doctor was a woodpecker.

SEVENTEEN. A CROW GETS A DRINK OF WATER

A crow was thirsty and was looking everywhere for water to drink.

The crow saw a bottle. There was water in the bottle. But the bottle was very deep and its mouth was small. There was not much water inside, and he couldn't get at it. What to do?

The crow, seeing that there were many small stones beside it, worked out a way.

The crow picked up the small stones in his beak one by one and put them into the bottle. The water in the bottle rose, and then the crow was able to drink it.

EIGHTEEN. A BALL FLOATS UP

Several children were playing ball in a field.

The ball gave a bounce and bounced into a hole in the ground. The hole was very deep, and they couldn't get the ball out. The children looked back and forth at each other. There was nothing they could do.

One of the children thought of a way. He got a basin and, filling it with water, he poured it into the hole. When the hole was filled with water, the ball floated up.

TWENTY-THREE. THE EAST IS RED

The East is red, the sun is rising.
China has produced a Mao Tse-tung.
He plans for the happiness of the people;
He is the savior of the people.
Chairman Mao loves the people;
He is the one who leads the way.
In order to build a new China,
He leads us in our advance ahead.
The Communist Party is like the sun;
Wherever it shines there is brightness.
Wherever the Communist Party is,
There the people are liberated.

TWENTY-FIVE. CARRY A MESSAGE TO PEKING

Swallow, swallow, please wait a moment;
Carry a message for us to Peking.
Please tell beloved Chairman Mao,
We here send our respects to him;
We are indeed studying hard and advancing upwards every day;
We will forever be his good students.
Please do not stop long,
And do not speak in a loud voice;
Let beloved Chairman Mao
Attend to his business in peace and quiet.
Swallow, swallow, please wait a moment;
Carry a message for us to Peking.

THIRTY-TWO. IN THE WHEAT FIELD

The team's wheat was drying in the field.

My little brother and I, each holding a bamboo pole, stood at the edge of the field keeping the chickens and the crows from eating the wheat.

Suddenly a chicken came over to the other side of the field. When we ran over to have a look, it turned out to be our family's big hen. We chased her, waving our bamboo poles. As my little brother ran after her, he said in a loud voice: "Get away from here at once! This is the team's wheat. You can't eat it!"

The big hen, flapping her wings, ran off, cackling as she went.

THIRTY-FIVE. THE BOY WHO TOLD A LIE

Once upon a time there was a little boy who often tended sheep on the mountains.

One day he called out from the mountain in a loud voice: "There's a wolf! There's a wolf!" When the people at the foot of the mountain heard him, they came running up the mountain at once. They asked him: "Where is the wolf? Where is the wolf?" The shepherd boy laughed. He said: "There's no wolf. There's no wolf. I was only joking."

The shepherd boy tricked them like this several times in succession.

One day, there really was a wolf. The shepherd boy called out in a loud voice: "There's a wolf! There's a wolf!" When the people at the foot of the mountain heard him, they said: "That boy is telling lies again. Don't pay any attention to him!"

The wolf killed and ate several sheep. The shepherd boy cried.

THIRTY-SIX. SZU-MA KUANG

Once upon a time there was a man called Szu-ma Kuang. Once, when he was little, he was playing in a flower garden with a large number of his little friends.

One of his little friends, who was not being careful, fell into a big cistern.

His many little friends were upset and ran about calling and shouting. Some ran off to look for adults.

Szu-ma Kuang did not run. He got a big rock and, with great effort, struck the cistern with it. The cistern broke, and the water flowed out from it. The little friend who had fallen into it did not drown.

THIRTY-EIGHT. A TELEPHONE CALL

The morning glory looks like a horn;
I'll make a telephone call into the horn.
Where will I call?
I'll call our worker uncles.

Thank you for your tractor,
Which plowed and seeded and harvested the crops.
Thank you for your water pump,
Which gave us a way to water and drain our fields.

Thank you for your generator,
On which we depended for light at the grinder.
Thank you for your chemical fertilizer;
Our grain and cotton production increased.

Goodbye, worker uncles.
I have one last word:
Please come down to the country after autumn,
To see our good crops.

SELECTIONS FROM
VOLUME 3 OF THE
READERS

(GRADE TWO)

THREE. AUTUMN IS HERE

Autumn is here; autumn is here;
And in the fields the crops have grown well.
The cotton blossoms are white;
The soybeans are plump;
The kaoliang is blushing red;
And the rice plants smilingly bend their waists.

Autumn is here; autumn is here;
In the orchards, the fruits have grown well.
The branches have borne persimmons;
Grapes are hanging from the trellises;
The pears are yellow;
The dates are red.

Autumn is here; autumn is here;
In the earth, the vegetables are growing well.
The winter melons are spread out like white threads;
The eggplants are wearing purple gowns;
The cabbages are in glossy strips;
The greens and reds are peppers.

Autumn is here; autumn is here;
And this year we've had a good harvest in our commune.
Everyone is hurrying about,
And everywhere voices are loud in song,
Singing about the rich harvest year,
Singing that the commune is good.

FIVE. DON'T WALK THROUGH HERE

One morning as I was going to school, I was passing by a vegetable garden when I saw a line of footprints in the garden. They were probably made by someone selfishly taking a shortcut. There was also a break in the irrigation ditch at the edge of the garden. I was thinking about taking the same shortcut and had just entered the garden when someone called out behind me: "Hey, wait a minute."

I turned around and looked. It was someone from the Shao-hsien brigade. I stopped and asked: "What is it?" He said: "Please don't walk through here. You might trample the vegetables!"

He was right. I said, "Right," and left the vegetable garden and went on to school on the highway.

After school let out, I passed by the garden again and remembered the morning's incident. I thought, if everyone went through the garden, many vegetables would be trampled! How could I remind people taking the shortcut? I decided to write a sign and place it at the edge of the garden.

I hurried home and asked my older brother to help me make a wooden sign, on which I wrote: "Please protect the cabbages— DON'T WALK THROUGH HERE."

I carried the sign on my shoulder to the vegetable garden. The man from the Shao-hsien brigade was banking up the earth by the irrigation ditch with a hoe. He raised his head and saw me carrying the sign and said with a smile: "Put that sign over here." He dug a hole quickly, and we put the sign up together.

After that, passersby never again walked through the vegetable garden.

ELEVEN. CHAIRMAN MAO SEES A PLAY

Once a theatrical company was putting on a performance at Yenan. Many people had come to the hall to see the play.

As the curtain was about to open, Chairman Mao arrived. When he saw that all the seats in front were taken, he found an empty place at the back and sat down. The people sitting in front saw that Chairman Mao had come, and everyone stood up, each wanting to give his place to him. Chairman Mao rose hastily and said: "Everyone sit in your own seat. Once you move, order will be destroyed."

Everyone still wanted to invite Chairman Mao to sit down front.

Chairman Mao saw that no one was willing to sit down. He then walked to the front and sat in the seat of a little boy. Chairman Mao picked the little boy up and let him sit on his lap.

The play began, and Chairman Mao and his little friend watched it together. During intermission they chatted like close friends.

FIFTEEN. A BUNDLE OF ARROWS

Once upon a time there was an old man who had ten sons. The ten sons were not of one mind and were always quarrelling with each other. The old man was very worried about it.

The old man became sick and grew worse from day to day until he was on the point of death. He called his ten sons before him. He asked someone to bring out ten arrows, one of which he gave to each son, asking them to break them.

They broke all the arrows easily.

The old man then asked someone to bring ten more arrows, which he tied into a bundle. Then he let them take turns at breaking it.

They each tried to break it for a long time, but could not.

The old man said:"These ten arrows are like you ten brothers. If brothers are united together, with everyone of one mind, their strength will be great."

After the old man finished speaking he closed his eyes and died.

His ten sons cried in grief. They looked at the bundle of arrows and thought about what their father had said. From that time on, they did not quarrel again.

SIXTEEN. THE FOX AND THE CROW

A crow had built a nest in a big tree.

Beneath the tree was a hole, and in the hole lived a fox.

One day, the crow flew out in order to hunt for something to eat for her children. She found a slice of meat, which she brought back in her beak. She perched happily on the small branch at my side.

At that time, the fox also came out to look for something to eat. He raised his head, and when he saw the piece of meat that the crow was holding in her beak, he drooled greedily.

He thought a while and then smiled at the crow and said: "How are you, Mrs. Crow?"

The crow did not utter a sound.

The fox spoke again: "Mrs. Crow, how are your children?"

The crow looked at the fox but again did not utter a sound.

The fox spoke again: "Mrs. Crow, your plumage is truly attractive, quite different from the sparrow's. Your voice is truly good, and everyone loves to listen to you sing. How about singing a song?"

When the crow heard what the fox had to say, she felt very proud and began to sing: "Wa..." No sooner had she opened her mouth than the meat fell out.

The fox picked up the meat in his mouth and crept back into his hole.

SEVENTEEN. A WOLF IN SHEEP'S CLOTHING

There once was a shepherd who tended a large flock of sheep. One day he discovered that one of his sheep was missing, and the next day he discovered that yet another was missing. This continued for several days running. He was very worried, but he did not know what had happened to the sheep.

One day, the shepherd had driven the sheep to a hillside. There was much tender grass on the hillside, and the sheep ate very hungrily. There was, however, one sheep that was always lying down and that did not eat any grass. He thought that this was very strange, and when he went over to take a closer look, he found that it actually was a wolf wearing a sheepskin.

The situation became clear. The shepherd raised the wooden stick in his hand and struck fiercely at the wolf, saying as he struck: "Death to you, you wolf in sheep's clothing! Death to you, you wolf in sheep's clothing!"

The wolf wanted to escape, but it was too late. In a moment, the shepherd had beaten him to death.

EIGHTEEN. EXAMINING A PASS

There was once a village in the Kiangsi Soviet called Wan-t'ai. Every day the members of the Pioneers in the village stood sentry in order to question passers-by.

One day, as two Pioneers were standing watch at the village gate, a stranger came by. They came down to question him, and the man took out a pass.

The two Pioneers looked at the pass. It was in order and had been issued by the government. However, when they examined it more carefully, they discovered that it bore an early date and that it had expired. What was even more suspicious was that no one should be passing through Wan-t'ai on the way to the destination written on the pass.

The two Pioneers then questioned the man closely about his origins (i.e., where he was from and his background). The man said that he was a peasant and that he lived in a place not far from Wan-t'ai. However, his bearing did not resemble that of a peasant, and when they heard him speak, he did not have a local accent.

The two Pioneers took the suspicious man to the People's Militia, and it was found that he was actually an enemy spy.

NINETEEN. "I AM THE DISTRICT CHIEF"

One day during the War of Resistance against Japan, the enemy suddenly surrounded Ta-wang Village and drove everyone in the village to a field at the eastern edge of the village. The enemy had come to capture the District Chief of the anti-Japanese government, and they had traced the District Chief to this village.

One of the enemy soldiers with a full beard flashed his bayonet at an old man and asked menacingly: "Who is the District Chief? Speak!"

The old man did not utter a sound.

"Speak up. If you don't talk, I'll..." The enemy soldier gave his bayonet a shake.

"I don't know," said the old man with his head held high. No sooner had he finished speaking than the bayonet had pierced his chest. The old man fell to the ground, onto which his blood flowed out.

The soldier then pressed the bloody bayonet to the chest of a young boy. The enemy soldier asked in a loud voice: "Who is the District Chief? Speak! If you don't, the same thing will happen to you!"

The young man clenched his teeth and paid no attention to him.

The enemy soldier was just about to raise his bayonet when District Chief Wang burst from the crowd and said: "I am the District Chief!"

The enemy soldier let the young boy go and ran towards District Chief Wang. At the same time, everyone began to shout: "I am the District Chief. I am the District Chief."

As they shouted, everyone surrounded the enemy soldier. The enemy soldier stared at them but could not pick out which of them was the District Chief.

Why did District Chief Wang rush out from the crowd? Why did all the people of Ta-wang Village shout: "I am the District Chief!"?

TWENTY. THE HAWKER

In the autumn of 1942, one of the towns which was a Japanese resistance base was occupied by the enemy.

In order to build an arsenal, the enemy tore down our one

elementary school. Whenever any of the enemy soldiers saw a child, he would say with a sneer: "Little Eighth Router (The term refers to the Eighth Route Army.—Trans.), are you still studying anti-Japanese books?" The children would clench their fists tightly but say nothing.

Ever since the enemy tore down the school, a hawker had appeared on the streets. Every day he carried a load of goods on his shoulders which he hawked on the streets. As soon as his drum sounded, the children would surround him, and the hawker would talk with them in a low voice. If a stranger came by, the children would start to shout, some saying, that the goods were too expensive, and some saying that they weren't any good. Then the hawker would shoulder his load and go off to another street.

The enemy often watched them, but didn't know that the hawker was actually Teacher Li of the Japanese Resistance Elementary School and that his drum was actually the class bell.

TWENTY-ONE. TAKING A PRISONER

One day, an enemy plane from Taiwan was discovered on the Fukien front. Our Air Force took off at once to do battle with the enemy plane. The rat-tat-tat of gunfire sounded from the sky. In less than three minutes the enemy plane was spiraling to earth spewing black smoke.

A white parachute suddenly appeared in the sky and fell slowly toward the earth. The pilot of the enemy plane had bailed out. Then the Militia men, who were working in the fields, grabbed their guns and surrounded him. As they ran, they shouted in loud voices: "Capture him! Capture him!"

The enemy airman had barely touched the ground before he was surrounded. The Militia men shouted in loud voices: "Don't move! Raise your hands!" The enemy airman was shaking with fear from head to toe. He hadn't expected that the Militia would be everywhere, and he raised his hands and surrendered at once.

A prisoner had been captured. Everyone was very happy, saying: "We have a strong Liberation Army, and we have a strong Militia too. Wherever the enemy appears, we will annihilate him."

TWENTY-TWO. LENIN'S OVERCOAT

It was winter, and although the north wind had brought a blizzard, Lenin was still wearing an old overcoat. He had been wearing the same old overcoat for many years, and it was patched in many places. His comrades, fearing that Lenin was cold, advised him to exchange it for a new one.

Lenin laughingly said: "Isn't everyone equally cold? Some of you don't have even old overcoats!"

Later, the Revolution was victorious. Some of his comrades said: "Comrade Lenin's overcoat can be put into the Revolutionary Museum."

One day, a comrade saw the old overcoat that Lenin was wearing and said to Lenin: "Comrade Lenin, please put on a new overcoat at once. Otherwise you will become sick from the cold."

Lenin grasped his comrade's hand firmly and said: "You think, then, that since the Revolution has been victorious we ought to dress a little better? True, the Revolution has been victorious, but we must still labor at construction. We must use our money for construction. What difference does it make if the clothes we wear are a little old?"

TWENTY-FOUR. DIALOGUE OF THE TABLE AND THE CHAIR

One morning, Hsiao Hua was the first to arrive at school. When he reached the classroom door, he could hear the chair on which he sat speaking. Then, he heard his table and chair start to talk.

The table said: "Brother Chair, why are you gasping?"

The chair said: "Ai! When my master sits on me, he shakes back and forth and hurts my legs. They really hurt!"

The table said: "Brother Chair, he is very bad to me too. Yesterday he cut into me several times with his knife, and it still hurts!"

At that time, the surrounding tables and chairs all became very angry. One table said: "Our masters wouldn't be like that. They all take care of us and have never hurt us. That's because they know that Uncle Laborer has to spend a lot of time to make tables and chairs. They also know that it is not easy to find wood to make tables and chairs."

As Hsiao Hua listened, he lowered his head and his face turned red.

TWENTY-SIX. MAN HAS TWO TREASURES

Man has two treasures,
A pair of hands and a brain.
With his hands he can work;
With his brain he can think.
Using the hands but not the brain,
Work cannot be done well.

Using the brain but not the hands,
There's nothing but a string of fantasies.
Using the hands together with the brain,
There then can be creation.
All creation depends on labor;
Labor must depend on the hands and the brain.

Read the text aloud. Memorize and recite the text.

TWENTY-EIGHT. WHY DOES THE POT COVER MOVE?

In England more than two hundred years ago there was the son of a laborer by the name of Watt.

One day when Watt was little, he saw a pot of water boiling on the stove. The pot cover was continually bouncing up with a pa-pa-pa sound. Watt watched inquisitively for a long time but could not figure out the reason for it. So he asked his grandmother: "What makes the pot cover bounce?"

His grandmother said: "When the water boils, the pot cover bounces."

Watt asked: "Why does the pot cover bounce when the water is boiling? What is it that's pushing it?"

His grandmother answered: "Who knows?"

After that, Watt often sat by the side of the stove and watched carefully. He saw that when the water was boiling, the steam in the pot rose and came out. He thought: it must surely be the steam that makes the pot cover move. He also thought: since the steam in the pot makes the cover move, if one used a very large kettle to boil water and made even more steam, wouldn't it be possible to move even heavier things.

Watt grew up, all the while thinking about how he could make use of steam. He conducted many experiments, studied the experiments of others, and invented the steam engine.

THIRTY-TWO. VISITING A STEEL PLANT

The teacher took us to a steel plant for a visit. The steel plant had very large buildings and very tall smoke stacks that could be seen from a great distance.

We first visited the refining room. As soon as we entered, we saw the smelting furnace spitting out red flames. The workmen were wearing white protective clothing and white protective caps. Some were also wearing blue protective glasses. The workmen who were wearing protective glasses were looking at the molten steel in the furnace. Everyone's face was red from the flames of the furnace.

A bell rang. The furnace chief walked up to the front of the furnace, raised his hands and said: "Pour the steel!" The flaming molten steel poured out, spurting hundreds of thousands of sparks.

We also visited other workshops and saw the workmen each busy at work. The Uncle Workman who was guiding us said: "We must smelt even more good steel to support agriculture and to hasten the establishment of Socialism!"

THIRTY-SIX. THE ANT AND THE CRICKET

As soon as autumn arrived, the ant began to busy himself, looking here and searching there to prepare food for the winter. The cricket saw him and said: "Brother Ant, the weather is so nice. Why don't we enjoy ourselves together?"

The ant said: "No, winter will soon be here and I want to prepare food to get through the winter. You ought to make some early preparations too."

The cricket said unhappily: "It's still early! Winter isn't here yet. Why be so hasty?"

The ant said: "If you don't prepare food now, you'll suffer from hunger this winter. It will be too late to be sorry then!"

The cricket paid him no heed and sang and hopped about, going off to have a good time by himself.

Winter arrived, and the cricket, with nothing to eat, was suffering from hunger. He crawled feebly to the ant's home and said to the ant: "Brother Ant, would you lend me a little food? Things are getting worse for me every day."

The ant said: "Now you know what it's like to have a hard time. Why didn't you listen to my advice earlier?"

The cricket, in his shame, could say nothing.

THIRTY-SEVEN. A BASKET

Grandmother once used this basket
For gathering leaves and grain.
The landlord saw her and did not let her,
And tore grandmother's ragged clothes.

Grandfather once used this basket
When he drifted into the city to beg for food.
He was kicked by a foreigner's boots
And the basket kicked to the edge of the road.

Now I use this basket
When I go to the fields to labor after class.
Picking grain and singing,
I fill the basket full with golden valley grain.

THIRTY-EIGHT. HUANG-P'U PARK

On Sunday, I went with some of my classmates for an outing to Huang-p'u Park. When we were tired from our play, we sat down on a long bench and watched the steamships on the Huang-P'u River. Then my grandfather came. We stood up at once and asked grandfather to sit down with us.

I said: "Grandfather, when you were small did you come here to play often?"

Grandfather said: "Did I come here to play when I was little? You're dreaming! At that time, Shanghai was an empire of the Imperialists. There was a sign hanging over the gate of this park with the words 'Chinamen and dogs keep out' written on it! They were so tyrannical that they didn't even consider us Chinese to be human."

When we had heard this, we were all extremely angry. Grandfather continued: "But that's in the past. Now that we are liberated, the Imperialists have been driven out. The New China is so strong that no one can ever again come to bully her." I said to grandfather: "If anyone dares to come to persecute us we'll beat them till blood flows from their heads!"

Grandfather said: "Right! That's how it ought to be. The people of many countries in the world are still suffering the persecution of the Imperialists, and we must join together with them to oppose Imperialism."

THIRTY-NINE. LIFE IN OUR FAMILY BEFORE THE LIBERATION

Before the Liberation, life was very hard for our family. According to Mother, the room where we lived was run-down and leaked, and sunshine never came into the room. No one in the family had enough to eat or wear, and we often suffered from hunger and cold.

Mother washed clothes for people from morning until night. There was no money in the house. My older brother could not go to school and went out every day to pick up cinders.

Father was a workman in a coal mine. His monthly wages were pitifully low, but he worked very hard, some ten hours a day. He dug out coal in the dark pits, using an open basket to carry out the coal on his back. The air in the mine shaft was extremely bad, and he could not stand it, and often fainted. Capitalists know only how to exploit workers and don't care whether they live or die.

Father did not get home from work each day until late at night. His health grew continually worse and he often spat blood. There was no money for seeing a doctor. One year before the Liberation, he died.

FORTY. WE MOVE INTO A NEW LABORERS' VILLAGE

After the Liberation, our life improved from year to year. My older brother worked in the coal mine, while I entered the mine's elementary school for dependents.

One evening older brother came home from the mine, and as soon as he entered the gate said: "The new village for the mine workers has been completed. In a few days we'll be moving in."

One Sunday morning we moved into the new laborers' village.

The new houses were built of red brick and laid out in orderly rows. The walls of the rooms were snow-white, and the window glass was very clear. How happy Mother must have been! She turned on a water faucet, and water came flowing out. She pulled an electric light switch, and lights began to shine. She laughed and said: "It's really handy." Everyone looked here and there, and if older brother had not called us, we would have almost forgotten to put the pile of things we had moved into order.

The whole family was busy all day. In the evening, we turned on the electric lights and sat in the bright room. Mother said over and over: "Think of how we used to live and how we're living now!"

SELECTIONS FROM VOLUME 4 OF THE READERS

(GRADE TWO)

FOUR. PLUGGING A HOLE

One autumn day toward evening, three elementary school pupils were coming home from school along the bank of a drainage ditch. Suddenly they heard the sound of flowing water. They looked and saw that there was a leak in the embankment. A stream of water was flowing from the leak and pouring out into the fields.

They were very worried. One of them ran off to tell the production team, while the other two jumped down from the embankment and hastily plugged the leak with mud. The water was very swift, and the leak grew bigger and bigger so that it could not be plugged. The two of them took off their clothes, rolled them up, and stuffed them into the leak. They also pressed their backs up against the hole and stopped the water.

The water was very cold, and the evening wind was blowing with a howl. The two shivered from the cold, but they kept at it, taking turns at pressing their backs to the hole.

After a while, the commune members received the report and hurried up. Everyone joined together in repairing the embankment.

The elementary school pupil who went to report was tired and out of breath, and everyone told him to rest. The two elementary school pupils who had plugged the hole were covered all over with mud. The commune members hurriedly pulled them up onto the embankment and gave them a change of clothes.

The embankment was repaired. On the way home, the production team chief praised them, saying: "You are really good boys.

If it weren't for you, the embankment would have been destroyed. Who knows how many crops would have been flooded and destroyed!"

SIX. HOW TO WRITE A DIARY

A diary is a record of our daily lives. However, it is only the more significant things that are material for a diary. What we have, what we have heard, what we have done, the books we have read, school activities, and events at home can all be written in a diary.

We should be selective about what we write in a diary. It's not important that there be a great deal, but it must be significant. It is all right either to write about only one event or to write about a few impressions.

In writing a diary, the date and the weather should be written down. Sentences should be smooth, and characters should be written clearly.

There are many advantages to writing a diary:

First, writing a diary every day gives daily practice in composition. With diligent practice, progress is quick and it is of very great help in composition.

Second, we can check over, at our convenience, what we have done right and what we have done wrong and can keep an eye on our progress.

Third, writing important things in a diary can be a help to our memories. If we have forgotten something, we can open the diary and find out what it was.

TEN. PLANTING CASTOR PLANTS

On the first day of April after school let out, we did not return home at once but did an interesting piece of work at school. We planted castor plants.

On an empty spot at the south side of the classroom, we got a piece of land ready. We buried the castor plant seeds in the ground and covered them with a layer of fine earth.

The next day, as soon as we got to school we ran out to see whether the castor plants had come up. The surface of the earth was the same as it was the day before. All we could see was earth, and nothing else. For the next several days we all went to look, but still all we saw was the earth. One of our classmates said: "Why haven't the castor plants come up yet?" The teacher said: "It's still early. You'll just have to wait patiently. It will probably take about half a month before they come up. Now the seeds are swelling in the ground."

One morning I saw that a few sprouts had come up through the earth. The sprouts had a pair of delicate leaves. I called out happily: "The castor plants have come up!" My classmates all crowded around to look.

The castor plants grew taller day by day until they were taller than the teacher. Each large leaf was like an opened hand. At this time, the castor plants blossomed, putting out strings of small light red flowers.

A few more days passed, and the castor plants bore fruit. Each fruit had three seeds.

When autumn came, we gathered many castor beans. The teacher told us to pick out some big, bright, full ones to serve as seeds. The teacher said: "We'll plant them next year."

ELEVEN. A STORY ABOUT PRACTICING CHARACTERS

Wang Hsi-chih was a famous calligrapher of ancient China. His accomplishments were attained through diligent study and practice.

Wang Hsi-chih was practicing writing characters at the age of seven. When he got to be eleven or twelve years old, he could already write characters very well. But he was not at all satisfied with himself. One day, he found a book on calligraphy in his father's room, which he took down and read. His father saw him and said: "You're still little. Wait until you have grown up and I will teach you." Wang Hsi-chih said: "Father, please teach me now. If I study when I'm grown up, won't it be too late?" His father then talked to him about the principles in the book. After this, his progress was even more rapid.

Wang Hsi-chih practiced writing characters every day without letup. Each time he finished writing, he took the brush and ink-slab to the pond in front of the gate to wash them. As time wore on, the water in the pond turned black.

Wang Hsien-chih was the son of Wang Hsi-chih, and he also practiced writing from the time he was little. One day, as he was practicing writing characters, Wang Hsi-chih walked softly up behind him and grabbed at the brush in his hand, but could not shake it loose. When Wang Hsien-chih wrote characters, he usually held the brush with a great deal of strength. At that time, Wang Hsien-chih was seven or eight years old and was as determined as that about practicing his writing. Later, the more he practiced, the better he got, and he ended up becoming as famous a calligrapher as his father. Everyone called the father and son the "Two Kings." (A play on words, the surname "Wang" also meaning "King."—Trans.)

TWELVE. GRINDING A PIECE OF IRON INTO A NEEDLE

Over a thousand years ago, there was a poet named Li Po. When Li Po was little he was fond of playing and afraid of hardship, so that he made very little progress in his studies.

One day, Li Po was walking by the side of a small stream when he saw a white haired old woman squatting beside a rock grinding a piece of iron and dipping it into the water. He felt that this was very strange and went up to the old woman and asked: "Auntie, why are you grinding this piece of iron?"

The old woman said: "To make a needle."

Li Po thought this was even stranger. "To make a needle? How can a piece of iron be ground into a needle?"

The old woman said: "It can, indeed it can. All you need is perseverance. If you do not fear hardship, a piece of iron can be ground into a needle."

Li Po listened to what the old woman said and understood the truth that no matter what one is doing one must have perseverance and that one must work hard. The more he thought the more ashamed he was. How could anyone like him, who liked to play and who feared hardship, ever be able to make any progress in his studies?

From that time on, Li Po studied hard and his progress was very rapid.

FOURTEEN. OUR GOOD FRIENDS

The swallow, who eats harmful insects, is one of our good friends. There are also many other birds that are our good friends.

One horned owl will eat more than a thousand field mice a year. One field mouse will spoil five or six catties of food a year. On this basis, we can calculate that one horned owl saves us five or six thousand catties of food a year. There are people who say that when a horned owl cries, someone will die. That is superstitious talk and shouldn't be believed.

The titmouse eats harmful insects on fruit trees as well as harmful insects on other kinds of trees. When the titmouse hatches its young, it catches insects to feed them. It feeds them more than a hundred times a day and destroys a good many harmful insects for us.

The cuckoo and the oriole like to eat all kinds of harmful insects. The thrush and the starling also like to eat all kinds of harmful insects. They are all of great benefit to trees and crops.

The swallow, the horned owl, the titmouse, the cuckoo, and the oriole are all beneficial birds. We should protect beneficial birds.

EIGHTEEN. THE SWALLOWS RETURN

Spring had come, and a little swallow was flying back north with his mother.

They were flying past a high mountain. A highway wound round the mountain, and on the highway trucks were coming and going. The little swallow said: "Mama, last year when we flew past this mountain, there wasn't any highway on the mountain and there weren't any trucks. We haven't lost our way, have we?"

His mother said: "Child, there's no mistake. The people have built a highway on the mountain, and the mountain has changed in appearance."

They flew past a large river. An iron bridge had been built over the river, and trains belching forth white smoke were crossing the bridge. The little swallow said: "Mama, last year when we flew past this river, there was no iron bridge over the river and there were no trains. We haven't lost our way, have we?" His mother said: "Child, there's no mistake. The people have built an iron bridge over the river. The river has changed in appearance."

They flew over a plain. On the plain were rows on rows of buildings and also many tall smokestacks. The little swallow said: "Mama, last year when we flew over this plain, where were all these buildings and smokestacks? We must have lost our way." His mother said: "Child, there is no mistake. The people have built factories on the plain. The plain has changed in appearance."

The little swallow flew along with his mother to the place they had lived the year before. They flew around over a new house. The little swallow said: "Mama, we've gone to the wrong house. Where we lived last year there was no new house like this." His mother said: "Child, there is no mistake. Look, don't you know everyone inside?"

When the children in the room saw that the swallows had flown back, they all ran outside to welcome them, clapping their hands and saying: "Our old friends have come back."

TWENTY-ONE. LITTLE HAMMER

At the time of the War of Resistance against Japan, there was in one of the militia units a young militiaman called Little Hammer. Little Hammer was then only fifteen years old. He was short and very sturdy. The militia unit chief often asked him to serve as a spy to go out and search for information.

Once, Little Hammer dressed up as a shepherd and was driving two sheep toward the base of South Mountain in order to stand watch. When he saw the enemy coming, he drove the sheep back hastily to report the news.

When the people in the village heard the news, they moved at once, leaving behind only their spy, Little Hammer.

The enemy pushed into the village. Little Hammer climbed on

top of the wall of the Li family's courtyard and got a clear view of the enemy's numbers and arms. He was just turning around, when he saw a Japanese officer holding a rifle jump down from a big white horse. Little Hammer calmly walked up and said to the officer: "There's grass in the courtyard. Why don't you go in and feed the horse? I'll go and get some water for you to give the horse to drink." The officer went into the Li family's courtyard, and Little Hammer went to get some water.

There was very little grass, and it wasn't enough for the horse to eat. Little Hammer said: "The horse is very hungry. Why don't I lead him out to eat some grass?" The officer struck Little Hammer's head with his rifle barrel and said angrily: "Feed my horse well, but if you deceive the Imperial Army, I'll kill you!" Little Hammer agreed and led the horse out of the courtyard to the rear of the house.

At the rear of the house was a strip of kaoliang. Little Hammer mounted the horse, rode through the strip of kaoliang, and raced straight into a gully. He raced up a low slope and then heard the sound of a rifle behind him.

Little Hammer, riding the big white horse, returned to his militia unit.

TWENTY-FOUR. THE GOLD AND SILVER SHIELD

Once there were two generals who went out together to buy a shield. The artisan who made shields took out a shield, showing one side to the left and one side to the right so that the two generals, who were standing at his sides, could see it.

The general standing at his left looked at the shield and said: "This golden shield is excellent." The general standing at his right also looked at the shield and said: "You're wrong! What golden shield? This is a silver shield." The general standing at his left said stubbornly: "It's you who are wrong, not I! This shield is clearly golden. How can you say it's silver?" The two generals began to argue, arguing until their faces and ears were red.

The artisan turned the shield around and said: "You're both wrong. Look, one side of this shield is golden and one side is silver. You looked only at one side and didn't look at both sides. Therefore, you were both wrong."

THIRTY-ONE. THE DAY KUO-HUA JOINED THE PIONEERS

Kuo-hua got up early. He looked in the mirror. His newly cut hair and his freshly washed white shirt and blue shorts were neat and clean. Everything was in order, and the hands of the clock were just pointing to seven. He set out with great strides, walking happily toward school.

This was Kuo-hua's day to join the Pioneers. He remembered what the director had said to him, that he wanted him to be an outstanding Pioneer member and to protect the honor of the Pioneers at all times.

The sun was pleasantly warm and the weather excellent. Kuo-hua felt that today everything all around him was especially likeable and especially close. The travelers seemed to be smiling at him, the trees seemed to be beckoning to him, and the roads too appeared genial.

He was walking along when he suddenly saw a book on the ground. When he picked it up he saw that it was a language textbook, and on it was written "Lin-chiang Elementary School, Grade One, Class A, Wang Ta-kang."

Kuo-hua thought: by now Wang Ta-kang must have discovered that he had lost his textbook and must be worried. Without his textbook, how could he go to class? A Pioneer ought to help others. Could he see the book without doing anything about it? But, if he took the textbook back to him and then went to school, he might be late. What should he do?

He hesitated for a moment. Finally he took the book and ran off in the direction of the Lin-chiang Elementary School.

When he reached the Lin-chiang Elementary School, he handed the textbook over to the person in charge of the message room, saying: "I picked this up on the road. Please give it to classmate Wang Ta-kang in Grade One, Class A." The person in charge glanced at the textbook. He raised his head to ask Kuo-hua what school he was from, but Kuo-hua was already well on his way.

Kuo-hua ran back to school very quickly, running until his whole body was hot and his face was covered with sweat. He had just gone through the school gate when the bell sounded. His heart was pounding hard, his legs ached, and he was very tired. But he felt a happiness that he could not express, because on the day that he was to join the Pioneers he had done the kind of thing that a Pioneer ought to do.

FORTY. THE STORY OF SISTER LI CH'UN-HUA

When I was little, my family was very poor, and often we could not get food to eat. Everyone in the family was so hungry that our faces were yellow and our flesh wasted away. One day, I was so hungry I cried. My mother said: "Ch'un-hua, don't cry. Mother will go and dig up a few wild vegetables and cook them for you to eat!" She couldn't keep from crying as she spoke.

The year that I was ten years old, our family couldn't pay the rent, so the landlord forced my mother to send me to his house to work. In the landlord's house, I looked after the children, washed clothes, made tea, and poured water. I got up every day at the fifth watch (3 to 5 a.m.—Trans.). I was as tired as a rice sprout during a drought and couldn't raise my head. I was often beaten and cursed. One day I ran away home secretly and said to my mother: "Mother, I'm not going back again." When my mother saw me, my body covered with scars and so thin I didn't look like myself, she was so sad she couldn't speak. The landlord found out and came at once, forcing me to return to his house.

When the Communist Party came, the landlord was overthrown. Paddy land and a house were distributed to my family. Things changed for the poor people. They didn't have to worry about food or clothing, and life got better from day to day.

One day, when my mother said she wanted to send me to school, I was so happy that I began to jump up and down. I thought of the old days when only the children of landlord families went to school. When would I ever have gone to school? After the Liberation I had books to read. Why wouldn't I have been happy?

After I finished school I worked in an agricultural cooperative.

When the communes were set up, I studied how to run a tractor and became a tractor driver. I am very grateful to the Party and to Chairman Mao. I will certainly labor actively and strive for production.

What changes were there in the life of sister Li Ch'un-hua before and after the Liberation?

SELECTIONS FROM VOLUME 5 OF THE READERS

(GRADE THREE)

ONE. SUMMER HAS GONE BY

Summer has gone by,
But I am still thinking of it.
Those delightful dawns and dusks
Appear before my eyes like a picture scroll.

Rising early, I opened my window and looked out.
The fields and meadows were green, and the sky was blue.
I thanked the night rain
For washing the earth so fresh and clean.

With the eye-dazzling sun shining on our heads,
We pulled weeds in the vegetable garden.
The old man in charge of the vegetable garden brought out a
    bucket of water for tea
And praised us for how fast and how well we were working.

Beneath the old elm there was a good place
Where I often rested and cooled myself.
I stretched out my legs to the little stream beside the tree,
And listened to the sounds of singing from the tree.

Once we spent the night in the melon patch;
Even at midnight no one wanted to go home to sleep.
We caught three little thieves,
Whose names were hedgehog.

Those delightful dawns and dusks
Appear before my eyes like a picture scroll.
Summer has gone by,
But I am still thinking of it.

Read the poem aloud.
Discuss the event that made you happiest during summer vacation.

TWO. PULLING WEEDS

Today the teacher took us out to take part in labor. First we looked for the production team chief. The team chief said: "It's good that you've come. The vegetable plot needs weeding. Why don't you weed it?"

We followed the team chief to the vegetable plot. The team chief told us that vegetable plots should be weeded regularly. If they aren't weeded, the weeds absorb the nutrients in the soil, and the growth of the vegetables is slowed. The team chief also said: "There are three points you should pay attention to when weeding: first, you should weed clean; second, you shouldn't hurt the sprouts; third, you should pile up the weeds that you've pulled."

Next, the teacher split us up into two groups, one group weeding in the turnip patch and one group weeding in the cabbage patch.

The labor began. Our two groups weeded very quickly and very cleanly. Where we had weeded, not one weed remained. We weeded until our hands were red and our legs ached, but everyone kept on working as hard as before because we were striving for a rich agricultural harvest.

The weeds in the turnip and cabbage patches had all been pulled out! It was time to eat. How tasty food is after one has labored!

Have you ever weeded in a vegetable plot? Discuss what you should pay attention to.

SIX. GATHERING RICE

Kuei-chen and Hsiao-chin were about to go out to the fields to play when they saw the team truck filled with husk rice coming towards them along the highway.

Suddenly they heard sounds of talk and laughter in the distance. They looked and saw that there were many children and Pioneers wearing red scarfs in a field where the harvesting of rice had just been completed.

Hsiao-chin asked Kuei-chen: "Why have all the elementary school pupils in our village come out to the fields? Have they come to help load the truck?"

Kuei-chen said: "No, they have come to gather rice."

Hsiao-chin said: "Let's go and gather some too!"

Then they ran to the field together.

The elementary school pupils who were gathering rice were moving forward together in rows gathering the fallen rice. Some of them put it into small baskets, and some put it into sacks.

Hsu Wei-min was the first to see Kuei-chen and Hsiao-chin. He said in a loud voice: "Kuei-chen and Hsiao-chin have come!" The other pupils all said: "Welcome! Welcome!"

Then the leader of the Pioneers walked over and said to everybody: "Kuei-chen and Hsiao-chin are still too young for school, but even they know enough to care about food and have come to help gather rice. They are really good children." She also said: "Let Kuei-chen and Hsiao-chin work with you. Everyone look carefully. When you see a shoot, pick it and don't drop even one, so that all the crop in our field will be harvested."

After a while, Hsiao-chin said anxiously: "I've cut a few, and one was broken. How come I've gathered so little?"

Kuei-chen patted his sack and said: "I haven't gathered much either."

The leader heard them and said with a laugh: "If you haven't gathered much, that's because the commune members have gathered it so carefully!"

Why didn't the pupils gather much rice? Read the text aloud, paying attention to the wording and expression.

SEVEN. AUTUMN IN PEKING

Peking is a beautiful city. When autumn comes it is even more beautiful.

When one climbs Ching Shan and stands at its highest point, the sky is a transparent blue, like blue glass that has just been washed with water. White doves, cooing and whistling, fly through the sky in flocks past ancient palaces and newly constructed buildings.

There are trees everywhere in the city of Peking. The rows of imposing big buildings are unusually beautiful under the golden sunlight. In the distance, big smokestacks of factories send out blue smoke. The smoke rises slowly, mingling with the white clouds.

In the parks, one can smell the fragrance of cassia blossoms and see chrysanthemums in full bloom. The leaves of the trees gradually turn yellow, and sometimes a light breeze blows, a few leaves falling from the trees.

On the outskirts, the rice is golden and the cotton blossoms are snow white. The grapes are ripe. The dates are red and the persimmons are yellow. All of this tells everyone that a rich harvest season has arrived.

When National Day draws near all Peking puts on a new holiday dress. Big red temple lanterns are hung from T'ien An Gate, and the Great Hall of the People and many neighboring buildings are all decorated with strings of electric lights. At night, it seems like a palace inlaid with pearls. Everywhere on the streets colored memorial gateways and big, high slogan placards can be seen. The people, in order to celebrate the great festival of their motherland, have dressed their capital city up to be even more beautiful.

What scenery can one see when looking at Peking from Ching Shan?

EIGHT. NATIONAL DAY

On National Day our school held a celebration.

The meeting place was the athletic field, on the south end of which we built a pine memorial gate and on the north end of which we built a speakers' platform. Two national flags were hung from the speakers' platform, and between them was a picture of Chairman Mao. In front of the platform, flowers of various colors were set.

The people taking part in the celebration arrived one after the other. Our classmates were all dressed neat and clean. The scarfs of the Pioneers looked especially fresh in the sunlight. The principal wore a golden advanced workers commemorative medal on his blue uniform. The commune manager came and many heads of households also came. They celebrated National Day with us and also wanted to watch us perform.

At three o'clock in the afternoon, the celebration began. Everyone sang the national anthem. There was an especially large number of people that day, and the singing was especially loud.

The principal spoke first. He spoke of the great accomplishments of socialist re-construction in our motherland. He encouraged us to study hard, to advance upward day by day, to build good bodies, to do our lessons well, to build a good character, and to labor well in preparation to serve our motherland.

Next, the commune manager spoke. He said that this year our commune had reaped a rich agricultural harvest and that the pupils had given a lot of effort to it.

Teacher Yin told us the story of the revolutionary struggle at Chingkang Mountain. He told us that the happy life of today was won only after many hard battles. Everyone should study the spirit of the revolutionary martyrs' hard struggles. Ch'ien Li's father is a model agricultural laborer and went to Peking last year to take part in the National Day ceremonies. The principal asked him to tell about National Day at Peking.

Next, the performance began. There was group singing, dancing, recitations of songs and poems, and little operas. Finally, everyone sang together "Socialism is Good."

From what places in the text can a view of the festival day be found? Tell how National Day was celebrated at your school this year.

NINE. CHAIRMAN MAO IS LIKE THE SUN

Chairman Mao, like the sun,
Shines bright and clear in all directions.

When you are here in spring, all the flowers are fragrant,
The wheat is green and the rape is yellow.

When you are here in summer, the growing rice flourishes;
A hundred thousand *mou* of fields and gardens put on a new
    dress.

When you are here in autumn, there is a good harvest,
And golden kernels of grain are piled high in the granaries.

When you are here in winter, we're not afraid of the cold,
And in the cold of the twelfth month, we are pleasantly warm.

We respect and love you, our leader Chairman Mao:
Your grace will never be forgotten.

TEN. CHU TEH'S CARRYING POLE

In 1928, Comrade Chu Teh led the Red Army to Chingkang
Mountain to join forces with Chairman Mao. The Red Army was
on the mountain, and the enemy was not far from the foot of the
mountain.

The Red Army wanted to hold the Chingkang Mountain base
and smash the enemy encirclement, so they had to stock sufficient
supplies of food. Not much food was produced on Chingkang
Mountain, and it was often necessary to pick out people to go to
Maop'ing to carry food back. It was 50 or 60 *li* from Chingkang
Mountain to Maop'ing. The mountain was high, and the roads
were steep and difficult to travel. Nevertheless, each time food
had to be carried, everyone vied with each other to go.

Comrade Chu Teh also went together with the soldiers to carry
food. Wearing straw sandals and a rain hat, he climbed up the
mountain with everyone else, carrying a full load of food.
Everyone thought that Comrade Chu Teh must be overtired,
working as busily as he did and also climbing the mountain
carrying food. Everyone urged him not to do any carrying, but he
didn't agree. Then one of his comrades hid his carrying pole. But
unexpectedly Comrade Chu Teh found another carrying pole and
wrote on it the characters: "Chu Teh's." When everyone saw this,
they respected Comrade Chu Teh but with embarrassment once
again hid his carrying pole.

Why did they hide Comrade Chu Teh's carrying pole?

FIFTEEN. THOUSAND-MAN-CAKE

One day, I went to my uncle's house. My uncle said to me: "Tomorrow afternoon I'm inviting you to eat thousand-man-cake. This cake goes through more than a thousand hands before it is completed." I thought that a cake made by more than a thousand people must certainly be as big as a house. I asked my uncle: "What is a thousand-man-cake like?" My uncle said: "You'll find out tomorrow."

The next afternoon after school, I ran very quickly to my uncle's house. As soon as I went through the door, I looked around thinking that I would see what the thousand-man-cake was like and how my uncle had prepared it. But there was no activity at all. I felt that this was very strange and wanted to take a look in the kitchen. My uncle said: "There's no use in going. The cake has already been made." As he spoke, my aunt brought out a plate of ordinary date cake. I asked hastily: "Is this thousand-man-cake?"

My uncle laughed and said: "This is thousand-man-cake. Do you know how this piece of date cake was made? To make cake, you need flour. Flour is ground from rice, and rice is husked from rice plants, which are planted by farmers. Figure now, how many hands did it go through from planting to the grinding of the flour? To plant rice, you need ploughs, and ploughs are made by iron-workers. How many hands do they have to go through from mining and refining to casting of the plough? To grind flour you need a mill, and mills are made by stonemasons. How many people's hands must it go through for this? To steam the cake, you need a steaming basket and a steaming basket is made of bamboo and wood. How many hands are needed to cut down the bamboo and saw the wood to make the steaming basket? Besides these, there are dates in the cake. How many people are needed to plant the date trees and transport the dates?"

Uncle continued: "There's still more. For us to steam the cake, miners are needed to supply the coal and iron workers are needed to supply the pot. When the cake is being steamed, cloth is needed on the bottom. And speaking of cloth, think of the people who plant the cotton, the people who pick the cotton, the people who spin the thread, the people who weave the cloth, and the people who make the spinning machines ... you really never realized how many people were needed! Think carefully. If it hadn't been for all those people laboring, could you be eating this piece of date cake?"

After I had listened to my uncle's story, I understood that a piece of cake or a bowl of rice depended on the labor of many people.

Read the text aloud. Discuss why an ordinary piece of date cake is called "thousand-man-cake."

EIGHTEEN. I LOVE OUR GREAT MOTHERLAND

I love our great motherland.
How vast and broad is our motherland.
I love our great motherland.
How flourishing and powerful is our motherland.

The Himalaya Mountains pierce the clouds;
The waters of the Yangtze River are vast.
Dams and power stations are scattered like stars;
Railroads and highways are as dense as spiders' webs.

I love the countless factories;
The sound of machinery has a rhythmic song
As they refine millions of tons of fine steel
And build millions of precision machine tools.

I love the fertile fields;
Tractors are busy day and night;
The gathered grain is piled high as mountains;
And everywhere are sung the songs of rich harvests.

I love our great motherland.
The Party and Chairman Mao nurture us as we grow.
We must study hard and labor hard
To build our motherland into a paradise of Communism.

Discuss systematically what facts are presented in this poem to show the greatness of our motherland. Memorize the poem. Write out the third and fourth stanzas.

TWENTY. GIVING LENIN SOMETHING TO EAT

Time:	A clear morning
Place:	The Kremlin, Moscow

Dramatis personae:

> Lenin. A woman secretary. A fisherman.

Setting:	An office with simple and neat furnishings. A long table, two chairs. On the table are official papers, a plate of black bread, and a cup of tea. Hanging on the wall are a big map and a telephone.
	(When the curtain opens, Lenin is sitting at the table having breakfast. A woman secretary enters.)
Secretary:	Comrade Lenin, there is a fisherman here who runs a fish business. He wants to see you.
Lenin:	Ask him to come in.
	(The secretary goes out. The fisherman enters. The fisherman is very hearty and is carrying a satchel in his hands.)
Fisherman:	Good morning, Comrade Lenin!
Lenin:	Thank you. Please have a seat.
Fisherman:	I have some important business that I want to talk over with you.
Lenin:	Fine. Please sit down and talk.
Fisherman:	The government wants us to improve the fishing industry, and I am naturally very happy. But there are many difficulties, and the work has not been accomplished. This makes me feel very ashamed.

Lenin:	Whatever difficulties there are, the government will certainly help you solve them.
Fisherman:	We've got to add to our fishing nets and repair the boats. Our problem right now is that we don't have any money.
Lenin:	Please don't worry. Although the government is having its difficulties too, money has already been set aside for this sort of thing.
Fisherman:	(Pauses for a moment, looking at the food on the table.) Ah, Comrade Lenin, how is it that you're eating black bread? You don't even have any butter!
Lenin:	(Smiling) Life is hard for everyone in the country now and no one is eating well. How could I allow only myself to eat well?
Fisherman:	My beloved Comrade Lenin, I'd like to give you a little something. (Opens his satchel.) Please accept this piece of fish.
Lenin:	It ... I can't accept it.
Fisherman:	I've brought it especially for you, and I certainly want you to accept it.
Lenin:	Thank you for your kind intentions, Comrade, but I can't ...
Fisherman:	You must accept it.
Lenin:	No, I can't. Think, life is hard for everyone in the country now. How could I allow myself only to eat well?
Fisherman:	You musn't say that. Comrade Lenin, you are serving everyone and have suffered a great deal. You should take care of your health! Whether you want to accept it or not, I would be happy if you would.
	(The fisherman asks him several times. Lenin presses his buzzer. The secretary comes in.)
Lenin:	Let's handle it this way. (To his secretary) Please take this piece of fish and send it to the kindergarten for the children to eat.

Secretary:	Yes. (Takes the fish and goes out.)
Lenin:	Comrade, let me thank you on behalf of the students.
Fisherman:	(Moved so that he cannot speak for a moment; then, after a moment) I must go.
Lenin:	After you go back, I hope that you will work hard. If you have any difficulties, the government will solve them for you. But if you come again, please be sure not to bring any gifts for me.
Fisherman:	Beloved Comrade Lenin, goodby.

(The curtain falls.)

Why did the fisherman want to give the fish to Comrade Lenin? How did Lenin handle the situation? Read the play aloud with different people taking the parts.

TWENTY-THREE. A BEAN'S JOURNEY

I am a little bean. Together with my comrades, I left a basket of beans, going first into a cooking pot and next onto a plate. Next, someone set me on a table. I was picked up by a pair of chopsticks and put into someone's mouth. In a person's mouth there are two rows of teeth. When the teeth chew, a great deal of saliva is secreted into the mouth, mixing the food together. This person ate so fast that he swallowed me without chewing me up.

I went down through the esophagus and came into a very spacious place. That place was the stomach. The stomach never stopped wriggling. My comrades who had been chewed up finely had all turned into a paste. But even after I had been there for several hours, I was still the same as before.

Going on from the stomach, I came to a winding tube. This tube was the small intestine. When my comrades got to the small intestine, they were all absorbed and sent out to every part of the person's body. I, who had not been chewed finely, made the journey in vain and, together with the other refuse, went along through the large intestine and came out the anus.

TWENTY-FIVE. INFORMAL NOTES

Informal receipts:

Today received:
The Battalion Headquarters of the Kang-Chuang Elementary School Pioneers delivered 148 catties of locust tree seeds and 69 catties of cypress tree seeds. These have been received.
> Youth Corps Committee, Hung Hsing
> People's Commune
> Ts'ai Yu-min, Manager
> October 24, 1960

Note of receipt:

Today received:
One steam engine, two chaff cutters.

> Wang Chi-hsien, Chief, Kang Chuang
> Production Team
> September 24, 1960

Borrowing note:

Today borrowed:
From the General Affairs Section, seven brooms, two winnowing fans, five cloths. Will return them as soon as finished.

> Lu Wen-hui, third grade
> April 29, 1962

TWENTY-SEVEN. I'LL WAIT A WHILE

Once upon a time there was a man who bought two big baskets of porcelain in the city and was carrying them home on his donkey.

At noon, he went into a small shop to have something to drink and to eat. The manager of the shop saw that the donkey's harness was twisted, and he said to the man: "The harness is twisted; you'd better fix it in a hurry!" He said: I'll wait a while. There's only about 20 miles to go before I'll be home, and it isn't causing any trouble." After he had finished eating, he went off, driving the donkey carelessly.

He had gone about ten miles when someone on the road said to him: "The donkey's harness is twisted; you'd better fix it in a hurry!" He said: "I'll wait a while. There's only about ten miles to go before I'll be home, and it isn't causing any trouble." As before, he went off, driving the donkey carelessly.

After he had gone a few more miles, the harness became even more badly twisted. An old man saw it and said, "You'd better unload and fix it right away, or you'll have an accident!" The man said: "I'll wait a while. There's only a few miles to go before I'll be home, and it isn't causing any trouble."

A little while later, he was going over the slope of a hill. A large number of women saw him and all shouted: "You'd better unload those things in a hurry; it looks like there'll be an accident!" The man said: "I'll wait a while; there's ..." Before he finished speaking, the harness fell, and the two big baskets of porcelain were thrown down and smashed to pieces. The man stood staring at the heap of broken porcelain, not able to say a word.

What principle does this story illustrate? Do such things happen in our everyday lives?

TWENTY-EIGHT. THE WOLF AND THE CAT

Once there was a wolf that ran out of the woods. He ran with all his might toward a village. He wasn't going there as a guest or to take care of any business, but to save his life. There was a hunter, with a hunting dog, chasing after him.

He ran and ran until he came to the gate of a house in the village. But when he looked, the gate was closed. He looked further, and found that the gates of all the houses in the village were closed. He was very worried.

Suddenly he saw a cat. In bewilderment, he ran up to the cat and begged, "My good cat, please tell me at once where the kindest peasant in the village lives. I want to ask him to hide me and save me. Please tell me at once!"

When the cat saw that it was the wolf, he said, "Why don't you ask Lao-shih? He is the kindest."

The wolf said, "It won't do for me to ask Lao-shih. Once I hate one of his fat hens, and he hates me."

The cat said, "Then ask Lao Yang. He's kind too."

The wolf said, "It won't do for me to ask Lao Yang either! I stole some of his geese, and he hates me too."

The cat said, "Then try Lao Lo. He's kind too."

The wolf said, "Lao Lo? That won't do either! I chewed up one of his sheep, and he wants to beat me to death!"

The cat said, "Ai! This is bad! Perhaps Lao Chang can protect you!"

The wolf said, "Ai-ya! That's even worse! A few days ago, I ate up one of his calves."

The cat glared at him and said, "If you're always doing bad things, how can you expect anyone to protect you!"

Why didn't anyone want to protect the wolf?

Read the text aloud, expressing the differing emotions of the wolf and the cat.

TWENTY-NINE. THE AXE AND THE FUR COAT

Once upon a time, Old Father Winter had two sons. One of them was older brother Blue Nose, and the other was younger brother Red Nose.

One day the brothers were out in the open fields, running back and forth through a thick woods.

Red Nose said: "Brother Blue Nose, why don't we look for someone to freeze so that we can show our powers?"

Blue Nose answered, saying: "Right! We ought to show our powers. Brother Red Nose, let's go out to the highway. There ought to be someone there."

The two brothers started to run. They ran, jumping first on one leg and then on the other. They ran very fast, howling through the pines and cypresses.

From one direction they heard a big bell ringing and gradually drawing closer, and from another direction a small bell ringing and drawing closer. The big bell was ringing on a rich merchant's new cart that was heading toward the city. The small bell was ringing on a toiling peasant's rickety cart that was heading towards the woods.

Red Nose said: "I'll chase after that peasant. I'll be able to freeze him in no time at all. The cotton coat and the hat that he's wearing are ragged. Why don't you go after that merchant? He's wearing a bearskin hat, a foxskin coat, and wolfskin boots. I couldn't cope with him."

Blue Nose, laughing, said: "Good. Let's do it that way."

They ran off, screeching, in separate ways.

In the evening, the two met again in the open fields. Elder Brother Blue Nose's face was covered with a smile and he was clapping his hands. Younger Brother Red Nose's brows were knit, and he was panting. Red Nose asked: "How did it go? Elder Brother Blue Nose, did you freeze the merchant?"

Blue Nose answered: "I froze him. I let him go after he became numb."

Red Nose was very much surprised and said: "How did you ever manage to freeze him? He was wearing a bearskin hat, a foxskin coat, and wolfskin boots!"

Blue Nose laughed and said: "As soon as I caught up with him I went right through his fur cap, right through his fur overcoat, and right through his fur boots. He didn't even jump down from the cart to stamp his feet or rub his hands. All he did was draw his overcoat more closely around his body. I just made my way straight through it until I reached his bones. How about you? How did you handle the peasant?"

Red Nose answered: "I couldn't cope with him. I wanted to freeze him on the road, but because he was so fond of his horse, he wasn't riding it. Instead, he was running behind the horse. How could I freeze him when he was running so hard? I thought: all right, I'll wait until the woods; it won't be hard to freeze you then. But it was even worse when he got to the woods. He started cutting brushwood with his axe, and the chips kept flying into my body. The more he chopped the warmer he got, just as if he didn't know there was anybody in the world like me. He took off his ragged cotton coat and his ragged cap, put them down on the ground, and started chopping brushwood again. I thought: now he'll pay some attention to me. Then I struck at his body. I went into his nose and I went into his ears, but he wasn't in the least afraid. There was nothing for me then but to work my way through his cotton coat and his hat. I thought: as soon as he puts on his cotton coat and his hat, then he'll know how bad I, Red Nose, am. But when he had finished cutting the brushwood, he picked up a piece of the wood and started beating the snow on his ragged overcoat. He beat and beat, beating all the harder as he went on, until I could barely run. My waist still hurts."

Blue Nose shook his head, saying: "Brother, you are still young, and there's a lot you don't know yet. Stay with me for a few more days, and then you'll know that an axe is a lot warmer than an overcoat."

Why was it said that an axe is much warmer than an overcoat?

Read the story with different people taking the parts.

Divide the story into sections, writing out the main idea of each section.

THIRTY-THREE. AT THE YENAN CENTRAL HOSPITAL

One day when Chairman Mao was in Yenan, he went to the Central Hospital to see Comrade Kuan Hsiang-ying.

Comrade Kuan was lying on his sickbed, his head sunk into a pillow and his body covered with a blanket. Comrade Mao shook his hand warmly and then sat down beside his bed. The two of them talked together quietly.

Suddenly the door screen lifted, and a young nurse came in. As soon as she saw that there was someone beside the bed, she said: "Comrade, please excuse me. The doctor has ordered that Commissar Kuan needs rest and quiet and that too much talk isn't good for him."

Chairman Mao turned and, smiling, said: "Ah, I'm sorry. I didn't know that the doctor had issued such an order." As he spoke, he rose hastily, said a few words of comfort to Comrade Kuan, and then left.

In the nurse's office next door, Chairman Mao again ran into the nurse he had just met.

"Little Comrade, what is your name? And how old are you?"

"Everyone calls me Hsiao Liu, and I'm sixteen. Please sit down, Comrade."

Chairman Mao asked her in detail about the sick man's condition and said warmly to Hsiao Liu: "Little Comrade, take good care of Commissar Kuan."

After Chairman Mao had left, Hsiao Liu went back to Comrade Kuan's sickroom. As soon as she entered, Comrade Kuan laughed and said: "Hsiao Liu, do you know who it was that just came?"

"I don't know. There was a guard outside, so he must have been a leader. It doesn't matter who he was. The doctor ordered that you must have rest and quiet, and I couldn't let him disturb you."

"That's right. But didn't you know that he was Chairman Mao?"

Hsiao Liu opened her eyes wide and cried out: "Oh, Chairman Mao!"

After that, whenever Hsiao Liu met anyone she always told how courteous, friendly and respectful Chairman Mao was.

How did Chairman Mao respect the system in the hospital and in what way was his attitude friendly? Pick out and write down the words concerned with this in the text. Memorize the text.

THIRTY-FOUR. BETHUNE

Bethune was a member of the Canadian Progressive Labor Party and was also a famous doctor. In 1937, China's War of Resistance against Japan broke out. Bethune, in order to help the people of China resist Japan, led a medical team that, scaling mountains and fording rivers, came to China from 30,000 li away. He worked in the Shansi-Chahar-Hopeh Border Region at the very front lines of the Anti-Japanese War.

He feared no danger in saving the wounded, sometimes running ten miles or more an hour. When he was at the front in Hopeh, a shell fell in front of him, but he continued operating on the wounded as calmly as ever. He looked on his own life very lightly and sometimes even gave his own blood to wounded who had lost much blood.

He often said: "The wounded are dearer than brothers because they are comrades."

In November 1939, he suffered an infection while treating one of the wounded and died in a village in Wan Hsien in Hopeh. In order to commemorate this great international friend, the name of the Hygiene School in the Shansi-Chahar-Hopeh Special District was changed to "The Bethune School."

Why is it said that Bethune was a great international friend? Recite the text from memory.

THIRTY-SIX. UNCLE, PLEASE ACCEPT

How are you?
Uncle guarding the frontiers of our motherland,
Please accept this small gift.
Please accept this pair of gloves!

Uncle, accept them.
The wool from which these gloves were woven I sheared myself.
It is as fresh and clean as the red flag itself.
You will certainly like them!

Uncle, accept them.
They were woven by me, stroke by stroke.
Mother and sister all weave far better than I.
I don't know if they should be smaller;
I know the hand holding the rifle is big and strong.

Uncle, accept them.
I know your weather there;
The wind blows so cold,
And the mountains wear white through the four seasons.

The hands holding the rifle
Cannot be numb for an instant!
Uncle, wear this pair of gloves;
Wear this pair of gloves!

SELECTIONS FROM VOLUME 6 OF THE READERS

(GRADE THREE)

ONE. CHAIRMAN MAO AT THE SHIHSANLING RESERVOIR WORK SITE

May 25, 1958 was a Sunday. On that day, our beloved leader Chairman Mao, together with a good number of leadership comrades, had gone to the Shihsanling Reservoir work-site in the outskirts of Peking to take part in voluntary labor.

That afternoon, the weather was very hot. The sun was hot and high, and there wasn't a breath of wind. Chairman Mao, wearing a straw hat, together with his comrades-in-arms, was riding on a train going toward Shihsanling Reservoir.

At twenty minutes past three, the train arrived at the command post of the work-site. The news that Chairman Mao and a large number of leadership comrades were taking part in voluntary labor spread at once over the entire work-site. The people at the work-site were overjoyed. Wherever Chairman Mao went, there arose the cry of greeting: "Long live Chairman Mao!"

Chairman Mao climbed to a high place on the eastern embankment of the reservoir to see the whole view of the reservoir. Then, he ascertained the progress of the work from the man in charge of the work-site.

"Can you guarantee that it will be completed before the floods come?" Chairman Mao asked with concern.

"Indeed we can!" Commissar Chao answered with great assurance.

"How many people are there working?"

"One hundred thousand. Every day they carry 500,000 blocks of earth to the large embankment."

Our beloved Comrade Mao, like a common laborer, picked up an iron shovel and began to shore up the earth and load it into a willow basket. The people at the work-site were overcome with happiness and pleasure.

There was an old peasant who, with tears in his eyes, said: "In the past, the emperor exploited the people and forced them to build a tomb here. Today, the Communist Party leads us here in building a reservoir so that we can grow more food and improve the life of the people. If Chairman Mao, who is so busy, can come to help us build the reservoir, we must redouble our efforts and finish the reservoir ahead of time."

At six forty-five, Chairman Mao and the leadership comrades left the work-site. But the people at the work-site were still overcome with happiness and pleasure.

SIX. A PATCH

One afternoon, Pao Shih-ying had finished his homework and was taking his younger sister out into the country to play. At the edge of the village there was a big melon field surrounded on all sides by a bamboo fence. As Pao Shih-ying was walking past the field, he suddenly saw that there was a hole in the fence and that there was a sheep in the field. He quickly made his way through the fence and went into the field to chase away the sheep.

Pao Shih-ying chased away the sheep and came out of the melon field. His sister saw him and said: "Oh dear! Look at your clothes. What a big hole you've torn in them!" When Pao Shih-ying looked down, he saw that his clothes had indeed been torn by the bamboo fence.

His sister started to scold, "Your clothes are torn. What are you going to do about it? What are you going to do about it?" Pao Shih-ying was very upset. After a few moments, he said: "It's not serious that I've torn them. I'll patch them myself."

"What you say sounds good, but I don't believe you know how to do it."

"Don't underestimate me. We'll go back home and you can watch me while I patch them."

At his age, Pao Shih-ying had only sewn on a few buttons and had never put on a patch before. But this time he decided to do the patching himself. He felt that he had torn his clothes himself and that, having said that he would patch them himself, he ought to do it.

When he returned home, he got a needle and a thread and asked his mother for a piece of cloth. He took off his clothes and began to sew. It was certainly not a simple matter. The needle would not obey his directions. When he held it tightly, he could not handle it nimbly, and when he held it loosely, he dropped it. Some of the stitches were long and some were short or crooked. When he had finished patching, he no sooner had put his clothes on than his sister broke out laughing and said: "The way you've patched it, it really looks terrible!" Pao Shih-ying felt ashamed and said to his sister: "I was impatient just now and didn't patch it well. I'll do it again and sew slowly. I'm sure I can do a good job."

He took off his clothes, took off the patch, and sewed it on again. This time he sewed carefully and, after a long time, had completed sewing on the patch. He put his clothes on for a look. The patch was flat and the stitches were close and straight. When his sister saw it, she ran happily to her mother and said: "Brother is really good! I want to learn from him so that I can patch my clothes myself too when they are torn!"

TWELVE. THE PARTY IS MY MOTHER

How happy life is today! But I will never forget the tragic days before the Liberation.

Then, in our family we ate only breakfast but did not have any afternoon meal. The reactionary government of the Kuomintang and the landlords didn't care what happened to us and frequently came to force us to pay taxes and rent. Their flunkies, who were like wolves and tigers, always beat people with whips. My father can't remember how many times he was cruelly beaten.

The year that I was eight, there was a bad drought in our village, and everyone in my family ate plant stalks and tree bark to satisfy their hunger. In September, my father and mother both died of starvation. My grandfather, in tears, sold me to Huang Lao-pa, the landlord, in exchange for money for coffins. He then buried mother and father. From then on, grandfather begged for food on the streets, and I became a slave to Huang Lao-pa.

Huang Lao-pa simply did not consider me a human being. I worked from early in the morning until late at night, without a moment of rest. Even so, Huang Lao-pa said that I loafed on the job. If he wasn't cursing at me, he was beating me, and very often he did not give me any food to eat. In the winter he gave me only a bundle of rice straw, and I was so cold I shivered. For one whole year I wore a single ragged and dirty gown. My hair grew long, but it was not cut. My face yellowed and my flesh melted away until I did not look human at all.

During the grave-visiting festival (Ch'ing-ming-chieh) when I was nine, Huang Lao-pa called me to him and said: "Your hair's as long as a dog's and you still havn't shaved it off. Come!" He grabbed me and dragged me away with him. Taking a kitchen knife in his right hand and grasping my hair with his left, he made a thrust. I shouted aloud from the pain, but he still did not let me go. He threatened me, saying: "If you cry or shout again, I'll kill you!" As he spoke, he dug the back of the knife into my neck. The more I thought about it, the more I hated him, and with a burst of strength I bore the pain and broke away from him. My hatred for him has always remained in my heart.

After the Liberation, Huang Lao-pa was overthrown and a house and land were distributed to our family. The two of us, grandfather and grandson, were reunited. We took part in a mutual aid group and later in an agricultural production cooperative. With the establishment of the People's Communes in 1958, our life improved from year to year. Grandfather was 75 years old, but he was still very vigorous, often shouldering a basket in order to collect manure. When the harvests were being gathered, if he wasn't helping to dry millet, he was sweeping out the storehouses. During the day he took part in productive labor, and in the evenings he studied culture in a spare-time school.

I have often felt that the Party is my mother. If it weren't for the Party, where would today's happiness be? I must work actively and study hard, forever going along with the Party!

Why does the writer say that "The Party is my mother"?
Memorize and recite the whole text.

THIRTEEN. INCIDENTS FROM TAIWAN

In a city in northern Taiwan, there was a twelve year old child named Ch'eng-kuei. His mother had been driven to an early death by toil and sickness. After the reactionary Kuomintang had escaped to Taiwan, his father was driven out of his sugar refinery by the capitalists and did not have any work. The father and son lived together in a shabby room. For their livelihood, there was nothing that Ch'eng-kuei could do but shine shoes on the streets, eking out a little money to get through their days.

The Kuomintang reactionaries were building a road for the American barracks, and they wanted to tear down a good many houses. The common people were not willing to move out. The reactionaries sent out troops with loaded rifles and fixed bayonets and forced them to move out. Then they set fire to and burned down their houses. Under the rule of the Kuomintang reactionaries, many of the common people had no homes to return to. Ch'eng-kuei and his father had nothing but the streets to wander on.

Ch'eng-kuei and his little friends deeply hated the American soldiers and the Kuomintang reactionaries, because it was on account of these bad eggs (*huai tan*) that the people of Taiwan were living a life of tragedy. Whenever children, in groups of three or bands of five, saw an American automobile, they would pelt it with stones and then run.

One day, several American soldiers were riding along the road in an automobile. Some children were hiding in an alleyway, waiting for the automobile to draw near. They hurled a rock at the automobile, smashing the glass in its window into little pieces. The American soldiers in the car jumped out, but the children had already run far away. The American soldiers couldn't catch the children, so they grabbed someone who was passing by and beat him up.

The children, with this experience, then picked times to smash the automobiles of American soldiers when there were few people on the streets.

One evening, a thoroughly drunken American soldier riding in a pedicab passed by. When he got to the door of a bar, he jumped off and left. The pedicab driver grabbed him, wanting him to pay the fare. The American soldier stared at him and, putting up his fists, struck the pedicab driver in the face. When the children saw this, they were extremely angry. As soon as they heard Ch'eng-kuei shout: "Go and beat him!" the children came up in a rush, pushing and shoving until they had knocked the American soldier to the ground. The pedicab driver, holding the American soldier's head down, clamped him firmly by the neck so that the children could punch and kick him. They gave the rotten thing a savage beating. They had beaten him until he was beginning to suffer, when the reactionary police came along. Ch'eng-kuei gave a warning whistle. The pedicab driver quickly took charge, seeing to it that the children scattered in all directions, while he himself peddled his pedicab away.

Read the story to yourself. Retell the story in the following sequence: Livelihood of Ch'eng-kuei and his father, burning of the houses of the common people by the Kuomintang, smashing of the automobiles of the American soldiers by the children, painful beating of the American soldier by the worker and the children. Why are the people of Taiwan living tragic lives?

FOURTEEN. TWO LOUISES IN AMERICA

A cold winter had come, and little Louise did not even have a cloth coat. Wearing thin and tattered clothes, she spent her days from morning to night hunting for trash in garbage cans or picking up cinders by the iron works with her cold, numb hands.

The little girl had no father, for he had been crushed to death in a capitalist's mine shaft. She lived with her mother in a New York slum. Her mother worked day and night, but they still couldn't get a full meal. Her mother was also burdened with debts.

One day, little Louise decided to go and look for a little something on the streets. She walked and walked until she came to a stop in front of a department store. She looked in amazement at the goods displayed in the windows. In one window there were meats and chicken; in another there were fur coats and cloth hats. She looked and looked, and the more she looked the colder and hungrier she felt.

Little Louise knew that only the rich could enjoy these things and that none of them would ever belong to her. She could stand there until tomorrow morning and it would all be in vain, for she wouldn't be able to get anything. She walked on.

As she was passing the door of a restaurant for dogs, she suddenly heard someone call: "Louise." Little Louise felt that this was peculiar and, turning her head, found that it was a rich woman. The woman had not been calling to little Louise, but had been calling a Pekinese dog. The rich woman was wearing a fur coat and fur gloves. Even her little dog Louise was wearing a fur coat.

The rich woman led the little dog back into the restaurant for dogs so that it could have its noon meal. The woman in charge of the restaurant for dogs was plump and thick-jowled, and she welcomed the little dog Louise attentively.

The little dog Louise's appetite was very good, and she ate sausage, soup, and even some very good biscuits.

A few pieces of dirty biscuit had been thrown out of the dog restaurant onto the sidewalk in front. Little Louise hurried to pick them up. As luck would have it, the little dog Louise ran out the door. The little dog began to bark fiercely, frightening little Louise so that she couldn't move. With a shout, the rich woman struck the girl with the palm of her hand. Little Louise started to cry with grief, but the rich woman did not stop, and angrily scolded her without letup. A policeman ran up, and the rich woman ordered him: "Grab her at once! This little brat hit my Louise and now she will have to go to the hospital!"

The policeman did not ask about the fine points, but seized little Louise and took her off to the police station. He said that she had criminally wounded the little dog Louise.

Three days later, little Louise returned to her home. With tears in her eyes, she asked her mother: "Why isn't a laborer as good as a dog?" When her mother heard this, she gritted her teeth and, clenching her fists, said not a word.

Using the wording of the text, discuss what kind of a child little Louise was and what kind of a person the rich woman was. What is the life of the American laboring people like? Why? Read the text aloud expressing emotion.

FIFTEEN. HOW TO PREVENT INFECTIOUS DISEASES

Question: Why do people get infectious diseases?

Answer: When bacteria, viruses, and parasitic worms invade the body, people get infectious diseases.

Question: What are bacteria, viruses, and parasitic worms?

Answer: Bacteria, viruses, and parasitic worms are small living things that are harmful to people. Bacteria and parasitic worms are very small and can only be seen under the microscope. Viruses are even smaller and cannot be seen at all under ordinary microscopes.

Question: How do they invade a person's body?

Answer: There are three routes by which they invade a person's body:

The first route is through the mouth. This is what we commonly speak of as "the sickness enters by the mouth." For example, if we eat food containing dysentery bacteria, we can get dysentery.

The second route is through the nose. For example, children who have not had measles can get the measles by breathing in measles viruses.

The third route is through the skin. For example, if we are bitten by an anopheles mosquito, we can get malaria.

Question: How can we prevent infectious diseases?

Answer: To prevent infectious diseases, the following three points should be followed:

First, the body should be kept in shape in order to increase its resistance. One should also take immunizing shots and be vaccinated at the right time.

Second, carry out personal and environmental hygiene. Flies should not be allowed to fall onto food. Spoiled things should not be eaten. Fresh water should not be drunk. The hands should be washed before eating and after defecation. One should bathe often. Clothes and bedding should be thoroughly washed and dried. Rooms and courtyards should be swept often. Doors and windows should be opened often so that air can circulate and so that there will be enough light. Rats, mosquitoes, flies, and bedbugs should be exterminated. Lice and fleas should also be exterminated.

Third, if someone catches a contagious disease, he should be isolated at once. Aside from those who are taking care of the sick person and the doctor, no one should come in contact with the sick person. The sick person's sputum and excrement should be sterilized with lime or liquid chemicals. The things the sick person has used should be disinfected. They may be steamed in a rice steamer, boiled in water, or left to dry under the sun. In this way, the illness cannot be given to other people.

SIXTEEN. FLIES, MOSQUITOES, AND BEDBUGS

Flies can transmit disease and are very harmful to people.

The feet, legs and mouth of the fly are covered with bacteria. When a fly falls onto food, these bacteria can stick to the food. When people eat it, they can easily become sick.

Flies lay their eggs and reproduce in dirty, evil-smelling places. The eggs turn into maggots, which bore down into loose soil and become pupae. The pupae in turn become flies.

To exterminate flies, good environmental hygiene work must be done. When you see a fly, kill it with a fly swatter. Lime or hot coals can be used to kill the maggots. The pupae should also be dug up and burned.

Mosquitoes can also transmit disease.

Mosquitoes lay their eggs on the surface of water. The eggs, after one or two days in the water, hatch into mosquito larvae.

After about a week has passed, the larvae turn into pupae. The pupae spend two or three more days in the water and then turn into small mosquitoes.

During the day, mosquitoes hide in clumps of grass or in dark places in rooms. Toward evening they come out to suck people's blood. Some mosquitoes, as they are sucking blood, also pass viruses or parasites into a person's blood, in this way spreading disease to people.

To exterminate mosquitoes, ditches should be filled in and cracks in trees filled up so that rainwater cannot collect in these places and so that the mosquitoes will have no place to lay their eggs and reproduce. If you discover any mosquitoes, they can be killed by spraying them with "DDT" or "666."

Bedbugs are very fond of human blood, and after a person has been bitten by one, his skin will swell and itch. Bedbugs usually keep a person from sleeping restfully, which has an effect on his health and work.

Bedbugs reproduce very quickly, one bedbug being able to produce one hundred to five hundred others. The larvae hatch after a period of six to ten days. The larvae also like human blood. After molting five times, they become adults.

Bedbugs and their eggs are hidden in the cracks of beds, tables and chairs, and walls. They can best be killed by scalding them with boiling water or by spraying them with insecticides.

NINETEEN. BEE GUIDES

In 1922, when Lenin was living on a hill near Moscow, he often sought out a local beekeeper to pass the day with.

Once Lenin wanted to talk with him about how to develop the bee industry. But the man he usually sent out to find the beekeeper had gone to Moscow, and none of the others knew where he lived. They only knew that it was not too far away. Lenin himself went out to look for the man.

Lenin walked through the countryside, observing as he went. Suddenly he saw a large number of bees in a clump of flowers. When he observed them more closely, he saw that the bees were gathering honey and then flying back to a flower garden nearby. In the flower garden there was a small house. Lenin then walked toward the small house and knocked on the door. The man who opened the door was none other than the beekeeper.

When the beekeeper saw Lenin, he said with surprise: "Good day, Comrade Lenin. Who brought you? Very few people know that I live here. How did you find me?"

Lenin laughed and said: "I had guides. Your bees led me here."

The beekeeper, with even greater surprise, said: "Comrade Lenin, no matter how difficult a problem is, in your hands you always have a way to solve it."

Lenin said: "All you have to do is be good at using each opportunity, observing carefully, and thinking earnestly, and you can work out correct decisions and find ways to solve problems."

Since Lenin did not know the beekeeper's address, how could he find him?

Memorize and recite the text. Write down Lenin's words in the final paragraph.

TWENTY. A GREAT HORTICULTURIST

Michurin was a great Soviet horticulturist.

Michurin's father was a man who loved gardens. Michurin often worked with his father in the orchard and loved gardens ever since he was little. In the orchard, he took a small piece of land as a vegetable garden, planting in it carefully selected seeds.

He always gave a great deal of attention to collecting seeds. If he saw a large cherry stone or plum seed, he would pick it up. His pockets were always filled.

Michurin's family was very poor and did not have enough money for him to go to school for very many years. He did not even graduate from middle school. In order to make a living, he had no choice but to leave school, and he went to work at the railroad station. But he did not forget the gardening work he loved, and every day after getting off from work, he would plant seeds, make grafts, and carry out experiments in his garden. In the evening he read books about horticulture. He wanted with all his heart to improve the orchards in his village and to grow new and superior fruit trees.

At that time, there was being produced in the south a large fragrant and sweet apple. In the cold north, however, this kind of apple had never been seen. Michurin wanted the people in the north to be able to eat big apples too. He used all kinds of methods and experiments. One by one and from year to year he kept on failing, but he did not become discouraged. After fourteen years, he succeeded in growing a new apple tree in the north that bore large fragrant and sweet apples.

After the October Revolution, he obtained the great interest and assistance of the Soviet Government. He succeeded in producing more than 300 kinds of new fruit trees. In Michurin's orchard there were rows on rows of trees bearing large, sweet cherries and large apples of over a catty in weight. There was a pear tree that could bear more than a thousand large pears that bent the branches low. There were also pear-apples, large grapes ... so many that you couldn't keep count!

Michurin used his life's energy in the study of horticulture, improved on nature, and made a great contribution to horticulture.

From what points can it be seen that Michurin was a person persistent in study? Break the story down into paragraphs and discuss the central idea in each paragraph.

TWENTY-FOUR. LIU WEN-HSÜEH

A good child of Chairman Mao and an outstanding Pioneer, Liu Wen-hsüeh was a fourth grade pupil in the Shuang-chiang

Elementary School in Ho-ch'uan Hsien of Szechuan Province. In order to protect the interests of the People's Commune he struggled with a landlord and sacrificed himself courageously.

Liu Wen-hsüeh was born into the family of a poor farmer. Before the Liberation, his family had suffered the cruel oppression of their landlord, and the evil heart of that bad egg landlord was early engraved in his mind.

After the Liberation, Liu Wen-hsüeh entered school, joined the Pioneers, and receiving the instruction of the Party, his awareness was further raised. He was obedient to the words of the Party and of Chairman Mao, loving study, loving labor, and loving the collective. He strove only to do something of benefit to the nation. He loved Socialism and he loved the People's Communes.

On the evening of November 18, 1959, Liu Wen-hsüeh was returning home happily after having finished his labor in the fields. Suddenly, he caught sight of a shadow moving in the pepper plot.

"Who could that be?" Liu Wen-hsüeh went over at once to take a closer look. It turned out to be a controlled landlord who was in the midst of stealing the Commune's peppers. Before the Liberation, this bad egg had devoted himself to abusing the peasants. After the Liberation, the government had turned him over to the people for supervision, but he was still dishonest and often carried out sabotage. A few days before, Liu Wen-hsüeh had exposed him as having stolen and sold the Commune's peppers and oranges, and now he had come back again to carry out some more sabotage!

"Why are you stealing the Commune's peppers?" Liu Wen-hsüeh called out in a loud voice.

"Ah! ..." The landlord couldn't answer. When he saw that it was a child, he said with mock fear: "The people on the boats want to eat peppers, and the Commune asked me to gather some."

"That's nonsense. If the Commune asked you to gather them, why didn't you do it in the daytime?" Liu Wen-hsüeh's voice was particularly severe.

By this time, the landlord realized that the person standing before him was Liu Wen-hsüeh. When Liu Wen-hsüeh had exposed his crime a few days before, he had been filled with hatred for him. He suddenly bent down and said quietly: "Look, isn't there someone over there stealing oranges?" As he was speaking, he started to gather his bag, which was filled with peppers.

Liu Wen-shüeh rushed up to him and, grabbing the bag in his hands, ran after the landlord. When they got to the orange tree and looked, there was no one there. That bad egg of a landlord had been deceiving him all along! Liu Wen-hsüeh was on the point of questioning him, when the landlord craftily broke out in a mocking smile and, taking a piece of money from his pocket, shoved it at Liu Wen-hsüeh and said: "Little brother, you are the only one who knows about this. If you keep quiet, then nothing's happened...."

"I don't want your stinking money!" Liu Wen-hsüeh hurled the money angrily to the ground, slung the bag over his shoulders, and grabbed the landlord's clothes, saying: "Come on. We're going to the Public Security Committeeman!"

"If you try it, I'll kill you!"

"Even if you kill me, I'll never let go of a bad egg like you!" Liu Wen-hsüeh answered bravely. He grabbed the landlord securely, letting out a loud yell: "Someone's stealing the Commune's peppers! ..."

The evil landlord, not waiting for Liu Wen-hsüeh to call out a second time, knocked him to the ground with his fists, whereupon he rushed at him and, sitting astride Liu Wen-hsüeh's body, gagged his mouth with one hand while he pressed his throat with the other.

Even at this tense and critical moment, the brave Liu Wen-hsüeh did not yield in the slightest, but bit the landlord's hand and used all the strength in his body in an attempt to turn over and scramble to his feet. But the landlord, like a crazed wolf, pressed down on Liu Wen-hsüeh like a dead weight, tightly closing shut Liu Wen-hsüeh's windpipe with his evil claws.

The brave Pioneer sacrificed himself heroically.

After three days, the Public Security Bureau arrested the wicked murderer and executed the bad egg by shooting.

Liu Wen-hsüeh's heroic deed moved his many young friends. The youths and children of Ho-ch'uan county held a memorial service for Liu Wen-hsüeh, at which they resolved to study Liu Wen-hsüeh's noble qualities of love for the Party, love for Chairman Mao, and love for Socialism, and determined to be good children of Chairman Mao.

How did Liu Wen-hsüeh struggle with the wicked landlord? Why was he able to do this?

TWENTY-FIVE. THE SUNFLOWERS SMILED

After a storm had passed, we found that two large branches of the ash tree in front of the door had been broken off. This made me think of the sunflowers that our company had planted—those more than a hundred sunflowers which were tended by us, shovel by shovel of earth and ladle by ladle of water. We had challenged the First Company to see whose sunflowers would grow the best. If they had been blown down by the storm, we would lose to the First Company. That would really be a disgrace! The more I thought the more worried I became, and I ran off as fast as my legs would carry me toward school.

Ai-ya! The sunflowers had just about been uprooted and were lying helter-skelter in the mud, the beautiful yellow flowers drooping their heads. At once, I propped up one of the sunflowers, but the sunflower, dripping with mud, would not stay standing. I decided to go back home and get some wooden sticks to support the sunflowers. Then I thought again and first went to see how the First Company's sunflowers were. Starting to run, I hurried over to the First Company's garden.

Strangely, the First Company's sunflowers had not been blown down, but were standing straight. To get a clearer view, I ran forward a few steps and discovered Wang Min, of our company, with sticks in one hand and rope in the other, propping up a sunflower. Her hair clung tightly to her face, and water was dropping from it. Her white shirt had become yellow, and she was soaking wet from head to toe. I stood there silently. She saw me coming and said: "You've come! Chih-liang! All that's left are these two. We'll prop them up together and then go and prop up ours." I didn't utter a sound. When she saw that I wasn't minding her, she said: "Chih-liang, what's the matter? Are you tired from running? Why don't you have a drink ..."

I was really furious and began to shout in a loud voice, "Enough, enough. Don't talk nonsense!"

"Chih-liang, what ...?"

"What ... what's the matter with me?" I said, interrupting her. "Don't you know that we've challenged the First Company? Why didn't you save our own first? Your arms are turned to the outside. It's clear you don't love your own company."

Wang Min's face was white with anger, and she said furiously: "Don't you know? Our classmates in the First Company live far away and it's not easy for them to make the trip here. Besides, their sunflowers are growing better than ours and ought to be saved first!"

"Then we should let ours spoil and rot?" I asked her.

"Who is saying that? Look, didn't I bring along a lot of sticks? After we're finished here, we'll go and prop ours up."

I was about to say a little more to her, when suddenly I heard the sound of running feet. I looked around and saw that it was Cheng P'ing and Lan Hua from the First Company. Both of them were running and gasping for breath. When they saw me and Wang Min and saw the sunflowers in the garden, they said with surprise: "Ai-ya! You've propped them all up for us. How can we ever be grateful enough to you!"

"There's nothing to be grateful for," said Wang Min with a smile. My face was hot, and I lowered my head, not saying a word.

Lan Hua gave me a hard push, saying: "What's got into you? You've done a good deed and your face is red!"

"Go, Chih-liang, and look after the ones in our company," said Wang Min, seeing that I was still hanging my head.

"What? You still haven't fixed yours but took care of ours for us? I'm going to tell the leader so that he can put you two on the honor roll!" What Cheng P'ing said almost started me crying.

"Lan Hua, let's go and help them!" As Cheng P'ing was speaking, she ran off, dragging Lan Hua after her like a train of smoke. I shamefully took Wang Min by the hand and ran off toward the garden too.

The sun had come out, and the sunshine after the rain shone with exceptional brightness. As I ran, I turned around and looked back. The First Company's sunflowers were smiling under the sunlight.

Why did Wang Min save the First Company's sunflowers first?

TWENTY-SIX. I'VE COME TO ESCORT YOU TO WORK

Every morning I ride the bus to work at the Metal Factory of the Blind. After I get off the bus, there is about a block before I reach the factory. At one time I had to grope my way by myself.

One morning last autumn I had just gotten off the bus when suddenly I heard a boy's voice, "Auntie Liu, good morning!" Then his small hand tugged at my arm. He wanted to escort me to the factory. This seemed strange, and I said: "Little friend, you've mistaken me for someone else. I'm ..." He broke in saying: "Auntie, isn't your name Liu? Aren't you going to the Metal Factory of the Blind to work? I've come to escort you to work."

How did this ever come about?

A few days before, while he was on his way to school, this boy had met one of our comrades from the factory on the street as he was tapping his way along with his cane. He went up to him and helped our comrade all the way to the factory. He also said to the comrade: "Your factory is not far from our school. I would like to escort you to work every day." The comrade said: "Thank you for your kind intentions. There's always someone in my family who escorts me every day. It is just today that I'm by myself. But since you would like to escort someone, you could escort Auntie Liu from our factory." The comrade then told him what time I got to the station every day.

The boy finished telling me all this in one breath and then went on: "Auntie Liu, would you like me to escort you to work every day?" For a moment I was so moved that I didn't know what to say. All I could do was to grasp his arm tightly and say, "You are really a good boy! You are really a good boy!"

From that day on, the boy came to the bus station every day to meet me and, supporting me carefully, escorted me to the gate of the factory. Whether the wind was blowing or whether it was raining, he never missed a day.

One morning last winter, there was a big snowfall, and I didn't go to work. Suddenly I heard someone knocking on my door. Then I heard a familiar voice calling: "Auntie Liu! Is Auntie Liu at home?" It was my little friend, who had come looking for me at home. I said quickly: "I'm home. Come in at once!" As soon as he entered, he said, panting: "Auntie, I didn't wait for you at the station. I thought that I had come late and that you had already gone to the factory. But when I went to the factory and asked, they said that you hadn't gone. I thought that with such a heavy snow you might have had some accident. So I came to your home."

I put on my overcoat quickly and went with him to the factory.

A year went quickly by, and the boy was promoted to middle school and couldn't escort me to work any more. He passed on the task of escorting me to work to his sister. The day before yesterday, as soon as I got off the bus, I heard the clear and gentle voice of a girl: "Auntie Liu, good morning!" The boy's sister had come to meet me for the first time. She touched my arm gently, saying to me as we walked: "Auntie Liu, now it is my turn to escort you to work. Later, when I go to middle school, my little brother will be able to escort you."

I do not know with what words to express the feelings in my heart. I've written these events down to tell it to the people I know and the people I don't know, to praise our children, and to praise the great mother who teaches our children to grow—Our Party.

Why did the brother and sister want to escort Auntie Liu to work?

TWENTY-SEVEN. THE SECRET OF THE GOD

There is a mountain in which there is a cave known as "the cave of the immortal." One year, the people began to talk about how the "immortal" in the cave had displayed divine powers and could cure disease.

There was an old man nearby who, when his family was struck by illness, bought incense, candles, and paper to burn before an idol and who, bearing an offering of food, went up onto the mountain to seek a "magic remedy."

When he reached the cave of the immortal, he first crawled into the cave, presenting his offering of food. Then, outside the cave, he burned incense and kowtowed. After this he took back a little of the offering. This he thought to be the "magic remedy" given by the immortal.

What was even more peculiar was that after the man who was seeking the "magic remedy" had offered the food in the cave and had finished kowtowing, there was only a little of the offering remaining when he took it out. The old man said: "It was eaten by the great immortal in the cave." Several young people found out about this event, and, being very suspicious, wanted to go up to the cave to investigate. However, the old people did not allow them to go and risk danger.

The news that there was an "immortal" in the cave spread farther and farther. There were people who travelled far and who spent much money coming to seek the "magic remedy."

One day an old woman came bringing her daughter-in-law in search of the "magic remedy." The old woman presented her offering and then kneeled outside the cave, kowtowing and praying: "O great immortal and protector, let my child's illness be better soon!" Then a voice suddenly came out of the cave: "All you need to do is send her to bed and cover her with a flowered quilt and she'll get well." When the woman and the girl heard this voice, they were frightened, crawled down, and ran away.

When some youths who were building a pond at the foot of the mountain heard of this event, they could contain themselves no longer and, wanting to see what was going on, ran up to the mountain. They made their way into the cave, where they seized the "great immortal." It turned out that the "great immortal" who had deceived a number of people, was nothing more than a local vagabond who was still unreformed after repeated instruction.

What actually were the divine powers of the "immortal"?

TWENTY-EIGHT—SELECTION TWO.
THE MAN WHO LOST HIS SHEEP

Once upon a time, there was a man who used to raise a few sheep. One morning when he went to let the sheep out, he discovered that one was missing. It turned out that there was a hole in the sheep pen and that during the night a wolf had come in through the hole and had carried off the sheep.

A neighbor advised him: "You'd better fix the sheep pen at once and patch up that hole."

He said: The sheep has already been lost, so what's the good of fixing the pen?" He did not accept the neighbor's advice.

The next morning, when he went to let the sheep out, he discovered that one more was missing. Once again the wolf had gone in through the hole and carried off a sheep.

The man was full of regret, for he should have taken the advice of his neighbor. He patched up the hole at once and repaired the sheep pen so that it was very sturdy. From then on, no more sheep were carried off by the wolf.

Study this allegory and discuss what educational value it has for us and how it should instruct us in our daily lives. Write out "The Man Who Lost His Sheep."

THIRTY-TWO. TUNG TS'UN-JUI GIVES HIS LIFE TO BLOW UP A BUNKER

Tung Ts'un-jui was an outstanding battle hero of our Liberation Army. Already having attained the Order of Great Merit four times and the Second Class Order of Merit twice, he offered up his own life heroically in the battle for the liberation of Lunghua in order to complete a difficult and glorious mission.

In May of 1948, our army liberated the county seat of Lunghua in Hopeh province. The troops entered the city. As they drew near to Lunghua Middle School, the enemy, who were holding a sturdy bunker, set up a heavy net of fire with about twenty machine guns and submachine guns, cutting off our army's advance. Two demolition squads had gone out to blow up the bunker, but neither had completed their mission. The general assault was about to begin, and the bunker had to be destroyed at once in order to open up a route of advance for the troops.

Tung Ts'un-jui clenched his fists and, with a firm glint in his eyes, said to the company commander: "Commander, I'll go and blow it up!" The company commander granted his request.

Under cover of a barrage of hand grenades, Tung Ts'un-jui, holding the explosives, dashed out into the smoke. He crawled forward, zigzagging from left to right. At about 40 meters from the bunker, the enemy fire was so thick that he could advance no further. Concealing himself in a hollow, he looked around carefully. He saw that the bunker was built on a bridge and that beneath the bridge there was a dry river bed. Thereupon he aimed a hand grenade at the bunker and, taking advantage of the thick smoke, dashed under the bridge.

The underside of the bridge was six or seven feet from the ground. There was no place along the bridge to set the explosives, and if he set the explosives on the ground, the blast would not reach the bunker. What could he do? In his anxiety, Tung Ts'un-jui's face was covered with sweat. At that moment, the call rang out for our army's assault party to begin their assault. Tung

Ts'un-jui knew that if he delayed one more minute many of his fellow soldiers might be sacrificed. Without stopping to think, with one hand he held up the explosives and with the other he pulled the pin.

"Hlung!" There was a great roar that shook the earth. The enemy bunker was smashed. Tung Ts'un-jui had gloriously offered his young life. Our troops burst into the enemy lines, and the Red Flag was raised above Lunghua Middle School. The enemy had been completely annihilated, and Lunghua had been liberated.

The leaders, in acknowledgement of the martyr Tung Ts'un-jui's being a battle hero and a model Party member, decided to name the squad that he had led while he was alive the "Tung Ts'un-jui Squad." The soldiers in the Tung Ts'un-jui Squad swore that "they would always preserve the hero's glorious and heroic spirit."

The People's Government, in order to commemorate this people's hero, changed the name of the "Lunghua Middle School" to the "Ts'un-jui Middle School."

Discuss Tung Ts'un-jui's blowing up of the bunker. Listen to and write the paragraph beginning with "The underside of the bridge ..." and ending with ". .. with the other he pulled the pin."

THIRTY-FIVE. PLASTICS

The word plastic sounds a little strange, but actually we see plastic very often. We have all seen bakelite bowls and glass toothbrushes. These things are all made of plastics.

There are many raw materials in nature which can be used to make plastics. For example, water, air, coal, oil, salt, limestone, and even kaoliang stalks and corn stalks can be used to make plastics. Of course it is not a simple business to manufacture plastics from these raw materials, but today, with the development of science and technology, plastics can be produced in large quantities.

Let's talk about making plastics from coal. The workmen first extract and refine the raw materials for making plastic from the coal. Then they heat the raw materials and chemicals together in a tank, making something that looks like molasses. This is called synthetic resin. After this, depending on requirements, various substances are added in order to make plastics having different properties. When fibers are added, the plastic is not easily broken. If asbestos is added, the plastic is heat-resistant. In order to make these products beautiful in appearance, various dyes can also be added. Many different kinds of plastics are made from different synthetic resins and from different ingredients.

There are very many kinds of plastics. Some are harder than steel, some lighter than wood, some as transparent as glass; some can be pressed into paper and some can be drawn out into thread. Plastic is a most obedient material and, like the clay with which children play, it can be made into any shape by the workmen just by pressing it into a mould.

Plastic can take the place of steel, wood, glass, and ceramics and can be made into many kinds of things. The combs, wallets, and pens that we use every day can all be made from plastic. Many parts of trains, automobiles, ships, airplanes, and even space rockets are made from plastics. Plastics can also be used to make houses and machines. Plastics have become a widely used material.

What uses does plastic have? What things in nature can be used as raw materials for plastics?

SELECTIONS FROM VOLUME 7 OF THE READERS

(GRADE FOUR)

TWO—SELECTION ONE.
EVERYONE LOVES MAO TSE-TUNG

The stars in the heavens cannot be counted.
All the stars face toward the North Star.
The people of China, six-hundred-million strong
All love Mao Tse-tung.

TWO—SELECTION TWO.
EVER SINCE THE PARTY LINE

Gold fills the earth and silver fills the hills;
Everywhere there are rivers of food.
Ever since we've had the Party Line,
The song of the Leap Forward has not ceased.

THREE. A WOUNDED MAN'S WISH

During the War of Resistance against Japan, there was a field hospital in a village to the northeast of Yenan. In the hospital there was a wounded man who had just been brought from the eastern bank of the Yellow River. His wounds were very severe.

The nurses taking care of him knew that his injury could not be healed, and they were very sad.

308

Suddenly the wounded man opened his eyes wide and called: "Chairman Mao, I want to see Chairman Mao!" After that, he kept muttering over and over: "Chairman Mao, Chairman Mao ..."

The nurses didn't know what to do but to soothe him said: "Do you want to see Chairman Mao? We will think of a way to tell him."

There were tears in the eyes of the wounded man, and with great effort he said: "Chairman Mao is very busy. I don't think he would have the time to come. But, still, I want to see him very much!"

The nurses thought that since Chairman Mao was busy all day with the affairs of the nation and since he lived some 40 *li* from the hospital, he couldn't come. But since the wounded man wanted to see him so much, there was no reason for not putting through a telephone call to tell Chairman Mao.

As soon as Chairman Mao received the call, he at once mounted his horse and raced to the hospital. When he arrived at the hospital gate, the horse was panting for breath and was covered with sweat.

Quickly Chairman Mao went in to see the wounded man. The wounded man had already lost consciousness. A nurse spoke into his ear: "Chairman Mao has come to see you!"

Suddenly the wounded man's eyes brightened, and he fixed his eyes on Chairman Mao. His lips moved as if to say: "Ah, it's Chairman Mao! I've seen you ... you ..."

He used up the last of his strength in trying to grasp Chairman Mao's hand. Chairman Mao bent down and, grasping his hand, said into his ear: "You are a good comrade of our Party. We will never forget you."

Chairman Mao observed the state of his wound. The blood had almost all flowed out of him. The wounded man slowly closed his eyes, and a smile appeared on his face.

From what sentences in the text can one see Chairman Mao's concern for the wounded man?

FOUR. A WOOLEN BLANKET

In February 1942, we escorted Comrade Liu Shao-ch'i to Shantung. Each time we bivouacked during the first few days, we first set up quarters for Comrade Shao-ch'i. But Comrade Shao-ch'i always waited until all of the soldiers had places to live before going into his room. Later, as soon as we arrived in a bivouac area, we set up the quarters for the soldiers so that they could rest a little earlier and so that we could ease the weariness of Comrade Shao-ch'i. Who could have known that this procedure would upset Comrade Shao-ch'i even more? He himself set up the quarters for the soldiers, giving the better rooms to them, while he stayed in a room of poor quality.

One evening, Comrade Shao-ch'i stayed in a tool shed. There was no door to the tool shed, and all he could do was hang up a ragged blanket to keep out the wind. The February nights were very cold, and the north wind blew at the blanket, rushing into the room. I was sleeping in another shed and fearing that Comrade Shao-ch'i would catch cold, I put on my clothes and went to see him. When I reached the shed, I saw a faint light coming through the holes in the ragged blanket. When I raised it and looked in, there was Comrade Shao-ch'i reading a book by candlelight. He read for a while and then put down the book. Rubbing his cold hands together, he looked at the guard curled up beside him and then gently placed the overcoat covering his legs over the guard. As I watched this scene, I was so moved that I wanted to shout: "Comrade Shao-ch'i, your health is important!" But, fearing that I might startle Comrade Shao-ch'i, I did not call out.

I hurried back and took the woolen blanket from my own bed, and, pulling up the ragged blanket that blocked his door, I went into the shed in which Comrade Shao-ch'i was staying.

Comrade Shao-ch'i looked at me and, putting his book down, asked: "Why aren't you sleeping yet?"

I nodded my head and covered Comrade Shao-ch'i's legs with the woolen blanket. Comrade Shao-ch'i refused it for some time before finally accepting it. I was very happy and, seeing on my way back that the soldiers were all fast asleep, I went to bed. Although I was short one blanket and my body was a little cold, my heart was warm.

I gradually fell asleep and in the darkness felt ever warmer as I drifted deeper into sleep. The next morning when I got up, I found the blanket that I had given to Comrade Shao-ch'i covering my body. When I went out and asked the sentinel on duty, I learned that as soon as I had fallen asleep Comrade Shao-ch'i had covered me with the woolen blanket.

When I went to see Comrade Shao-ch'i, he didn't mention the blanket. The first thing he asked was: "Did the soldiers sleep well?"

I answered: "They slept very well."

Comrade Shao-ch'i nodded his head, smiling.

From what passages in the lesson can one see Comrade Liu Shao-ch'i's concern for the soldiers?

SEVEN. CLEANING A WALL

Every time I walked down the lane by the school, I felt unhappy. On the wall, which had once been very clean, someone had scribbled pictures and had written characters with chalk. What made me the most angry was one crooked chalk line several feet long. It was probably drawn by someone as he walked along and who had stopped once the chalk was used up. I often thought about how it might be possible to get the wall clean again.

At one of the group meetings of the Pioneers, I brought up this problem. After a discussion, everyone decided that on Sunday afternoon the whole group would get to work and clean the wall in the lane. We also talked at the meeting about how to clean it and how to divide the work.

When Sunday afternoon came, all of our classmates in the group gathered in front of the school gate. We had all kinds of tools: water buckets, brooms, brushes, rags. As soon as the group leader gave the order, everyone began to work on the section for which he was responsible.

Lu Chien-wen, Chao Shu-fang, and I were responsible for the south half of the lane. We started working diligently. Chao Shu-fang was patient and precise. He dipped his brush into the water and brushed bit by bit until in a little while there were no chalk-written characters to be seen and there was not a trace of the pictures. Lu Chien-wen, who is by temperament too hasty, would throw a whole bucket of water at the wall all at once and then scrub. Not only did this waste water, but it also did not get things clean. Once the water dried, some of the chalk marks reappeared and the wall had to be scrubbed again. Our other classmates were very diligent, but some of them were too excited, and their bodies and faces got all covered with mud. The one who scrubbed the fastest and the best was Sun Shou-jung. He was responsible for brushing a section of the wall that was made of broken bricks. That section of the wall was very difficult to scrub because it was covered with bumps. He rubbed them with a wet rag through the tips of his fingers, rubbing them rapidly and rubbing them clean. The group leader told everyone to study from him if they wanted to find a way to complete their task better and faster.

While we were cleaning the wall, there were a number of children living nearby who crowded around us to watch. As the group leader scrubbed, he said to them: "Look how much work has to be done to scrub the wall! After this, if you see anyone drawing on the wall, explain to them and tell them not to draw." The children all agreed, and one of them said: "After this, I won't draw on the wall any more."

By four o'clock we had completed our work victoriously. When we looked at the wall, which had been scrubbed so clean, we felt an inexpressible happiness in our hearts.

NINE. MAILING BACK A KITCHEN KNIFE

In October 1949, when the Liberation Army was advancing toward the southwest, one of its divisions was following a highway westward. One day they marched 80 *li* and bivouacked in a market town.

The cooking squad comrades opened up their oil and salt packs and prepared to cook. Suddenly, Lao Ch'ien, one of the cooks, took a kitchen knife from Hsiao Wang's pack and said anxiously: "Oh, no! Oh, no! What are we going to do?"

"What's the matter?" asked the chief cook anxiously.

"Last night I borrowed this kitchen knife from an old man in I-chuang, and when I finished using it I put it down on top of the pack. We travelled rapidly today, and Hsiao Wang has carried it here." When he had said this, everyone was stunned.

"80 *li*, that's 160 coming and going. If we go back, we won't be able to catch up with the division," someone said.

The chief thought a while and said: "I have it! I just saw a post office on the east side of the town, so we can mail the kitchen knife back to the old man. We can go to the post office and discuss whether this will work."

Fortunately, the lights in the post office were still lit. Someone was sitting there sorting letters and putting on the postmarks. The squad chief went in and said: "Comrade, we'd like to send a kitchen knife, registered mail. How much will it be?" As he spoke, he placed the kitchen knife on the counter.

The man in the post office was startled and for a moment did not answer. The squad chief, who was afraid that he might not be willing to send it, quickly told him the reason, explaining: "In our division, to borrow an old man's things and not return them is a violation of the law of the masses, so we must send the knife back!"

"Ah, that's what it's all about. Well, then, the mailman will take it back."

Lao Ch'ien explained that the owner of the knife lived in I-chuang, that his gate faced south and that it was the fourth house from the west end of the town. The man in the post office wrote this address on a piece of paper. After that, Lao Ch'ien began to argue with the man in the post office over the matter of postage. Lao Ch'ien said: "The Liberation Army preaches fairness. What reason is there for mailing something without paying for it?" But the man in the post office was firm about not accepting payment and said: "Comrades, please go ahead with your army with an easy mind. We guarantee to send this knife back to its original owner."

The man in the post office waited for Lao Ch'ien and his group to leave and then added one sentence to the piece of paper: "The Liberation Army takes not so much as a needle or a thread from the masses."

The next day the mailman handed the knife and the note to the original owner of the knife.

What does the story of mailing back the knife show?

TEN. THE WATERMELON BROTHERS

During the War of Liberation, there were in our village two brothers named Li, who made their living from growing watermelons. Lao Ta's melon field was at the edge of the highway to the east of the village, while Lao Erh's melon field was at the edge of the highway to the southwest of the village.

Once when the watermelons were ripe, a unit of the Kuomintang reactionary troops came along the highway to the east of the village. When they saw the watermelons in Lao Ta's field, they ran at once into the field and began picking and eating the melons. In a little while, they had eaten up more than a *mou* of watermelons. All that was left were the rinds and seeds.

Not long after, the People's Liberation Army came. They were walking along the highway to the southwest of the village and passed by Lao Erh's melon field. When Lao Erh heard that troops were passing through, he was so worried he didn't know what to do. He thought: "Now my melons will be done for." He took a knife and ran quickly to his melon field, where he sat down, saying to himself: "I'll sit here and watch. If anyone picks one of my melons, I'll drive him away!"

The Liberation Army went by.

"How well these watermelons have grown!" "Good melons—they must weigh more than 20 *chin* a piece!" "There aren't many watermelons as big as these!" said the soldiers in praise of the melons.

When Lao Erh heard the soldiers praising how well his melons had grown, he was even more frightened. But the strange thing was that, even though they talked like that, they kept marching ahead without stopping. Lao Erh looked at the column. He couldn't see the head of the file of troops, nor could he see the end. He said to himself: "This must be the Liberation Army!" He stood up and, picking some of the biggest melons with his knife, cut them open, their fresh red flesh exposed, and placed them at the side of the road.

Lao Erh said to the passing soldiers: "Have some watermelon, Comrades!" But no one answered.

Lao Erh thought that the soldiers hadn't heard him, so he raised his voice and said very loudly: "You're thirsty from marching. Have one!"

The soldieers said in unison: "We won't eat any. Thank you, old man!"

Lao Erh was upset and shouted loudly: "When I saw the Liberation Army, I cut open these melons. Why won't you eat them?"

A sixteen or seventeen year old signalman was passing, and he asked Lao Erh: "Old man, are you selling melons here?"

Lao Erh said: "I don't want money for these melons. Take one if you want!" As he spoke he held out a melon to the signalman.

"I won't take it! I won't take it!" said the signalman as he passed by without stopping.

Lao Erh stood holding up the watermelon in astonishment. The soldiers kept on marching shoulder to shoulder toward the southwest. To the front he could not see the head and to the rear he could not see the end.

Why did Lao Erh fear that the soldiers would eat his melons and then in the end hold up the melons to give to them?

ELEVEN. THE LITTLE MESSENGER

During the War of Liberation, there was in one of the cavalry companies of the Chinese People's Liberation Army a fourteen year old messenger boy by the name of Ma-lin.

Once, Ma-lin received orders to scout out Pa-li Village, which was being held by the Kuomintang reactionaries. He disguised himself as a boy collecting firewood and carrying a bamboo basket went along picking up firewood. Near the village he sat by a ditch to rest, keeping an eye out for enemy activity.

Suddenly, an enemy soldier ran out from a blockhouse and pointing at Ma-lin with his leather whip, said: "What are you up to?"

Ma-lin calmly pointed to the bamboo basket at his side and said: "Gathering firewood."

"Nonsense! You're a little spy and you've come to look for information for the Communist Party!" The enemy soldier was shouting loudly and had a fierce look in his eyes. Then he looked around and with a grunt said: "Where do you live?"

"At the east of the village."

"Well, then, take me to see where you live," said the cunning enemy soldier with a sneer. Tapping the pistol at his side, he said menacingly: "Little thing, if you're lying, I'm going to shoot you on the spot!"

"This is bad! What am I going to do now? Could the enemy soldier have found out I'm a spy?" Ma-lin stood up, the skin of his scalp tight, and walked toward the east end of the village. As he walked, he thought: "He can't have. The enemy soldier can't have found out. But I don't know anyone in this village. Who can cover for me?" When this thought occurred to him, he became very worried.

When they reached the east end of the village, Ma-lin saw a thatched hut and pointed to it, saying: "That's my house."

By chance a woman came out of the hut, and Ma-lin rushed up to her crying: "Mother! He wants to shoot me. He says I'm a spy and that I'm looking for information for the Communist Party."

Ma-lin's unexpected action gave the woman a start. But she understood very quickly. She held Ma-lin tightly as if he were her own son and even called him by her son's name. She said: "Camel, don't be afraid! What does a child know about spying? The officer here is just teasing you!"

There was nothing the enemy soldier could do and, giving the woman an angry stare, he turned and went.

Ma-lin, under the woman's protection, completed his scouting mission. The next day, pretending to leave the village to gather firewood, he went back to the cavalry company, where he reported the information he had discovered to the company commander and to the political officer.

The following night, the cavalry company surrounded Pa-li Village and completely annihilated the enemy.

From this time on, the soldiers in the cavalry company affectionately called Ma-lin by his new name—"Camel."

How did Ma-lin get his new name, "Camel"?

TWELVE. TO SAVE A FISHERMAN'S LIFE

One afternoon in the winter of 1957, a Class 8-to-9 gale suddenly arose in the Chou-shan fishing grounds. Many of the fishing boats that had been out to sea were not able to get back in time and were caught and driven by the violent winds and giant waves.

When the Chou-shan Naval Installation heard this news, it immediately sent some dozen gunboats out to the rescue.

The gunboats directed their powerful searchlights out into the blackness of the night and, avoiding the shoals, groped their way ahead in an attempt to rescue the fishermen in distress.

"There's a black shadow ahead!" This was the report of a soldier on watch on one of the gunboats. This soldier had already been on watch for several hours. The storm was so bad that to keep himself from being carried away by the huge waves he had tied himself tightly to an iron post with hemp rope. His eyes were swollen from the sea water, but he stuck to it. This was the fourth time he had found a fishing boat in distress. The mast of the fishing boat was broken, and the five fishermen on the boat were helpless before the wind and the waves. The soldiers thought of every means they could and finally tossed out a line, with which they steadied the fishing boat and by means of which they rescued the fishermen one by one.

Another of the gunboats, Boat No. 23, which was very light, was itself tossed up and hurled down as the giant waves rose and fell. The men on the boat, paying no heed to their danger, successively saved five fishing boats that were about to sink. As the storm grew more violent, Boat No. 23 again discovered a fishing boat that was being spun round and round in the eddies made by the giant waves. The boat captain abruptly issued the order: "Prepare your life-jackets and your lines. Forward! Boat No. 23 sped to the fishing boat like an arrow. Suddenly it was submerged by a series of waves, but in a moment it worked its way out of the waves and made the fishing boat fast.

With the help of the navy, all of the fishermen escaped from danger. But this storm resulted in heavy damage to the fishing boats. The navy units sent out many of their engineers to help the fishermen repair their boats. The fishermen said with emotion: "The Liberation Army is truly the army of the people."

Why did the soldiers save the fishing boats in distress? Why did the fishermen say that the Liberation Army was truly the army of the people?

THIRTEEN. WHY WE MUST PREDICT THE WEATHER

When elementary pupils want to go out on a trip, they wake up in the morning and ask: "How is the weather today? Is it a clear day or a cloudy day? Is it going to rain? Is it going to be windy?"

When sailors prepare to set sail or aviators prepare to take off, they must know what the weather is going to be like. When there is a heavy fog, it is very dangerous on the sea. Ships that cannot see what is around them move ahead blowing their fog horns so that other ships will know they are there. If one is careless and runs into another boat, the boat may be damaged and sink, and people may be injured or lose their lives. Flying is also very dangerous in a heavy fog. If a pilot cannot see clearly, he will have a great deal of difficulty landing.

Storms that arise suddenly are also very dangerous to sailing and aviation. If we can know beforehand that there is going to be a gale or that there is going to be a rainstorm, then we can avoid the danger. When the weather is about to turn bad, steamships do not set out to sea and airplanes do not take off.

If the weather is not appropriate to the season, agricultural crops may be endangered. If it doesn't rain in the spring and summer, and if watering is not done in time, then the crops may wither and die. If there is too much rain during the harvest season and the crops are not gathered in time, they may become damp and rot. Typhoons, rainstorms, hail, frost, and cold waves are also very dangerous to agriculture. If we know in advance what changes there will be in the weather, then we can make preparations against drought, heavy rains, wind, and freezing, and can plant and harvest at the proper times.

Before the Liberation, there were few weather observatories and weather stations in our nation. After the Liberation, there was a rapid development in meteorology, and weather observatories and weather stations were set up all over the country. Many of the people's communes also established weather outposts. There are even weather observatories and weather stations in such thinly populated places as the Tibetan and Tsinghai plateaus, the Pamir Plateau, and the Gobi Desert. The weather observatories and weather stations usually send out weather reports, in this way safeguarding shipping and aviation and benefiting agricultural production. The damage from typhoons, rainstorms, hail, frost, and cold waves can also be greatly diminished.

FOURTEEN. MOUNTAIN SONG OF A RICH HARVEST

In October the rice is ripe and yellow,
And the fields and the earth flash with gold.

The commune members are happy;
They rise early and rest late, busy with the harvest.

The rice plants bend like golden hooks,
Each golden hook reflecting the sun.
From the distance it is a golden sea,
And in the communes there is another rich harvest this year.

The mountain harvest songs sound over the land,
Each person singing in his own way;
The songs are different but the thought is the same,
All thanking Mao Tse-tung.

There is no end to the singing of the mountain songs,
Just as rivers flow on and on.
Forever following the Communist Party
Assures a rich harvest of food.

SIXTEEN. FOOD CROPS

Crops that are planted in the fields and which serve as food for people are called food crops. Wheat, rice, corn, sorghum, millet, and sweet potatoes are food crops.

Wheat

Wheat is one of the major food crops and, for the most part, is produced to the north of the Yangtze River.

The roots of wheat are fibrous roots. The stalks of the wheat plants are hollow and have nodules. The wheat leaves are narrow and long, and the lower leaves are wrapped around the stalk. The flowers of the wheat plant are not colorful, the buds being small with many buds clustered together. After the flowers fade, the wheat grows out from the flowers.

There are two kinds of wheat. The kind that is planted in the fall and that is harvested at the beginning of summer in the following year is called winter wheat. The kind that is planted in the spring and that is harvested at the end of the summer in the same year is called spring wheat.

Wheat is ground into flour, from which many kinds of foods can be made, such as cakes, steamed rolls, vermicelli, etc. The wheat stalks can be woven into mats and straw hats and can be fed to cattle.

Rice

Rice is our nation's major food crop and is produced for the most part to the south of the Yangtze River.

Rice is very much like wheat in appearance but differs from it in its habits and in the methods by which it is cultivated.

Rice likes warmth and usually is grown in wet paddy fields.

Rice is planted mostly in the spring. It is first planted in seed beds and, after the young plants have grown, replanted in the wet paddy fields. Early rice ripens in the summer, while middle and late rice ripens in autumn.

The rice is cut and dried. The milled kernels are the rice. This rice can be made into cooked rice. When the rice is ground into a powder, it can also be used to make various kinds of foods. Rice straw can be made into paper, straw sandals, straw cushions, and can be fed to cattle.

Corn

Corn is produced in all parts of our nation. The greatest amount of production is in North China, South China, and the Southwest regions.

Corn stalks grow as tall as a person, the ears of corn being attached to the stalk. The corn grains are very good to eat and are rich in nourishment. Not only is corn an important food, it is also an important industrial raw material. The leaves and stalks of the corn can be fed to cattle and can also be used to make paper, as fertilizer, and as fuel.

SEVENTEEN. ECONOMIC CROPS

Cotton

Cotton is an important economic crop and is the principal raw material of the textile industry.

There are many places in our nation where cotton may be planted. It can be planted in the Yangtze River valley, in the Yellow River valley, and in the Liao River valley.

Strong sunlight, fertile earth, and ample water are needed for the growth of cotton. A great deal of work must be done in planting cotton, such as preparing the ground, spacing the sprouts, banking up the earth, cultivation, applying fertilizer, and pruning. Once this work has been done, the cotton can grow well and there will be a rich harvest.

Cotton blossoms are very big and fade not long after they open out, after which the cotton buds grow out. Within the cotton buds is a white wool that is called fiber. The finer and longer the fiber is, the more difficult it is to break and the better the cotton is. As soon as the cotton buds are ripe, they can be broken open to reveal the white fibers that look like clumps of snow. At this time it can be picked. The cotton that has been picked is called seed cotton. When the seeds are removed, it is called cleaned cotton. When the cleaned cotton is drawn, it can then be spun into thread for cloth.

Peanuts

Peanuts are also an important economic crop. Peanuts contain a great deal of oil, which can be pressed from them.

There are swellings on the roots of the peanut. After the flowers blossom, fine tubes extend from them. These work their way into the soil, and the fruit grows from them. Therefore, they are also called "fallen peanuts."

Peanuts are adapted to planting in sandy soil. If the sand is loose, the tubes from the blossoms can easily work their way into the soil and produce peanuts.

The oil that is pressed from the peanuts, besides serving as food, also has many industrial uses. The sediment left over after pressing the oil can be used as fodder and as fertilizer.

Sugar Cane

Sugar cane has been planted in our nation for more than 2,200 years. At first it was eaten as a fruit, but later it was made into sugar.

The stalk of the sugar cane is from three or four feet to ten feet tall. There are nodules on the stalks like those on bamboo. Within the stalk there is abundant syrup. When the syrup is pressed out it can be boiled into sugar.

Sugar cane likes to grow in hot, rainy places, and a great deal is produced to the south of the Yangtze River. Taiwan is the place in our nation where the most sugar is produced.

Planting sugar cane is like planting crops. The soil must be turned over, fertilizer applied, cultivation carried out, weeds removed, and the fields irrigated.

NINETEEN. LENIN AND THE GUARD

The Smolny Institute in Petrograd was the headquarters of the October Revolution, and Lobanoff was a guard at the Smolny Institute. One day he was standing before the gate inspecting passes. Anyone entering had to take out his pass so that it could be inspected. At that time, the revolution had just been brought to a victorious conclusion, and if careful inspections were not carried out, secret agents might sneak in. Therefore it was necessary to be especially vigilant.

Lobanoff was a Red Guard and came from a working class family. He was extremely dedicated to the revolution and for that reason was called upon to stand guard at this important post.

He said to everyone entering: "Please wait a moment, Comrade! Let me look at your pass."

Without exception, each person took out his pass and let Lobanoff look at it. After Lobanoff had inspected the pass, he would raise his hand in a salute and say: "Please enter."

Lenin arrived at the Smolny Palace. He was wearing a plain fall jacket and a cap. As he walked along he was thinking about some matter, and when he came to the palace gate he started to walk straight in.

At that time, there were very few pictures of Lenin, and since Lenin had just arrived in Petrograd, Lobanoff did not recognize him. Lobanoff said to him: "Please wait a moment, Comrade! Let me look at your pass."

Lenin, who was deep in thought, suddenly hearing that someone wanted to see his pass, said: "Ah, that's right, my pass. Excuse me, Comrade, I'll take it out for you to see." As he spoke he pulled the pass from his pocket.

At this time a man with a short beard arrived. When he saw that the guard had not let Lenin enter, he said angrily: "This is Comrade Lenin! Let him go in!"

Lobanoff said to the man in a low voice: "If he didn't have a pass, I couldn't let him enter. Besides, I don't know who you are either, and I must look at your pass too!"

The man grew even more angry and shouted loudly: "Let Comrade Lenin in at once!"

Lenin said severely: "Don't shout like that. What he has done is perfectly correct. No matter who a person is, he must respect the regulations."

Lenin handed his pass to Lobanoff, who opened it, examined it carefully, and found that the man really was Lenin.

Lobanoff raised his hand in salute to Lenin and said: "Please forgive me, Comrade Lenin!"

Lenin said: "Comrade, what you did was correct. One ought to serve in this conscientious way. Thank you!"

When Lobanoff wanted to inspect the pass, what was the difference between Lenin's attitude and that of the short-bearded man? Who was right and who was wrong? Who was correct? Who was incorrect?

TWENTY-ONE. WEIGHING AN ELEPHANT

In the time of the Three Kingdoms, there was a man called Ts'ao Ch'ung. One day when he was seven years old, he went with his father, Ts'ao Ts'ao, to see a big elephant.

There were several people estimating the weight of the elephant. Some said 1,000 catties, and some said 2,000 catties. They argued among themselves unendingly. Ts'ao Ts'ao asked: "How much does this big elephant actually weigh?" This question brought everyone to a halt, and they could give no answer. In order to find out exactly how much the elephant weighed, it would have to be weighed on a scales. But where was there a pair of scales that big?

Then Ts'ao Ch'ung thought of a good solution. He said: "Lead the elephant onto a large boat and see how deep the boat sinks and make a mark on the side of the boat. Then lead the elephant back to the bank and pile stones into the boat. When the boat sinks to the same depth, unload the stones and weigh them separately. When you add the weights together wouldn't that be the weight of the elephant?"

When everyone heard this, they all said: "That's right. That is really a good solution."

TWENTY-TWO. LOOKING FOR A CAMEL

Once upon a time there was a merchant who had lost a camel and who had looked for it everywhere but could not find it.

The merchant saw an old man ahead and, running up to him, asked: "Sir, you haven't seen my camel, have you?"

The old man said: "Is your camel lame in his left leg and blind in his right eye?"

"Yes."

"Was it carrying honey on its left side and rice on its right?"

"That's right."

"Does it have a missing tooth?"

"That's it. You've seen where it went. Please tell me at once."

The old man said: "That I don't know."

The merchant said angrily: "Don't try to fool me. You must have hidden my camel away. If you haven't, how could you know about it in such detail?"

The old man said slowly: "What is there to be angry about? Listen to what I have to say. I was walking along the highway just now when I saw the footprints of a camel. The right side was deep and the left side shallow, so that I knew the camel was lame in the left foot. I also saw that quite a bit of the grass on the left side of the road had been eaten, but that not a bit had been eaten from the right side, so I knew the camel was blind in his right eye, seeing only the grass on the left side, but not the grass on the right side. I also saw many flies on the left side of the road and many ants on the right. When I looked more carefully, the flies were eating honey, and the ants were carrying rice. Therefore I figured out that the camel was carrying honey on his left side and rice on his right. I also saw the marks of the camel's teeth on the leaves it had chewed, so that I knew it was missing one tooth. I have deduced all this from what I have seen. As to where the camel has gone, you should follow his trail rather than ask me."

When the merchant heard this, he expressed his thanks and began his search in the direction pointed out by the old man.

TWENTY-FOUR. KICKING A "GHOST"

When Lu Hsün was teaching school in his native village, he liked to chat at a friend's house in the evenings, returning to the school very late from his conversations. The road from his friend's house to the school was several miles in length and passed through a cemetery.

Once Lu Hsün was returning very late. Luckily there was moonlight and it was not very dark. He was walking along very rapidly and staring absently into the distance when he saw a white shadow.

Lu Hsün, who was a student of medicine, had often dissected dead people, and he neither feared the dead nor believed in ghosts, so he continued walking ahead as before.

After he had walked a few more steps, the white shadow in the distance disappeared. A few steps later, he saw it again. Sometimes it looked tall, sometimes short, sometimes big, and sometimes small, just like the ghosts of traditional tales.

Lu Hsün continued to walk ahead, with the intention of seeing what it actually was. When he came up beside the white shadow, the white shadow shrank, squatting down beside a burial mound.

That day Lu Hsün was wearing a pair of thick leather shoes, and he directed a vigorous kick at the white shadow.

The white shadow let out a yell. When Lu Hsun looked more carefully, he found that it was a grave robber.

What did Lu Hsün do when he saw the white shadow in the cemetery? What was the result?

THIRTY. THE GREAT WALL

We set out from Peking by train on the Ching-pao Line (i.e., the Peking-Paotou Line). After we had passed Nan-k'ou Station, we could see a line of wall. The wall followed the undulations of the mountain topography, being built along high and steep mountain ridges, and was extremely imposing and beautiful in appearance.

The Great Wall was a defense construction project of antiquity. Its construction was begun during the period of the Warring States. At that time, the various countries in north China each built separate sections of wall. During the Ch'in Dynasty, Ch'in Shih Huang, in order to prevent the attacks of outsiders, joined the original sections of the wall together, this construction becoming the Great Wall. The building of the Great Wall was an immense undertaking. In order to complete the construction, hundreds of thousands of laboring people, under the oppression of Ch'in Shih Huang, worked for many years and spilled much blood and sweat. Many lives were sacrificed. From that time forward, the emperors of many dynasties have levied the laboring people to repair the Great Wall, in some places adding on new sections and in some places changing its original course. Therefore, the Great Wall that we see today is the result of several thousand years of collective labor by countless numbers of the laboring people.

The Great Wall arises in the eaast at Shan-hai-kuan and extends to Chia-yū-kuan in the west, crossing more than 5000 *li.* At the passes and at strategic points there are often several layers of wall. The Great Wall has an average height of about 30 feet and is 15 to 20 feet wide. If the bricks making up the Great Wall were used to build a wall seven feet high and four feet wide, it would encircle the earth. The Great Wall is not only long; it is also solidly built. Even though it has undergone the attacks of winds and rain for some thousands of years, even now it is still largely intact, and its foundations are very firm.

The Great Wall is one of the great constructions of ancient China, and this structure is famous all over the world.

Why is it said that the Great Wall is the result of several thousand years of collective labor by countless numbers of the laboring people?

THIRTY-ONE. THE GRAND CANAL

The Grand Canal was one of the great construction projects in our nation's history. It begins at Peking in the north and extends southward to Hangchow. It is more than 1,700 kilometers in length.

More than 1,300 years ago, Yang Ti of the Sui Dynasty, in order to strengthen his control over the south and to travel to the south for pleasure and amusement, levied several million laboring people and from Loyang in Honan built a canal through to Yangchow in Kiangsu. The millions of laboring people, using shovels to dig out the mud and stones, opened up new waterways and dredged out old waterways. Under the oppression of reactionary control, they labored incessantly and within half a year had opened up the canal. Along the canal, broad embankments were built, and willow trees were planted along one section of the embankment.

A few years later, Yang Ti again levied the laboring people to build a canal from Loyang to Peking and to build a canal from Chenchiang in Kiangsu to Hangchow in Chekiang. These two canals were joined with the canal from Loyang to Yangchow, making what was called the Grand Canal.

During the Yüan Dynasty, the Grand Canal was rebuilt, an intermediate section of canal being built across Shantung. In this way, ships could sail directly from Peking to Hangchow.

The laboring people of ancient times in our nation, under extremely difficult conditions of material life and of technology, opened up the Grand Canal, making communication between north and south much more convenient. In the last one hundred years, because it had not been dredged, the canal was blocked to travel, there being several places through which ships could not pass.

After the Liberation, the people on the banks of the canal, under the leadership of the Party, carried out a great deal of dredging work. Now, the canal has been thoroughly reconstructed for the convenience of communication, the irrigation of farm lands, and the supply of water or industry. In short, it can now better serve socialist re-construction.

What has been the effect of the Grand Canal on history? Why is it said that the Grand Canal is one of the great construction projects in the history of our country?

THIRTY-TWO. KUANG'S BISCUITS

Over 400 years ago, during the Chia Ching period of the Ming Dynasty (Trans. Note: 1522-1567), the coastal regions of Fukien and Chekiang were often attacked by the dwarf pirates (Trans. Note: Refers to the Japanese pirates, the Japanese being called "dwarfs" by the Chinese.) The dwarf pirates burned, killed, and plundered everywhere they went, and the common people suffered greatly.

There was at that time a military officer by the name of Ch'i Chi-kuang. He was born into a poor family and from a very young age was very ambitious. He studied military affairs with great effort and learned the skills of commanding an army. When he saw that the government troops were inefficient and incompetent, he enlisted a new army of three thousand soldiers from among the common people and in person led them in the attack against the pirates.

In battle, Ch'i Chi-kuang was always at the head of his troops. Once, he was in the fore alone assaulting the enemy positions. One of the pirate chiefs saw him and was so frightened that both of his hands trembled. With one blow, Ch'i Chi-kuang slashed his arm. The pirate chief, in pain, lay down on his horse and quickly escaped. Ch'i Chi-kuang, who was following close behind him, fired three arrows in succession and struck him down from his horse. When the soldiers saw how brave their leader was, they killed pirates right and left with little thought for their own safety.

Not only was Ch'i Chi-kuang very brave in battle; he was also very clever. Once, the pirates who were invading Fukien had occupied a small island. At high tide, the island was surrounded on all sides by water and at low tide by mud. When horses and men walked over the mud, they sank into it. The pirates thought that Ch'i Chi-kuang's army could certainly not cross over and made no defensive preparations whatsoever. Ch'i Chi-kuang studied the terrain carefully and then ordered each of the soldiers to prepare a bundle of straw. One evening when the sky was blanketed by fog, he sent his war-ships in the direction of the island. The soldiers, throwing the straw that they had prepared into the mud, made a road of it and in this way launched their attack on the island. The pirates could not rise to the defense in time, and every one of them was taken prisoner.

At that time, communications were very inconvenient, and it was very difficult to supply food to Ch'i Chi-kuang's troops, who were fighting day after day along the coast. In their pursuit of the enemy, the soldiers often could not eat on time, and this affected their fighting. So Ch'i Chi-kuang thought of a solution. He made biscuits of rice flour, and in the middle of each biscuit he made a hole, through which he tied them together with string. When the soldiers were fighting, they tied strings of these biscuits to their bodies. They were very convenient to carry, and it was very easy to pull off the biscuits in order to eat.

Ch'i Chi-kuang's troops fought very bravely and were well-disciplined. The common people supported them very well and, in a few years, they had driven the invading bandits out.

Later, in order to commemorate Ch'i Chi-kuang, the common

people of the region made biscuits with holes in the middle, which they called "Kuang Biscuits."

THIRTY-THREE. LI CH'UANG WANG CROSSES THE YELLOW RIVER

Over 300 years ago, at a time when the ruling classes of the Ming Dynasty were most corrupt, the emperor and the government officials were cruelly exploiting the peasants to the point where they had no means of livelihood. There was at that time a peasant leader, Li Tzu-ch'eng, who led a revolt in Shensi and whom the people called Ch'uang Wang. Ch'uang Wang was leading a peasant army in readiness to cross the Yellow River and annihilate the greedy and corrupt officials and landlords and bullies who were bringing calamity to the nation and to the people in order to avenge the common people for their hardships and sufferings.

At that time, the weather was that of early winter, and the rushing waters of the Yellow River blocked the peasant army's route of advance. Ch'uang Wang could only order the whole army to a halt. The next day, Ch'uang Wang sent two men to see whether the Yellow River had frozen over. The two men returned, reporting that the Yellow River had not yet frozen. Ch'uang Wang was so distressed that half of his hair turned white. The third day, Ch'uang Wang again sent the two men out to see whether the Yellow River had frozen over. The two men returned, reporting that the Yellow River, as before, had not yet frozen. Ch'uang Wang was so distressed that the rest of his hair turned white.

The fourth day, Ch'uang Wang once again sent the two men out to look. When they arrived at the river bank and heard the sound of the water lapping, they knew that the Yellow River had still not frozen over. One of the men said: "Our Great Chief wants the Yellow River to freeze over so that he can save the common people from their suffering. All of his hair has turned white in two days' time on hearing that the Yellow River has not frozen over. If we go back today and tell him that the Yellow River has not frozen over, he will be even more upset. We've got to figure out the best thing to do."

As the two men were talking, the boatmen on the banks of the Yellow River heard them and were all very much moved. They said to the two men, "We've got a solution. The Yellow River won't freeze, so we'll make a floating bridge that will let the army cross. You go back and say that the Yellow River has frozen over."

The two men hurried back to report. As soon as Ch'uang Wang heard, he was extremely happy and immediately issued orders to the army to cook at the fourth watch and set out at the fifth watch. They arrived at the river bank and, hearing the lapping of the water, knew that it had not in the least frozen over. But boats were lined up in the river, end to end and deck to deck, making a wide floating bridge. Ch'uang Wang thought this was strange. Several boatmen came up to him. One of the boatmen said: "We are Yellow River boatmen, and when we heard that the Great Chief wanted the Yellow River to freeze over so that he could save the common people from suffering, we were very happy. We saw men coming every day to see whether the Yellow River had frozen over, and we knew that you were anxious to cross the river. So, in a night's work, we built this floating bridge."

Ch'uang Wang thanked the boatmen and led the army in a victorious crossing of the Yellow River.

Why did the boatmen want to build a bridge for the peasant army led by Li Ch'uang Wang?

THIRTY-SIX. HSIANG HSIU-LI

Hsiang Hsiu-li was a worker in a drug manufacturing plant in Canton. She worked in the chemical workshop.

On the evening of December 13, 1958, an unfortunate incident took place in the workshop. A bottle of alcohol tipped over and a large amount spilled out. When it came into contact with the hot air from the coal stove, it immediately caught on fire, the blazing flames quickly burning their way toward some metallic sodium. If the fire had reached the sodium, it would have exploded, and the blast would have severely damaged the plant as well as endangering the lives and property of the people in the neighborhood.

A serious accident was about to occur. Just at this critical moment, Hsiang Hsiu-li, with no thought for her own safety, rushed up to the fire, blocking off the alcohol with her body so that it could not flow towards the sodium. The flames set her clothes on fire and burned her hands. At that time, Hsiang Hsiu-li had only one thought in her mind: that no matter what happened, she could not let the sodium explode and could not allow the property of the nation to be damaged.

The fire grew bigger and bigger, and as the workshop filled with flames and smoke, Hsiang Hsiu-li's whole body caught on fire. But she still held fast, using her body to block the fire.

The plant's Party Branch Secretary and the Workroom Chief rushed in leading the workers, everyone rushing forward to put out the flames covering her body. She said: "Don't bother with me; save the sodium at once!"

The fire was extinguished and the plant saved. But the young Communist Party member Hsiang Hsiu-li had been seriously injured, and she lost consciousness.

When Hsiang Hsiu-li awoke in the hospital and saw the Party Branch Secretary, the first thing that she asked was: "Did the sodium explode? Was the plant damaged?" When she heard that the plant had not been damaged, she smiled happily.

Hsiang Hsiu-li had been severely injured, and every move seemed like a knife cutting into her. But she never groaned aloud. When anyone went in to see her, she said: "I'm fine. It doesn't hurt. Don't worry about me."

The Party and the people tried every means to save Hsiang Hsiu-li's life, but her injuries were too severe. She sacrificed herself gloriously.

Although Hsiang Hsiu-li was sacrificed, her lofty Communist spirit and her heroic self-sacrifice for the people will always live on in our hearts.

In what ways was Hsiang Hsiu-li's lofty Communist spirit exemplified?

SELECTIONS FROM
VOLUME 8 OF THE
READERS

(GRADE FOUR)

THREE. THE TA-HSÜEH MOUNTAINS

Not long after the Red Army Troops on the Long March (1934-1935) crossed the Tatu River, they reached the Ta-hsüeh Mountains.

The Ta-hsüeh Mountains are in western Szechuan. There are no people, no flowers and trees, and not even any roads there. Throughout the four seasons of the year, the mountains are covered by thick snows. In summer, when people in other places are fanning themselves in the heat, snowflakes are still flying and cold winds pierce one's bones on the Ta-hsüeh Mountains.

The air on the Ta-hsüeh Mountains is extremely thin. On the mountains it is hard to breathe, and one' has to stop to get one's breath at almost every step. Moreover, the weather is very strange, for sometimes there are heavy snows, sometimes hail-storms, and sometimes even violent winds and heavy rains. The shrieking winds can spin a person around as if he were a leaf on a tree or hurl him from the top of the mountain to its base.

The Red Army had set out from Kiangsi and had been on the way for eight months. Their clothes were worn out and their straw sandals had rotted. They had no jackets, no padded shoes, no caps, and no gloves. How could they pass through as cold and snow-filled a mountain as this? No difficulty, however, could impede the heroic Red Army. In order to go northward to resist Japan, in order to overthrow the reactionaries, and in order to secure the liberation of all the people, the Red Army had to battle with an evil enemy and with an evil natural environment. The Red Army had to conquer the Ta-hsüeh Mountains and cross over them.

332

When the Red Army troops reached the foot of the Ta-hsüeh Mountains, each soldier opened his bundle and put on everything that it was possible to wear. Those with blankets wrapped their bodies in them, and those with oilcloth put the oilcloth over their heads. Some of the soldiers found strips of cloth and rice straw, which they tied to their feet as wadded shoes. Some of the soldiers found pieces of sheepskin, which they put over their bodies as overcoats.

Before they went up onto the mountain, each soldier drank a bowl of pepper soup. It is said that pepper soup can stimulate blood circulation and warm the body so that it can withstand cold mountain winds.

The Red Army set out, file after file, one after the other, advancing toward the snow-covered Ta-hsüeh Mountains.

The snowflakes, driven by the wind, like ten thousand prancing horses, shrieked down from the top of the mountain, blowing the soldiers about like tree branches, so that they could not keep their balance. Black clouds brought hail, and the hailstones, as big as chicken eggs, sounded like a rattle on the tin buckets being carried by the cooks. As soon as the blizzard had passed, there was a heavy rain. Freezing rain soaked their clothes and ran under their collars onto their chests until their bodies were completely soaked. The courageous Red Army, braving hail and driving rains and treading through snow up to their knees, advanced, step by step, towards the snow-covered mountaintop.

The closer they got to the top, the colder it became and the more difficult it was to breathe. The soldiers' lips were frozen white, and their teeth chattered. They walked on, the young supporting the old, the strong supporting the weak, the men supporting the women, and the children holding onto the horses' tails. They walked on! Getting across the Ta-hsüeh Mountains would be a victory!

The Red Army's information corps was for the most part made up of young fellows. They stood halfway up the mountain, beating gongs and drums and waving red flags in order to stir everyone into advancing.

Thousands upon thousands of the Red Army, following the Red Flag and following Chairman Mao, advanced on the snow-covered mountain. From morning until noon and from noon until dusk they advanced and advanced, until finally they had made their way over the first of the Ta-hsüeh Mountains—Chia-chin Mountain.

At the foot of the Chia-chin Mountain was a market town called Ta-wei. The lead group of the four-part army was waiting there for the branch of the Central Red Army to come from Kiangsi. The two branches of the Red Army joined forces at the foot of the Ta-hsüeh Mountains. Dancing, singing, shouting, and embracing each other, everyone was so happy that tears flowed from their eyes.

SEVEN. WRITE MUCH AND REVISE MUCH

When we wish to write well, we must write diligently and practice a great deal.

When one is beginning the study of writing, one should not be afraid of writing poorly. In whatever one does, one progresses from bad to good, from unfamiliarity to familiarity. When a child is learning to walk, he can't avoid falling down. If he is not afraid of falling and practices every day, gradually he will learn to walk. Studying writing is like that.

Not being afraid of writing poorly is to have the courage to write. When one participates in labor, sees some significant event, hears a good story, or has any impressions in one's mind, these can be written out. Keeping a diary, keeping notes, writing copy for wall newspapers, and writing reports for periodicals are all good methods of practicing writing.

Just writing by itself is not enough. It is also necessary to repeatedly revise what has been written. When one has finished writing an article, it should be examined carefully to see whether or not the central idea of the article is clear and whether the viewpoint is correct. If there are places that are unsatisfactory, careful thought should be given to them and they should be revised. When revising, the following four points should be observed:

1. First, see whether what one wished to write has been written clearly. If there are places that are obscure, they should be corrected. Then one should see whether what one wished to write has been written completely. If there are places where there are omissions, these should be filled in.

2. One must see whether the order is clear. When one narrates an event or expresses an opinion, it must be done systematically

and in a clear order. It cannot be confused and disorderly. If one feels that it would be better to shift the last part to the beginning, then it should be revised. If the ideas in two paragraphs repeat each other, then they should be combined into one paragraph, or one of the paragraphs should be eliminated. If one paragraph contains several ideas, and they are involved and complex, then it should be revised into several paragraphs.

3. One must see whether or not the wording is satisfactory. One should read aloud what one has written. Any sentence that does not run smoothly or which is not stated clearly is an unsatisfactory sentence and must be revised. If a word is not used properly, then another word should be used in its place. If a sentence is not well constructed, replace it with another. Once it has undergone revision in this way, it can be expressed accurately.

4. One should see whether there are wrong characters, incorrectly written characters, and incorrect punctuation. Even if an article is well written, if there are many wrong characters, incorrectly written characters, or incorrect punctuation, it will be difficult for people to read clearly and it may even lead to misunderstandings. Therefore, it should be examined carefully, and wrong characters, incorrectly written characters, and incorrect punctuation revised.

If one writes much and revises much, then one can raise one's writing ability very quickly.

EIGHT. SIX INK BOTTLES

Lenin was leading the working class in carrying out the revolutionary struggle in St. Petersburg. The Czarist government was trying everywhere to capture him.

Once, Lenin was arrested by the Czar's police and put into prison. But how could a prison shut in a revolutionary mind like Lenin's? In prison, he carried on his revolutionary work as before.

Life in prison was bitter and depressing, and his room was dark and without air. Some people could not endure it and spent the whole day moaning and sighing, with mournful expressions on their faces. Lenin was not like this. His heart was filled with enthusiasm for the revolution, and he lived bravely and happily. This optimistic spirit stimulated his other comrades.

There was a library in the prison from which the prisoners could borrow books. Each time that Lenin went there, he borrowed a big stack of books. When his fellow prisoners heard that there was someone walking through the corridors lugging a big basket of books, they knew that this must be Lenin. Who besides Lenin would be reading so many books?

Lenin studied under hardship in prison, collecting data and making careful investigations. Prison became his place of study and work. One day, Lenin's elder sister came to call on him and told him: "I've heard that your case will soon be closed and that you'll be allowed to leave soon." Lenin smiled, saying: "How soon! I haven't got my data collected yet!"

In prison, Lenin wrote the Party Laws of the Russian Communist Party and wrote many pamphlets and leaflets which he sent out secretly in order to lead the revolutionary struggle on the outside.

If Lenin had been discovered writing these secret articles in prison, that would have been a "crime" on top of a "crime," and he might have been executed by hanging. He thought of a way. He wrote in milk on the blank spaces of books. Once they were sent outside, his comrades heated the books over a fire, and the words appeared. For his "ink bottles" he used bread filled with milk. When he was writing with his head bowed, as soon as he heard a sound he would put his "ink bottle" into his mouth and swallow it. The military police came several times a day to inspect, but they never discovered his secret. Once, he wrote humorously in a letter to one of his comrades: "I really didn't go far today. I ate six bottles of ink in a row!"

How did Lenin carry on revolutionary struggle in prison? Memorize and recite the text.

THIRTEEN. THE CAMEL

For several thousands of years, on the vast deserts, the camel has been the principal means of transportation.

The body structure and habits of the camel are closely related to desert life.

The camel is very tall, has a long neck, and is able to see for long distances on the desert. The camel's nose is very large and it has an especially keen sense of smell for water. Wherever there is water, a camel can smell it. Travellers on the desert frequently rely on the camel's sense of smell to find water. The camel can also close its nose tightly to keep out the hot winds and blowing sand.

Sometimes travellers go for six or seven days over the grassless and waterless desert without their camels eating or drinking anything at all. But the camels walk ahead undisturbed, feeling neither thirst nor lack of strength.

At these times, the humps on the back of the camel gradually grow smaller day by day. The humps are storehouses of fat. Under favorable conditions, a great deal of fat gradually collects in the humps. After several days without food and water, the fat in the humps is gradually consumed, and they therefore become smaller.

The camel eats the leaves of plants, grass, and also plants bearing thorns.

The sole of the camel's foot is broad and thick, with two toes. When the feet strike the ground, the two toes spread apart. Therefore, it cannot sink into the loose, shifting sands.

There are thick calluses on the camel's legs. The desert sands are often heated boiling hot by the sun, and, with the calluses, it is not burned when it walks through the sand.

Not only can the camel endure heat, it can also endure cold. When the weather is severely cold, the camel is often out in the open, but no one has ever seen a camel so cold that its teeth were chattering.

Camels have been living on the desert for thousands of years, and they have adapted to the characteristics of the desert. Since people travelling on the deserts have used the camel as a means of transportation, it is no wonder that it has been called "the ship of the desert."

FIFTEEN. CROSSING A BRIDGE

From behind the hills to the west of the bridge there arose the sound of trucks. Some dozen large trucks drawing heavy artillery began to rumble out from behind the hills.

One by one, the trucks easily crossed the bridge. As the last truck was crossing the bridge, one wheel of the artillery carriage that it was drawing went off the edge of the bridge and hung in mid-air, stranding the gun on the bridge. The two trucks rumbled and roared, but they could not budge, and the wheel of the gun carriage could not be pulled back up onto the bridge.

The trucks ahead all came to a stop. Scores of soldiers jumped down from the trucks, running up to the gun and looking at it. They pushed and pulled, keeping at it until everyone was tired and their faces were covered with sweat, but the gun could not be budged.

One of the soldiers said: "Don't work blindly. There's no use trying to lift this fellow up without a crane!" The platoon leader said: "Don't talk nonsense! Doesn't Chairman Mao teach us that when we have a problem we must talk it over with the masses? Let's ask some old local people to come at once and help us think out a solution!"

Several of the soldiers ran over to the neighboring village and brought back a few peasants. The platoon leader told them of the difficulty and asked them to help in working out a solution. The peasants looked at the gun carriage, some of them saying that they could haul it out with cattle, some of them proposing that the bigger of them lift it out, while some of them said nothing, but tried to push it forward. For a while, the platoon leader could not decide which method to use. An old man was standing at one side, a pipe between his teeth, looking at the gun carriage and not saying a word. The platoon leader asked him: "Sir, what do you think would be best?" The old man said: "The methods they have suggested will hardly do. As I see it, we ought to borrow a big boat and some thick boards and, by making use of the force of the water, we may be able to push this fellow up." Then he explained the method to everyone in detail.

Everyone agreed to use the old man's method. Several of the peasants and soldiers ran to the village and borrowed a big boat and several pieces of board.

They placed the boat near the edge of the bridge and, bucket by bucket, poured water into its hold. After the boat had sunk down into the water several feet, they piled the boards onto the boat, which was beneath the wheel that was hanging in mid-air. The pile of boards grew higher and higher. After they had come into close contact with the wheel, everyone poured the water from the boat's hold back into the river. As the amount of water in it grew less, the boat began to float slowly upward, the boards touching the wheel also slowly rising until finally the wheel was pushed upward.

"Good!" the peasants and the soldiers called out in unison.

The driver at once jumped aboard the truck. The truck started up, and the gun carriage crossed the bridge steadily.

When they left, the soldiers said to the peasants: "Sirs, many thanks for your help!" The platoon leader said to the old man: "We are very fortunate that you thought out this method."

The old man waved his hand and said: "Not at all. When there are many people, one can work out good ideas."

TWENTY. THE ABUNDANT HSI-SHA ARCHIPELAGO

The Hsi-sha Archipelago is a group of islands in the South China Sea. It is a place of beautiful scenery and abundant products. It is a delightful place.

In the region of the Hsi-sha Archipelago, the sea water gives off many colors, deep blue, light blue, green, light green, and apricot yelow, all interchanging with one another in exceptional beauty. This is because there are high peaks and deep valleys in the ocean floor, the depth of the water not being uniform. Seen from the surface, it is of different colors.

The rock on the sea floor is filled with coral of various colors. There are sea-slugs everywhere, undulating lazily. Great lobsters, their bodies covered with armor, slide by with a majestic air. School upon school of fish thread their way through the forests of coral. Some have long, striped bodies. Some have red spines on their heads. There is a kind of flying tiger fish that appears to have its body surrounded by fans, and which is extremely pretty when swimming. There is a kind of lung-fish with round eyes and a long body covered with spines. When it swells out with air, it is as round as a leather ball. There are so many kinds of fish that it is hard to keep count of them. For this reason, people say that one half of the sea in the Hsi-sha Archipelago is water and the other half is fish.

On the beaches, there are many kinds of beautiful shells, big and small, of all colors and shapes. They are truly amazing, and there is no spot without them. The most interesting are the sea-turtles. In April and May of each year, giant sea-turtles crawl ashore in schools to lay their eggs. Fishermen flip the sea-turtles over so that their legs are in the air, making it difficult for them to move.

The Hsi-sha Archipelago is also a kingdom of birds. There are strips of tall forests on the islands, and many kinds of sea birds nest in the woods. There are eggs of sea birds everywhere. Beneath the trees, there are piles of bird droppings as high as mountains. This is a valuable manure for agricultural production.

In the past, the Hsi-sha Archipelago was very desolate, but after the Liberation, the Party and the government sent many scientists and workers to the islands to work. As a result of their hard labors, the Hsi-sha Archipelago has become an extremely attractive place.

TWENTY-THREE. LI SHIH-CHEN

Li Shih-chen was one of our nation's great doctors and pharmacologists. He was a native of Ch'i-ch'un in Hupeh during the Ming Dynasty. His family had been doctors by trade for generations. His grandfather was a "bell doctor," who spent the year away from home, going along the rivers and the lakes. His father was a people's doctor, who had set out his shingle and treated the sick in a temple that was called the "Monastery of the Abstruse." When Li Shih-chen was a little boy, he studied at his father's side. Those that asked his father to treat them were all poor people. They could not pay the fees for treatment and could not ask other doctors to treat them. How happy they were to be able to come to the Monastery of the Abstruse and receive free treatment from his father! Li Shih-chen, on seeing this, from that time forth resolved to treat the poor.

During the Ming Dynasty, medicine was an occupation that was looked down on. All families of "status" wanted their children to study the "eight-legged essays" in preparation for the imperial examinations so that they could become officials and glorify the family. They were not willing for them to study medicine. Li Shih-chen's father had had a difficult life, having borne decades of distress, and hoped that his son would take the examinations.

But Li Shih-chen, his resolve fixed on studying medicine and with no concern for hardship or the scorn of others, persuaded his father and persevered in his study with him. When he reached 22 years of age, he began to treat the sick. One year there was a great flood in Ch'i-ch'un, the waters of the Yangtze River pushing their way into the Ch'i River, flooding farm lands and destroying homes. After the waters had withdrawn, an epidemic broke out. Li Shih-chen saved lives and helped the injured day and night with no thought of reward. There was no one treated by him who was not grateful. Because he usually treated the poor, there were many peasants, fishermen, and hunters who were his friends.

As Li Shih-chen practiced medicine, he also studied drugs. In his thirty-fifth year, he began to compile his *Materia Medica (Pents'ao kang-mu)*. In the beginning the work went smoothly, but later he experienced difficulties. He found many old drug books that were not complete and some in which only the names of the herbs had been written down without descriptions of their shape and habits of growth. In order to clarify these problems, he decided to collect herbs from every location himself. He feared neither high mountains nor remote paths, severe cold nor intense heat, travelling to all of the famous mountains where raw drugs were produced. He made friends everywhere who helped him enthusiastically, telling him about the growth habits of plants, telling him of much knowledge that could not be found in books, and helping him to gather each kind of herb.

Li Shih-chen spent a full twenty-seven years reading many kinds of herb books, journeying ten thousand *li*, and listening to the suggestions of thousands of people before finishing his *Materia Medica*. In order to improve the book even further, he made three revisions, each of which was almost total. His writing desk was piled several feet high with notebooks on which he wrote down his raw data. These materials were in part copied from ancient books, in part what he had heard from others, and in part what he had written down while gathering herbs. After repeated study and meticulous revision, his great work, the *Materia Medica*, was at last completed.

All his life, Li Shih-chen, cherishing his great ambition, kept to his arduous labors. Not only did he make an outstanding contribution to our nation's medicine and to pharmacology, but his work has received respect in international medical circles. This great work, the *Materia Medica*, has been translated into Russian, English, Japanese, German, and French.

After the Liberation, the Party and the government, in their great respect for the contributions of Chinese traditional medicine and herbs to the health of the people of the nation over thousands of years, summoned those in medical circles to carry out research on traditional medicine and herbs. Li Shih-chen's *Materia Medica* has had a great effect on this research.

TWENTY-FIVE. A STORY ABOUT BORROWING A PICTURE BOOK

Our school has a small library, in which there are three people who take turns in supervising the work of lending and returning books. I am one of these three supervisors.

Our library has a rule: Because there are many people who look at picture books, they can look at them only in the library and cannot take them outside. Cheng Li, who is in our class, violated this rule, and I criticized him in class. Whenever he saw me, he always pouted, and it seemed as if he bore a resentment against me.

Cheng Li was my neighbor; we lived in a courtyard. Before, we almost always went to school and came home together. Ever since he came under my criticism, we each went our own way.

The day before yesterday, my little brother climbed up into a tree to pick some mulberry leaves for the silkworms, and in his carelessness fell, breaking his leg. The doctor put medicine on it and applied a cast, telling him over and over again that he must lie down in bed and not get out without the doctor's permission.

This was very hard on little brother, who lay on his bed all day fussing and complaining.

Mother said to me: "Ying-ying, why don't you bring home some picture books for him to look at."

As soon as he heard this, little brother at once said: "I want to look at picture books. I want to look at picture books." I said: "All right, I'll bring back a picture book for you!"

Having spoken, I thought to myself: "Ai-ya, how will this do? How can I bring a picture book home?"

Yesterday it was my turn to be on duty in the library. After school had let out, only one person remained in the library. At that moment, I really didn't know what would be the best thing to do. If I were to take some of the books home, I would be

violating the rule; but if I didn't take any home, how disappoint-
ed little brother would be! I paced back and forth in front of the
bookcases, unable to make up my mind. For the sake of little
brother, I wanted to take down some picture books from the
bookcase, but I also felt that this was something that I shouldn't
do. It seemed as if the eyes of all of my teachers and classmates
were fixed on me and as if their eyes were saying: "Others have
to obey the rules, but you're special! You don't observe the rules
that you yourself set up ..." At last I gave up the idea of
borrowing the picture books, straightened things up, and went
home.

As I drew near the door to his room, little brother must have
heard the sound of my footsteps, and from his room he was
calling excitedly: "Big sister, are you back?"

I walked into his room. Little brother stretched out both of his
hands from under his coverings and said: "How I've been waiting
for you to come! Quick, give me the picture books!"

I lowered my head. What could I say in answer to him? Little
brother, seeing the expression on my face, guessed that I had not
borrowed any picture books for him. In anger, he turned his face
to the wall and started to cry.

In a little while someone knocked on the door. When I opened
the door, to my surprise it was Cheng Li! In his hand he was
carrying two picture books. He walked quickly up to little
brother's bed and said to little brother: "Lin-lin, look, I'm lending
these two picture books to you." After he finished speaking, he
ran out with rapid strides.

Today, when I went to school and saw Cheng Li, I felt very
uncomfortable. Yesterday when he abruptly came with the picture
books for little brother, I hadn't even said thank you.

Before class in the afternoon, I had just walked into the
classroom when my classmates suddenly surrounded me. One of
my classmates handed me a picture book, saying: "For your little
brother." Another classmate also gave me a book, saying: "For
your little brother." Before long I had received more than 30
books. I looked from classmate to classmate, not knowing how to
express my thanks. It was strange. How could they have known
that my brother had been hurt and was lying in bed wanting to
look at picture books?

After school, I put my satchel in order and returned home. My
satchel was bulging. When I reached the school entrance, Cheng
Li was waiting for me! With what seemed like a great effort, he
said something like the following: "Let's walk home together
today."

"Fine!" I said happily.

On the way, I asked him why he brought the picture books for little brother yesterday and why everyone in the class lent little brother the picture books. At first he didn't want to tell me, but after I had asked him several times he finally spoke. "I knew about what happened when you returned home yesterday. I heard Lin-lin crying, and I knew that he had asked you for picture books and that you had not brought him any. I was very moved at that moment. You were a library supervisor, and it would have been very easy for you to take out a few picture books, but you didn't do it. And I ... it just wasn't right for me to be angry at you about the books I borrowed. So I gave him my own picture books. When I knew that you hadn't borrowed any picture books yesterday, I thought I would ask our classmates to help you. This morning, while you were out of the classroom, I told everyone about it. By afternoon, everyone had brought back picture books from their own homes."

"How very kind of you, Cheng Li!" I said, very much moved.

"What's so good about me? Everyone says you're an outstanding library supervisor."

"No. In order to borrow some books for little brother, I almost committed an error." I told Cheng Li about how I was planning to take some picture books home to little brother yesterday.

On arriving home, I quickly pushed the door open and went in. I wanted to hand the picture books to little brother as quickly as possible. And I wanted to tell little brother all the details of what Cheng Li and our classmates had done.

Why didn't Ying-ying bring home the picture books for her little brother after promising to do so? Was what she did correct or not?

TWENTY-SEVEN. THE CHINESE AND RUSSIAN PEOPLES ARE
ETERNAL BROTHERS

In the summer of 1953, an exhibition of our nation's industrial and agricultural accomplishments opened at the Gorky Cultural

Park in Moscow. Every day many people came to visit it. I was responsible for making explanations about it in the exhibition hall.

One day after the completion of my work, I was just walking out the gate of the exhibition hall when I saw a woman well along in years walking by slowly with the help of a cane. I asked her how she was and made way for her. I was preparing to continue on my way, but the old woman called to me and said that she wanted me to do a little something for her. She said that she had come from the outskirts of Moscow by train and that she had a husband even older than she. After they learned the news that a Chinese exhibition was opening in Moscow, they both wanted to come. However, because the way was so far and his age so great, he sent his wife in his place to see it and to tell him about it when she came back. Several days before, the old woman had come to see it and had told her husband the details of what she had seen and heard. After her husband had listened to her description, he scolded her for not bringing a few Chinese things for him to see. Even a piece of paper with a few Chinese characters on it would have done. Having related this, the old woman smiled kindly and said: "It's for this that I've made one more trip. My good friend, would you write a few of your characters for my husband? Anything will do." As she spoke, she took a book from her purse. Even now I still remember clearly that it was a red book containing stories about Lenin. The old woman touched my shoulder and repeated sincerely: "My good friend, would you write a few of your characters for my husband? Anything will do." I was so moved that, although I was pressed for time, I gave it a great deal of thought.

An ordinary farmer from a Soviet collective farm was as enthusiastic as this about our country. She had come here, without regard for the distance or for her advanced years, in order for us to write a few Chinese characters. There is not merely one person in the Soviet Union like this, but thousands upon thousands. Of course I'd write something for her. I wanted to tell her of the love of our people for the people of the Soviet Union. I opened the book and prepared to write something for the old woman on the first page, which was blank. In my excitement, my hand shook a little. What should I write? I thought for a while, and then neatly wrote the following words: "The Chinese and Russian peoples are eternal brothers." In order that the old woman might understand what I had written, I translated it into

Russian. When we parted, I recall vaguely that we shook each other's hands and that she kissed me several times.

This minor incident happened several years ago. But every time I remember it, it is as if it had just taken place, the kind old woman appearing before my eyes.

Why is it said that the Chinese and the Russian peoples are eternal brothers? Explain using the incident in the text.

TWENTY-EIGHT. LO SHENG-CHIAO

One winter's morning, the Korean countryside was covered by a thick, white snow. Lo Sheng-chiao of the Chinese People's Volunteers had finished drill and was walking along the bank of a river. There were many Korean children skating on the ice over the river. Suddenly he heard a call: "Ai-ya!" A Korean boy by the name of Ts'ui Ying had fallen through a hole in the ice. The children along the edge were frightened and began to cry.

Lo Sheng-chiao ran over quickly, taking off his clothes as he ran. As soon as he reached the hole, he jumped in. How cold the water was! Lo Sheng-chiao was so numb with cold that his body was purple and his face white. Again and again he grasped Ts'ui Ying, but the ice was too thin. As soon as Ts'ui Ying emerged from the water, the ice gave way and he sank once again. Lo Sheng-chiao set his mind on saving Ts'ui Ying and with all his strength he pushed Ts'ui Ying out of the water using his own head. Ts'ui Ying was saved, but Lo Sheng-chiao was sacrificed.

Lo Sheng-chiao was a good soldier of Chairman Mao. He loved his motherland, and he loved the Korean people. In order to save a Korean boy who had fallen into the water, he gloriously offered his own precious life.

The Korean people, in order to honor the memory of Lo Sheng-chiao, changed the name of the village where he had sacrificed himself to Lo Sheng-chiao Village, changed the name of the river to Lo Sheng-chiao River, and changed the name of the mountain on which he was buried to Lo Sheng-chiao Mountain. Moreover, before his grave they raised a high tombstone on which are carved in large characters the words written by General Kim Ilsung, the leader of the Korean People: "The international spirit of the hero Lo Sheng-chiao will live forever among the Korean people."

THIRTY. RATHER DEATH THAN SUBMISSION

On February 1, 1923, the Chinghan (Peking to Hankow) Railroad Labor Federation held its inaugural meeting. The warlord Wu P'ei-fu, in order to repress the workers' movement, sent his soldiers to surround the meeting hall and demolished the meeting place of the Labor Federation. In order to resist oppression and obtain freedom, the Labor Federation resolved to hold a strike on the Chinghan Line beginning on February 4. At the same time, they decided to move the Labor Federation to Hankow and Chiang-an and to carry on their work at separate meetings.

On the third day of the strike, more than ten thousand workers met at Chiang-an, shouting the slogan: "Long live the Chinghan Labor Federation!" "Proletarians of the world, unite!" The warlord and the imperialists were very frightened, and, conspiring with each other, prepared to use the most despicable measures to slaughter the workers.

February 7 was the fourth day of the strike. The Labor Federation received a communication from the warlord saying that he would accept all of the workers' demands and that he wanted the Labor Federation to send representatives for negotiations to a meeting place in Chiang-an that day at five-thirty in the afternoon to await his arrival. When the appointed time came, the reactionary military police surrounded the meeting place at Chiang-an and, opening fire, slaughtered the workers. The brave workers, unarmed, fought hand-to-hand with the enemy. More than thirty persons were sacrificed and more than two hundred wounded by the wild enemy fire.

At the same time, the enemy surrounded the workers' dormitory, capturing workers everywhere. The Chairman of the Chiang-an Branch Committee, Comrade Lin Hsiang-ch'ien, was captured on the night of February 7. Lin Hsiang-ch'ien was a member of the Communist Party. During the days of the strike, the enemy had tried every means to capture him, but under the protection of the workers and the masses, he had evaded the poisonous hands of the enemy several times. But that night he was captured and tied to a telegraph pole at the Chiang-an railroad station. The enemy pressed Comrade Lin Hsiang-ch'ien to issue the order to resume work, but Comrade Lin Hsiang-ch'ien firmly refused. The enemy ordered the executioner to slash Comrade Lin Hsiang-ch'ien with his sword, asking viciously: "Will you or will you not go back to work?"

"No!" Comrade Lin Hsiang-ch'ien, through his pain, answered in a firm voice. "You can cut off my head, but we're not going back to work!" He cursed: "Pity our good China if it ends up in the hands of you running dogs of imperialism! ..."

Comrade Lin Hsiang-ch'ien was sacrificed heroically.

Comrade Lin Hsiang-ch'ien, for the benefit of the working class and for the cause of the liberation of the Chinese people, considered hardship of little importance and "looked on death as going home," fully demonstrating the incomparably noble qualities of the vanguard of the proletariat. He sacrificed himself for the revolutionary struggle, and his courageous and heroic spirit will always live on in the hearts of the millions of our people.

What places in the text show Comrade Lin Hsiang-ch'ien's spirit of preferring death to submission? Divide the text into sections and outline the major content of each section.

THIRTY-ONE. THE MARTYR FANG CHIH-MIN

The Communist Party has brought us a happy life. But, young friends, do you know what kind of a person a Communist Party member is? Do you know how the older generation of the Revolution, for the Liberation of China, struggled bitterly, even to spilling their last drops of blood?

Now let me tell you some stories about the martyr Fang Chih-min, who was an heroic and outstanding member of the Communist Party.

"Strike"

Once, Fang Chih-min was going from Shanghai to Nanch'ang on an imperialist steamer. On board the steamer he saw three poor Chinese people who, because they could not afford to buy boat tickets, were being tormented cruelly by the foreign slaves. The foreign slaves used strips of rattan and bamboo to beat them and, tying them together with rope, hung them over the hull, the foam of the waves striking their faces like a driving rain. They cried out in pain, but the heartless foreign slaves only danced and laughed on the deck, saying over and over: "What fun! What fun!"

"Strike!" Fang Chih-min, unable to endure it further, began to call out to the foreign slaves.

"Who shouted 'strike'?" the foreign slaves asked with round, evil eyes.

"Strike!" shouted some scores of the passengers all together. As soon as the foreign slaves saw that the situation was unfavorable, they quickly slipped away.

"We Will Not Go"

In 1923, Fang Chih-min joined the Chinese Communist Party, undertaking many activities. In 1927, he was directing the revolutionary movement and organizing peasant revolts in Kiangsi Province. The reactionaries sent a large number of troops to attack them. At that time, the Red Army was very small, and the situation was extremely critical.

Some people were afraid and said: "Let's disperse the Red Army, bury our rifles, and hide in the cities!" Fang Chih-min did not agree, saying "If we bury our rifles and run away in the face of difficulty, how will we ever gain the respect of the masses? Anyone who wants to leave is not a Communist Party member! We will not go! We must live and die with the masses, suffering hardships in common and keeping on together!" His comrades all agreed with his opinion.

In this way, they overcame various difficulties, the relieved areas in Kiangsi Province grew larger and larger and the Red Army grew stronger and stronger.

"You're Mistaken"

In January of 1935, Fang Chih-min had the misfortune of being captured during a battle. The Kuomintang soldiers searched his body from head to toe, from his collar to the tip of his socks, in the hope of finding some foreign money. But although they searched a long time, they did not find even one copper.

One of the soldiers picked up a hand grenade and shouted: "Give us your money at once or I'll blow you to pieces!"

"There's no need to look so fierce! I don't even have a copper. If you think you're going to get foreign riches out of me, you're mistaken!" Fang Chih-min said with a smile.

"Who are you trying to fool? How could it be that such a big official wouldn't have any money?" The soldier holding the hand grenade didn't believe him. Another of the soldiers, arching his back, felt Fang Chih-min's belt and the crevices of his clothes in the hope of new discoveries.

"Don't waste your time! We aren't like your Kuomintang officials, who are all rich. Our revolution isn't for getting rich," said Fang Chih-min.

Fang Chih-min, during the long revolutionary struggle, continually led an extremely plain and simple life. Usually he didn't have any money in his pockets. The socks that he wore were patched over and over, and when the enemy attacked, he often hid them in a mountain cave.

In Prison

The enemy shut Fang Chih-min up in prison and used various cruel punishments in order to force a confession from him. When firmness didn't work, they switched to gentleness, trying to persuade him to surrender for money and position.

Fang Chih-min answered them in a tone that could cut metal in two: "Surrender? What are you Kuomintang people? A bunch of executioners who slaughter the workers and the peasants! ... You can cut off our heads, but you can never shake our faith!"

Fang Chih-min, knowing that sooner or later he would be killed by the enemy, gave his thoughts to what more he could do for his motherland! Every day he wrote letters to his comrades, writing of his work experiences in the past and inspiring his comrades to continue in their struggle. He said: "I can give up everything, but as long as the cause of the revolution is remembered in my heart, I cannot give up." He also said: "What torments me the most is that I have lost my chance to work for the Party!"

In July 1935, Fang Chih-min was heroically sacrificed. As he was about to die, he lifted up his head and swelled out his chest, showing his great spirit of devotion to the cause of Communism.

More than twenty years have passed, and our nation's revolution, having attained its great victory, is advancing toward Socialism and Communism. The blood of the martyr, Fang Chih-min, was not shed in vain.

Beloved young friends, having heard these stories about the martyr Fang Chih-min, what are you thinking of? What do you want to say? Let us tell the martyr Fang Chih-min: "We, the young generation of the New China, like you, love our motherland and its people and will be outstanding members of the Communist Party. We shall take up your cause and carry it through to the end."

Discuss what aspects of Martyr Fang Chih-min's revolutionary spirit we ought to study.

Read the text. Listen to and write out the section "Strike," dividing it into paragraphs.

THIRTY-TWO. GENERAL LIU CHIH-TAN'S NOTEBOOK

At the time of the agrarian revolution, the commander-in-chief of the Northern Shensi Red Army, General Liu Chih-tan, was victorious again and again. The major reason for this was the extreme importance he gave to investigation and research.

Each time that General Liu Chih-tan arrived in a place, he always opened out his maps and studied them carefully. Then he would look for villagers to talk to, asking them about this and about that. In 1934, he led a part of the Northern Shensi Red Army, stationing them at Hua-an Monastery in Ch'ing-chien County. The chief of the food ministry in Ch'ing-chien County also lived in the village. One day, General Liu Chih-tan, pointing toward Ma-chia-t'a village, asked the ministry chief: "Do you know how many people there are in that village? How many kilns? How many cauldrons?" The ministry chief, having been asked this, felt very embarrassed. Then he asked General Liu Chih-tan: "Do you know how many there are?" General Liu Chih-tan then told him in detail. The food ministry chief was a little skeptical and went to ask the chief of the Poor Peasants Society in the village. There was no discrepancy between what he and what General Liu Chih-tan said.

This incident aroused the interest of the ministry chief, and he thought: "How did General Liu Chih-tan have such precise knowledge?" He also thought: "He must have known about the situation in that village from the beginning, but he doesn't necessarily know about any of the other villages."

Once, the troops set out from Yuan-chia-kou, returning to Hua-an Monastery by way of Teng-chia-t'a. When they arrived in Teng-chia-t'a, the ministry chief found the chief of the Poor Peasants Society in Teng-chia-t'a and inquired of him how many people, how many kilns, and how many cauldrons there were in Teng-chia-t'a. The chief of the Poor Peasants Society ran off to look, after which he told him in detail. Thereupon, the ministry chief asked General Liu Chih-tan: "Do you know how many people there are in Teng-chia-t'a? How many kilns? How many cauldrons?" General Liu Chih-tan laughed and, pulling a notebook from his coat pocket, he looked at it, telling him of the conditions, the population, the kilns, the cauldrons, the cattle, etc., in Teng-chia-t'a. There was not the least error, and even the chief of the Poor Peasants Society, who was present, was astonished. From that time on, everyone respected the fine investigative work that General Liu Chih-tan did.

In every place that General Liu Chih-tan came to, he investigated all aspects of its conditions, gathered all kinds of data, and wrote this down in his notebook. When necessary, he thumbed through it, immediately finding what he needed. This was extremely convenient. Many of his comrades were influenced by him, and they all came to respect investigation and research.

THIRTY-FOUR. THE WOLF AND THE LAMB

By chance, a wolf and a lamb came to drink water by the edge of a brook at the same time. The brook flowed down from a mountain.

The wolf wanted very much to eat the lamb, but he thought that, inasmuch as they were face to face, it would be better to find a pretext first.

The wolf then purposely picked a quarrel, saying angrily: "How dare you come to the bank of my brook and make my water dirty so that I can't drink it? What are your intentions?"

The lamb, startled, said goodnaturedly: "I don't see how I could have gotten the water dirty. You're standing upstream, and the water flows down from you toward me, not upstream from me to where you are."

"That may be right," said the wolf. "But you're a bad fellow. I hear that you said bad things about me last year behind my back."

"Ah, my dear Mr. Wolf," shouted the unfortunate lamb. "That can't be. Last year I hadn't been born yet!"

The wolf, feeling no need for further argument and flashing his teeth and roaring, drew close to the lamb and said: "You little rotten egg! You're not the one who said bad things about me. It was your father. But it's all the same." As he spoke, he rushed on the lamb, grabbed him, and ate him up.

When a bad person has it in his mind to do an evil and cruel act, it is very easy for him to find a pretext for it.

What is the implication of "The Wolf and the Lamb?" Explain using the content of the lesson as evidence.

Memorize and recite the text.

SELECTIONS FROM VOLUME 9 OF THE READERS

(GRADE FIVE)

ONE. WE MUST PRIZE THE HAPPY LIFE OF STUDY

(An Old Laborer's Story)

I am now more than fifty years old, and my hair has already grown white. When I see my two grandchildren skipping off carrying their books, many events of the past well up within me.

My life when I was young can't be compared with that of today's children!

Our family lived in a poor mountain valley, depending for our livelihood on a few *mou* of land rented from a landlord. My father would go away to do odd jobs, and there would be no news of him once he had gone. My mother, who took care of me, earned the living. Day and night she thought about her desire to have me go to school. One day, when I was eight years old, she found a piece of tattered cloth and, wrapping up a book in it, sent me to attend a private school. Patting my head, she said: "Child, there has been no one in our family for generations who has been to school or could read. Today, I'm sending you to study. You must really study hard!"

My mother, in order to pay the school fees for me, went every day to a field several miles away to cut grass. The summer sun was merciless, as if it wanted to bake her. Around her head there were darting swarms of big mosquitoes, and at her feet were holes of stinking, putrid water. If one did not pay attention and stumbled into a hole, then one would be bitten by leeches until the blood ran. My mother covered her head with a piece of cloth to protect her from the bites of the mosquitoes and, her waist bowed, cut grass energetically. Her arms were scarred by wounds from the grass. Toward evening, my mother returned home carrying the grass on her back, and I often went to meet her. How unbearable it was for me to see her trudging along, step by step, her face yellowed, her waist bent, and her head almost between her knees under the weight of the large bundle of grass on her back. Even though I was small, I always carried a little of the grass for my mother as I returned with her.

At that time I studied very hard, as I was afraid of doing poorly and grieving my mother. With my mother suffering such hardship, eating less and being frugal, not even being able to make one set of clothes for herself, so that I could go to school, how could I have wished to grieve her?

I was a little unhappy in the private school. The teacher in the private school was very severe, incessantly pounding a board and shouting at us. Sometimes he used the board to beat us, and beat us until the palms of our hands swelled. My seat faced the teacher, and I didn't dare to move the whole day. I just sat there and studied hard. Once, the teacher lost his temper with me for some reason and, with a sudden swoop, angrily threw a broom at me. The broom struck the side of my face, injuring my eyelid. It began to bleed, and my eye hurt so much that I couldn't open it. My eyes filled with tears, but I didn't dare make a sound. If I were to cry, the teacher would certainly beat me.

The year that I was eleven, my father was so old that he couldn't work the fields any more. He said to me: "There can't be many books in a poor man's house. It's working in the fields and struggling for food to eat that's important." From that time on, I did not go to school again. First I worked for the landlord, and later I went to work on the railroad.

As soon as I think about these things, my heart becomes heavy. I envy you children today. How fortunate you are! The Party and government have immense concern for you and have set up excellent schools for you. The teachers are warm and pleasant to you so that you can study and learn the skills of labor without fear and anxiety. How you ought to prize such a happy life of study!

Speaking of the concern of the Party and of the government, there is one more event I want to tell you about. After the Liberation, in order to raise the culture of the working people, I also went to school. This old worker became an old student. I had grown old, and, as if my eyes were covered with a film, the characters in the books appeared blurred. I at once was fitted with a pair of glasses. Because I was old, my memory was bad, but, although there were some things that I just could not remember, I obstinately kept at my studies. On Sundays, when the dormitory was peaceful and quiet, I moved up a stool and, sitting by the foot of my bed, turned over the pages of my little notebooks. I had filled the notebooks with problems. These were the problems that I had not been able to work out each day. I "attacked" them one by one. When I defeated one, I would mark it off with a red pencil. Through study I raised my culture quite a bit. Now I can even write essays.

You don't mind my chattering, do you? You must understand that the pleasant life of study today was not easily come by. I hope that you will be obedient to the Party, toughen your bodies, strive in your studies, labor hard, respect your teachers, and, uniting in friendship with your classmates, become outstanding successors to the building of Socialism and Communism. You must indeed accomplish the mission of study given to you by your motherland and must not be unworthy of the hopes that our older generation has for you!

THREE—SELECTION ONE.
BECAUSE THERE IS THE COMMUNIST PARTY

The cassia gives off its fragrance to the earth;
The song of the Leap Forward is spread everywhere;
Desolate mountains and impoverished villages are becoming rich towns,
Because there is the Communist Party.
Birds depend on trees, and fish depend on ponds;
The hundred flowers depend on the sun to bloom;
A happy life has come,
Because there is the Communist Party.

FOUR. SUNRISE AT SEA*

In order to see the sunrise aboard ship, I purposely got up very early. At that time, the sky still had not grown light, and it was

---

*This selection is from Pa Chin's *Hai-hsing tsa-chi.*

tranquil on all sides, with only the sounds from the engine room to be heard.

The sky turned to a blue, a pale, pale blue. In the twinkling of an eye, a streak of red cloud appeared on the horizon that gradually grew in size and grew more intense in its brightness. Knowing that the sun would be rising there, I watched without moving my eyes.

As expected, in a little while the edge of the sun emerged there, very red, but not bright. The sun, as if it were bearing some heavy burden, slowly strove to ascend. At last it broke through the red clouds and leapt out in full form onto the surface of the sea. Its color was a delightfully pure red. In an instant, this deep red thing suddenly put forth an eye-dazzling light that pained the eyes when it struck them and that at the same time brilliantly colored the neighboring clouds.

Once, the sun entered the clouds, its rays shining through directly onto the surface of the sea. At these times, it was hard to tell which was sky and which was sea, because all one could see was a strip of light.

Once, there were thick layers of black clouds on the horizon, and the sun could not be seen. From behind the black clouds, the sun's rays framed them with a golden border of light. Finally, the sun penetrated its encirclement, appearing in the sky and turning the black clouds purple and red. At that time, it was not only the sun, the clouds, and the sea that were bright, but I as well.

NINE. THE DEVELOPMENT OF YEN-WO ISLAND

Yen-wo Island is in the southeastern part of Heilungkiang Province and is a solitary island in the great northern wilderness. It is surrounded entirely by marshes. Although they look like ordinary land, as soon as a person steps onto them, he sinks down into deep mud.

Yen-wo Island has 5,000 hectares of fertile land that had not been developed for thousands of years. Under the Party's call for the development of the northern wilderness, a group of outstanding young men and women of our motherland, the demobilized service people, courageously resolved to go to the northern wilderness to set up farms. They resolved to remake the great northern wilderness into a great granary for our motherland and decided to develop Yen-wo Island first.

Once all of the preparatory work was completed, the brave and battle-hardened warriors formed into a survey team and set out. Tractors hauled sleds on which food and fuel were carried. When the old native villagers saw them, they said: "How many years we have wanted to develop this valuable island! Now that the Communist Party has come, it is at last really going to be started."

When they set out, the weather was very clear, but in the afternoon a fierce northern wind began to blow, piling up high drifts of snow into the sky and driving fiercely at their bodies and faces. For a time the sky and earth darkened so that not even the old hunter who was their guide could tell east from west or north from south. They walked in circles until they finally found a large tree that could serve as a road marker. Then they continued to advance.

Once this survey team had arrived on the island, there were snow storms day after day, the temperature falling to 40 degrees below zero and at times burying their tents in deep snow. All they could do was to squat down inside their tents and wait. On the fifth day, the blizzard stopped. They grasped that long-awaited day of clear weather to begin their surveying.

From their preliminary survey, they found that there were dense forests and a broad wilderness that could be opened. But the materials needed for the whole year had to be prepared during the winter. Otherwise, when the weather grew warm and it began to thaw, the circumference of the island would become marsh again, and traffic cut off. Nine or ten strong young men were picked from the farms to make up a transportation team. Bulldozers opened up the road ahead, and tractors hauling sleds filled with materials packed it down. Close behind there followed trucks and horsecarts. They set out for the isolated island day and night without stopping.

Spring came, and the ice and snow began to melt, the island slowly taking on a green spring dress. All kinds of birds and animals began to come to life. This is the "kingdom" of the wild goose. If two people go out for a day, they can easily return with several thousand goose eggs the size of a man's fist. If one goes out in a small boat, with very little effort one can return with a boatload of small geese. There are as well such wild animals as spotted deer, wild pig, black bear, and white-eyed wolves that can be caught at will. Fish are the easiest to catch. When one goes to the bank of a stream with a basin to wash one's face, one can catch several fish in the process. Just as the people of the great northern wilderness say: "We kill deer with our cudgels and scoop up fish with our gourds, and pheasant fly into our cooking cauldrons."

The developers of the desolate island battled obstinately against nature. The roar of the tractors broke the island's ancient stillness. The black mud was turned over, and seeds were sown in the newly opened earth.

Autumn on Yen-wo Island was a season of abundance. In the newly opened fields, the ears of wheat were more than a foot in length, the soy beans had grown knee high, the turnips were as big as pumpkins, while the pumpkins looked like small mill-stones. When the wilderness developers saw these abundant fruits of their labors, they were overjoyed. They caught thirty or forty thousand catties of fish, which they dried and set aside in preparation for the winter. Chopping down trees and cutting grass, they built more than seventy new houses in preparation for welcoming the second group of their wilderness-breaking companions. They resolved to use their own two hands to build Yen-wo Island into a basin of gems in which nothing was lacking.

THIRTEEN. EIGHTEEN BRAVE SOLDIERS

In May of 1935, the Workers and Peasants Red Army on the Long March arrived at the Tatu River.

The Tatu River pours down from high mountain ranges, rolling on in great billows and forming whirlpools everywhere. The waves strike the black rocks on its banks with a roar that can be heard even more than ten *li* away.

One hundred years ago, Shih Ta-k'ai, the I Wang ("Righteous Prince") of the Heavenly Kingdom of Great Peace (*T'ai-p'ing t'ien-kuo*), leading tens of thousands of troops of the T'ai-p'ing Army, was surrounded and defeated at the Tatu River by the troops of the Ch'ing Dynasty. Chiang Kai-shek dreamt that the Red Army might also meet a fate like that of Shih Ta-k'ai's T'ai-p'ing Army. He sent out tens of thousands of White Army Troops, a part of them pursuing from the rear and a part of them cutting off the route ahead, thereby hindering the advance of the Red Army.

The Red Army decided to seize An-shun-ch'ang on the south bank of the Tatu River and force their way across the Tatu River there, thus continuing their advance northward.

In an assault, the Red Army quickly occupied An-shun-ch'ang, annihilated the enemy troops there, and captured a boat. This was the only boat there, and their hopes of getting across the river were entrusted to this single boat.

The Hung-i Regiment of the First Battalion gloriously accepted the mission of breaking across the river. It was a difficult mission, for they had to cross the river, capture the positions on the beachhead, and cover for the troops to follow.

The officers and men of the entire battalion assembled on the bank of the Tatu River. The commander ordered mobilization for battle, saying: "Who is willing to take the lead in crossing the river?" The whole battalion stepped forward, everyone wanting to take the lead in crossing the river. Finally, eighteen brave soldiers were selected and organized into an assault party.

As soon as the common people of An-shun-ch'ang, who had suffered daily from enemy extortion, heard that the Red Army wanted to cross the river to annihilate the enemy, each of them rubbed their hands together. Those who could row came up in large numbers to register their names, asking that they might escort the Red Army across. The Red Army agreed to their requests, and they all came happily and enthusiastically to the bank of the river.

The crossing began. The eighteen brave soldiers were carrying eighteen machine guns, eighteen pistols, eighteen bayonets, and, in their chests, eighteen resolute hearts.

The boat was too small for so many people. The eighteen brave soldiers crossed the river in two groups. The first group of nine boarded the boat. The boatman pushed off from the bank with his pole, and the boat shot out toward the opposite bank like an arrow.

As they rowed on and on, the enemy opened fire, sweeping them with thick fire from behind the rocks on the opposite bank. The bullets, flashing red, whizzed past the heads and bodies of the brave soldiers. Next, enemy artillery shells began to fly past, falling into the river and raising high columns of water. The brave soldiers sat calmly in the boat, grasping their weapons tightly and looking toward their landing place on the opposite bank.

At that time, our army on the south bank also opened fire on the enemy. Machine gun bullets fell like hail on the enemy position, forcing the enemy to crawl down into their positions without daring to lift their heads. The artillery shells fired by our crack gunners burst one after another over the heads of the enemy.

While both sides challenged each other in battle, the boat bearing the nine brave soldiers rushed ahead, rising and falling with the turbulent billows. As soon as it struck the bank, the brave soldiers jumped vigorously ashore, each of them rushing energetically toward the ford on the enemy side. In one assault, the enemy was scattered and repulsed, and the brave soldiers occupied the enemy's beachhead fortifications.

The boat returned, and the second group of nine brave soldiers continued the crossing. The enemy in the mountains on the opposite bank concentrated all of their fire power on bombarding the surface of the river, hoping to block our army from continuing its crossing. The counterattack by our army grew more intense, artillery and machine guns firing in unison and repressing the enemy fire power.

The boat advanced across the river, striking gigantic wave after gigantic wave and avoiding round after round of bullets. Just as it appeared that they were about to reach the bank, a string of bullets pierced the hull, a stream of water spurting up through the bottom like a spring. The brave soldiers plugged up the hole in a flurry. Just then, a wave struck, driving the boat swiftly onto the rocks. "Jump out quick! Jump out quick!" one of the boatmen called as he jumped out onto the rocks. Several of the brave soldiers followed him in jumping onto the rocks. Everyone stood in the water, pushing with their hands, holding the boat off with their shoulders and raising it up with their backs, so that it could get around the rocks. They then boarded it again.

The second group of nine brave soldiers landed. The first group of brave soldiers, who were holding the beachhead fortifications, were just in the process of resisting an enemy counter-assault. The second group of brave soldiers rushed up. The enemy, unable to resist them, scattered in confusion into the hills on the north bank.

The crossing had been accomplished. The eighteen brave soldiers were in control of the north bank of the Tatu River. The troops following to the rear crossed the Tatu River without difficulty.

SIXTEEN. THE FOOLISH OLD MAN WHO REMOVED THE MOUNTAINS*

There is an ancient Chinese fable called "The Foolish Old Man Who Removed the Mountains." It tells of an old man who lived in northern China long, long ago and was known as the Foolish Old Man of North Mountain. His house faced south and beyond his doorway stood the two great peaks, Taihang and Wangwu, obstructing the way. He called his sons, and hoe in hand they began to dig up these mountains with great determination. Another greybeard, known as the Wise Old Man, saw them and said derisively, "How silly of you to do this! It is quite impossible for you few to dig up these two huge mountains." The Foolish Old Man replied, "When I die, my sons will carry on; when they die, there will be my grandsons, and then their sons and grandsons, and so on to infinity. High as they are, the mountains cannot grow any higher and with every bit we dig, they will be that much lower. Why can't we clear them away?" Having refuted the Wise Old Man's wrong view, he went on digging every day, unshaken in his conviction. God was moved by this, and he sent down two angels, who carried the mountains away on their backs. Today, two big mountains lie like a dead weight on the Chinese people. One is imperialism, the other is feudalism. The Chinese Communist Party has long made up its mind to dig them up. We must persevere and work unceasingly, and we, too, will touch God's heart. Our God is none other than the masses of the Chinese people. If they stand up and dig together with us, why can't these two mountains be cleared away?

What instruction do we receive on reading the story "The Foolish Old Man Who Removed the Mountains"? Write out the text.

SEVENTEEN. THE REORGANIZATION AT SANWAN

In September 1927, the Autumn Harvest Uprising failed, and the Red Army retreated from Hunan toward Kiangsi.

---

*This essay was taken from *The Foolish Old Man Who Removed the Mountains, Selected Works of Mao Tse-tung*, Vol. 3.

The enemy, wishing to exterminate completely the seeds of revolution, kept vigorously at the heels of the Red Army, and such reactionary military groups as the militia and the guard units hampered it along its route. After several successive days of forced march, the Red Army reached Sanwan in Yunghsin County of Kiangsi. In order to readjust its forces and fill out its strength for further battles with the enemy, the Red Army carried out a reorganization at Sanwan.

The comrade who was leading this branch of the Red Army assembled the forces for a talk. He announced the reorganization order reducing the army to two battalions. When the soldiers heard this, they became extremely heavy-hearted. Suddenly a comrade stepped up to introduce Comrade Mao Tse-tung's speech.

From the crowd, a tall man stepped forward. He was wearing a short jacket and leggings, and on his feet he wore a pair of sandals. This was Comrade Mao Tse-tung. Comrade Mao Tse-tung, a full smile on his face, walked out in front of the troops. The soldiers clapped their hands in excitement.

Comrade Mao Tse-tung said to everyone: "Comrades, the enemy is firing on us from the rear, but what's so amazing about that? .... Everyone is born of a woman. The enemy has two legs and we have two legs too.... Comrade Ho Lung began with two kitchen knives, and now he has become an army commander in charge of an army of men. We now are not merely two kitchen knives. We are two battalions of men. Do we have to be afraid we can't beat them? .... You are all the products of rebellions. One of you is worth ten of the enemy, and ten of you are worth a hundred. With our hundreds of troops, what have we go to be afraid of? .... If there are no obstacles and defeats, there can be no accomplishments...."

This talk got everyone to nodding their heads and smiling. After the meeting had dispersed, the soldiers began to hold discussions in groups. Someone said: "Comrade Mao Tse-tung is not afraid. What have we got to be afraid of?" Someone said: "Comrade Ho Lung began with two kitchen knives. Can't we begin with a few hundred men?"

With this, the troops carried out the reorganization. From this time forward, the troops established Party organizations at all levels. The squads had groups, the companies had branches, and the battalion had a Party committee and set up Party representation at all levels above the company. This force of young workers and peasants grew stronger from day to day.

Questions and Exercises: How did Chairman Mao's speech resolve the ideological problems of the soldiers?

NINETEEN. A RED SUN BLAZING LIKE A FIRE*

A red sun is blazing like a fire;
The rice in the fields is half withered and scorched.
The farmer's heart is like boiling soup;
Gentlemen and descendents of princes wave their fans.

How does the life of the peasant in the past appear as seen from the poem *A Red Sun Blazing Like a Fire?* Memorize and recite the poem.

TWENTY—SELECTION ONE.
THE SILKWORM WOMAN†

Yesterday I went into the city,
And returned, my kerchief soaked with tears.
It is not those adorned in fine silks
Who raise the silkworms.

Discuss the life of the peasant during the Sung Dynasty on the basis of this poem and the poem following. Write out this poem. Write out this poem in everyday language.

---

*This poem was taken from Chapter 16 of "Shui-hu," (*The Water Margin*, also translated as *All Men Are Brothers*—Trans.) and was sung by Pai Sheng, the good man of Liang Shan.

†The author of *The Silkworm Woman* was the Sung Dynasty poet Chang Yu.

TWENTY—SELECTION TWO.
THE BRICK BURNER*

When I've burned all the earth before my gate,
There's not one strip of tile for my roof.
He whose ten fingers are not stained with mud
Lives in a great mansion covered with scales. †

The author of *The Brick Burner* was the Sung Dynasty poet
Mei Yao-ch'en.

TWENTY-EIGHT. AN URGENT MESSAGE

(Part 1)

Hai-wa was fourteen years old. He was the leader of the
Pioneers in Lungmen Village. One day, Hai-wa was standing
sentry beneath a small tree on the mountain, a red tasselled spear
in his hand and a sheep whip stuck in his waist.

A man came climbing up the path from Yangpo, shouting from
the distance, "Hai-wa! Hai-wa!" Hai-wa, on recognizing his
father's voice, hastened to meet him. His father pulled a letter
from his shirt and said: "Go at once to Sanwang Village and
deliver this to Company Commander Chang at the command
post." It was a chicken feather letter. Three chicken feathers were
stuck through a corner of the letter, and Hai-wa knew that it was
an urgent message of great importance.

Hai-wa, driving his flock of sheep, turned from the precipice,
thinking to follow the path, but suddenly the "news tree" on West
mountain fell. This was bad! The enemy had been discovered on
that side of the mountain. Hai-wa thought that if he could not
take the path, then he must take the highway. But in the distance
beyond the mouth of the great river, a band of enemy soldiers was
coming, plundering grain.

---

*Brick burner—kiln worker. Here indicates a workman who bakes
brick and tile.

†scales—The tile covering the roof of a large mansion was laid on in
strips resembling the scales of a fish.

The enemy came closer and closer. Hai-wa grew nervous. Where could he hide the urgent letter? Seeing a sheep's bushy tail, he got an idea. He rushed to the front and, throwing his arms around the sheep, tied the urgent letter under the sheep's tail with two strands of wool from the base of its tail. Hai-wa, who was afraid of nothing, drove past the enemy, snapping his whip.

"Halt!" one of the enemy soldiers called out, raising his rifle with a shout and pointing it at Hai-wa's head. A wry-mouthed fellow in a black uniform ran up, grabbed Hai-wa by the neck, and dragged him in front of a man with a small beard. Hai-wa, not in the least afraid, intentionally tilted his head, opened his mouth wide, and gazed at the bearded man with a foolish expression on his face. The bearded man said: "Search him!" The wry-mouthed black dog at once set to work, feeling the bindings and crevices of his clothes and even taking Hai-wa's shoes off. But he could find nothing. The bearded man, who was intent on heading into the mountains to plunder grain, roared at Hai-wa: "Scram! Scram!"

Hai-wa went on, cracking his whip as he went and regretting that he could not fly away. But in a moment, the wry-mouthed dog came chasing after him again. Stopping the flock of sheep, he demanded under the threat of his rifle that Hai-wa drive the sheep back into the mountains. The black dog squinted his eyes and, with a twisted smile on his wry mouth, said: "The Imperial Army has not eaten! These sheep will be good for several meals."

The enemy troops came to a stop before a small mountain village. The enemy quickly slaughtered a sheep on a threshing floor, roasted it, and ate its flesh. Hai-wa, whose concern was not for his sheep, stealthily lifted the tail of the old sheep and, seeing the urgent letter still hanging there, called out to himself: "You're still here."

The enemy devils ate to the full and, rubbing their stomachs, went inside to sleep. The wry-mouthed black dog first ordered Hai-wa to drive the sheep into their pens and then, grabbing Hai-wa by the neck, dragged him into the sleeping room. The enemy devils and the black dogs slept on dry straw holding their rifles, squeezing Hai-wa tightly in among them.

Hai-wa could not sleep. He thought: "The devils will probably want to kill more sheep tomorrow. If I can't get away tonight, the urgent message may be lost. Hai-wa, Hai-wa, what good are you? You can't even deliver a letter! ..." As he was thinking, he suddenly heard the guard outside call out: "Who's there?" Someone said: "The cattle feeder!" The guard did not answer. In the distance, a rooster crowed. Once it had crowed two times, Hai-wa could not stay lying down, and he sat up. The guard at the door was dozing. Hai-wa stood up and, gently pushing aside the wry-mouthed black dog's arm with the tip of his left foot, he climbed over the bearded man, slipped up beside the door, stepped stealthily over the guard's legs, and picked his way to the road in the direction of the village. "Who's there?" called out the guard on the road. "The cattle feeder," Hai-wa answered in a coarse and heavy voice. The guard did not answer. Hai-wa walked into the pen, grabbed the sheep, and, untying the message from beneath its tail, put it into his bag. He tightened his belt and, letting loose, ran in one breath to the crest of the hill behind the village.

When Hai-wa was captured by the enemy, was his concern for the sheep or for the urgent message? Answer, citing phrases from the story.

TWENTY-NINE. AN URGENT MESSAGE

(Part 2)

The day dawned.

Hai-wa was running along the spur of the hill when he heard someone shouting ahead. On the crest of the hill one of the enemy soldiers was holding a white flag and waving it at Hai-wa. Hai-wa took off his white cloth jacket and, in imitation of the enemy, waved it back and forth too. Finally, he disappeared. Once he had gone around the spur of the hill, Hai-wa ran with one breath to the opposite hilltop and sat down. Hai-wa was very happy, for before him was Sanwang Village. But when he stuck his hand into his bag he began to tremble all over. The urgent letter was gone. Hai-wa groped through the bag again, but it was not there. He took off his jacket to look for it, but it was not there either. He looked among the cracks in the stones around him, but he still could not find it. Hai-wa immediately went back to look for it. He climbed the big hill in one breath and crawled along the edge of the spur. The urgent letter was lying on the spot where he had just been waving his jacket. Hai-wa nearly died of joy.

Hai-wa put the letter into his bag and was just about to run back, when suddenly a man shouted behind him. It was the wry-mouthed black dog. He grabbed Hai-wa, fired a series of rifle shots, and again ordered Hai-wa to lead the way for the devils.

The bearded man flourished his sword, and the devils and the black dogs again set out. Hai-wa was in the middle, driving the sheep. They passed by the big mountain and were approaching Sanwang Village. Hai-wa remembered that the "news tree" had fallen, which meant that Company Commander Chang knew the devils were coming.

The enemy devils, who sensed nothing, were resting in a ravine, smoking and eating sheep flesh. Once they had rested enough, the black dogs set out in the lead, intending to take the path to the village. Suddenly there was a sound of rumbling from the hillside, and columns of black smoke rose up. The black dogs had stepped on some land mines. The bearded man abandoned the black dogs with no concern and, pointing at the path, said to Hai-wa: "You take the lead. The Imperial Army will follow. Do you understand?"

Hai-wa walked far in advance of the devils. In the forest, the road split into two forks, a small path and a sheep trail. He drove the sheep onto the sheep trail. The black dogs below shouted: "That's the wrong way!" Hai-wa shouted back: "No. I've gone this way before ... It's the right way. Don't worry!" The sheep trail grew steeper and steeper and more difficult to travel, the devils walking and halting by turns and falling far behind. The bearded man shouted: "Slower!" Hai-wa, pretending not to have heard him, ran ahead step by step. The enemy devils shouted: "Halt! If you go any farther, we'll shoot!" Hai-wa did not stop, but instead cracked his whip and ran on ahead with all his might. The devils opened fire. Hai-wa sped on with the flock of sheep. When he could run no longer, he fell down in the grass, shouting at the top of his lungs: "The devils are coming! Strike! Strike at once!"

Suddenly there was a round of firing from the village, followed by a second round. When Hai-wa heard the sound of his own people's rifle fire, the energy returned to his legs and, crawling to his feet, he rushed into the village. Suddenly his hands spread open and with a cry of "Ai-yao!" he fell into a clump of grass and said nothing more.

At that time, a guerrilla soldier ran out from the village and picked Hai-wa up. When Hai-wa opened his eyes, Company Commander Chang of the Command Post was sitting beside him.

Hai-wa's wound was extremely painful. He opened his mouth and said: "Urgent message ... message ..." Then he lost consciousness again.

When Hai-wa awoke again, he was lying on a warm *k'ang* (combination bed and stove made out of brick—Transl.), his body covered by a soft cotton blanket. The sun was shining in through the window onto the *k'ang*.

Company Commander Chang, with a smile, asked Hai-wa: "Are you better? Does it still hurt?"

Hai-wa, giving no thought to his pain, asked Commander Chang: "Where am I?"

Company Commander Chang began to laugh loudly, saying as he laughed: "Have you forgotten? Didn't you bring an urgent message yesterday? That was a report from your father. On the basis of that report, our troops broke out their guns!" Hai-wa then recalled bringing the urgent message.

Company Commander Chang, stroking Hai-wa's head, said: "You are really a little Eighth Router, our little hero!"

Hai-wa blushed. He asked at once: "Have the rifles been delivered?"

Company Commander Chang said: "A big bundle of shiny brand new 38 rifles have been delivered!"

Hai-wa said happily: "Send me one!"

In what places are Hai-wa's cleverness and courage shown?

THIRTY. THE SONG OF THE NIGHTINGALE*

A battle just concluded, a small group of German soldiers entered the village. Broken pottery and tile lined both sides of the street, and burned out trees were bent over with a downcast air.

The song of a nightingale broke the deep silence of the summer day. The song stopped for a while and then began again, growing more and more vigorous.

The soldiers and their lieutenant, listening attentively, looked at

---

*This is a story from the Soviet Union's Great Patriotic War.

the surrounding thick undergrowth of trees and at the white birches at the edges of the road. They suddenly discovered that very close by there was a child sitting on the bank of a stream, his legs hanging down. He was bareheaded and wearing a green coat almost the color of the leaves. He was holding a piece of wood, on which he seemed to be whittling.

"Hey, you come!" the lieutenant called to the child in awkward Russian.

The child hastily put his knife into his coat pocket and, shaking off the shavings clinging to his coat, walked up to the officer.

"Hey, let me take a look!" the German officer said.

The child took a small toy from his mouth, which he handed to him, watching him with happy eyes.

It was a whistle made from white birchbark.

"Not a bad toy that you've made." The lieutenant nodded his head and, with a thin sneer on his dark face, said: "Who taught you to blow the whistle like that?"

"I taught myself. I know how to imitate the cuckoo's call too."

The child imitated a few cuckoo's calls. Then he put the whistle into his mouth and began to blow.

"Are you the only one left in the village?" The lieutenant continued his interrogation, lifting his field glasses to his eyes.

"You can't say that I'm the only one left! There are a lot of sparrows, and crows, and partridge. But there's only one nightingale."

"You good for nothing!" the lieutenant cut the child short. "What I asked was if any people were still here."

"People? There's been no one here since the war started," the child answered casually. "As soon as the shooting started, the village caught on fire, and everyone ran away shouting 'The wild beasts are coming, the wild beasts are coming!' "

"Fool!" the lieutenant thought, with a contemptuous sneer passing over his face.

"Hey, do you know the road to Sumengtaszu (Chinese transliteration of a Russian place name—Transl.)?"

"Of course I know it." the child answered in a trusting tone. "There's a mill there, and I often go to the slope near the mill to fish. The dogfish there are bad. They eat little geese!"

"Fine, fine. Take us there, then. If you take us the right way I'll give this little thing to you." As the lieutenant spoke, he pointed to his cigarette lighter. "But if you take us to some other place, I'll twist your head off. Do you understand?"

The troops set out, their field stove in the lead, the child and the lieutenant walking side by side in the rear. At times the child imitated the song of the nightingale and at times the call of the cuckoo, breaking off branches of trees with flings of his arms, bending down to pick up cones, or kicking them with his feet. It seemed as if he had completely forgotten the enemy at his side.

The forest grew thicker. The winding path wove its way through a dense growth of white birch, through open spaces grown up in clumps of grass and up hills covered with spruce.

Deep within the forest were several guerrillas lying in ambush, their submachine guns set up beside the trees. They looked out from the cracks between the spruce branches, from which they could see the winding path. Once in a while they spoke a few brief words, spread the branches open cautiously, and looked intently into the distance.

"Did you hear that?" one of the guerrillas suddenly said. In the distance a bird seemed to be calling, a weak and indistinct sound brought on the wind to the spruces. He straightened up and, cocking his head to one side, listened in the direction of the calls. "The nightingale!"

"You aren't mistaken, are you?" another of the guerrillas asked. The first of them to speak grew tense and listened carefully, but heard nothing more. Nevertheless, he picked up four hand grenades from beneath a gree stump and placed them in front of him in preparation for combat.

"Can you hear it now?"

The song of the nightingale grew louder.

The man who had first heard the nightingale's call was standing still, as if nailed to the spot. He counted slowly: "One, two, three, four ..." clapping his hands as he counted.

"Thirty-two enemy devils ..." he said finally, noting each bird call one by one. Only the guerrillas knew the meaning of the calls. The nightingale's call stopped and was followed by two cries of a cuckoo. "Two machine guns," he added.

"We can take care of them!" said a fellow with a full beard, who was carrying a submachine gun. When he had finished speaking, he tied his cartridge belt around his waist.

"We can take care of them!" the man who had first heard the call said. "I and Uncle Stefan will drive them out. After you've opened fire, we'll hit them from the rear. If anything happens to us, be sure not to forget the little nightingale ..."

After several minutes, the German soldiers appeared to the rear of the spruce grove. The nightingale was still singing merrily, but the guerrillas knew the meaning of the song.

When the Germans entered the spruce grove, someone suddenly let out a whistle from deep within the forest, answering the child as if it were an echo. The child turned suddenly, making his way deep into the forest, where he disappeared. The sound of rifle fire broke the stillness of the forest. The lieutenant, who had not grabbed his pistol in time, rolled to the edge of the path. The German soldiers, wounded by the submachine gun, fell to the ground one by one. For a time the forest was filled with the moans and shouts of the German soldiers and the commands of the guerrillas.

The next day the child was again wearing his green coat and sitting by the edge of the stream whittling, from time to time turning his head to look at the road to the village as if he were waiting for someone.

From the child's mouth there flew out the persuasive song of the nightingale. His call could not have been distinguished from that of a real nightingale even by those accustomed to the calls of birds.

What method did the "little nightingale" use to tell the guerrillas how many German soldiers there were and how many machine guns they had?

THIRTY-THREE—SELECTION ONE.
THE FARMER AND THE SNAKE*

Once upon a time, on a cold winter day, there was a farmer who saw a snake, numb from the cold, on the road. The farmer, who pitied the snake, loosened his clothes and placed it next to his bosom.

As the snake grew warm, he gradually awoke. As soon as he awoke, he bit the farmer. The farmer, poisoned, said as he was on the point of death: "A snake is something harmful to man and ought not to be pitied. Since I took pity on something harmful to man, I should receive an evil retribution."

---

*This fable is taken from *Aesop's Fables*.

Discuss the implications of this fable. What instruction do we receive from it? Write out this fable.

THIRTY-FOUR. OPEN FIRE ON THE GOD OF PLAGUES

The waves of the Taiwan Strait foam on,
Raising a Class-12 gale.
The heavens shake and the earth shudders in the cannon fire;
The mountains cry out and the seas scream in the light of the
    flames.
The heroic cannons roar,
And heroic soldiers shout out in rage:
Push Eisenhower back.
Open fire!
Push the American invaders out of Taiwan;
Open fire!
Push them out of Japan;
Open fire!
Push them out of Korea;
Open fire!
Push them out of Asia;
Open fire!
We must liberate our nation's territory, Taiwan;
Open fire!
Topple American imperialism;
Open fire! Open fire! Open fire!
Open fire on the god of plagues!
Open fire on the evil and barbarous plunderers.
Open fire on the common enemy of the world's peoples.
Open fire on the number one war criminal!
In June of 1950,
American arms invaded Taiwan;
In June of 1960,
American troops still shamelessly remained on Taiwan.
Taiwan,
Bright pearl of our motherland,
You have sunken into mud and have been stained with blood;
Taiwan,

Precious island of our motherland,
A sea of fire and disaster on disaster.
Our sisters on Taiwan,
Cut off from the mainland, their tears never dry;
Our brothers on Taiwan
Have lit the flames of hate.
Taiwan has had its volcanoes from ancient times,
And now the volcanoes are set to explode.
Injustice has its source, a debt has its claimant,
And a debt of blood must be returned in blood!

Our Brothers and Sisters of Taiwan,
Six hundred million compatriots are at your side,
And a strong, armed force is at your rear.
Listen,
The roar of tens of thousands of cannon shake the earth,
The shouts of six hundred million people reach the Heavens,
Calling the god of plagues to flee,
Calling the war criminals to terror.
We want them to understand:
The People of China will not stand for oppression!
The territory of China cannot be occupied easily!

The waves of the Taiwan Strait foam on,
Raising a Class-12 gale.
For our brothers and sisters on Taiwan,
Open fire!
For the fresh blood on the streets of Tokyo,
Open fire!
For the raging fires of Seoul and Pusan,
Open fire!
For the righteous struggles of the peoples of Asia, Africa, and
    Latin America,
On Eisenhower,
On American Imperialism,
Open fire! Open fire! Open fire!

Why is it said that the American invaders are gods of plague,
evil and barbarous plunderers, the common enemy of the world's
peoples, and the number-one war criminals?

SELECTIONS FROM VOLUME 10 OF THE READERS

(GRADE FIVE)

EIGHT. GIVING CONVENIENCE TO OTHERS

One day when the bell ending the shift rang, the girls in the fine-yarn room, with happy smiles on their faces for having fulfilled their quotas, came out of the work room talking and laughing. Chao Meng-t'ao, who had been following along with the happy group, had walked a ways when suddenly she stopped. She had discovered that Hsiao T'ang of their group had not come out. Chao Meng-t'ao called out to the girls with whom she was walking and then turned and ran back to the work room. Just as she ran in the entrance, Hsiao T'ang came walking out, her head lowered. Chao Meng-t'ao shouted, "Hsiao T'ang!" and Hsiao T'ang, not waiting for her to say anything more, came up to her. Grasping her hand and holding back the tears in her eyes, she said: "Meng-t'ao, what shall I do? I used all the strength of my whole body, and I still couldn't fulfill my quota ..." As she spoke, she lowered her head, brushing away her tears.

Hsiao T'ang's words pierced Chao Meng-t'ao's heart like a needle. She thought: "I am a Communist Party member and an advanced production worker too. If there is someone in the group who cannot fulfill her quota, isn't it because I haven't fulfilled my responsibilities?"

Chao Meng-t'ao knew Hsiao T'ang as if she were her own sister. Hsiao T'ang was a good comrade sincerely willing to work, but because she was inexperienced and because her two machines were not good, she broke many threads. By putting out 70 or 80 ounces of waste cotton a day, her production mission could not be fulfilled, and this affected the production quota of the entire

375

group. Chao Meng-t'ao had given Hsiao T'ang a great deal of help in technique, but now it appeared that she had still not been able to solve her problem.

Chao Meng-t'ao, looking into Hsiao T'ang's face, which was covered with clouds of grief, thought a while and then said with sincerity: "Don't worry. I've got a solution."

The next day, at the group meeting, Chao Meng-t'ao mentioned that she wanted to exchange machines with Hsiao T'ang. Her comrades listened with surprise, for although Hsiao T'ang could fulfill her quota once the machines were exchanged, what about Chao Meng-t'ao?

Chao Meng-t'ao went to the production group chief to make her request. The group chief thought a while and said: "Meng-t'ao, your machine is very good, but we still ought to study this a little more. Hsiao T'ang is not unwilling to work, but the machine is hard to run. If you give up yours, can you fulfill your quota?"

Chao Meng-t'ao said: "I've been running the machines for a fairly long time, and I'm quite familiar with the technique. If we exchange machines, I'll still be better than someone inexperienced. Besides, Hsiao T'ang can't fulfill her quota, and we can't go on without doing something about it!"

The group chief thought it over for a while and gave his consent. But one of the older girls on the same shift said: "Meng-t'ao, you are a labor model for the entire nation. Once you exchange machines, you won't be able to exceed your planned daily quota. Won't you lose face?"

In regard to this problem, Chao Meng-t'ao had gone through ideological struggle. Before suggesting the exchange of machines, she had thought that if, because of the exchange of machines, she could not fulfill her quota and could not fulfill the guarantee that she had made, what a bad effect that would produce! While she was still undecided, the words spoken to her by the Party Branch Secretary when she entered the Party rang in her ear: "A Communist Party member cannot think only of his own good. It is the responsibility and the duty of a Communist Party member to help others to advance to his level ..." These words gave Chao Meng-t'ao an inexhaustible strength, and she resolved to exchange machines with Hsiao T'ang, thinking: "Even if it's the most difficult machine to run, I must keep my guarantee to exceed my daily quota."

Chao Meng-t'ao, on hearing what the girl on her shift said, at once answered firmly: "Elder sister, it is the cause of the Party that is important for a Communist Party member, not his own reputation or position. I'm not afraid of not being an advanced production worker, and I want to help others catch up with the advanced."

Chao Meng-t'ao resolutely left her machine and went over to work on Hsiao T'ang's machine. She first studied the condition of the machine and ascertained what was causing the breakage. She found that the major deficiencies in Hsiao T'ang's work were that the coarse thread was mixed up, that the machine spun slowly, and that her cleaning work was not done well. Once she had seen through the situation, Chao Meng-t'ao came on duty early every day. When she went into the work room, she first inspected the machine, repaired what she could repair, made a note of what she could not repair, and cleaned the machine. After the machine had started operating, she kept it revolving continually with light and nimble touches of her foot, assaulting those places where break-age was worst. Whenever she had a free moment, she grasped it for cleaning work, so that her machine was always clean.

To be sure, Chao Meng-t'ao's mind was not completely at ease. Especially during the first few days, when the broken threads grew to large piles, she became so nervous that the sweat dripped from her face. But she was not frightened. Thinking of the firm and resolute spirit of the Liberation Army soldiers during battle, she encouraged herself: "You mustn't be nervous. Calm down. This is just like a war in which those who die bravely win! Even if the threads keep on breaking, your thought musn't get disordered ..." Thereupon, she kept it turning with even greater diligence, working with even greater care.

After Chao Meng-t'ao changed to this machine, as always, she exceeded her daily quota and fulfilled the state plans, and waste cotton decreased. At the same time, Hsiao T'ang also fulfilled her quota. With the help of Chao Meng-t'ao and the other girls, she made rapid progress, becoming a skilled machine worker.

"Keep difficulties for oneself, and give convenience to others." This was Chao Meng-t'ao's predominant characteristic. She changed machines with others some ten times in succession, and the most difficult to operate of machines in her hands became obedient and orderly. Those who had been helped by Chao Meng-t'ao and who had been influenced by Chao Meng-t'ao's advanced thought, similarly helped other comrades. One helping the other became the spirit of the whole group. Year after year, the group exceeded the quotas of the state plans and every year was judged to be the factory's model production group.

ELEVEN. STARTING FROM REALITY

If there is a date tree outside the classroom window, it can be seen on opening the window.

If, however, there were no date tree outside the window, would we be able to see a date tree on opening the window? No, we would not. If we are to see a date tree, there must be a date tree.

There is, then, a date tree outside the window. If we close the window and cannot see it, can we say that there is no date tree outside the window? We cannot. Whether you can see it or not, the date tree is always standing outside the window.

Whether or not there is a date tree outside the window must be determined by starting from reality. If there is one, one cannot say that there isn't one, and if there isn't one, one cannot say that there is one.

This truth is very clear. But when we are working, we sometimes do not start out from reality and do not investigate the actual situation, relying on our own methods of thought to make an evaluation, with the result that it does not tally with reality and our work is done incorrectly.

In work, one cannot rely only on one's own methods of thought, but must start from reality, emphasizing investigation and research. Here is an example.

Once upon a time there was a man who had lost an axe and who suspected that one of his neighbors had stolen it. When he then observed the neighbor, he felt that his gait and the tone of his voice were different from those of ordinary people. In short, from first to last he seemed very much like a thief. Later, he found his axe, which he had dropped while chopping firewood on the mountain. When he once again observed his neighbor, he felt that his gait and the tone of his voice did not seem like those of a thief.

The man who had lost his axe had not carried out investigation and research and thus thought that his axe had been stolen by his neighbor. He had blamed his neighbor falsely. Later, having found his axe, in face of the actual facts his error was corrected.

No matter what one is doing, one must start from reality and must not rely solely on one's own ways of thought. When one relies solely on one's own ways of thought, which may not tally with the actual situation, one may commit errors.

What is starting from reality? Explain, citing an incident from every day life as in the text.

TWELVE. TWO IRON BALLS STRIKE THE EARTH AT THE SAME TIME

Galileo[a] was a great scientist of the seventeenth century. He was born in Italy and was versatile and talented from an early age. When he was in school, people called him the "Debater" because he was most fond of arguing over problems with others. The questions that he brought up were very unusual, and some of them could not be answered even by his teachers.

At that time, students of science all believed in and followed Aristotle,[b] a Greek philosopher of 2000 years before. All that Aristotle had said was taken to be immutable truth, and no one had ever doubted him. Whoever doubted Aristotle would be subjected to the following sort of reprimand: "What is your intention? Can it be that you want to violate the truths of mankind?"

Aristotle had said that if two iron balls, one weighing ten pounds[c] and the other weighing one pound, were dropped from a high place at the same time, the velocity of the ten pound ball would be ten times that of the one pound ball. Everyone had always believed this statement, but Galileo doubted it. He wanted to try an experiment to find out whether this statement was really a truth after all.

At that time Galileo was already a professor. By means of his experiment he proved that Aristotle's statements could not be relied upon. When two iron balls are dropped from a high place at the same time, they strike the earth at the same time, the weight of the ball having no relationship to the velocity of descent. He announced the results of the experiment to his students and set a date for carrying out a public experiment from the Leaning Tower of Pisa,[d] to which he invited everyone.

When the day arrived, the Leaning Tower was surrounded by many people who had come to watch the experiment and to watch the contest of scientific principles.

Who was to be the victor in the contest? Was it to be the ancient philosopher, Aristotle, or was it to be the twenty-five year

---

a. Galileo (1564-1642)—A famous physicist.

b. Aristotle (384-322 B.C.)—A Greek philosopher.

c. Pound—The pound is roughly equivalent to somewhat more than 9 Chinese liang.

d. Pisa—A city in central Italy.

old professor, Galileo? Everyone felt that the two opponents were not in the least evenly matched.

"This young fellow is really all mixed up. He's really sure of himself to think that he could catch Aristotle in error!"

"Just wait a while and he won't be so sure of himself. Cold facts will make him lose face!"

Galileo appeared at the top of the Leaning Tower. In his right hand he held a ten pound iron ball, and in his left hand he held a one pound iron ball. The two iron balls left his hands at the same time and fell through the air. In a moment the people surrounding the tower could not keep from shouting out in amazement. Everyone saw that, just as Galileo had said, the two iron balls struck the earth at the same time.

What was the difference in the viewpoints of Galileo and Aristotle on the subject of two iron balls striking the earth? Why did Galileo win?

THIRTEEN. RECOLLECTIONS FROM SIXTEEN YEARS AGO

(Part 1)*

April 28, 1927 is a day that I shall never forget. That was the day my father was executed. That was sixteen years ago.

Father was captured on April 6, which was the day of the Grave Visiting Festival. We rose early and, as the weather was very warm, I and my sisters happily changed into new clothes. Father, on seeing us, said quickly: "Why don't you go out and enjoy yourselves? It's really spring."

Father was very busy those days and had very little spare time to talk with us. He came home very late at night each day, and I have no idea what time he left in the morning. Sometimes he stayed at home, busying himself in putting books and articles in order. I often sat at his side, silently watching him as he threw books and papers with writing on them into the fire. On touching the fire, the books and papers turned into ashes, fluttering in the

---

*This essay was written in 1943 in memory of her father by the daughter of the martyr, Li Ta-chao.

air like gray butterflies. Father's face was very severe. I thought: was he sad that these books and papers which were his companions had been innocently burned? But why would he burn them even if he didn't care about them? I thought and thought, but, not being able to find a satisfactory reason, I asked father: "Father, why are you burning them? It seems a pity."

Pausing for a moment, father answered: "I don't want them, so I'm burning them. Silly child!"

Father was always very kind and had never scolded us or beaten us. I had always asked father many silly and childish questions. No matter how busy he was, he was always very interested in my questions and always talked to me patiently. But for some reason, that time father answered me in this vague way.

Later I learned from my mother's lips that in a few days the reactionary warlord, Chang Tso-lin, was going to send someone to investigate. Two days later misfortune arrived. One of father's fellow workers, Yen Chen, had gone out shopping early and had not come back by evening. The next day, father and the others found out that Yen Chen had been seized and taken to the police station. We were all ill at ease and very worried about his fellow worker.

The situation grew more serious, and father's work grew more intense. But he did not become despondent or disillusioned because of the worsening of conditions. When he had finished working, he still said a little something to make people laugh. Father was always optimistic in the face of his difficult revolutionary tasks.

Father's friends often came to persuade him into leaving Peking. Father did not pay any attention to their advice. Naturally, mother was worried about father and frequently remonstrated with him, but to not the least effect. Father said to mother very firmly: "Haven't I often told you? I can hardly leave Peking ... You must know what the time is and how important the work here is. How can I leave?" He talked frankly, and mother closed her mouth, remaining silent. Although I was sad, I was still a child, and when I was playing happily, I could put everything to the back of my mind. I never was sad all day like mother. During those days, we lived in that sort of uneasiness.

The moment that we had feared came. On the morning of April 6, my sister put on her new clothes, and mother took her out for a stroll in the children's playground by the troop barracks. The weather was fine, and they set out happily, not even eating breakfast. In his room, father sat writing at his black table. I sat outside reading the newspaper on a long bench. I had barely read a word when I heard a few sharp bursts of gunfire, followed by the confusion of shouting from the area of the Boxer Indemnity Committee headquarters. After that, I heard several people jump into our courtyard over the low wall surrounding it.

"What is it, Father?" I asked, staring with startled eyes.

"It's nothing. Don't be afraid. Hsing-erh, come out and take a look with me." He calmly withdrew a shining pistol from his drawer and went out into the courtyard. We had just gone out the door when we saw a good many empty-handed young people rushing back and forth, unable to find a suitable way out. Staying close behind father, I walked out of the full and frightening courtyard until we found a quiet, out-of-the-way house, where we could be at ease for a while.

Father was sitting on a chair. His expression was very cold, and in his hand he held his only weapon. It appeared that he was going to put up a resistance if he could. I too grew a little more courageous.

Outside there came the sound of heavy boots. My heart began to beat wildly. I barely breathed and just stared at father, my eyes full of terror.

"Don't let even one of them get away!" There was a harsh shout outside the window. A moment later, a military policeman wearing a gray uniform and high boots, a scout wearing plain-clothes, and a policeman wearing a black uniform dashed in, filling the little room. Like a throng of devils, they surrounded us. Each of them held a pistol in his hand, which they pointed at father and me. Among the military and police I found our fellow worker, Yen Chen, who had been captured a few days before. He was being dragged along by a fat detective wearing plain-clothes, who had tied his arms up with a rope. His white face showed from between his long, flowing hair. He had obviously been tortured. They had brought him along so that he could identify people.

The big, fleshy-faced detective, with an insidious look in his eyes, pointed at father and asked Yen Chen: "Do you know him?"

Yen Chen shook his head, indicating that he didn't.

"Ach! You don't? I know him." The detective, with a cunning smile, ordered the men under him: "Watch carefully. Don't let him kill himself. Take his gun away first!"

They immediately took father's pistol away. Then they searched father all over. Father, maintaining his customary stern and dignified air, did not tell them any truth, because he understood that there was no truth that they could be told.

The cruel bandits tied father up and dragged him away. I was taken away by them too.

On the basis of the content of the text, discuss why the martyr Li Ta-chao was always optimistic about the revolution.

FOURTEEN. RECOLLECTIONS FROM SIXTEEN YEARS AGO

(Part 2)

In the courtyard of the police station, which was surrounded by a high brick wall, I saw that mother and sister had also been brought in. We were shut up in the women's detention house.

Some ten days passed, during which we did not see father or hear any news of him. Mother and I spent each day in worry. One day, about eleven o'clock in the morning, we were just earing lunch. We had not yet finished gnawing on the coarse bread in our hands when I heard the police shout the names of my mother and me, calling us out for the trial.

In the court we met father. He was, as always, wearing his old gray cotton gown, but he did not have his glasses on. Beneath his disordered long hair I saw his tranquil and kind face.

"Father!" I couldn't keep from crying out. Mother was crying, and sister began to cry too.

"Silence!" The judge took up his gavel and rapped loudly on the table.

"Silence!" his subordinate responded in reprimand.

Father looked at us, but said nothing to us. He had an extremely calm and grave expression on his face. His heart was filled with a great strength. This strength was his faith in the revolutionary task about which he talked to us every day.

"That is my wife," he said, pointing to mother. Then he pointed to me and sister. "These are my two daughters."

"Is she your eldest child?" the judge, pointing to me, asked father.

'Yes. I am his eldest child." I don't know where the resourcefulness or courage came from, but fearing that father would mention brother, I spoke out hastily.

"Don't interrupt!" The judge rapped angrily several times with his wooden stick.

"Don't interrupt!" his subordinate also shouted imperiously.

Father, who had understood what I intended, then said: "Yes, she is my eldest child. My wife is a country girl, and my children are little. They do not understand anything. They have no connection with anything." After father had said that, he did not speak again, but looked at us again and again.

The judge ordered us to be taken out in custody. Therefore, we met father just once before we were hurriedly separated.

There was no way to find out anything about father's circumstances after that. Every day mother and I thought and worried in anxiety and uneasiness.

At dusk on April 28, the police called out the names of my mother and me for the second time, telling us to pack our bags and leave the detention house. In confusion, I helped mother, setting our few items of tattered clothing in order with shaking hands. A police officer pushed us out the gate. Anxiously wanting to find out about father, I asked the police officer in a low voice: "Mr. Policeman, there's something I'd like to ask you. Do you know how ... my father is?" My voice was trembling a little, and there were tears in my eyes.

"You'll find out when you get home," he said coldly.

We went out through the black iron gate. When we reached home, it was already dark. Standing in front of the quiet and lonely gate, I felt an inexpressible strangeness. My uncle—the brother of my father's mother—opened the main entrance and, on seeing that it was us, with unexpected happiness, shouted in a loud voice into the courtyard: "They've come back!" Yu-tzu, the nurse who helped mother look after the children, was so happy she couldn't keep her mouth closed. All she said was: "It's the gods who have protected them!" When mother saw that three of her children were still at home, she could not help feeling a pang of grief.

The next day, uncle went out to buy a newspaper. The old man came in from the streets crying and holding a paper limply in his hands. When I saw the headline in large characters: "LI TA-CHAO AND OTHERS EXECUTED BY HANGING YESTERDAY," I suddenly felt a haze over my eyes, and I fell in a faint on my bed. When I awoke, there was a disordered group in mother's room. Mother fainted three times, fainting again each time just after she awoke.

We children gathered in a group around mother's bed.

"Mother, mother ... We're here," we called beside mother's ear.

"Remember, yesterday was the day your father was executed. What was the date yesterday?" mother, who had come-to, asked us in a low voice.

I was crying too and picking up the newspaper from the floor and holding it in front of my eyes, I forced myself to read it, hardening my heart and biting my lips. It was clearly announced that twenty people, my father among them, had been hanged yesterday.

I threw the newspaper onto the bed and said to mother in a low voice: "Mother, yesterday was April 28."

Mother nodded her head slightly.

A few days later, we dressed father's body for burial and laid his coffin temporarily at Che-chiang Hall outside of Hsuan-wu Gate. Mother returned to the country to live, taking me and my two younger brothers and two younger sisters with her. Brother also left Peking.

Divide the entire selection, "Recollections from Sixteen Years Ago," into sections and explain the main idea in each section.

SIXTEEN. BREAKING THROUGH THE WU RIVER BARRIER

(Part 1)

On January 2, 1935, the advance party of our Red army crossed the Wu River Barrier.

It was a stormy day, with both wind and rain.

At six o'clock in the morning, we arrived at the Wu River Ford. According to the information of our guide, there was an enemy regiment on the opposite bank who were under the illusion that the advance of our army could be blocked by the Wu River Barrier.

The Wu River can truly be called a barrier of heaven. Great mountains several hundreds of meters high rise like walls from both banks, giving it the appearance of having been cut out with a knife. The river is 100 meters wide, with whitecaps billowing and roaring. Just standing on the bank is enough to frighten a brave fighter, to say nothing of crossing the river.

As soon as our advance guard battalion stepped into the shallows, the enemy opened fire on us with a *"pa, pa, pa."* Fortunately the mountains were steep, and as we were standing to the rear of a hollow, the enemy fire could not reach us. To test them, I ordered the artillelry company to open fire on the enemy at the top of the opposite mountain. With three blasts from the artillery, the enemy fortifications on the mountain top blew sky high. Through the telescope, a band of the enemy could be seen crowding down the back of the mountain.

We had suppressed the enemy's fire power temporarily, but what could we do about the river that was spread before us?

Commissar Li and I went to a neighboring village to investigate. There was not even a single boat there, only an oar. It was difficult to find something even resembling a piece of board, the enemy having taken them away already.

As for swimming, the river was so swift that as soon as a person stepped into it he would be swept away by the water. There was no use in talking about building a bridge. Where were there any materials? The river was deep and the current swift, there was no bridge, and there were no boats. Nevertheless, all of our comrades in the regiment had to cross.

"We must cross. We must!" After obtaining the agreement of Commissar Li, I ordered the troops to organize their forces and go out to the surrounding villages to buy boats and wood. I myself went out to ask various local townsmen about their experiences in crossing the river. The townsmen in the neighboring villages told us that there are three necessary conditions for crossing the Wu River: very clear weather, large wooden boats, and boatmen thoroughly familiar with the nature of the river. We could not satisfy even one of these conditions. The wind was blowing, it was raining, we didn't have any boats, and we didn't have any boatmen.

The men who had been sent out returned, having been unable to find any boats in the neighboring villages and not having found a boatman.

The wind was still howling, and the rain was falling harder and harder. From time to time I shook the rainwater from my rain hat, walking back and forth, not caring whether I slipped in the slippery mud. I had racked my brain, thinking of everything that could be thought of, but there was still no solution.

It was already afternoon. Everyone was soaked by the rain, and we still had not worked out a solution. The enemy had probably guessed that we were stuck and were firing their rifles at us stealthily in ridicule. I was just about to check the enemy situation on the opposite bank through the telescope when suddenly something drifted in front of my eyes. I fixed my eyes on it and saw that it was a stick of bamboo. The bamboo was floating in the middle of the river, spinning with the waves. Even though a series of waves forced it under the water, it would in the end come floating back up.

"Lao Li!" Shoving the commissar, who was at my side, I pointed with my hand at the bamboo. "What is that?" I almost shouted out in excitement. "Come with me!" Not waiting for the commissar to answer, I wiped the rainwater from my face and ran to the village behind the mountain.

In the village we found many pieces of bamboo, dry, wet, big, little, long, and short. Everyone scurried to tie them up together. Since there was no hemp, we used straw rope, and finally we used everyone's leg laces. In about three hours we had tied three bamboo rafts together. Ha! These were really big fellows, ten feet in width and twenty feet in length, thick and looking just like skin rafts blown up with air.

We decided to make a first trial crossing. From the advance guard battalion, we picked eight soldiers familiar with the nature of rivers. Each of them was fully equipped with weapons, but, lacking oars, had to row with twigs of bamboo and sticks of wood.

It had already grown dark. The rain was still falling heavily, and nothing could be seen clearly beyond a few meters. The bamboo rafts were moved to the shoals by about twenty soldiers.

Gunfire was still sounding sporadically from the opposite bank. The eight soldiers jumped onto the bamboo raft. We decided that when the rafts reached the opposite bank, two shots would be fired as a communications signal.

The bamboo raft slowly left the shoals. Everyone on the bank of the river stared after it. Everyone's hearts were as taut as strung bows.

Ten meters, fifteen meters, the bamboo raft, with difficulty, plunged through one dangerous wave and then through another. Suddenly, in the middle of the river, the bamboo raft dipped two times in the water. A mountainous wave covered the raft and all of the men on it. I was covered with perspiration. Then the raft emerged from the water with the eight men still on it.

"Keep on!" Standing on the riverbank, I heard the voice of the raft squad leader call. I could not keep from feeling a reverence and a gratitude for them rise up in my heart. I felt pride that we had such brave soldiers.

The bamboo raft was struggling on in the water. Each wave

made those of us on the bank tense, just as it did the men on the raft. After the raft had been out for some twenty minutes, we were all very nervous.

"Give it the gas!" I cried out silently in my heart, regretting that I couldn't run out and give them a push. How much I wanted to hear the sound of rifle fire when they had the opposite bank beneath their feet!

Two or three minutes passed. Suddenly there was a cry of "Ai-ya" from someone in the crowd on the bank. I looked quickly toward the middle of the river, where I could see dimly that the raft had been upset in the water. I rushed forward a few steps, but all I could see was the bamboo raft slipping rapidly down-stream with the swift current. Several black spots in the middle of the river which, needless to say, were our comrades from the bamboo raft, were struggling in the waves. Without calling for help, they were swept up silently into a whirlpool.

The wind was still blowing and the rain was still falling. Everything was as it had been a moment before, except that everyone's hearts were oppressed by a heavy pain.

What conditions were necessary in order to cross the Wu River? What difficulties did the Red Army meet when they crossed the Wu River?

SEVENTEEN. BREAKING THROUGH THE WU RIVER BARRIER

(Part 2)

"I must find a solution. We've got to get across!" I resolved. I gave the task of continuing the crossing to the commander of the first battalion.

There was a burst of activity on the shoals as everyone busied himself with preparations. When the soldiers heard that we were going to continue with the crossing, they came from all sides to request the assignment from the battalion commander. The battalion commander, who had all he could do to talk them all down, selected about a dozen soldiers.

The crossing began again. The soldiers jumped onto the bamboo raft. From the opposite bank there came a round of machine gun fire. Everyone looked at the enemy facing us with anger and hatred. The battalion commander movingly said what was in everyone's heart: "Comrades, we must cross. Even if only one of you remains, you must get across. The hopes of the whole regiment are on you!"

"We can cross, indeed we can!" one of the soldiers answered in a loud voice.

"Advance!" The battalion commander issued the order.

The sky was black as ink. Not even the closest things could be seen. The bamboo raft left the shore. At first, we could still hear the slapping sound of the water, but gradually even the sound of the water became indistinct.

"How are you doing?" Everyone was anxious for their comrades on the bamboo raft. Everyone wanted to see clearly, but the sky was so black that nothing could be seen.

I waited silently, praying that they would succeed in crossing the river.

It had been almost an hour, and I began to grow anxious.

The wind and the waves were still roaring. "How are they doing? Probably they have ..." I dared not keep on with my thoughts. I felt as if a stone weighing a thousand catties were pressing down upon my shoulders.

"P'ang." Was it the sound of a rifle? I was aroused from my heavy thoughts. I raised my head, but all I saw was a flash of light from the top of the opposite mountain. It was not our communications signal, but rather a rifle fired by one of the enemy.

"P'ang, p'ang." Two shots. Commissar Li, who was standing beside me, called out: "Lao Yang, did you hear? Two shots from the foot of the mountain!"

"Ah, they're ours!" I simply could not believe my ears. "Yes, they're ours."

'Well, let's launch this 'boat' too!" I looked toward the opposite bank excitedly. The third bamboo raft, which had already been prepared, moved out.

We directed a heavy barrage of machine gun and rifle fire toward the opposite bank. A red glare was reflected from the surface of the river. The bamboo raft advanced under the light.

Before too long, flashing red light came from the mountain top opposite us. After that, the sounds of rifles, machine guns, explosions, and fighting were mixed together.

"Lao Li, we've succeeded!" I excitedly gave Commissar Li a painful clap on the shoulder. As the palm of my hand clapped Commissar Li's coat, there was a spray of water.

"Lao Li, you're wet!"

"And you?"

I heard him laughing in the darkness. Grasping his hand tightly, I said with emotion: "We're both as wet and hungry as if we had been floating on the bamboo raft together!"

"Right!" The commissar grasped my hand tightly. "We're both wet and hungry as if we had been floating on the bamboo raft together!"

The wind was still blowing and the rain was still falling. By the red light glimmering from the river surface, the bamboo raft could dimly be seen floating in the water.

"The Wu River Barrier has finally been broken!" Looking toward the center of the river, I felt an inexpressible happiness.

The bamboo raft crossed back and forth again and again, and the number of our men on the opposite bank gradually increased. A little after eleven o'clock the following morning, our whole regiment had crossed the Wu River.

Where can the heroic spirit of the Red Army soldiers in their determination to complete their mission of crossing the Wu River be seen?

NINETEEN. AN EXTRAORDINARY FORTY MINUTES

In the summer of 1958, the remnants of the Kuomintang reactionaries holding Quemoy were firing again and again, bombarding our fishing ships and coastal villages. The soldiers of the coast artillery units could not restrain their fury and had asked for the order to fire in order to punish that bunch of criminals.

One evening, the company commander was telling the soldiers on the hillsides about the battle of Samkum Ridge. A young soldier, An Yeh-min, was captivated by the story told by the company commander. Moonlight fell upon his face, and beneath his thick eyebrows his eyes flashed. After the story was finished, the soldiers gradually dispersed, but he still remained there deep in thought. The company commander came up to him and, clapping him on the shoulder, asked with concern: "What are you thinking about?" An Yeh-min turned his head and said resolutely: "Company Commander, I guarantee to you that, just like the heroes of Samkum and no matter what tests I am put to, I shall strive to be a glorious member of the Communist Party."

On August 23, orders came down from General Yen Ch'eng.

An Yeh-min, restraining his excitement, sat behind the semicircular shell plate, carrying out his first battle mission. He felt deeply the importance of his responsibility. If there is even a slight error in the operation of the aiming circle, the shells will not burst over the heads of the enemy, and if the following movement is even a little slow, the shells will not be fired in time. At this time, the company commander took pains to advise everyone: "In battle, whenever there is a temporary cessation of firing, you must rurn the barrels of your guns in the direction of concealment!" An Yeh-min bore these words firmly in his mind.

Our artillery opened intense fire. Tens of thousands of shells flew across the straits, and tens of thousands of thunderclaps bombarded Quemoy's Liao-lo Bay. The earth shook, the waves roared, and thousands of columns of water sprang up around the enemy ships.

"We've hit an enemy ship!" "An enemy ship's on fire!"

A cry of joy arose from the position, and everyone's battle morale swelled even further. This artillery group seemed like a sharp sword jabbing at Quemoy's Liao-lo Bay, threatening the lives of the enemy. The enemy artillery concentrated their fire on An Yeh-min's position. A bullet struck the gun captain's leg. So that his comrades would not see it, he rolled down his trouser leg without a sound, covering the wound. But a soldier who was standing opposite him, discovering the blood flowing from his leg, called out: "Gun captain, you've been wounded!"

"Don't shout!" the gun captain said in a low voice.

In an instant, the ammunition supply to the right rear of the gun was struck by a shell, and bright flames suddenly ignited above the position.

"Cease fire temporarily and disperse at once!" the gun captain ordered.

An Yeh-min, thinking of what the platoon leader had said, quickly turned both hands toward the aiming circle. Flames were lapping at the gun shield, lapping at the barrel of the gun, and lapping fiercely at his body, but the gun barrel was still turning! His whole body had caught fire, and the barrel of the gun was still turning! When the barrel had been turned toward the place of concealment, An Yeh-min was a ball of fire. He burst from the gun emplacement and rolled several times on the ground, his comrades surrounding him and beating him until the fire enveloping him had been extinguished. When everyone looked, An Yeh-min's eyebrows and hair had been burned off and the ashes of his sailor's jacket stuck to his flesh. Almost all of his body had been burned. He felt that the earth and sky were revolving and a severe and unbearable pain. Then he fainted.

Amid the whine of the shells, An Yeh-min opened his eyes and saw the battalion commissar standing in front of him. The battalion commissar gave him a cup of boiled water and said: "Rest quietly. Your comrades will avenge you!"

An Yeh-min suddenly heard the gun captain's order: "Continue the battle! Strike the enemy fiercely! Give the enemy ten shots for every one he fires!"

"Right! We'll never give the enemy a chance to get tough!" An Yeh-min, giving no heed to his burned body, rushed forward to the gun emplacement and rapidly and accurately let loose a volley of shells.

"An Yeh-min, the commissar sent me to take your place. Get down. II'll handle it!" The assistant gun captain came running up from the magazine to take his place.

An Yeh-min, without turning his head, said: "Report to the chief that I can complete my mission!"

Ten minutes later, the commissar again sent the assistant gun captain to take his place. As before, he answered firmly, saying: "Please tell the chief not to worry. I guarantee that I will fulfill my battle mission completely!"

An Yeh-min's red, swollen eyes glittered. Without blinking, he fixed his eyes on the pointer, his two burned arms pressing tightly onto the aiming circle, his waist held straight, like a giant cast of iron. Fifteen minutes, twenty minutes, thirty minutes, forty minutes. This giant kept on until the battle reached a victorious conclusion.

From Quemoy Island smoke and flame filled the sky. The enemy guns fell silent.

After the firing stopped the soldiers began to clean the gun. An Yeh-min's burned face began to swell, and he could not open his eyes. The assistant chief brought a stretcher, on which he was placed to rest. He quickly grasped the cleaning rag at his side and said: "No. I can see. I'll clean the gun!" But when he tried to extend his hand to clean the gun, he was unable to.

"An Yeh-min, you are a member of the Communist Youth Corps and you must obey orders. Wait until your wounds are healed and then return to fight." When An Yeh-min heard the assistant chief's words, he left the position.

An Yeh-min lay in the company first aid room. In his confused state, he felt that someone was wiping the blood from his face.

"Who?" An Yeh-min wanted to look, but he could not open his eyes.

"I'm ... Hsiao Hung." Hsiao Hung was a woman militia member who helped them in battle. When she saw how badly injured An Yeh-min was, she could not keep from crying.

"Hsiao Hung, don't cry. It's not serious. I'll be able to fight again tomorrow. Hsiao Hung, do you like to sing? Let's sing the "Coast Artillery Song!"

Hsiao Hung struggled to keep from crying.

An Yeh-min, clenching his teeth fiercely, began to sing in a broken voice.

"The coast artillery are brave ... and ... firm." Hsiao Hung began to sing along with him.
"Our motherland has ... given ... the coast ... to us,
The coast ... is ... our common life ..."

Relate briefly what An Yeh-min guaranteed to the company commander and how he realized this guarantee in action.

TWENTY-TWO. AT THE FOOT OF MOUNT MEI

From the time I was very young, I had no mother. When I was little, grandmother used to hold me in her lap and say to me: "Ah, you are a girl without a mother, and I am a mother without a daughter." She did not dare to speak loudly and stared out the door as she spoke.

Where had mother gone? Grandmother was not willing to tell me.

At that time I used to call second aunt Erh-shen. I asked Erh-shen if she had seen mother or not. Erh-shen was not willing to say either and only cried. I began to grow afraid. Why did everyone act so strangely when I mentioned mother? After some time, Erh-shen finally said: "Your mother is a good person. After you've grown up, learn from her!"

I was eight years old at the time and felt that I was already grown up and able to learn from mother. But what would I learn from mother? Erh-shen was not willing to talk about that either.

The year that I was twelve, we heard that there were guerrillas of the Liberation Army in our Tapieh Mountain. Grandmother said that the guerrillas were all good people and that the poor families in the mountains all liked the guerrillas. Grandmother often went out visiting from door to door, and sometimes she got up in the night to go out and talk quietly with other families.

One night, grandmother woke me, saying that my father had sent someone to see me. Grandmother said: "It's your father. Your father's sent someone. Everyone said he was dead long ago, but he's actually alive! Go at once! Go at once!"

Grandmother pulled me into a thatched hut. There were several men with guns standing at the door, and inside there sat a stranger wearing a short coat and pants. He was surrounded by a large number of men, and I thought that he must have been the man sent by my father. Everyone called him County Chief Pai.

County Chief Pai pulled me up to him and looked at me from head to toe. I was not in the least afraid of strangers, and I asked County Chief Pai, "My father?"

"Your father is fighting the reactionaries, but he gave me a message for you. I've also brought along your mother's earrings," County Chief Pai said lightly.

Grandmother's face turned white, and she sat down on a bench. County Chief Pai looked at her, saying: "I'll tell her, Aunt. The child has grown up, and she is strong. Her father said that she should know what happened."

Grandmother, holding back her tears, nodded her head and, taking me in her lap, said softly: "Child, listen carefully."

Everyone in the room was listening.

This is the story that County Chief Pai told:

Just twelve years ago, your mother was buried alive by the Kuomintang. Your three brothers, one seven, one five and the other three, were also killed at the same time. You were just a few months old then, and your grandmother hid with you in the mountains for over a month so that they wouldn't find you. They beat your mother, because they wanted her to tell them where your father was and who the members of the Communist Party were. Even your three brothers were beaten. Your mother closed her mouth firmly, and not even the hammer could force a word out of her.

After that, the secret agents dug a big pit on the shoals of the Shih River at the foot of Mount Mei and pushed your mother and three brothers toward it. Your mother raised her head and, holding your three brothers, walked on with determined steps. Your elder brother asked: "Mother, where are we going?" Smiling slightly, she said: "We're going to your father."

The reactionaries also drove the village elders out to the shoals.

Your mother glanced toward her fellow villagers. She stood at the edge of the pit, grasping your older brother with one hand and holding your second and third brothers with the other hand.

The chief of the secret agents said to your mother: "Are you going to talk? This is your last chance. If you talk, we'll let the four of you go. If not, we'll root you out."

Your mother looked up to Mount Mei, where the pines are green through the four seasons, and where orchids bloom every year. She answered him: "Root us out? As easy as that?"

The evil secret agent struck your mother. Blood dripped from the corners of her mouth.

"You are a hard-hearted woman. Don't you take into account your own cheap life, and don't you care about these three children?"

Your mother's face changed color and, pointing at the agent's nose, she asked: "Is it my heart that's hard?" Squatting down and taking your second and third brothers in her arms, she said to the villagers: "Uncles, Aunts, where is there a mother who does not suffer for her own children? What crime have these little children committed? Who of you is willing to take them for me? I'll give them to you to be your own children!"

Several women came forward, but they were blocked by the agents.

The chief of the agents spoke angrily, and the agents pushed your mother. Your mother said: "Don't hit me. I can go in by myself!" As she spoke, she jumped down into the pit. She wanted your three brothers to squat down so that she could kiss them. She knew that the reactionaries had already made the evil decision to "root them out."

Your mother looked at the pit. It was too big for burying just one person. The chief of the agents, knowing that your mother understood their evil intentions, asked, his teeth protruding: "Aren't you going to save these three children?"

Your mother could not keep herself from cursing at them: "You're still asking me, you evil dogs! You killers!"

The three children looked up at their mother, their arms extended. The chief of the agents walked over and kicked them into the pit one by one. Your mother took each of them and embraced them. The villagers wanted to draw closer, but the agents levelled their rifles at them, blocking the way. Then they began throwing sand rapidly into the pit. Your mother said to the villagers: "Uncles and Aunts, remember this and tell their father when the Red Army comes by."

After that, it always seemed to the villagers that they often heard your mother's voice and heard her say these words.

Find relevant passages from the words of County Chief Pai, and discuss the cruel oppression of the Kuomintang and the invincible spirit, even in the face of death, that the mother displayed to the enemy.

Divide the text into sections and write a title for each of them.

TWENTY-SIX—SELECTION TWO.
SETTING OUT EARLY FROM PAI-TI*

At dawn I bade farewell to Pai-ti, among colored clouds.
Over the thousand *li* of river, I will return in one day.
Monkeys cry without end from the banks on either side,
And my frail boat has already passed the ten-thousand-layered mountains.

TWENTY-SEVEN. K'UNG-MING (CHU-KO LIANG) BORROWS SOME ARROWS

Chou Yü, who was jealous of Chu-ko Liang's talents, thought of a way to make trouble for him.

One day, Chou Yü assembled his generals in his tent and ordered someone to ask Chu-ko Liang to come for a conference on military matters. Chu-ko Liang came happily.

Chou Yü said to Chu-ko Liang: "We want to go into battle against Ts'ao Ts'ao's army. What weapons would be best for a water battle?" Chu-ko Liang said: "Bows and arrows." Chou Yü

---

* Li Po (d. 762—Transl.) is also the author of this poem. Pai-ti is on a mountain in eastern Feng-chieh county in Szechwan Province.

said: "Correct. What you say, Sir, agrees with my thoughts. At present the army is short of arrows, and I have been planning to ask you to assume the responsibility for making 100,000 of them. I hope that you will not decline." Chu-ko Liang said: "Whatever the military governor entrusts to me, I shall naturally carry out. When do you need these 100,000 arrows?" Chou Yü said: "Could you complete them in ten days?" Chu-ko Liang said: "You must go into battle at once. If I finish them in ten days, there will be a delay in a major campaign." Chou Yü said: "Sir, in how many days do you think you can finish them?" Chu-ko Liang said: "All I need is three days." Chou Yü said: "In the army we cannot joke." Chu-ko Liang said: "How could I dare to joke with the military governor? I am willing for military orders to be drawn up, and if I do not finish them in three days, I shall voluntarily submit to punishment." Chou Yü was very happy and had military orders drawn up for Chu-ko Liang on the spot. He then arranged a banquet for his entertainment. Chu-ko Liang said: "It's too late today. I'll begin making them tomorrow. Three days from tomorrow please send 500 soldiers to the bank of the river to pick up the arrows." Chu-ko Liang drank several cups of wine and then left.

Lu Su said to Chou Yü: "He can never make 100,000 arrows in three days! Can Chu-ko Liang be lying?" Chou Yü said: "That is what he himself said. I didn't force him. I will order the army artisans not to prepare any materials for him that are necessary for making arrows. In that way, he will surely miss his date. Then, when we set his punishment, there will be nothing that he can say. First, sneak around and try to find out what he is planning. Then come back and report to me."

Lu Su went to see Chu-ko Liang. Chu-ko Liang said: "In order that I may make the 100,000 arrows in three days, I would like to ask for your assistance." Lu Su said: "That is your own task. How can I help you?" Chu-ko Liang said: "I hoped that you could lend me twenty boats, each with thirty soldiers on board, and each covered with blue cloth curtains. I would also like to have over a thousand straw targets, for which I have a suitable use. I guarantee that on the third day I will have 100,000 arrows. But I cannot let Chou Yü know about this. If he finds out, my plans cannot be realized."

Lu Su consented. However, he did not understand Chu-ko Liang's intentions, and when he returned and reported to Chou Yü, he did not mention the matter of lending the boats, telling him only that Chu-ko Liang did not need bamboo, feathers, glue, or varnish. Chou Yü said suspiciously: "When the time comes, we shall see how he has managed."

Lu Su, on his own authority, allotted twenty fast boats, each with thirty soldiers on board and each arranged with blue cloth curtains and straw targets as requested. Then he waited to see what Chu-ko Liang was going to do with them. On the first day, Chu-ko Liang did not seem to be taking any action. Nor did Chu-ko Liang take any action on the second day either. During the fourth watch on the third day, Chu-ko Liang secretly invited Lu Su to come to his boat. Lu Su asked him: "Why have you asked me to come?" Chu-ko Liang said: "I've invited you to collect the arrows with me." Lu Su said: "Where are we going to get them?" Chu-ko Liang said: "Don't ask. You will know soon." Chu-ko Liang issued orders to tie the twenty ships together with rope and set out toward the north shore.

At the time, there was a heavy fog covering the skies, and there was a thick mist over the river, so that the other bank could not be seen clearly. Before dawn, the boats had already drawn near Ts'ao Ts'ao's fleet. Chu-ko Liang issued orders to turn the bows toward the west and the sterns toward the east, in a straight line. He then told the soldiers on the boats to beat their drums and shout loudly. Lu Su said, startled: "If Ts'ao Ts'ao's troops come out, what will we do?" Chu-ko Liang said with a smile: "With this thick a fog, Ts'ao Ts'ao will certainly not dare to send out his troops. All we need do is drink wine and enjoy ourselves and go back once dawn has come."

When Ts'ao Ts'ao, in his fortress, heard the beating drums and the shouts, he ordered: "There's a very heavy fog over the river. The enemy navy has suddenly arrived and they must be lying in ambush. We mustn't move out recklessly. We'll just order the archers to fire their arrows at them." He sent someone to the shore fortress to call out 6,000 archers to the river bank to assist. Over 10,000 archers shot their arrows toward the river, and arrows were flying like falling rain. Chu-ko Liang then issued orders to turn the boats around, with their bows facing east and their sterns facing west, and to press closer to Ts'ao Ts'ao's fleet in order to collect their arrows, beating drums and shouting all the while.

The sun rose, but the fog had still not dispersed. At that time, the straw targets on each boat were stuck full of arrows. Chu-ko Liang then ordered all of the soldiers on the boats to shout in unison: "Thank you for the arrows, Prime Minister Ts'ao!" He then ordered the twenty boats to speed back. By the time Ts'ao Ts'ao had found out what had happened, by virtue of their lightness and of the swiftness of the currents, the boats had already made more than twenty *li*, and he could not catch them. Ts'ao Ts'ao was exceedingly angry.

When the twenty boats drew near to the south bank, the five hundred soldiers that Chou Yü had sent to pick up the arrows had already reached the bank of the river. Chu-ko Liang ordered the soldiers to come aboard to get the arrows. Each boat had five or six thousand arrows, and all together there were more than 100,000. The soldiers carried the 100,000 arrows to the central tent and delivered them to Chou Yü. When Lu Su saw Chou Yü, he told him of how the arrows were borrowed. Chou Yü sighed deeply and said: "I don't have brilliant schemes and subtle plans as good as those of K'ung Ming."

In a while, Chu-ko Liang arrived. Chou Yü came out of his tent himself to welcome him, saying: "My respects! My respects!" He ordered a banquet set up and invited Chu-ko Liang into his tent for wine.

TWENTY-NINE. A MAN WHO WAS GOOD AT BUTCHERING OXEN

Many years ago, there was a man who was good at butchering oxen. His carving knife, after nineteen years of use and after having butchered thousands of oxen, looked as if it had just been cast and sharpened.

When he was butchering an ox, the movements of the knife, the movements of his hands, feet, shoulders, and knees, and the sounds of the pieces of flesh being cut off one by one all had a rhythm like that of beautiful music. He said, "When I first began butchering oxen, all I saw was the whole ox. Three years later, it was different. What I saw was not the whole ox, but a heap of flesh and bones collected together. Between muscle and muscle, between bone and bone, and between flesh and bone, there appeared to be wide empty spaces. The blade of my knife is very thin, and there are spaces between the bones and the flesh of the ox. When my very thin knife blade goes into the spaces, it simply travels as it pleases without hitting the least obstacle. Therefore, although I have used my knife for nineteen years and have butchered thousands of oxen with it, it looks like new.

"Naturally, I know that it is not particularly easy when one runs into places where muscle and bone are joined together, and if one is not careful, the knife may be broken. The important thing in a case like this is to be cautious and not to be hasty. If you move the knife gently, when an opening is suddenly found, a large piece of meat falls off just like a clump of dirt. When I have been victorious in my work, I feel very happy. Then I wipe my knife clean and put it away."

This is an allegory that has been told in our nation from ancient times. From this allegory it can be seen that in butchering an ox, the ox cannot be considered as an entity to be struck at wildly. It is necessary to understand the organization of each part of the ox's body and find the places where the knife should enter if one is to butcher the ox well. Similarly, in doing one's work, one cannot have a confused knowledge of the matters involved in it, but must analyze them, find the places in which to begin, and discover the openings by which difficulties can be overcome. Then the work can be accomplished.

Doing work badly, not doing it thoroughly, or making something good into something bad, is called running into a nail. If the nail is very small in area and there are no others near it, why is it that you did not strike places where there was no nail rather than strike the nail? This is not because you wanted to strike your head and bleed, but because you did not see the nail when it was in front of you and struck it with a cry. It is here that you should learn from the man who butchered oxen. "Be cautious, don't be hasty, and move the knife gently." As soon as an opening is found, pull the nail out. Then the work can proceed more smoothly than you would have ever expected.

Failure to analyze a matter clearly and to hesitate in unwillingness in setting to work for fear of running into nails is called a "slowdown." People who engage in a slowdown are not as good as people who dare to run into nails. People who dare to run into nails broaden their knowledge with each misfortune they meet and after that do not meet with difficulty again. People who slow down work can never make any progress.

"There are no difficult tasks on earth, only people who are afraid to try." What is spoken of here as "trying" means, for one thing, to be decisive, and for another, to be diligent. Work must be done well. That is one aspect. The ability to do the work well is another aspect. When the two are joined together, there are no difficult tasks on earth.

What truth does the ancient allegory in this text exemplify?

Having read this allegory, how do you think that things can be done well?

THIRTY-ONE. SAMBO

Sambo was a Negro. He lived in central Africa. He worked on a rubber plantation belonging to a colonialist—a white man. At that time, Africa was still a colonialist empire, and the Negroes suffered cruel oppression and exploitation. Sambo had to work twelve to fourteen hours a day. He was frequently beaten savagely by the overseer, and all that he received was a few pence.

There were many people in Sambo's family. He had seven children. He had no choice but to work with all his life's force in order to wrest the money to raise his family. But the unexpected frequently happened. If he wasn't fined by the overseer, one of his children would be taken sick, of if not that, his small thatched hut would be damaged by the rain. The few pence that he did have would be used up, so that there wouldn't be anything left even for food.

One day, several white "tourists" arrived in Sambo's village. They brought along a machine and a big stack of luggage. One of the "tourists" saw Sambo and, after looking him over carefully, asked him: "Are you strong? Can you run fast? Can you carry heavy things?" He also said: "I'll talk to your overseer so that he'll let you work for me. The wages I will pay will be far above those on the plantation."

Sambo went to work for his new masters. He returned to the village, telling of his new experiences to his wife, children, and neighbors. He said: "This white man has an amazing machine. He uses the machine to make pictures. In these pictures you can see all kinds of things: people, dogs, flying birds, running animals, trees, rivers ... All the people in the pictures can walk. The dogs can bark. It is really amazing."

On the fourth day, the master asked Sambo to take a small

package to the place where the master was living. He set out carrying the package. As he walked, he thought that once he had finished that day's work, he would take his wages home to his wife right away, as his wife was waiting for him.

The place where the master lived was not far away. All that remained was to pass through a woods along a short path beside the main road.

Sambo had no sooner entered the woods, when he heard a frightening sound. A lion jumped out at him. Sambo dropped the package and ran away in haste. He raced toward the master's house with all his strength. He knew the master had a gun. He ran and ran. Suddenly, he saw two white men waiting in a tall tree. One of them was his new master, who was holding a rifle in his hands, and the other, his face stuck out in the direction from which Sambo was running, was holding the machine in his hands. Sambo, out of breath and panting, called out: "A lion ... fire at once ... I'm Sam ... bo ..."

The lion came at him. The lion's claws were already on Sambo's shoulders. Sambo struggled, raising his head to call out for help to the two white men. But the two white men only laughed. One held the rifle without moving, while the other, his head sticking out toward Sambo, held the machine. In an instant, all was lost for Sambo. The lion rushed at him and tore his body to pieces.

Two months later, the two white men returned to Europe. They brought back with them an amazing sound film: "A Real Lion Eats a Real Man." As soon as the film was shown, it made a great stir throughout the entire city. A reporter interviewed the two brave photographers, asking them: "How could you risk such a great danger? This is really a marvelous sound film. We would like to know how you arranged it all."

"Ah, that was very easy." One of the photographers lit a cigarette and said with a smile: "I had a Negro carry a little something to the place where we lived. Near the path that he had to take, we set out a cage with a lion shut up in it. As the Negro came up, we opened the cage and let the lion out. That's all there was to it."

He smiled thinly, drawing in a puff of smoke, and, raising his voice, said: "What's important is to pick out a strong and agile Negro. Then the film will be powerful and moving and will sell seats."

THIRTY-THREE. A LETTER TO COMRADE HSÜ T'E-LI

You were my teacher twenty years ago, you are still my teacher now, and you will certainly be my teacher in the future. When the revolution failed, many Communist Party members left the Party, and some even ran off to the enemy. But you joined the Party in the fall of 1927 and took an extremely positive attitude. During the long and bitter struggle from that time until the present, you have been even more positive than many youths and young adults, you have not feared difficulties, and you have studied many things in a disinterested manner. "Age," "infirmities of body and spirit," and "hardships and obstacles" all submit to you. But to some others? In contrast, they make cowardly excuses for not going ahead. You understand a great deal but always think that it's not enough. But there are those who have only a "half bucket of water," and who "spill a great deal."* What you think, you speak and write. But there are those who, in the corners of their minds, have filthy things that must be concealed. You are always with the masses. But there are those who appear to take pleasure in being dissociated from the masses. In all things, you show that you yourself follow the pattern of rules of the Party and of the revolution. But there are those who appear to feel that rules are binding on others but not upon themselves. You put the revolution first, work first, and others first. But there are those who put making a name for themselves first, who put resting first, and who put themselves first. You always pick the difficult tasks to do and never evade responsibility. But there are those who are willing only to pick the light tasks and who hide when responsibility must be taken. It is for all of these characteristics that I respect you and for which I am willing to learn from you continually and am also willing for the whole Party to learn from you. I am writing this letter to congratulate you on your sixtieth birthday, to wish you health, to wish you long life, and to wish

---

* Have only a "half bucket of water," and who "spill a great deal"— This means that they understand little but put on airs of understanding a great deal. "T'ang" (to drip) has the connotation of "tang" (agitated, dissipated), indicating that the water in the bucket shines and ripples.

that you may become a model for all revolutionary Party members and for the entire people. Revolutionary greetings!

Mao Tse-tung

January 30, 1937 at Yenan

DATE DUE

A fine of TEN CENTS will be charged for
each day the book is kept overtime.

RETURNED MAY 9 1973			